Zhang Wenguang's Chaquan Volume II

Further Styles Within The Chaquan System - Hua, Pao, Hong, And Tui

Available from **tgl books**

Translated from the Chinese by Andrea Mary Falk
Jiang Rongqiao's Baguazhang
Li Tianji's The Skill of Xingyiquan
Yan Dehua's Bagua Applications
Di Guoyong on Xingyiquan: Volume I, Foundations
Di Guoyong on Xingyiquan: Volume II, Forms and Ideas
Di Guoyong on Xingyiquan: Volume III, Weapons
Zhang Wenguang's Chaquan
Zhang Wenguang's Chaquan: Volume II, Further Styles
Zhang Wenguang's Chaquan: Volume III, Weapons

Researched and written by Andrea Mary Falk
A Shadow on Fallen Blossoms: The 36 and 48 Traditional Verses of Baguazhang
Falk's Dictionary of Chinese Martial Arts
Beijing Bittersweet
Shadowboxing in Shanghai

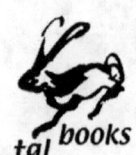

www.thewushucentre.ca

Zhang Wenguang's Chaquan

Volume II
Further Styles Within The Chaquan System – Hua, Pao, Hong, And Tui

张文广

中国查拳

translated and edited

by Andrea Mary Falk

霍安娣翻译，主板

Translation copyright © 2024 by Andrea Mary Falk

All Rights Reserved

ISBN 978-1-989468-38-8

Originally published by Zhang Wenguang as Zhongguo Chaquan. Published by Shandong Jiaoyu Chubanshe, Jinan, Shandong province, China, 1985.

Translated and edited by Andrea Falk,

2024 in Morin-Heights and Quebec City, QC, Canada.

This is volume two of a three volume translation set on Chaquan.

The techniques described in this book are performed by experienced martial artists. The author, translator, and publishers are not responsible for any injury that may occur while trying out these techniques. Please do not apply these techniques on anyone without their consent and cooperation.

TABLE OF CONTENTS

About the Author (from the original book) vii
Zhang Wenguang's Preface to the Original Chaquan Book viii
Translator's Preface ix

CHAPTER ONE: FIRST FORM HUAQUAN 1
CHAPTER TWO: SECOND FORM HUAQUAN.. 21
CHAPTER THREE: THIRD FORM HUAQUAN (B)... 39
CHAPTER FOUR: THIRD FORM HUAQUAN (A) (IMAGES ONLY)......... 65
CHAPTER FIVE: THIRD FORM PAOQUAN.. 95
CHAPTER SIX: SIXTH FORM PAOQUAN... 117
CHAPTER SEVEN: NINTH FORM PAOQUAN... 153
CHAPTER EIGHT: FIRST FORM HONGQUAN 177
CHAPTER NINE: FOURTH FORM HONGQUAN..................................... 203
CHAPTER TEN: SEVENTH FORM HONGQUAN.................................... 229
CHAPTER ELEVEN: THIRD FORM HONGQUAN (IMAGES ONLY).......... 259
CHAPTER TWELVE: FIRST FORM TUIQUAN 289
CHAPTER THIRTEEN: SECOND FORM TUIQUAN 317

Mandarin Pronunciation of *pinyin* 339
About the translator 341

ABOUT THE AUTHOR

Professor Zhang Wenguang was born in 1916 in Tongxun county, Henan province. As a child, he first learned Chaquan from the famous master Zhang Fengling, from Guan county, Shandong province. From 1929, he continued to learn the Chaquan system from the great teacher Chang Zhenfang. In 1933, he entered the Nanjing Central Guoshu Academy, where he studied many martial styles and weapons. He was selected to the Chinese Wushu touring troupe in 1935, which performed in Hong Kong, Singapore, Malaysia, and the Philippines. In June 1936, he performed at the eleventh Olympic Games in Germany. Professor Zhang Wenguang is an all-round martial artist – proficient in many styles and exceptional at Chaquan. From 1936 on, he has been a martial art professional.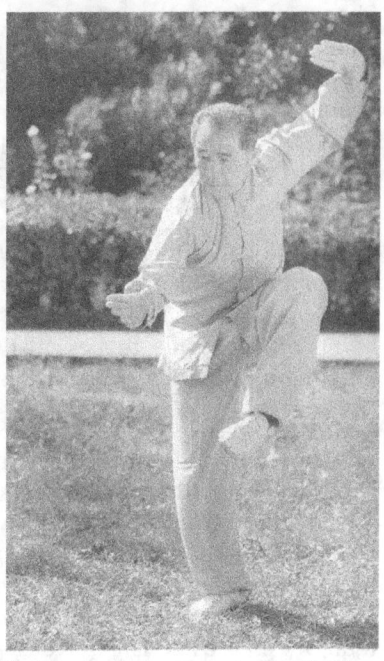
From 1953 on, he has worked in the Wushu department at the Beijing Physical Culture Institute. Professor Zhang Wenguang is a professional wushu teacher.

Over thirty years, Zhang has been responsible in the committees that wrote the national wushu regulation forms and competition rules and the curriculum for the national Physical Culture Institutes. He was the editor of the sport chapter of the China Encyclopedia. He has written many books, including Youth Fist, and China's Wrestling.

Professor Zhang has had the responsibility of head judge at many national wushu competitions. In 1960, he was the coach of the national sport troupe that went with Premier Zhou Enlai to Malta. In 1980, Professor Zhang was the head of the wushu troupe that visited Japan.

Now (1983) he is the vice-chairman of the National Wushu Association.

PREFACE TO THE CHAQUAN BOOK

Chaquan is one of the exceptional traditional wushu styles. Its origins are in Luxiguan county, and it is widespread in Shandong and Hebei provinces. In the martial world, it is said that the south does fists, the north does legs, and Shandong does Chaquan. In the complete system there are ten Chaquan forms, three Huaquan, three Paoquan, four Hongquan, and two Tuiquan. In order to give materials for martial arts professionals and enthusiasts, we have written up the main solo barehand forms of the Chaquan system.

This book is written by Zhang Wenguang, vice-chairman of the national wushu association and professor at the Beijing Physical Culture Institute. In order to draw on the collective wisdom of Chaquan masters, we invited seven other people to be involved in the writing: Zhang Ziying, Zhang Yinming, Li Weiqing, Wu Guixiang, Xu Qingshan, Yang Encheng, and Yang Hengtai.

The forms in different regions differ, some moves differ quite a great deal, and sometimes the structure takes on quite different patterns. We have taking this into consideration in our analysis of the forms, to keep the traditional nature of Chaquan while working to popularise it and bring it into the sporting world. With much discussion, we looked at the content of each form and the manner of performance, and arrived at agreement. In total, we have established twenty-four forms (twenty-two different names). Finally, sixteen professors at Beijing Physical Culture Institute took part in the writing up of the forms. Those are: Zhang Wenguang, Men Huifeng, Gong Wanmin, Wang Huafeng, Wang Yulong, Zhu Ruiqi, Liu Yuping, He Ruihong, Chen Xiulong, Zhu Yuming, Yang Li, Yang Bolong, Xia Bohua, Xu Weijun, Kang Gewu, and Kan Guixiang.

During the work of discovery for the writing of the Chaquan forms, we visited Jinan, Liaocheng, Guan county, Yanggu, and Linqing in Shandong province; Kaifeng, Tongxu, and Zhoukou in Henan province; Daming in Hebei province, and over twelve cities and counties such as Shenyang, Chengdu, and Beijing. In addition, during the National Wushu Exchange Meet held in Lanzhou in 1984, we interviewed some masters from the north-west region. We have had the support of many party organs, sports committees, traditional masters, for which we are very grateful. We hope the reader will excuse the weaknesses of this book.

TRANSLATOR'S PREFACE

I published the Chaquan forms of Zhang Wenguang's 1985 book on Chaquan in 2023. In this volume I have translated the other forms that were in his book. These are the styles of Huaquan 滑拳, Paoquan 炮拳, Hongquan 洪拳, and Tuiquan 腿拳. Chaquan is a style from the area around Shandong and Henan provinces, and the history of these styles been linked to that of Chaquan, making them part of the Chaquan system. Hua, Pao, Hong, and Tui styles also grew from popular styles in the area, and share many of Chaquan's characteristics and techniques. Note that the Huaquan in this book is not the better known style of Huaquan 华拳, Paoquan is not the better known style of Paochui 炮捶, Hongquan is not the better known style of Hongquan 红拳, and Tuiquan is not the better known style of Tantui 弹腿.

There are a few origin stories for Chaquan, but professor Zhang feels that it is likely that Chaquan developed from Ming dynasty General Qi Jiguang's style, itself developed from the variety of styles from Shandong province. If Chaquan existed in the Ming dynasty, it would certainly have been mentioned in General Qi Jiguang's book, and it is not. General Qi discussed postures and techniques of sixteen styles popular in the area, and used them to create his Qi style. General Qi did discuss Tantui, a style of long fist that was known for leg techniques, and Tantui was likely later incorporated into Chaquan. Professor Zhang suggests that if General Qi himself did not create Chaquan, perhaps a general Sha Liang developed it from General Qi's study. Sha is the first historically verifiable person who taught Chaquan, and it has been suggested that Cha is simply a mis-pronunciation of Sha.

Professor Zhang (1915-2010) was the head of the martial arts department at the Beijing Physical Culture Institute (Beijing Sports University) from 1953 to 1994, and was actively involved in writing this book when I was a student there, from 1980 to 1983. I learned the Chaquan fourth form at the Beijing Physical Culture Institute in 1982, but did not learn the other styles.

There is a lot of content, so I formatted this volume a bit more compactly than the first volume, but there is still too much to translate fully. For this reason, I only provide names and images for two of the longer forms. Those comfortable with the styles might be able to figure out these forms, and I thought it was better than leaving them out entirely.

As usual, while going through the book I corrected some typos and errors that were in the original Chinese text. I should also mention that in the text 'forward' and 'in front' sometimes means 'in the direction of travel' and sometimes 'in relation to the way the torso is facing.' You can tell which by context and the images.

I hope that you enjoy this book.

Andrea Falk

(Aka Huo Andi 霍安娣)

Morin-Heights and Quebec City, QC, Canada

June 2024

FIRST FORM HUAQUAN

头路滑拳

Names Of The Movements

Position Of Preparation
Section One
1. Facing Fists
2. Step Forward Close The Fists
3. Embrace With The Fists
4. Left, Right Wind The Arms And Straight Punch
5. Left, Right Flash Palm
6. Thread The Hand And Slap
7. Stamp To Bow Stance, Chop With Hand
8. Drop Stance, Separate The Hands
9. Closed Stance, Palm Carry
10. Bow Stance, Scooping Snap
11. Bow Stance, Chop With Hand
12. Drop Stance, Separate The Hands
13. Closed Stance Palm Carry
14. Bow Stance, Crossed Hands
15. Turn Around, Bow Stance, Sideways Strike
16. Bow Stance, Crossed Hands
17. Turn Around, Bow Stance, Sideways Strike

Section Two
18. Wind The Arms And Chop
19. Scooping Snap, Snap Kick
20. Scooping Snap, Snap Kick
21. Scooping Snap, Snap Kick
22. Jump Step To Hammerfist
23. Horse Stance, Straight Punch
24. Drop Stance, Thread The Hand
25. Bow Stance, Flowers
26. High Empty Stance, Flash Palm
27. Raised Knee, Hooked Hand
28. Jump To Drop Stance Press Down
29. High Empty Stance, Stab With The Hand
30. Reverse Bow Stance, Chop With Hand

Section Three
31. Bow Stance Chop With Hand

32. Closed Stance Crossed Hands
33. Horse Stance Straight Punch
34. Jump To Horse Stance Straight Punch
35. Drop Stance Thread The Hand
36. Raised Knee Inverted Hooked Hands
37. Jump Step And Slice Upwards
38. Wheel Over And Chop With Hand
39. Jump Step And Chop With Hand
40. Horse Stance Straight Punch

Section Four

41. Drop Stance, Thread The Hand
42. Raised Knee Flash Palm
43. Walk Slicing Upwards
44. Bow Stance Scooping Snap
45. Turn Around, Flash Palm
46. Turn Around, Chop With Hand
47. Closed Stance Lash
48. Stamp To Drop Stance, Thread The Hand
49. Bow Stance, Slice Up With A Hooked Hand
50. Empty Stance Flash Palm
51. Withdraw, Press Down
52. Closing Posture

Position Of Preparation   yùbèi shì   预备势

Stand to attention with the legs together, the feet turned slightly outwards, and the arms hanging naturally at the sides. Look forward. (image 1.0)

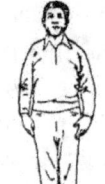

Section One

1. Facing Fists   duì quán   对拳

Circle the hands around to the front and clench them, facing each other in front of the belly, fist hearts down, about a fist-length apart, with the arms slightly bent. Reach the chest slightly forward. Look to the left. (image 1.1)

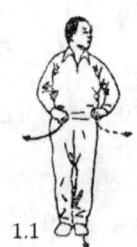

FIRST FORM HUAQUAN

2. **Step Forward Close The Fists**   shàngbù bīngquán   上步并拳

Push off with the right foot to shift forward and step the left foot a half-step forward, raising the right heel to touch the ball of the foot on the ground. Unclench the hands and open them out to circle to either side until the arms are angled downwards and the palms face forward. Look to the left. (image 1.2a) Take a half-step forward with the right foot while clenching the hands and circling them until the arms are extended in front of the shoulders with the fists together, about two fist-widths apart, fist hearts down. Look forward. (image 2b)

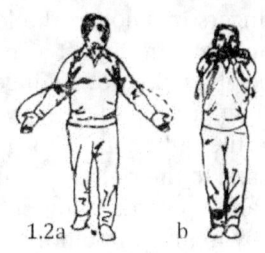

3. **Embrace With The Fists**   bàoquán   抱拳

Without moving the body, bring the fists to the waist, fist hearts up. Look forward. (image 1.3)

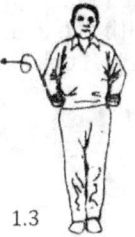

4. **Left, Right Wind The Arms And Straight Punch**
   zuǒ yòu ràobì chōngquán   左右绕臂冲拳

Without moving the body, circle the right fist to the rear at the right side, drawing a full circle, then punch out to the right side with a straight arm, fist at shoulder height with the fist eye up. Look at the right fist (image 1.4a) Circle the left fist back at left side, drawing a full circle, then punch out to the left side, arm straight, fist at shoulder height with the fist eye up. Look at the left fist. (image 4b)

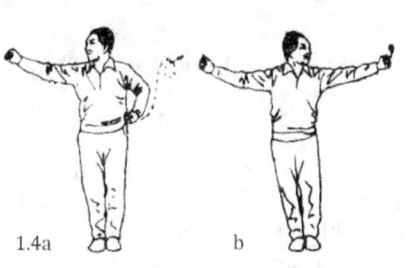

5. **Left, Right Flash Palm**   zuǒ yòu liàngzhǎng   左右亮掌

Without moving the body or the right fist, unclench the left hand and snap the fingers up to flash the palm at the left, palm angled to the forward left. Look at the left hand (image 1.5a) Unclench the right hand and flash the palm at the right side, fingers up, palm angled forward. Look at the right hand

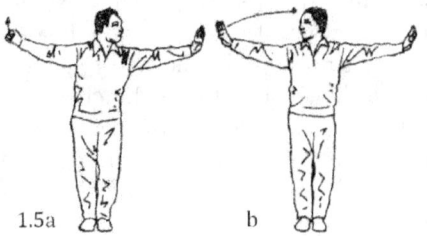

(image 5b)

6. Thread The Hand And Slap   chuānzhǎng pāijī   穿掌拍击

Bend the right arm to bring the right hand to the right ear, palm forward, fingers in. Look at the left hand. (image 1.6a) Thread the right hand along underneath the left arm to the left side until the arm is straight at shoulder height, palm down, fingers pointing left, and draw the left hand inside the right arm, palm down, fingers pointing in. Twist the torso leftward and look at the right hand. (image 6b) Twist the torso rightward and bring the right hand to the right ear, palm forward, fingers pointing left, and thread the left hand upwards to the left until the arm is straight at shoulder height, palm down, fingers pointing to the upper left. Look at the left hand. (image 6c) Twist the torso leftward and slap the right hand onto the left arm. Look at the hands. (image 6d) Twist the torso rightward and lift the right hand at the left side, passing over the head to circle over to the right to chop down with the arm at shoulder height, fingers up, palm angled to the forward right. Look at the right hand. (image 6e)

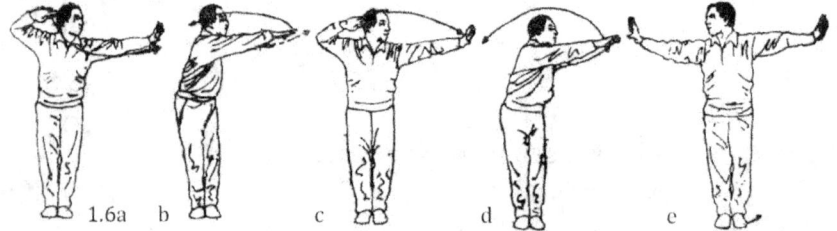

7. Stamp To Bow Stance, Chop With Hand

tà gōngbù pīquán   踏弓步劈掌

Pivoting around the palms, turn the body to the left, lifting the right heel. Look to the left. (image 1.7a) Settle down, bending the left leg and standing on it, lifting the right knee. Look to the left. (image 7b) Stamp with the right foot, quickly lifting the bent left knee, bending the right knee slightly to support the weight. Look to the left. (image 7c) Step the left foot back, touching the toes down with the heel up. Bend the left arm and bring the hand to the chest, palm down, fingers pointing right. Look forward. (image 7d) Turn the torso to the left to set into a right bow stance. Raise the right hand upwards to pass over the head then chop down in front with the arm straight at shoulder height, fingers up, palm angled to the forward left. Circle the left hand past the chest, forward and down to the left hip, then raise it to shoulder height behind the body, arm straight, fingers up, palm angled to the rear left. Look at the right hand. (image 7e)

FIRST FORM HUAQUAN

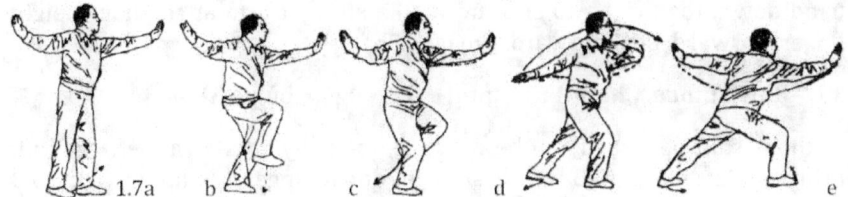

8. **Drop Stance, Separate The Hands** pūbù fēnzhǎng 仆步分掌

Push with the left foot and turn to the left, bending the left knee and straightening the right leg to take a bow stance. Circle the hands down to either side, bringing them in to cross in front of the belly, right hand on top. Look to the lower front. (image 1.8a)

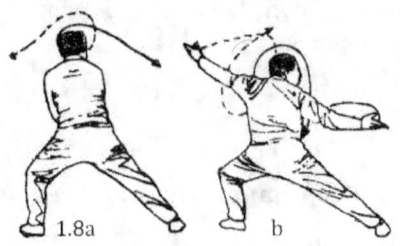

Sit down, squatting on the left leg and extending the right leg. Circle the hands up past the head, then open out to either side, finishing with the right arm angled downwards and the left arm angled upwards, both hands facing up. Look to the right. (image 8b)

9. **Closed Stance, Palm Carry** bīngbù tuōzhǎng 并步托掌

Push into the right leg and turn to the left, bring the right foot in beside the left in a closed stance, and stand up. Medially rotate the right arm and circle the right hand down at the right then up at the left, drawing a full circle, then placing the hand with the thumb on the belly. Raise the left hand at the left and circle it past the head and down to the right, drawing a full circle, stopping the hand above the head, palm up, fingers pointing right. Look to the right. (image 1.9)

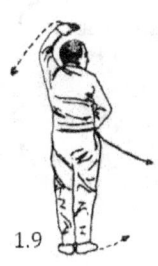

10. **Bow Stance, Scooping Snap** gōngbù tiǎozhǎng 弓步挑掌

Squat fully on the left leg and extend the right leg. Slide the right hand along the inside of the right leg to thread to the lower right, palm forward, fingers pointing to the lower right. Hold the left hand out at the left side and reach the torso towards the right. Look to the lower right. (image 1.10a) Push into the left foot and shift to the right into a right bow stance. Circle the right hand, thumb side leading, down, to the right, then up past the head to scoop up to the upper rear, fingers back. Circle the left

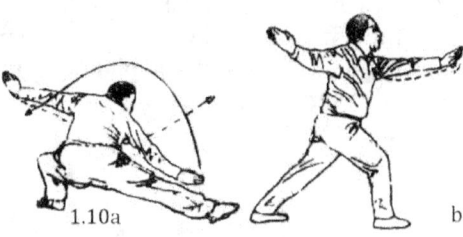

hand down, then right, to slice up with a straight arm at shoulder height, fingers forward. Look forward. (image 10b)

11. Bow Stance, Chop With Hand gōngbù pīzhǎng 弓步挑掌

Without shifting out of the bow stance, medially rotate the left arm and bring the left hand in to the chest, palm down, fingers pointing back. Look forward. (image 1.11.a) Circle the left hand forward then down past the left hip to raise it out behind the left side, arm straight at shoulder height, palm down, fingers pointing to the rear. Circle the right hand upwards over the head to chop down in front, arm straight at shoulder height, fingers pointing forward, palm angled down. Look at the right hand. (image 11b)

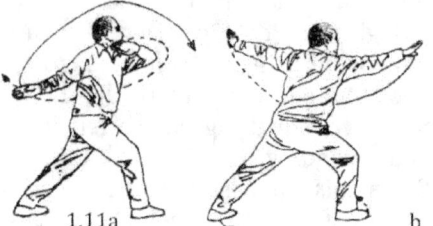

12. Drop Stance, Separate The Hands pūbù fēnzhǎng 仆步分掌

Push into the right foot and turn left, bending the left knee and straightening the right leg to a side bow stance. Circle the hands down at each side until they cross in front of the belly, right hand on top. Look to the lower front. (image 1.12a) Squat on the left leg and extend the right leg to sit into a drop stance. Circle both hands up over the head then out to either side, the right arm angled down and the left arm angled up, palms up. Look to the right side. (image 12b)

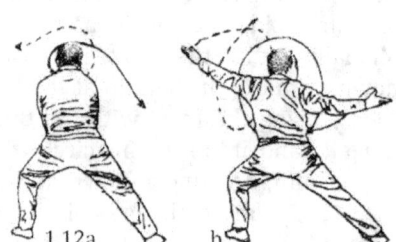

13. Closed Stance Palm Carry bīngbù tuōzhǎng 并步托掌

Push into the right foot and shift to the left, bringing the right foot in beside the left in a closed stance, standing straight up. Medially rotate the right arm and bring the right hand down the right side then up on the left, drawing a full circle, finishing with the thumb on the belly. Circle the left hand up over the head then down on the right, drawing a full circle and stopping with the hand raised above the head, palm up, fingers pointing to the right. Look to the right side. (image 1.13)

FIRST FORM HUAQUAN

14. Bow Stance, Crossed Hands   gōngbù shízìshǒu   弓步十字手

Squat down on both legs to a half-squat, reaching the torso slightly forward. Lower the left hand to cross the hands in front of the chest, fingers up, right hand on the outside. Look forward. (image 1.14a) Push into the right foot and step the left foot forward, bending the knee to take a bow stance. Lower the hands in front then raise them. Look forward. (image 14b) Step the right foot forward, bend the knee, and extend the left leg with the heel off the ground. Circle the hands out to the sides, fingers pointing out to the sides, palms down. Look forward. (image 14c) Step the left foot forward into a left bow stance. Circle the hands down at each side, then forward to cross in front of the chest, right hand inside, fingers up. Look forward. (image 14d)

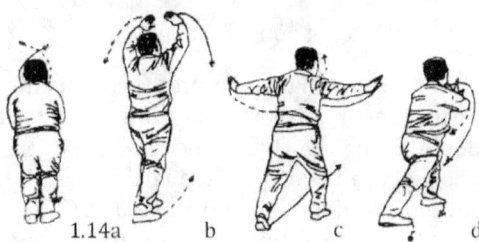

1.14a   b   c   d

15. Turn Around, Bow Stance, Sideways Strike

     zhuànshēn gōngbù héngzhǎng   转身弓步横掌

Push into the left foot and turn right to sit into a right drop stance. Circle the right hand as the body turns, to smear to the lower right, fingers pointing left, palm down. Bring the left hand to inside the right arm and lean the torso to the right. Look to the front lower right. (image 1.15a) Push into the left foot and shift forward to take a right bow stance. Circle the right hand up to the right, palm angled to the forward right, fingers pointing up. Set the left hand at the right chest, fingers up, palm to the right. Look at the right hand. (image 15b) Without shifting out of the bow stance, strike the left hand across to the left side with the arm straight at shoulder height, fingers up, palm facing the forward left. Look at the left hand. (image 15c)

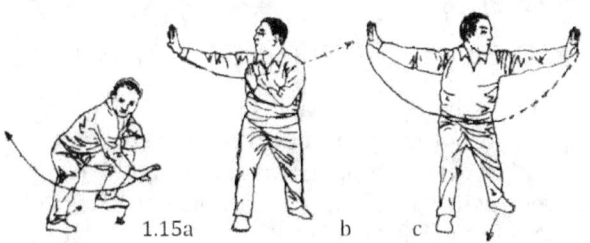

1.15a   b   c

16. Bow Stance, Crossed Hands   gōngbù shízìshǒu   弓步十字手

Push into the right foot and shift forward, stepping the left foot to the forward left, bending the knee. Circle the hands down at the sides, then cross them in front of the belly, palms in, right hand on the outside. Look to the forward lower left. (image 1.16a) Push into the right foot and shift forward, stepping the right foot to the forward left to take a right bow stance. Lift the hands above the head then separate them down and out to either side, palms back, fingers down. Look to the forward left. (image 16b)

Without shifting from the bow stance, circle the hands up and out at their respective sides, finishing by crossing in front of the chest, fingers up, left hand on the inside. Look to the forward right. (image 16c)

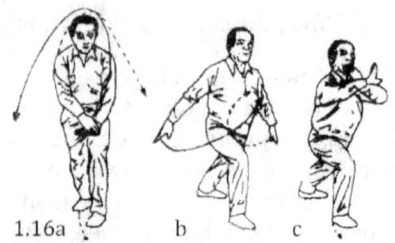
1.16a b c

17. Turn Around, Bow Stance, Sideways Strike
zhuànshēn gōngbù héngzhǎng   转身弓步劈掌

Push into the right foot and turn left into a left drop stance. As the body turns, smear the left hand down to the left, fingers pointing right, palm down. Bring the right hand inside the left arm. Reach the torso to the left. Look to the lower forward left. (image 1.17a) Push into the right foot and shift forward into a left bow stance. Circle the left hand to raise it to the left side, fingers pointing left, finishing at the left side with the palm facing the forward left, fingers pointing up. Bring the right hand to the left chest, fingers up, palm facing the forward right. Look at the left hand. (image 17b) Do a sideways strike with the right hand out to the right side to shoulder height, arm straight, fingers up. Look at the right hand. (image 17c)

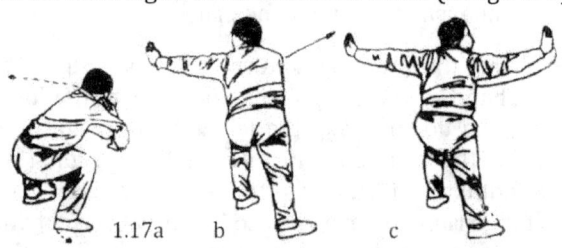
1.17a b c

Section Two

18. Wind The Arms And Chop   ràobì pīzhǎng   绕臂劈掌

Push into the right foot and shift forward, taking a half-step forward with the right foot to touch the ball of the foot to the ground, the heel raised. Medially rotate the right arm and bring the hand to the chest, palm down, fingers pointing left at shoulder height. Look to the right. (image 1.18a) Push into the left foot and shift to the right, turning right and lifting the left heel, keeping the ball of the foot on the ground. Circle the right arm up, then down to the right until it is behind the body at the right side, palm facing right. Laterally rotate the left arm and circle it on the left side, up over the head then down to chop to the right, palm forward,

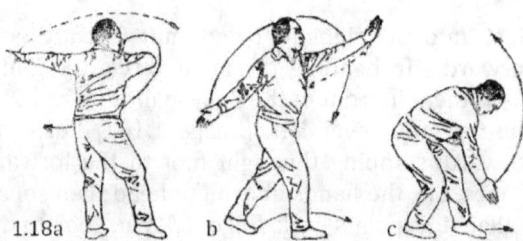
1.18a b c

fingers up. Look at the left hand. (image 18b) Step the left foot a half-step forward, touching down the ball of the foot with the heel up, and bend both legs, leaning forward. Circle the right hand from the back, up over the head then chop down in front, palm facing left, fingers pointing down. Bring the left hand in under the right arm. Look to the lower front. (image 18c)

19. Scooping Snap, Snap Kick   tiǎozhǎng tántuǐ   挑掌弹腿

Step the left foot forward a half-step and stand up. Circle the right hand up from below with a scooping snap with the arm straight, fingers up, palm facing left. Bring the left hand to the right chest, palm in. Look forward. (image 1.19a) Push into the right foot and shift forward. Raise the right knee, then quickly snap the lower leg forward with the ankle plantar-flexed. Scoop the right hand to the rear, arm bent, fingers up. Circle the left hand forward to do a scooping lift at shoulder height, arm straight, palm facing right, fingers pointing forward. Look forward. (image 19b)

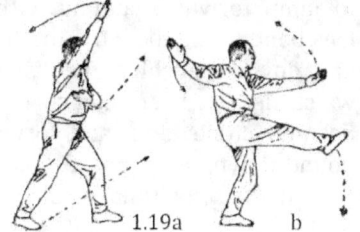

1.19a   b

20. Scooping Snap, Snap Kick   tiǎozhǎng tántuǐ   挑掌弹腿

Land the right foot forward and shift forward, lifting the left heel, keeping the ball of the foot on the ground. Circle the left arm upwards, palm facing forward, fingers back. Lower the right arm at the rear right so that it is angled downwards. Look forward. (image 1.20a) Push into the left foot and shift forward, lifting the left knee then snapping the lower leg quickly forward with a snap kick, ankle plantar-flexed. Do a scooping snap forward with the right hand, arm straight, palm facing left, fingers forward. Lift the left hand at the rear left, fingers up. Look forward. (image 20b)

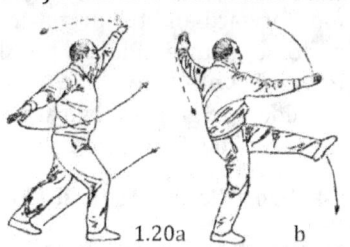

1.20a   b

21. Scooping Snap, Snap Kick   tiǎozhǎng tántuǐ   挑掌弹腿

Land forward on the left foot and shift forward, bending the left knee and extending the right leg, pushing the ball of the foot into the ground, lifting the heel slightly. Circle the right hand upwards with a scooping lift to the back, fingers up, palm left. Lower the left hand to angle down, fingers down. Look forward. (image 1.21a) Push into the right foot and shift forward, lifting the knee then snapping the lower leg quickly forward to kick with the ankle

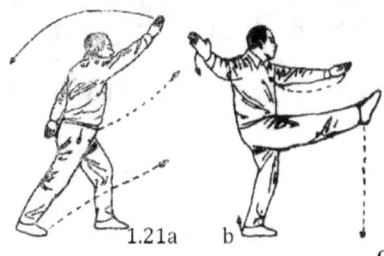

1.21a   b

plantar-flexed. Swing the right hand over the head to the lift to the rear. Circle the left hand down and forward with a scooping lift at shoulder height, arm extended, fingers forward, thumb up. Look forward. (image 21b)

22. Jump Step To Hammerfist   tiàobù záquán   跳步砸拳

Land the right foot forward and bend the knee. Bend the left knee and raise the heel to push the ball of the foot into the ground. Bend the left arm with the forearm flat, palm down, fingers pointing right. Lower the right arm slightly. Look forward. (image 1.22a) Push into the right foot to jump up, taking off with the left, then the right to jump forward, landing with both legs bent. Circle the left hand forward and down, clenching the fist at the waist, fist heart up. Clench the right fist and circle it up and forward to pound down, arm bent, fist heart up. Look to the right. (image 22b)

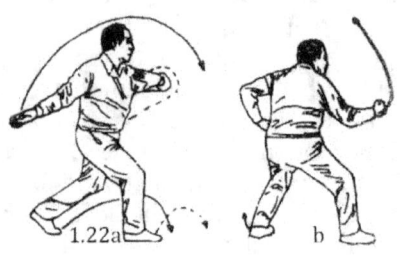

23.   Horse Stance, Straight Punch   mǎbù chōngquán   马步冲拳

Push into the left foot and shift to the right, turning right, lifting the left heel to push into the ball of the foot. Medially rotate the right arm and circle it up with a framing block at the right, fist heart forward, fist eye down. Look forward. (image 1.23a) Step the left foot forward and turn right to sit into a horse stance. Punch the left fist forward with the arm straight at shoulder height, fist eye up. Look to the forward left. (image 23b)

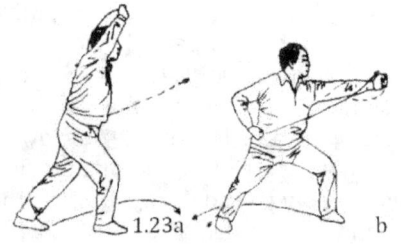

24. Drop Stance, Thread The Hand   pūbù chuānzhǎng   仆步穿掌

Shift back then step the left foot back, turning left to sit into a right bow stance. Unclench the right hand and thread the hand forward inside the left arm until the arm is straight at shoulder height, fingers up, palm forward. Unclench the left hand and place it inside the right arm. Look at the right hand. (image 1.24a) Turn the torso left and lean to the side, sitting down into a left drop stance. Thread the left hand along the inside of the left leg, palm facing right, fingers forward. Look to the lower left. (image 24b)

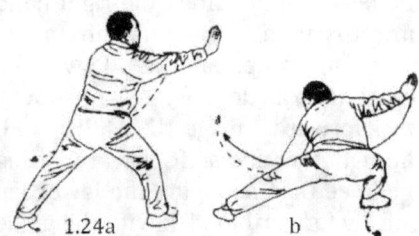

FIRST FORM HUAQUAN

25. Bow Stance, Flowers   gōngbù wǔhuāshǒu   弓步舞花手

Push into the right foot and shift to the left, turning left into a left bow stance. Thread the left hand forward and up, bending the arm, fingers up. Hook the right hand and circle it down and forward to rise with a slice up to by the left hand, the hook pointing down. Look forward. (images 1.25a) Without changing the bow stance, unhook the right hand and draw a circle to the left with the hands, pivoting around the wrists, until the right hand is on top. Look at the hands. (image 25b) Again pivoting around the wrists, draw another circle with the hands, to the right. Look at the hands. (image 25c)

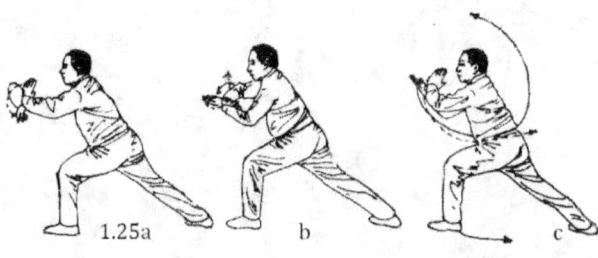

26. High Empty Stance, Flash Palm   gāoxūbù liàngzhǎng   高虚步亮掌

Push into the left foot and shift back, stepping the left foot back a half-step into a left high empty stance. Circle the right hand down, back, then up at the rear right to raise it over the head at the right side, palm up, fingers pointing left. Hook the left hand and circle it to the left and down to do a hook with the arm slightly down, the hook pointing to the rear. Look forward. (image 1.26)

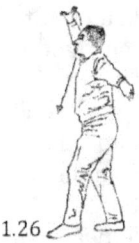

27. Raised Knee, Hooked Hand   tíxī gōushǒu   提膝勾手

Sit down and lean forward. Circle the right hand down in front with the arm straight, fingers down, palm facing left. Look at the right hand. (image 1.27a) Stand up and lift the bent left knee, ankle plantar-flexed. Laterally rotate the right arm and hook the hand up, bringing the hook up in front of the chest, arm bent, hook facing in. Look forward. (image 27b)

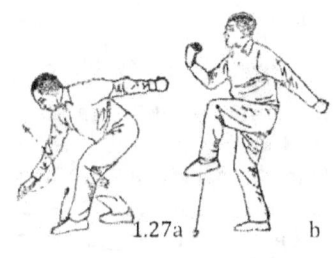

28. Jump To Drop Stance Press Down   tiào pūbù ànzhǎng   跳仆步按掌

Land forward on the left and bend the knee, straightening the right leg. Look forward. (image 1.28a) Push into the right foot and shift forward. Unhook the left hand, palm up, and circle it up over the head to the front, palm forward, fingers right. Look forward. (image 28b) Push into the left foot and jump up, landing on the right foot with the leg slightly bent, lifting the bent left knee. Lift the right hand from the waist to the rear, fingers back. Press down with the left hand down in front with the arm bent, palm down, finger to the right. Look to the lower front. (image 28c) Land forward on the left foot and sit to a drop stance. Clench the right fist and bring it to the waist, fist heart up. Press the left hand down by the left leg. Look to the lower front. (image 28d)

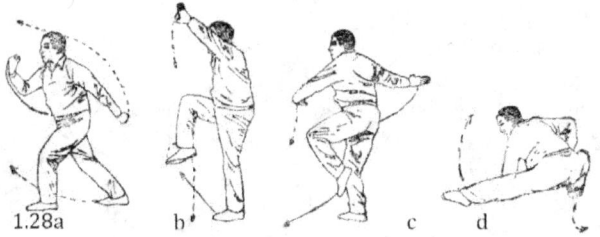

29. High Empty Stance, Stab With The Hand

gāoxūbù chāzhǎng   高虚步插掌

Land the right foot and shift forward, bending the left knee and extending the right leg. Turn the torso leftward and circle the left hand up past the front to do a framing block above and in front of the head, palm up, fingers right. Look forward. (image 1.29a) Push into the right leg and shift forward, stepping the right foot a half-step forward to take a high empty stance. Turn the torso leftward and bring the right hand from the waist to thread up, extending the arm straight out at shoulder height, palm down, fingers forward. Look forward. (image 29b)

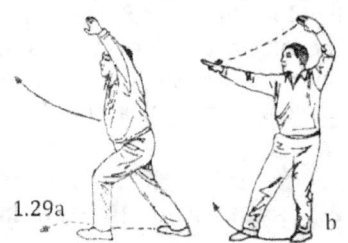

30. Reverse Bow Stance, Chop With Hand

àogōngbù pīzhǎng   拗弓步劈掌

Push into the left foot and shift forward, turning rightward and stepping the left foot forward with the foot hooked in and keeping both legs slightly bent. Slap the back of the right hand with the left palm. Look forward. (image 1.30a) Push into the right foot and shift forward, to step the right foot out to the left side, passing behind the left foot in a back insertion step, touching the ball of the foot down with the heel raised. The legs are crossed and slightly bent. (image 30b) Turn rightward and step the left foot back to take a right bow

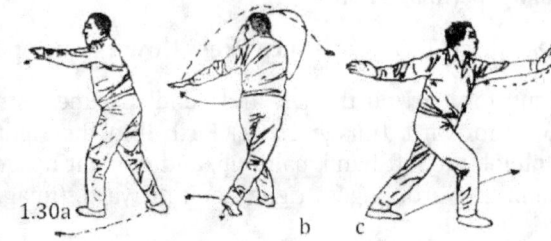

stance. Circle the right hand up past the head then down on the right side behind the body on the right, fingers pointing back. Laterally rotate the left arm and circle the left hand over the head to chop down in front, on the right with the arm straight at shoulder height, fingers up. Look at the left hand. (image 30c)

Section Three

31. Bow Stance Chop With Hand   gōngbù pīquán   弓步劈掌

Push into the left foot and shift forward, stepping the left foot forward and bending the knee, straightening the right leg. Bend the left arm with the forearm flat, palm down, fingers pointing back. Look forward. (image 1.31a) Step the right foot forward and turn left, taking a right bow stance. Circle the left hand back to the rear left. Circle the right hand over the head to chop forward. Both arms are straight at shoulder height, fingers up. Look at the right hand. (image 31b)

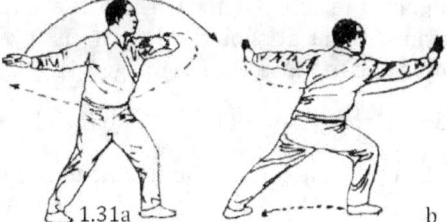

32. Closed Stance Crossed Hands   bīngbù shízìshǒu   并步十字手

Push into the right foot and shift to the left, turning the body slightly. Bring the right foot in by the left and bend both legs, touching the ball of the right foot down with the heel raised. Circle the hands from the sides to cross in front of the chest, right hand on the outside. The fingers of both hands point upwards. Look to the right side. (image 1.32)

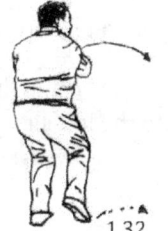

33. Horse Stance Straight Punch   mǎbù chōngquán   马步冲拳

Step the right foot out to right side, bending both legs and turning right. Smear the right hand flat across to the right with the arm almost straight, palm to the right, fingers angled upwards. Clench the left fist and bring it to the waist, fist heart up. Look to the right side. (image 1.33a) Step the left foot to the right side and turn the torso to the right, bending both legs. Laterally rotate the right arm, clench the fist, and circle it in to the waist, fist heart up. Punch the left fist out to the left side, arm straight at shoulder height, fist eye up. Look to the left side. (image 33b)

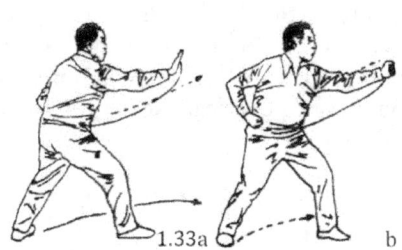

34. Jump To Horse Stance Straight Punch

tiào mǎbù chōngquán 跳马步冲拳

Push into the right foot and shift left, bending the right knee and raising it. Turn the torso slightly to the left. Unclench the right hand and reach forward under the left arm, palm forward, fingers left, preparing to grab. Bend the left arm to bring the fist in beside the right forearm. Look forward. (image 1.34a) Push off the left foot to jump up, landing the feet right, then left, a little forward, turning the torso right to sit into a horse stance. Laterally rotate the right arm and clench the fist, bringing it to the waist, fist heart up. Punch the left fist forward to the left, arm straight at shoulder height, fist eye up. Look to the left side. (image 34b)

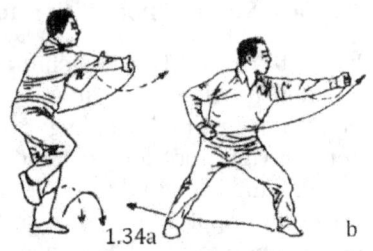

35. Drop Stance Thread The Hand   pūbù chuānzhǎng   仆步穿掌

Push into the left foot and shift to the right leg, pivoting on the ball of the right foot to turn back to the left, retreating the left foot back to take a right bow stance. Unclench the fists and thread the right hand up on the right side along the left arm, fingers up. Bring the left hand to inside the right arm. Look at the right hand. (image 1.35a) Turn the torso leftward and sit down into a left drop stance. Slide the left hand along the left leg to thread to the left, thumb side on top. Look to the lower left. (image 35b) Push into the right leg and shift to the left into a left bow stance. Thread the left hand up to the left side, fingers up. Look to the left side. (image 35c)

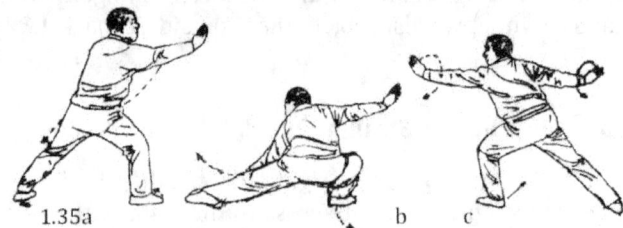

36. Raised Knee Inverted Hooked Hands   tíxī fǎngōushǒu   提膝反勾手

Push into the left foot and turn right, bending the left knee and lifting it. Draw small circles inwards with both hands to form upside-down hooks, the hooks pointing to the rear. Reach the torso forward to the left. Look to the lower right. (image 1.36)

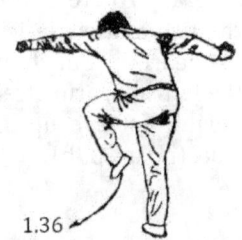

FIRST FORM HUAQUAN

37. Jump Step And Slice Upwards   tiàobù liāozhǎng   跳步撩掌

Land on left foot to the left side and bend the knee, extending the right leg. Look to the lower right. (image 1.37a) Push into the right leg to jump up. Look back and down, to what was the front. (image 37b) Land the feet right, then left, to the left side, bending the left knee and straightening the right. Lean the torso to the left. Look to the lower right. (image 37c) Without moving the feet, turn the torso leftward and lean forward. Unhook the right hand and circle it down then slice up on the left side, using the thumb side as the point of contact. Circle the left hooked hand to the rear, angling up. Look at the right hand. (image 37d)

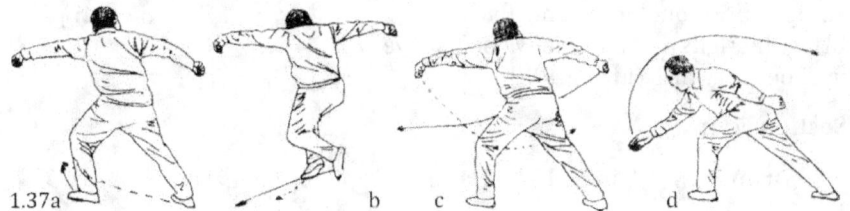

1.37a   b   c   d

38. Wheel Over And Chop With Hand   fǎnshēn pīzhǎng   反身劈掌

Push into the left foot and shift back, turning rightward. Circle the right hand from the lower left, up over the head, then chop down to the right, fingers up. Unhook the left hand and slice up on the left side, fingers down. Look at the right hand. (image 1.38a) Turn rightward, bending the right knee and straightening the left. Circle the right hand down, then up to the rear right, palm down. Circle the left hand up over the head then chop down at the right side, arm straight, fingers up. Look at the left hand. (image 38b)

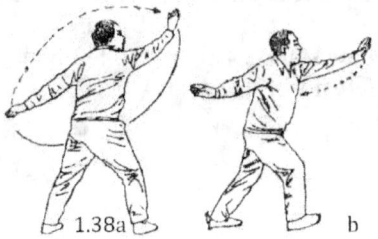

1.38a   b

39. Jump Step And Chop With Hand   tiàobù pīzhǎng   跳步劈掌

Push into the left foot and shift forward, bending the right leg, lifting the left heel to push the ball of the foot into the ground. Medially rotate the left arm and bring the hand in to the waist, palm down. Look forward. (image 1.39a) Bend the left knee and lift it. Lift the left hand slightly. Look forward. (image 39b) Push into the right foot to jump up, landing the feet left, then right, moving forward and bending both legs. Circle the left hand down then back to lift at the rear, fingers up.

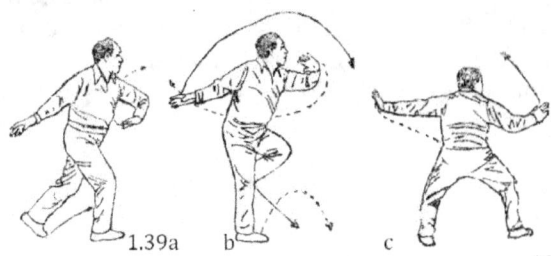

1.39a   b   c

Circle the right hand past over the head to chop down at the front at waist height, fingers up. Look to the right side. (image 39c)

40. Horse Stance Straight Punch   mǎbù chōngquán   马步冲拳

Push into the left foot and shift to the right, turning slightly to the right. Clench the left fist and bring it to the waist, fist heart up. Clench the right fist and raise the bent arm up in front. Look forward. (image 1.40a) Step the left foot forward and turn the torso rightward, to sit into a horse stance. Punch the left fist forward with the arm straight at shoulder height, fist eye up. Bring the right fist in to the waist, fist eye up. Look forward. (image 40b)

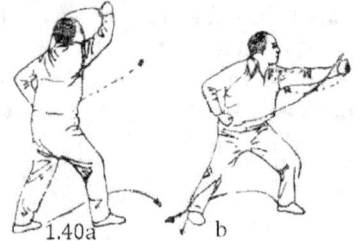

Section Four

41. Drop Stance, Thread The Hand   pūbù chuānzhǎng   仆步穿掌

Push into the left foot and shift to the right leg, pivoting on the right foot to turn around to the left, then retreat the left foot one step. Unclench the right hand and thread it forward along the left arm, fingers up. Unclench the left hand and bring it to the inside of the right arm. Look at the right hand. (image 1.41a) Turn leftward and sit down into a left drop stance. Thread the left hand along the inside of the left leg, palm facing right. Look to the lower left. (image 41b) Push into the right foot and shift to the left into a left bow stance. Thread the left hand up to the left, fingers forward. Look to the left side. (image 41c)

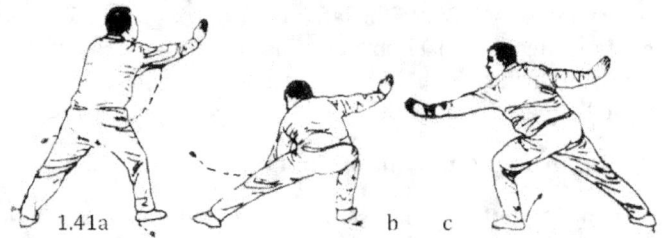

42. Raised Knee Flash Palm   tíxī liàngzhǎng   提膝亮掌

Push into the left foot to shift to the right leg, lifting the bent left knee with the ankle plantar-flexed. Hold the arms out to front and back, fingers up. Look forward. (image 1.42)

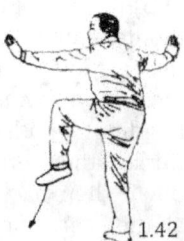

FIRST FORM HUAQUAN

43. Walk Slicing Upwards   xíngbù liāozhǎng   行步撩掌

Land forward on the left foot, bending the knee and straightening the right leg. Look forward. (image 1.43a) Push into the right leg to shift forward, then step the right foot forward with the foot turned out slightly, bending the left leg to lift the heel and push the ball of the foot into the ground. Bend the left arm to bring the hand to in front of the face, fingers up, palm facing right. Look forward. (image 43b) Step the left foot forward into a left bow stance. Circle the left hand from below to slice up to the front with the arm straight, fingers up. Look forward. (image 43c)

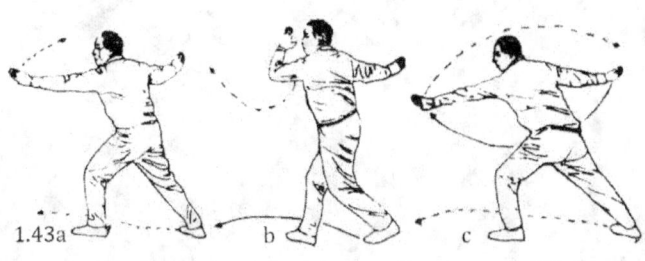

44. Bow Stance Scooping Snap   gōngbù tiǎozhǎng   弓步挑掌

Push into the right foot and shift forward, turning the torso leftward, and stepping the right foot forward into a right bow stance. Circle the left hand back, passing over the head, to finish raised behind. Circle the right hand down past the leg to slice up in front. The arms are straight at shoulder height, fingers up. Look at the right hand. (image 1.44)

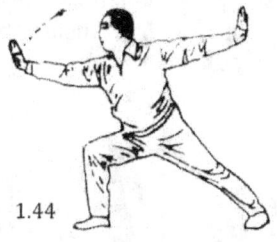

45. Turn Around, Flash Palm   zhuànshēn liàngzhǎng   转身亮掌

Turn the torso left without moving the feet. Circle the right hand up above the head, arm bent, palm up, fingers back. Look to the right side. (image 1.45)

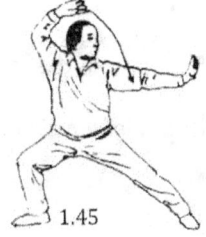

46. Turn Around, Chop With Hand   zhuànshēn pīzhǎng   转身劈掌

Push into the right foot and shift left, bending the left knee and straightening the right. Circle the right hand to press down inside the left arm. Look down. (image 1.46a) Press into the left foot and shift right, pivoting on the right foot and turning around to the right. Step the left foot across in front of the right foot to a closed stance, standing up with the legs slightly bent. Circle the hands from the left side down, past the belly, then up at the right side. The right hand finishes raised above the head, the left arm is raised out to the side. Look to the left. (image 46b) Pivoting on the left foot, turn around to the right and retreat the right foot to take a left bow stance. Circle the right hand towards the right and down to behind the body at the right. Circle the left hand to chop at the right side then chop down. Both arms are straight and at shoulder height, fingers up. Look to the left side. (image 46c)

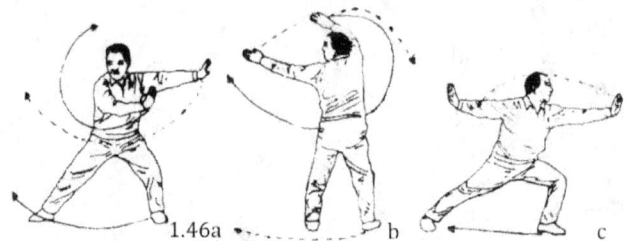

47. Closed Stance Lash bīngbù bǎizhǎng 并步摆掌

Push into the left foot and shift right, turning right and stepping the left foot in beside the right. Circle the left hand up and over to inside the right arm, fingers up. Look at the right hand. (image 1.47)

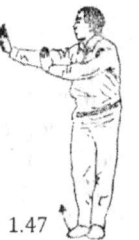

48. Stamp To Drop Stance, Thread The Hand
  tà pūbù chuānzhǎng 踏仆步穿掌

Sit down slightly and lift the right knee. Look at the right hand. (image 1.48a) Stamp with the right foot and half-squat on both legs. (image 48b) Step the left leg out to the left side and sit into a left drop stance. Thread the left hand along inside the left leg. Look to the lower left. (image 48c)

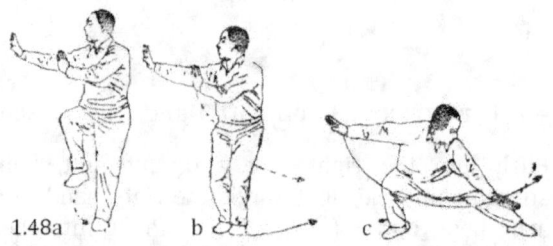

49. Bow Stance, Slice Up With A Hooked Hand

gōngbù liāogōu 弓步撩勾

Push into the right foot and shift to the left, turning the torso slightly left, to take a left bow stance. Hook the right hand and circle it up to meet the left hand with an upward slice, hook pointing down. Look forward. (image 1.49)

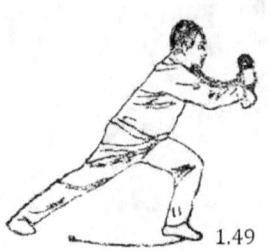
1.49

50. Empty Stance Flash Palm   xūbù liàngzhǎng   虚步亮掌

Push into the left foot and shift right, turning the torso to face half-on to the right. Retreat the left foot a half-step in, placing the ball of the foot on the ground, the heel raised, to take a left empty stance. As the body turns rightward, bring the hands along to the right side. Look to the forward right. (image 1.50a) Without changing the stance, unhook the right hand and raise it above the head, placing the arm curved, fingers pointing left. Push the left hand slightly forward, fingers up. Look to the forward left. (image 50b)

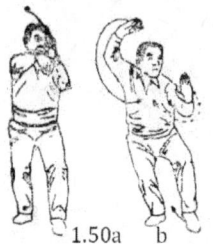
1.50a   b

51. Withdraw, Press Down   chèbù ànzhǎng   撤步按掌

Push into the left foot and shift right, retreating the left leg one step, bending the right knee and straightening the left, touching down the ball of the left foot with the heel raised. Turn the torso slightly to the right. Circle the hands from the sides, down, then thread up to the front, palms up. Look forward. (image 1.51a) Shift back and retreat the right foot a half-step back to place the feet together. Circle the hands down and out to the sides, palms facing forward. Look forward. (image 51b) Bring the left foot in to a closed stance by the right foot and stand up. Circle the hands from the sides up, then down, to press down in front of the belly, palms down, fingers pointing to each other. Hold the chest up slightly. Look forward. (image 51c)

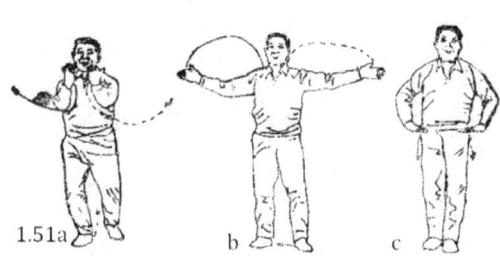
1.51a   b   c

52. Closing Posture   shōu shì   收势

Stand to attention, letting the arms hang by the sides. Look forward. (image 1.52)

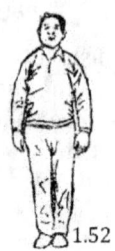

SECOND FORM HUAQUAN
二路滑拳

Names Of The Movements

Position Of Preparation
Section One
1. Stand To Attention, Punch To The Sides
2. Support The Wrist, Reverse Slap
3. Left Chop
4. Stand To Attention, Framing Block And Thread The Hand
5. Stand To Attention, Right Chop
6. Horse Stance Vertical Palms To The Sides
7. T Stance, Framing Block, Stab
8. T Stance Flash Palm
9. Palm Carry And Snap Kick
10. Leap To Bow Stance Push

Section Two
11. T Stance Tuck In
12. Plum Blossom Hand, Empty Stance Scooping Snap
13. Horse Stance Chop
14. Drop Stance Thread The Hand
15. Crossed Arm Slap Kick

Section Three
16. Turn Back, Snap Kick
17. Leap To Bow Stance Forward Slice Up
18. Turn Back, Horse Stance Chop
19. Empty Stance Check

Section Four
20. Leap To Horse Stance Chop
21. Turn Around, Back Sweep
22. Bow Stance Three Stabs
23. Left T Stance Slice Up
24. Leap To Insertion Stance Threading Hand
25. Spin Around To Bow Stance Stab
26. Right Empty Stance Tuck In
27. Bow Stance Plant A Punch

Section Five
28. Turn Around, Closed Stance Crossed Hands
29. Bow Stance Spread The Arms

CHAQUAN, VOLUME II

30. Turn Around, Horse Stance Flash Palm
31. Empty Stance Aligned Punch
32. Turn Around, Closed Stance Punch Upwards
33. Bow Stance Spread The Arms
34. Turn Back, Swing The Arms To Crossed Hands
35. Bow Stance Spread The Arms
36. Snap Kick Close The Hands

Section Six

37. Withdraw To Horse Stance Thread The Hand
38. Right Empty Stance Tuck In
39. Jump To Insertion Stance Thread The Hand
40. Turn Around To Closed Stance Hack
41. Bow Stance Scooping Snap
42. T Stance Crossed Hands
43. T Stance Flash Palm
44. Closing Posture

0. Position Of Preparation yùbèi shì 预备势

Stand to attention with the arms slightly bent. Clench the hands in fists at the hips, fist hearts to the rear. Look to the left. (images 2.0a, 0b) Look forward, then step forward towards the right three times, first right, then left, then right again. Then bring the left foot up beside the right foot to stand to attention, and look to the left. (images 0c, 0d, 0e, 0f) Laterally rotate the forearms and bring the fists to either side of the waist, fist hearts up, then medially rotate the arms to punch forward to shoulder width and height, fist hearts down. Look forward. (images 0g, 0h) Unclench the hands and spread the thumbs out, palms forward. then clench the fists again and bring them to either side of the waist, fist hearts up. Look forward. (images 0i, 0j)

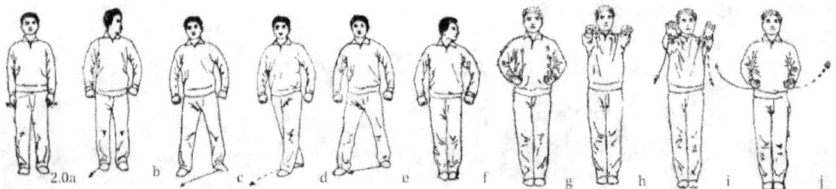

Section One

1. Stand To Attention, Punch To The Sides

bīnglì cè chōngquán 并步侧冲拳

Lower the fists to their respective sides, then circle them upwards and forward until the arms are out to the sides at shoulder height, the fist hearts turned towards the shoulders. (image 2.1a) Pull in the fists quickly into

SECOND FORM HUAQUAN

either side of the waist. (image 1b) Then punch out to the sides, fist eyes up. Look at the right fist. (image 1c)

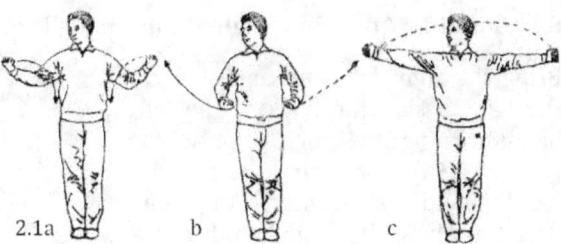

2. Support The Wrist, Reverse Slap   fúwàn fǎn pāizhǎng   扶腕反拍掌

Unclench the hands. Circle the left hand up and over to meet the right, pressing down to on top of the right wrist. (image 2.2a) Once it touches, bend the right wrist to lower and roll the hand over. Circle the right hand up, flipping the hand over to slap at shoulder height, palm up. Look at the right hand. (images 2b, 2c)

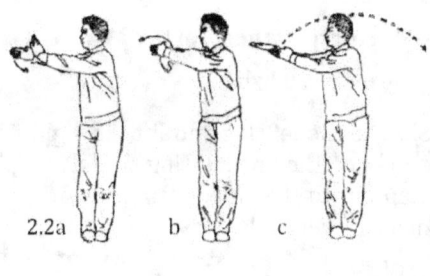

3. Left Chop   zuǒ pīzhǎng   左劈掌

Circle the left hand up and over to the left, to chop down at shoulder height. Both palms face forward, the palm edges down. Look at the left hand. (image 2.3)

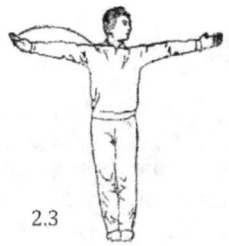

4. Stand To Attention, Framing Block And Thread The Hand
bīnglì jià chuānzhǎng   并立架穿掌

Bend the right elbow to bring the hand in to the right jaw, palm down. (image 2.4a) Stab the right hand out to the left side to shoulder height, thumb up, turning the torso slightly to the left and bending the left elbow to place the left hand in the right elbow crease. Look at the right hand. (image 4b) Turn the torso to the right and circle the right hand up, then right to do a framing block above the head, palm facing forward and up. Stab the left hand out to the left, palm down. Look at the left hand. (image 4c)

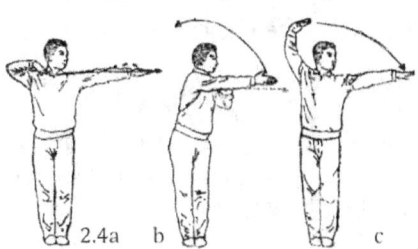

23

5. Stand To Attention, Right Chop   bīnglì yòu pīzhǎng   并立右劈掌

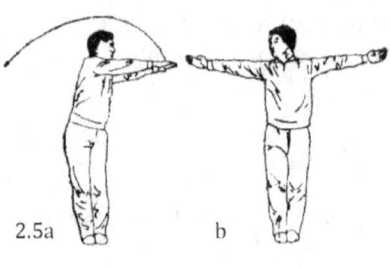

Bring the right hand up and over to the left, to slap the back of the left hand, turning the torso rightward. (image 2.5a) Then circle the right hand up and over to the right to chop down at shoulder height. Both arms are straight out to the sides, the palms facing forward. Look at the right hand. (image 5b)

6. Horse Stance Vertical Palms To The Sides
   mǎbù cè lìzhǎng   马步侧立掌

Shift to the left leg and lift the right foot. (image 2.6a) Stamp the right foot and bend the knee, lifting the left foot. (image 6b) Then quickly take a large step out to the side, sitting down into a horse stance. Snap both wrists to make vertical palms. Look at the left hand. (image 6c)

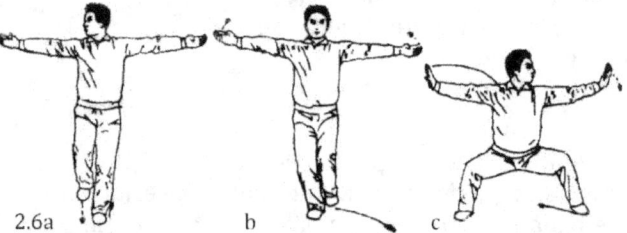

7. T Stance, Framing Block, Stab   dīngbù jià chōngquán   丁步架穿掌

Turn the torso slightly leftward and shift to the right leg, bringing in the left foot a bit to take a left empty stance. Bend the right elbow to place the hand above the right shoulder, palm down. Press the left hand down and continue to turn leftward. (image 2.7a) Bring the left foot in beside the right foot and touch the ball of the foot down to take a left T stance. Stab forward with the right hand to shoulder height, arm straight, palm down. Do a framing block up above the head with the left hand, palm angled up and forward. Look at the right hand. (image 7b)

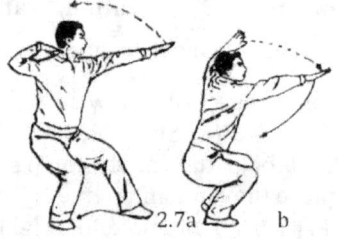

8. T Stance Flash Palm   dīngbù liàngzhǎng   丁步亮掌

Bring the left hand down to press on the back of the right hand, then press down with both hands in front of the knees, palms down. (image 2.8a) Separate the hands out to either side then circle them up. the right hand finishes above the head at the right, palm flashing up. The left arm is at shoulder height, fingers up, palm angled to the forward left. Look forward. (image 8b)

SECOND FORM HUAQUAN

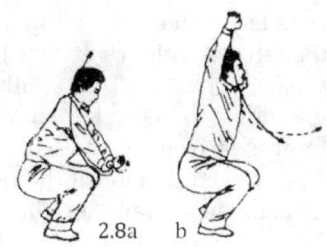

9. Palm Carry And Snap Kick   tuōzhǎng tántuǐ   托掌弹腿

Circle the left hand down, forward, then to the right to carry, palm up. Circle the right hand right, down, forward, then left to carry, tucked into the left elbow crease, palm up. The hands are about chest height. Look at the left hand. (image 2.9a) Push into the right leg and extend the left leg to kick forward, ankle plantar-flexed. Look past the left foot. (image 9b)

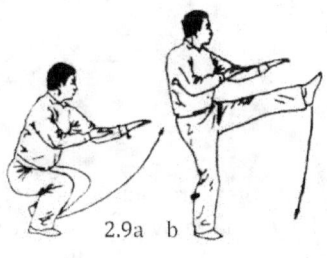

10. Leap To Bow Stance Push   yuè gōngbù tuīzhǎng   跃弓步推掌

Land forward on the left foot and shift to the left leg, then push off strongly to jump up, swinging the right leg forward and up with a jump. Swing the hands forward and up. Land the right foot, then the left, and turn right to take a right bow stance. Swing the arms right, then down, bending the right arm slightly and snapping the wrist to make a vertical palm. Place the left vertical palm at the right elbow. Look at the right hand. (images 2.10a, 10b, 10c) Sit down on both legs and turn the torso slightly leftward, bringing the hands in to the chest. Turn leftward and push into the right leg to shift to the left leg, taking a left bow stance. Extend the vertical palms out to either side to eyebrow height. Look at the right hand. (images 10d, 10e)

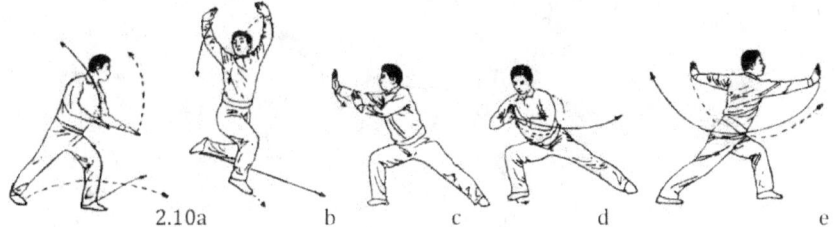

Section Two

11. T Stance Tuck In   dīngbù yǎnzhǎng   丁步掩掌

Turn the body around to the right, circling the right hand down, right, then up to above the head with a vertical palm. Circle the left hand down, left, then up to the side, also in a vertical palm. The palms face out. Shift to the right leg to take a right bow stance. Look at the left hand. (image 2.11a) Step the left, then the right foot forward to the left, then shift to the right leg. (images 11b, 11c) Take another step forward with the left foot, touching the toes down to take a left empty stance. Circle the left hand down to the right to pass in front of the left knee, then continue on, bending the elbow, to place a vertical palm at the right side of the chest, palm forward, fingers up. Look to the forward left. (images 11d, 11e)

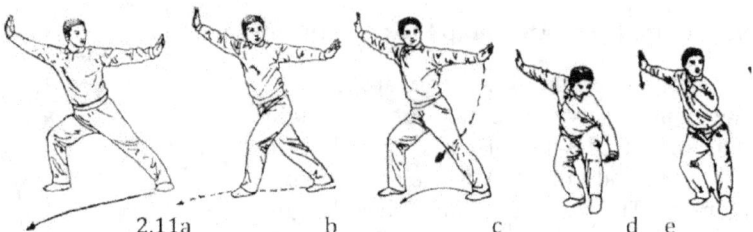

Shift completely onto the right leg and straighten it, lifting the left knee. Flip the left hand over to circle the back of the hand past the left knee then out to the left and up to above the head, palm out. (images 11f, 11g) Land the left foot out to the forward left, to take a left bow stance. Look at the right hand. (image 11h)

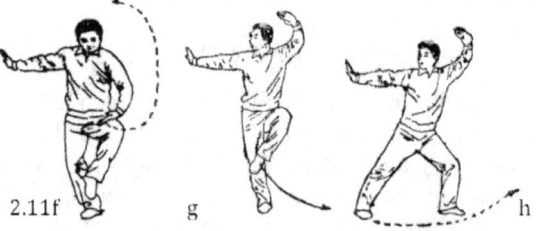

Step to the forward left with each foot, first right, then left, then shift to the left leg and step the right foot forward again, touching the toes down to take a right empty stance. Circle the right hand down to the left to pass in front of the left knee, then continue on, bending the elbow, to place a vertical palm at the left side of the chest, palm forward, fingers up. Look to the forward right. (images 11i, 11j, 11k, 11l)

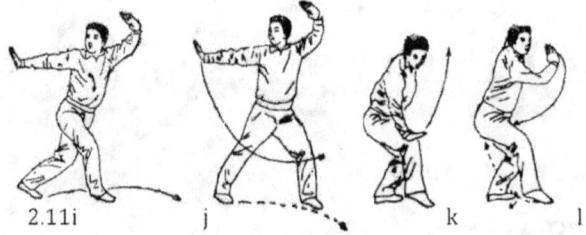

Shift completely onto the left leg and straighten it, lifting the right knee. Flip the right hand over to circle the back of the hand past the right knee then out to the right and up to above the head, palm out. (images 11m, 11n) Land

SECOND FORM HUAQUAN

the right foot out to the forward right to take a right bow stance. Look at the left hand. (image 11o)

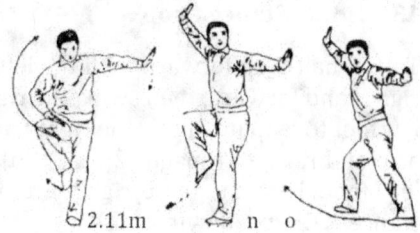

Step to the forward right with each foot, first left, then right, then shift to the right leg and step the left foot forward again, touching the toes down to take a left empty stance. Circle the left hand down to the right to pass in front of the right knee, then continue on, bending the elbow, to place a vertical palm at the right side of the chest, palm forward, fingers up. Look to the forward left. (images 11p, 11q, 11r, 11s)

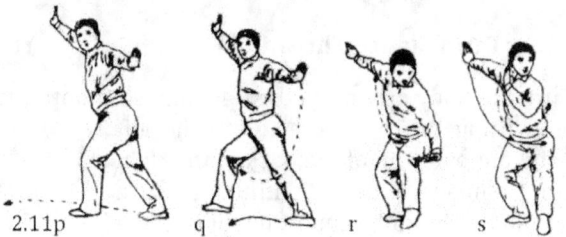

12. Plum Blossom Hand, Empty Stance Scooping Snap

méihuā shǒu xūbù tiǎozhǎng 　　　　　　　　梅花手虚步挑掌

Turn the body slightly to the left and lower the hands in front of the belly, thumb webs facing each other. The left palm faces up, fingers pointing right, while the right palm faces down, fingers pointing left. Look at the left hand. (image 2.12a) Pivoting at the heels of the palms, laterally rotate the left arm and medially rotate the right arm, so that the hands draw counter-clockwise circles until the left palm flips to face up and the right palm flips to face down. The right hand is now on top. (image 12b) Then lean the torso slightly forward, laterally rotate the right hand to turn the palm up, and circle it to the left, then right, then down past the left knee to do a scooping snap up in front at the right, fingers at nose height, body upright. Circle the left hand down, to the left, and back, palm facing the forward left, fingers back. Look past the right hand. (images 12c, 12d)

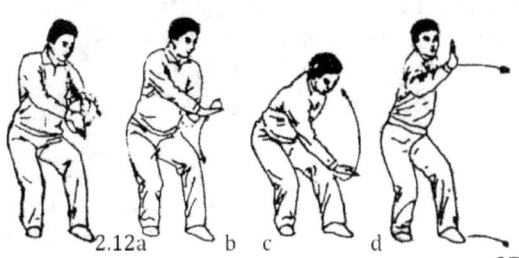

13. Horse Stance Chop   mǎbù pīzhǎng   马步劈掌

Take a half-step forward with the left foot and shift to the left leg. Stab the right hand forward, then swing the right leg forward and up, pushing off the left foot to leap up. Circle the right hand down and to the rear. Bend the left arm and raise it. (images 2.13a, 13b) Land on the right foot, then land the left, foot. Turn the torso rightward and sit into both legs to take a horse stance. Chop downwards with the left hand so that the arms are in a straight, level, line. The thumbs are on top and the palms face forward. Look at the left hand. (image 13c)

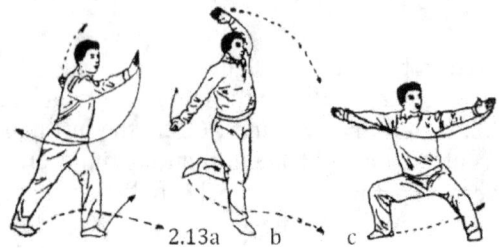

14. Drop Stance Thread The Hand   pūbù chuānzhǎng   仆步穿掌

Turn the body around to the right and shift onto the left leg, straightening it and lifting the right knee. Stab the left hand out over top of the back of the right hand. (image 2.14a) Continue to turn around to the right, squatting fully on the left leg and extending the right leg to take a right drop stance. Thread the right hand down and out along the inside of the right leg, extending the left arm angled upwards. (image 14b)

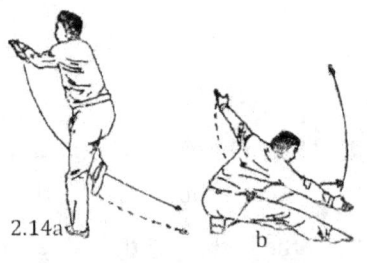

15. Crossed Arm Slap Kick   shízì pāijiǎo   十字拍脚

Shift to the right leg and extend it, pushing off with the left leg to lift it, standing up and turning right. Raise the right arm up and lower the left arm. Then land forward on the left foot into a left bow stance. Lower the right hand to the forward right, then left. Circle the left hand from the lower left to the upper right to cross with the right arm in front of the belly. The right arm is on top. Look to the lower front. (images 2.15a, 15b) Circle the right hand to the left, up, down, then left again, bending the elbow to finish in front of the belly, palm down. Circle the left hand to the left, forward, up, then slap down. Lift the right leg to kick with the ankle plantar-flexed, slapping the foot with the left hand. Look at the right foot. (image 15c)

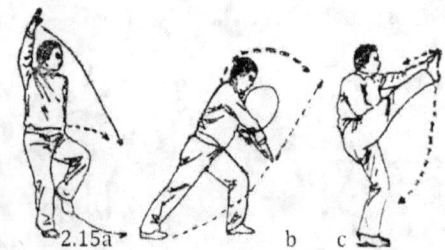

SECOND FORM HUAQUAN

Section Three

16. Turn Back, Snap Kick huíshēn tántuǐ 回身弹腿

Lower the right foot, keeping the knee up and bent. Cross the arms in front of the head, palms out, left hand inside the right. (image 2.16a) Then stamp with the right foot and lift the left foot, turning a bit to the left. (image 16b) Open out the arms upward to either side. Turn the torso a bit more to the left. and do a snap kick to the left with the left foot, spreading the arms out to the rear. Look at the left foot. (image 16c)

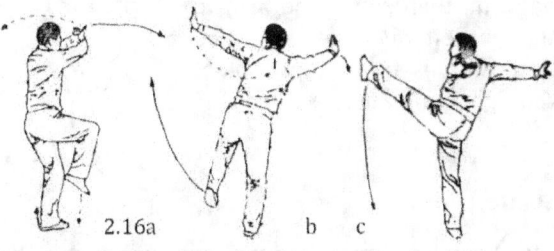

17. Leap To Bow Stance Forward Slice Up

yuè gōngbù qián liāozhǎng 跃弓步前撩掌

Land forward on the left foot and shift to the left leg, then swing the right leg forward and up and push off the left leg to jump forward. (images 2.17a, 17b) Land on the right foot, then land the left, to take a left bow stance. Slice the right arm forward and up to shoulder height, thumb on top, fingers forward. Extend the left arm to the rear. Look at the right hand. (image 17c)

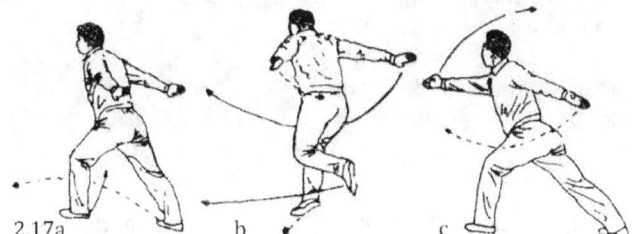

18. Turn Back, Horse Stance Chop

huíshēn mǎbù pīzhǎng 回身马步劈掌

Turn around to the right, swinging the right arm up and to the right. The left arm extends to the lower rear. (image 2.18a) Step the left foot forward and turn the torso to the right to take a horse stance. Swing the right arm down, back, then up. Swing the left arm up, then chop down. The arms are extended straight out to the sides. Look at the left hand. (image 18b)

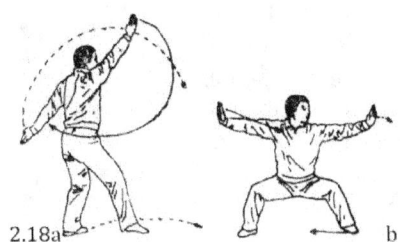

19. Empty Stance Check   xūbù cuòzhǎng   虚步挫掌

Straighten both legs slightly and turn the torso leftward to take a left empty stance. Bend the right elbow to bring the right hand to the right shoulder. (image 2.19a) Stab the right hand forward at shoulder height, rubbing the left palm as the hands pass. Bend the left elbow to bring the hand in, then swing the arm to the rear left, raising it to the side. Both thumbs are on top. Look at the right hand. (image 19b)

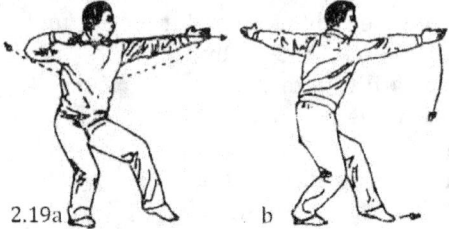

Section Four

20. Leap To Horse Stance Chop   yuèshēn mǎbù pīzhǎng   跃身马步劈掌

Take a half-step forward with the left foot and shift to the left leg. Medially rotate the right forearm and lower it in a hooking action, then swing the right leg forward and up and push off with the left leg to jump forward, swinging the right arm upwards. (images 2.20a, 20b) Land on the right foot, then land the left, and turn the torso to the right to take a horse stance. Swing the left arm up, left, then down to shoulder height. Swing the right arm down and back to shoulder height. Both hands are vertical palms. Look at the left hand. (image 20c)

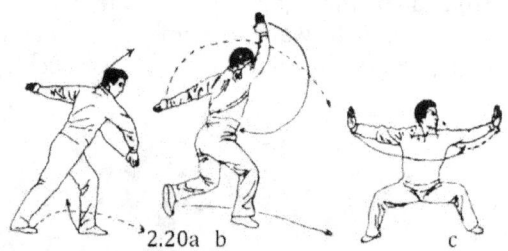

21. Turn Around, Back Sweep   zhuànshēn hòusǎo   转身后扫

Straighten the right leg, turning the heel out, and shift to the left leg. Turn the torso to the left, swinging the right hand down to the left, bending the elbow to place the hand in front of the left chest. (image 2.21a) Turn the torso further rightward and place both hands on the ground inside the left foot, right fingers pointing back, left fingers pointing to the right. Squat fully on the left leg and extend the right leg, then pivot on the ball of the left foot to complete a full back sweep with the right leg. Look at the right foot. (images 21b, 21c)

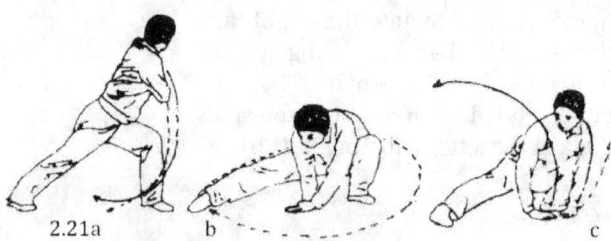

SECOND FORM HUAQUAN

22. Bow Stance Three Stabs   gōngbù sānchuānzhǎng   弓步三穿掌

Shift to the right leg, standing up. Brush aside with the right hand to the right, and swing the left hand back to level. Circle the right hand down, left, then bring it in to the waist, palm up. Turn the torso slightly rightward and swing the left hand up, forward, and down to press down at belly height, palm down. Look at the left hand. (images 2.22a, 22b) Shift forward to take a right bow stance, reaching the torso slightly forward. Stab to the lower front with the right hand, passing over the back of the left hand, thumb on top. Stab with the left hand and bring the right hand back to the waist, palm up. Then stab the right hand forward and down again, passing underneath the left hand, and bring the left hand back to the waist, palm up. Look at the right hand. (images 22c, 22d, 22e)

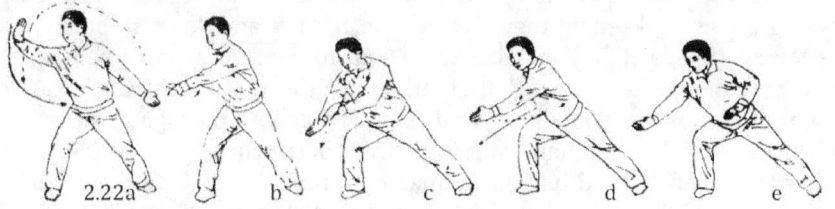

23. Left T Stance Slice Up   zuǒ dīngbù liāozhǎng   左丁步撩掌

Turn left and lean slightly, shifting to the left leg. Laterally rotate the left hand and circle it down past the left knee. (image 2.23a) Then shift to the right leg and sit, bringing the left foot back to take a left empty stance. Continue to circle the left hand left, up, and right to take a vertical palm in front of the chest. Extend the right arm out to the right. Look to the forward left. (image 23b)

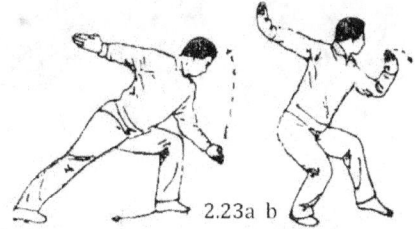

24. Leap To Insertion Stance Threading Hand

yuè chābù chuānzhǎng   跃插步穿掌

Roll the left hand over to the left, palm up. (image 2.24a) Take a half-step to the left with the left foot and shift to the left leg, threading the left hand out to the left. (image 24b) Swing the right leg up to the left and push off with the left foot to jump up, threading the right hand out past the left palm. (image 24c) Land on the right foot and shift to the right leg, then step the left foot forward behind the right leg with an insertion step, heel up. The right hand is at shoulder height, and the left hand is in front of the chest, palm up. Look at the right hand. (image 24d)

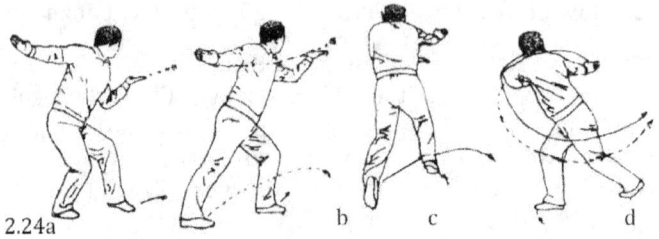

25. Spin Around To Bow Stance Stab

xuànyāo gōngbù chāzhǎng 旋腰弓步插掌

Lean the torso forward and spin around to the left, shifting onto the left leg. Swing the arms, keeping them straight, to the left and down to below the left knee. (image 2.25a) Arch back and shift to the right leg in a half-squat, spinning the torso over to the left then again lean forward. As the torso spins, the arms circle left, back, and right. Finish with the right hand at the right waist, and the left hand upright in front of the chest. (images 25b, 25c) Shift to the left leg and half-sit to take a left bow stance, turning the torso leftward. Clench the left hand and bring the fist to the waist. Stab to the lower left with the right hand, thumb side up. Look at the right hand. (image 25d) Unclench the left hand and stab it to the lower front, thumb up. Bring the right hand to the waist, palm up. Look at the left hand. (image 25e)

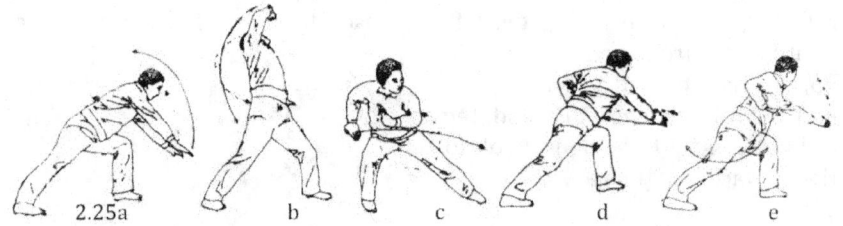

26. Right Empty Stance Tuck In   yòu xūbù yǎnzhǎng   右虚步掩掌

Shift to the right leg and turn rightward. Circle the right hand down and to the right to in front of the right knee, palm up. (image 2.26a) Shift to the left leg and sit down, bringing in the right foot with the knee slightly bent to take a right empty stance, the torso upright. Continue to circle the right hand right, up, and to the left, then bend the elbow to bring the palm in to the chest. Hold the left arm out to the side. Look to the forward right. (image 26b)

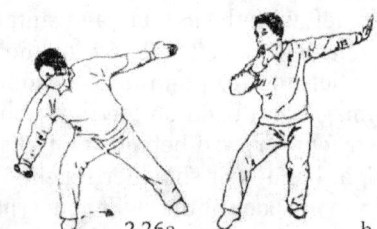

SECOND FORM HUAQUAN

27. Bow Stance Plant A Punch   gōngbù xiàzāiquán   弓步下栽拳

Step the right foot a half-step forward towards the left and shift to the right leg, then push off and swing the left leg up to jump up. Land on the left foot, then land the right, and shift to the right leg into a right bow stance. Push forward with the left hand and bring the right hand to the waist. (images 2.27a, 27b, 27c) Circle the right hand back and up and swing the left hand down and left, holding the arms angled up and down. Lean the torso forward and clench the right hand, bend the elbow, then punch downwards inside the right foot, knuckles near the ground. Clench the left hand and raise it up. Look at the right fist. (images 27d, 27e)

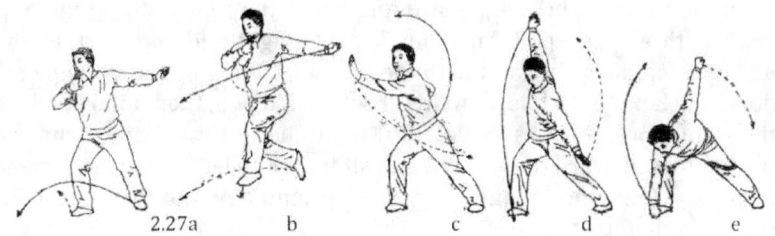

Section Five

28. Turn Around, Closed Stance Crossed Hands
   huíshen bīngbù shízìshǒu   回身并步十字手

Stand up, swinging the right arm forward and up while swinging the left arm back and down. Step the left foot forward to the right side and turn rightward, standing up with the feet apart. Circle the right arm up and right and the left arm down, left, and up to extend the arms out to the sides. (images 2.28a, 28b) Bring the right foot in to meet the left foot and stand upright. Swing the left arm up and the right arm down, bending the elbows to cross the forearms in front of the chest, left inside right, palms out. Look forward. (image 28c, and from behind)

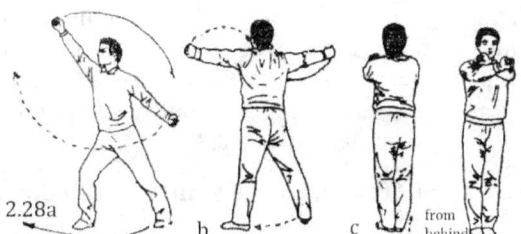

29. Bow Stance Spread The Arms   gōngbù zhǎnbì   弓步展臂

Shift to the left leg and bend the knee, lifting the right foot. (image 2.29a) Stamp the right foot and shift to the right leg, bending the knee. Lift the left foot, then step it out to the side and turn left to take a left bow stance. Spread the straight arms out to either side to extend them downwards and back, fist eyes up. Look forward. (images 29b, 29c)

CHAQUAN, VOLUME II

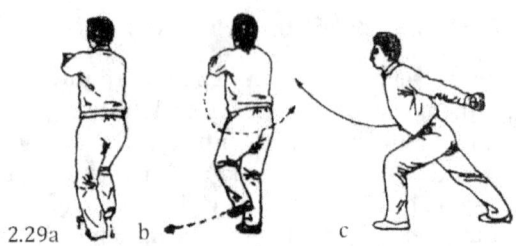

2.29a   b   c

30. Turn Around, Horse Stance Flash Palm

zhuànshēn mǎbù liàngzhǎng   转身马步亮掌

Turn the torso slightly rightward and lower the right fist, swinging it up in front with a slice up. Turn around to the right and shift to the right leg, unclenching the right hand with the turn and swinging the arm up and over, down to slap the right leg. Circle the left arm down, then up to level. Look to the right front. (images 2.30a, 30b) Continue to turn to the right and step the left foot forward to the right and sit into both legs, taking a horse stance. Swing the left hand up and over, forward and down to the left thigh. Raise the right hand at the right, then snap the wrist with a flash palm above the head at the right, palm up. Look to the left. (image 30c)

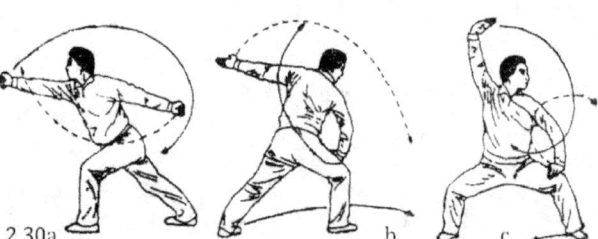

2.30a   b   c

31. Empty Stance Aligned Punch   xūbù shùn chōngquán   虚步顺冲拳

Turn slightly to the left and shift to the right leg, squatting and bringing the left foot in to take a left empty stance. Clench the right hand and chop down, then bring it to the waist. Clench the left hand and raise it past the chest, then punch out to the left, fist eye up. Look at the left fist. (image 2.31)

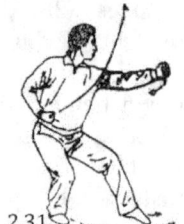

2.31

32. Turn Around, Closed Stance Punch Upwards

zhuànshēn bīngbù shàng chōngquán   转身并步上冲拳

Stamp with the left foot and shift to the left leg. Step the right foot in front, hooked in, and turn one-eighty degrees to the left, shifting to the right leg. Bring the left foot in beside the right and stand up. Punch the right fist straight up, passing by the right side of the chest. Unclench the left hand and tuck it into the right armpit. Look forward, to the left. (image 2.32)

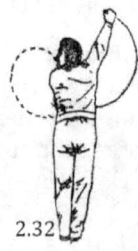

2.32

SECOND FORM HUAQUAN

33. Bow Stance Spread The Arms　　gōngbù zhǎnbì　　弓步展臂

Circle the right arm to the right, down, left, then up. Clench the left hand and circle it down, left, then up, so that the arms cross in front of the chest with bent elbows, left inside the right, fist hearts facing out. (image 2.33a, and from behind) Lift the right foot then land with a stamp, lifting the left foot and stepping it out to the side into a left bow stance. Turn the torso to the left and lean forward, spreading the arms to hold them low behind, fist eyes up. Look forward. (images 33b, 33c, 33d)

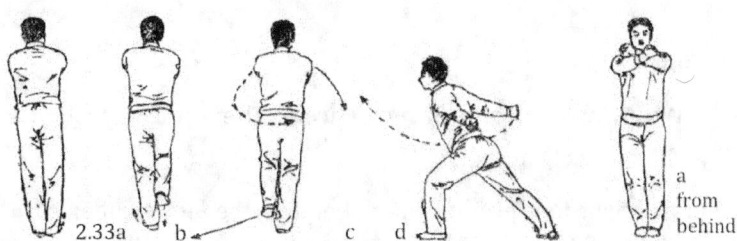

34. Turn Back, Swing The Arms To Crossed Hands

huíshēn lūnbì shízìshǒu　　回身轮臂十字手

Slice upwards to the front with the right arm. Turn one-eighty degrees around to the right, swinging the right arm up, right, and down. Swing the left arm down, left, then up, shifting to the right leg. (images 2.34a, 34b) Step the left foot forward, hooked in, landing in front of the right foot, turning the body ninety degrees to the right. Bring the right foot in beside the left and stand up. Swing the left arm down to the right and the right arm up to the left, bending the elbows to cross the forearms in front of the chest, left outside the right. Both fist hearts face out. Look at the left fist. (image 34c)

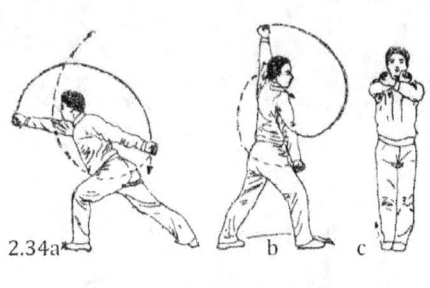

35. Bow Stance Spread The Arms　　gōngbù zhǎnbì　　弓步展臂

Shift to the left leg, bending the left leg. Lift the right foot then land with a stamp, shifting to the right leg. (images 2.35a, 35b) Lift the left foot and step it out to the side, turning left into a left bow stance. Separate the arms, keeping them straight, until they are held low behind, fist eyes up. Look forward. (image 35c)

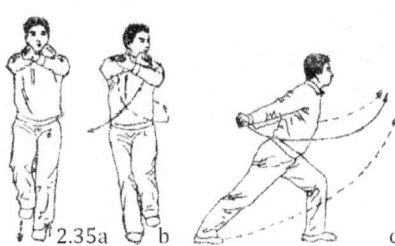

36. Snap Kick Close The Hands tántuǐ hézhǎng 弹腿合掌

Shift to the left leg and stand up, lifting the right leg to do a snap kick, ankle plantar-flexed at belly height. Unclench the hands and swing the straight arms forward, bringing them together in front of the body at shoulder height. Look at the hands. (image 2.36)

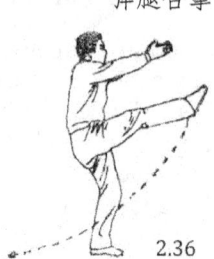

Section Six

37. Withdraw To Horse Stance Thread The Hand
chè mǎbù chuānzhǎng 撤马步穿掌

Land the right foot firmly behind, bending the left leg, then turn the body around ninety degrees to the right to take a horse stance. Flip the left hand to palm up and thread it forward past the back of the right hand to push, palm out, fingers up at nose height. Bring the right hand in to the waist, palm up. Look at the left hand. (images 2.37a, 37b) Withdraw the left foot and turn the body around one-eighty degrees to the left into another horse stance. Thread the right hand out along the back of the left hand to push, palm out, fingers up at nose height. Look at the right hand. (image 37c)

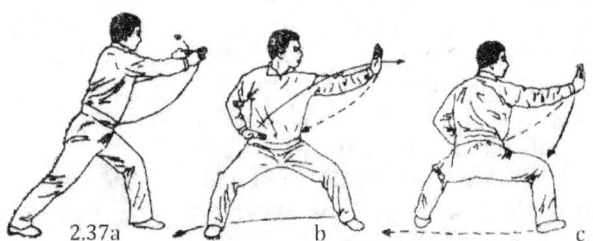

38. Right Empty Stance Tuck In yòu xūbù yǎnzhǎng 右虚步掩掌

Withdraw the right foot to the left and bend the knee, turning the body around one-eighty degrees to the right, straightening the left leg. Thread the left hand up past the back of the right hand then bring the right hand down to the right knee, palm up (image 2.38a) Continue to swing the right hand to the right and up, bending the elbow to cover towards the left in front of the chest, palm out, fingers pointing back. Snap the left wrist to take an upright palm, palm out, fingers up. Push into the right leg to sit back into a left empty stance. Look to the forward right. (image 38b)

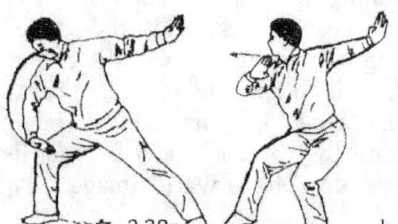

SECOND FORM HUAQUAN

39. Jump To Insertion Stance Thread The Hand

yuè chābù chuānzhǎng   跳插步穿掌

Laterally rotate the right forearm and bend the elbow, turning the palm up. Take a firm step forward with the right foot, bending the knee and straightening the left leg, shifting to the right leg. Lean forward and stab the right hand forward. (images 2.39a, 39b) Push off with the right leg to jump, swinging the right leg forward and turning right. Land with the left foot, then the right, stepping it behind the left leg with an insertion step. Thread the left hand directly forward, passing above the right hand, palm forward, fingers to the left. Bring the right hand in to the left side of the chest, palm up. Look at the left hand. (image 39c, 39d)

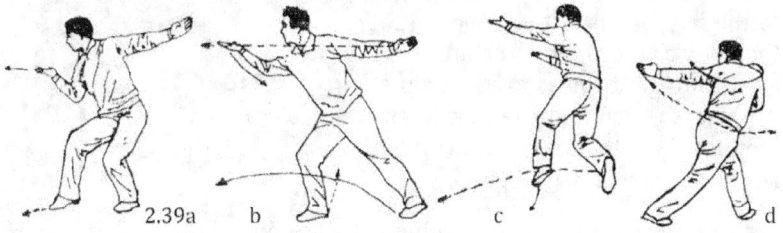

40. Turn Around To Closed Stance Hack

zhuànshen bīngbù kǎnzhǎng   转身并步砍掌

Pivoting on the heel of the left foot and the ball of the right foot, turn around to the right one-eighty degrees. (image 2.40a) Bring the left foot in beside the right and stand up. Whilst turning, swing the right arm forward, right, up and over, then down, bending the elbow in front of the chest with the palm down, and swing the left arm down, right, then up. Bend the left elbow in front of the chest, tucking the palm into the right armpit, palm down. (image 40b) Chop out to the side with the edge of the right hand, palm down. Look at the right hand. (image 40c)

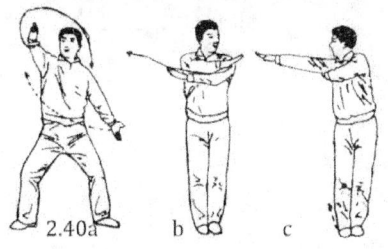

41. Bow Stance Scooping Snap   gōngbù tiǎozhǎng   弓步挑掌

Lift the right foot then land with a stamp and bend the knee, lifting the left foot then extending it out to the left into a drop stance. Thread the left hand along inside the top of the left leg to the foot, palm forward. (images 2.41a, 41b, 41c) Push into the right leg and extend the leg, standing up and turning the torso to the left to take a left bow stance. Do a scoop up to the left with the left hand, fingers at eyebrow height. Snap the right wrist to turn the fingers up. Look at the left hand. (image 41d)

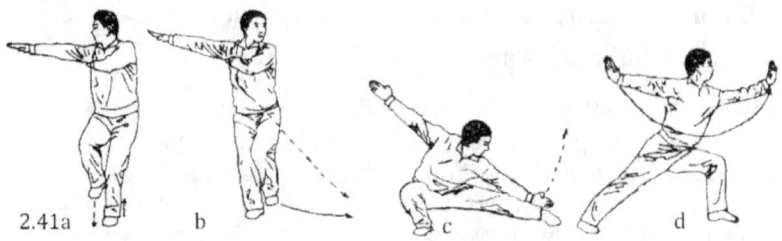
2.41a   b   c   d

42. T Stance Crossed Hands   dīngbù shízìshǒu   丁步十字手

Turn the torso slightly to the left. Circle the right hand down, forward, then up, bringing the wrist to the left wrist so that they cross in front of the chest, right outside the left, palms out. (image 2.42a) Turn the body to the right and shift to the right leg, bending the knees to a half-squat, and bringing the left foot in beside the right foot, touching the toes down in a left T stance. Look to the left. (image 42b)

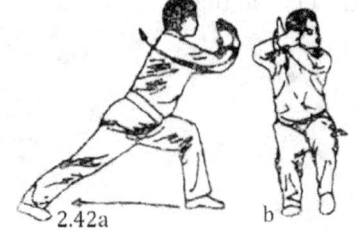
2.42a   b

43. T Stance Flash Palm   dīngbù liàngzhǎng   丁步亮掌

Lean the torso forward slightly and lower the hands to the left knee, then separate them to their respective sides. Continue to circle them up at the sides until the right hand does a flash palm above the head, palm angled up, and the left hand does a scooping snap with an upright palm at the left side, palm out. Look at the left hand. (image 2.43a, 43b)

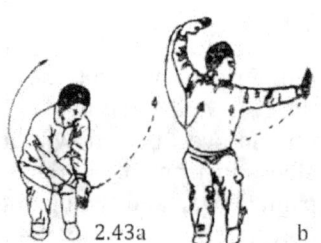
2.43a   b

44. Closing Posture   shōu shì   收势

Withdraw the left foot. Bring both hands in to the sides of the waist, then thread them forward, palms up. (image 2.44a) Withdraw the right foot and clench the fists. (image 44b) Withdraw the left foot to beside the right and stand up, medially rotating the forearms and bringing the fists to the hips, fist hearts angled to the back. Look to the left. (image 44c) Unclench the hands and let the arms hang naturally at the sides. Turn the head to look forward. (image 44d)

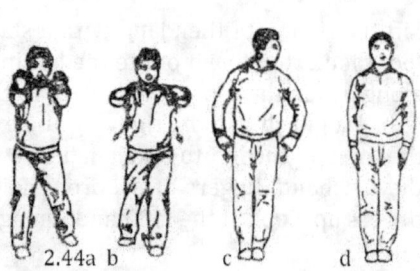
2.44a   b   c   d

THIRD FORM HUAQUAN (B)
三路滑拳（乙）

Names Of The Movements

Position Of Preparation
Section One
1. Bow Stance Flash Palm
2. Bow Stance Stab
3. Empty Stance Tuck
4. Jump To Bow Stance Chop
5. Turn Back, Right Bow Stance Left Push
6. Left Bow Stance Right Push
7. Right Bow Stance Left Push
8. Left Bow Stance Right Push
9. Turn Around, Left Empty Stance Tuck
10. Right Empty Stance Tuck
11. Left Empty Stance Tuck
12. Jumping Turn, Left Empty Stance Lash And Hook

Section Two
13. Right Empty Stance Lash And Hook
14. Left Empty Stance Lash And Hook
15. Withdraw, Bow Stance Cut
16. Turn Around, Open Bow Stance Elbow Butt
17. Turn Around, Open Bow Stance Elbow Butt
18. Snap Kick, Bow Stance Double Punch
19. Turn Around, Open Bow Stance Elbow Butt
20. Snap Kick, Bow Stance Elbow Butt
21. Bow Stance Hook And Punch
22. Right Empty Stance Tuck
23. Jump To Horse Stance Chop
24. Turn Around, Bow Stance Chop
25. Turn Around, Open Bow Stance Elbow Butt
26. Snap Kick, Bow Stance Double Punch
27. Left Empty Stance Tuck
28. Jump To Horse Stance Chop
29. Turn Around, Horse Stance Double Push
30. Step Forward To Bow Stance Double Push
31. Turn Around, Horse Stance Double Push
32. T Stance Framing Block And Hook

Section Three
33. Turn Around, Thread To Horse Stance Flash Palm
34. Turn Around, Thread To Horse Stance Flash Palm
35. Turn Around, Thread To Horse Stance Flash Palm
36. Turn Around, Thread To Horse Stance Flash Palm
37. Jump To Insertion Stance Stab
38. Turn Around, T Stance Framing Block And Planting Punch
39. Turn Around, Horse Stance Chop
40. Turn Around, Bow Stance Low Intercept
41. Turn Around, T Stance Framing Block And Planting Punch
42. Squat And Pounce
43. Squat And Pounce
44. Squat And Pounce
45. Turn Back, Bow Stance Elbow Butt

Section Four
46. Bow Stance Hook And Punch
47. Right Empty Stance Tuck
48. Empty Stance Brace
49. Horse Stance Push
50. Bow Stance Punch
51. Jump To Horse Stance Push
52. Turn Back, Bow Stance Punch

Section Five
53. Empty Stance Elbow Carry
54. Jump To Bow Stance Chop
55. Two Rising Kicks
56. Wheel Over, Drop Stance Reverse Slap
57. Step Forward, Drop Stance Reverse Slap
58. Step Forward, Drop Stance Reverse Slap
59. Back Sweep Kick

Section Six
60. Raised Knee Double Hooks
61. Hitting Hop-Step, Turn Around, Bow Stance Lash And Hook
62. Hitting Hop-Step, Turn Around, Bow Stance Lash And Hook
63. Hitting Hop-Step, Turn Around, Bow Stance Lash And Hook
64. Whisk Hand, Closed Stance Flash Palm
65. Closing Posture

0. Position Of Preparation yùbèi shì 预备势

Stand to attention. Step the left foot sideways to the left to take an open stance. Clench the fists and medially rotate the forearms, bending the elbows to lift the fists at either side of the hips, fist eyes inward. Look to the

THIRD FORM HUAQUAN (B)

forward left. (images 3.0a, 0b) Shift to the right leg and take two steps, first the left foot, then the right foot, forward towards the right. Then bring the left foot in a half-step to stand beside the right foot in an open stance. (images 0c, 0d, 0e) Laterally rotate the forearms and bend the elbows further, bringing the fists to either side of the waist, fist hearts up. (image 0f) Medially rotate the fists and punch straight forward to chest height, shoulder width, fist hearts down. (image 0g) Unclench the hands and cock the wrists to form vertical palms with the tiger's mouths facing each other. (image 0h) Finally, clench the fists again and bring them to either side of the waist, fist hearts up. Look forward. (image 0i)

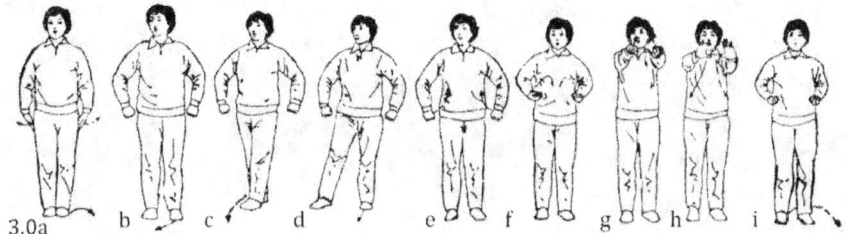

Section One

1. Bow Stance Flash Palm gōngbù liàngzhǎng 弓步亮掌

Turn the body slightly rightward and shift to the left leg, inserting the right foot behind the left leg, stepping towards the left. Then take a sideways step to the left with the left foot. Look to the lower left. (images 3.1a, 1b) Turn the torso slightly to the left and shift to the left leg, bending both legs. Medially rotate the left forearm and unclench the left hand, to press down on the left knee with the tiger's mouth facing in. Then pivot on the ball of the right foot to turn the heel outwards and straighten the leg, turning the torso leftward to take a left bow stance. Unclench the right hand and circle it right, up, then left to stop above the head with a flash palm, palm angled up. Look forward. (images 1c, 1d)

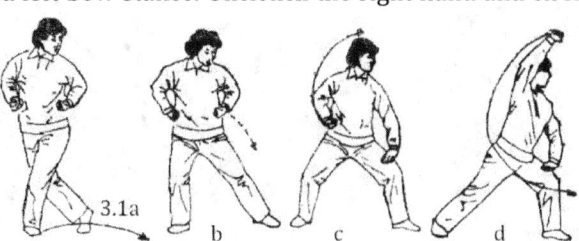

2. Bow Stance Stab gōngbù chuānzhǎng 弓步穿掌

Lean the torso forward and circle the right hand right and down to in front of and below the left knee. Then straighten the torso up and circle the hand up to the left to in front of the left temple. Look forward. (images 3.2a, 2b) Continue to circle the right hand up and to the right, bending the arm to bring the hand to the waist, palm up. Circle the left hand down, back, up, and rightward to above and in front of the head. Look forward. (images 2c,

41

2d) Lean the torso forward and continue to circle the left hand until it is below the left knee, then hook it back on the left, bringing it to hook and lash out to the side, fingers pointing left. Straighten the torso up and turn leftward, stabbing the right hand forward, fingers forward. Look at the right hand. (images 2e, 2f)

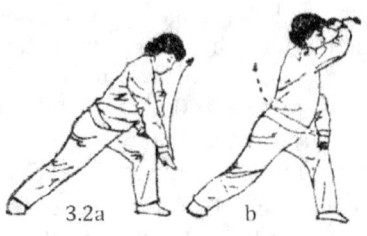

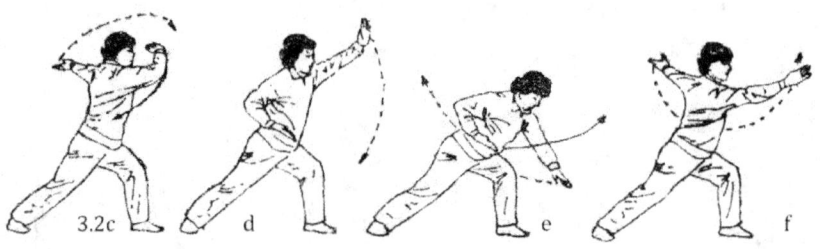

3. Empty Stance Tuck   xūbù yǎnzhǎng   虚步掩掌

Turn the torso slightly to the right and bend the left elbow, bringing the left hand past the left side of the waist then threading it out above the right forearm. Turn around to the right and shift to the right leg into a right bow stance, bringing the right hand down and to the right, laterally rotating to lash down, palm up. Look at the right hand. (images 3.3a, 3b) Straighten the torso and shift back, squatting on the left leg in a right T stance. Continue to circle the right hand past below the right knee, to the right, up, then left, then bending the elbow to place a vertical palm in front of the left ear, palm out. Look to the forward right. (images 3c, 3d)

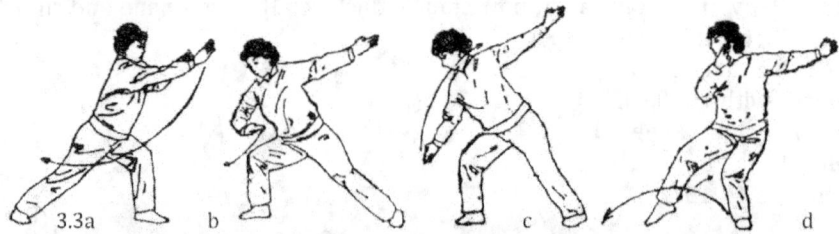

4. Jump To Bow Stance Chop   tiào gōngbù pīzhǎng   跳弓步劈掌

Land the right foot and shift to the right leg, then push off with the right leg and swing the left leg forward and up to jump. Land on the left foot, then land the right foot forward into a right T stance. Look to the forward right. (images 3.4a, 4b) Turn the torso rightward and shift forward to a right bow stance, bringing the right hand to the waist, palm up, and bringing the left hand overhead to chop forward. Turn the torso slightly left and swing the

THIRD FORM HUAQUAN (B)

right hand back, then up and over to chop down in front, bringing the left hand to the waist, palm up. Look at the right hand. (images 4c, 4d)

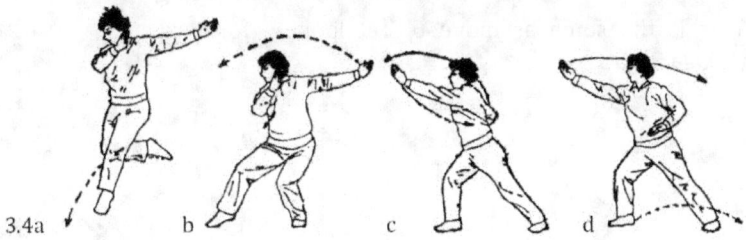

5. Turn Back, Right Bow Stance Left Push

huíshēn gōngbù zuǒ tuīzhǎng   回身右弓步左推掌

Turn the body around to the left one-eighty degrees and step the right foot forward into a right bow stance. Swing the right hand over with the turn to in front of the body. (image 3.5a) Turn the torso to the right and push the left hand forward with a vertical palm, bringing the right fist in to the waist, fist heart up. Look to the rear right. (image 5b)

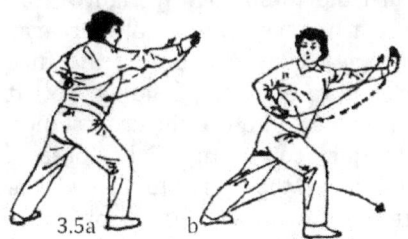

6. Left Bow Stance Right Push

zuǒ gōngbù yòu tuīzhǎng   左弓步右推掌

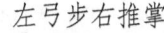

Step the left foot forward and turn the torso to the left to take a left bow stance. Unclench the right hand and push forward over the left forearm with a vertical palm, bringing the left fist in to the waist. Look to the rear left. (image 3.6)

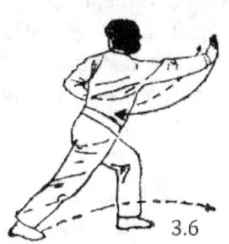

7. Right Bow Stance Left Push

yòu gōngbù zuǒ tuīzhǎng   右弓步左推掌

This is the same as move 6, just transposing right and left. (image 3.7)

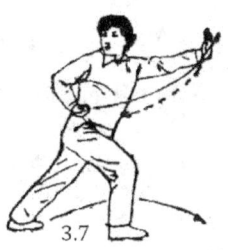

8. Left Bow Stance Right Push

zuǒ gōngbù yòu tuīzhǎng 左弓步右推掌

This is the same as move 6, but looking forward. (image 3.8)

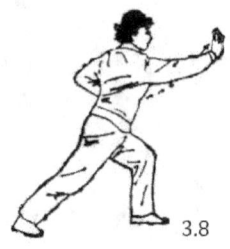

9. Turn Around, Left Empty Stance Tuck

zhuànshēn zuǒ xūbù yǎnzhǎng 转身左虚步掩掌

Turn the torso slightly rightward, unclench the left hand and thread it forward over the right forearm. (image 3.9a) Continue to turn around to the right, bending the left knee to sit into a right drop stance. Laterally rotate the right forearm and bend the wrist to thread the fingers down then right. Look at the right hand. (image 9b)

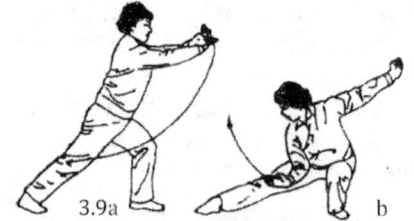

Turn to the right and push off the left leg to shift forward. (image 9c) Take three steps, first left, then right, then left, to the forward right, stopping in a left T stance. Continue to thread the right hand right and forward, coming up, then swinging over to extend to the rear. Swing the left arm down, forward, then left and up, then bend the elbow to place a vertical palm in front of the right ear. Look to the forward left. (images 9d, 9e, 9f, 9g)

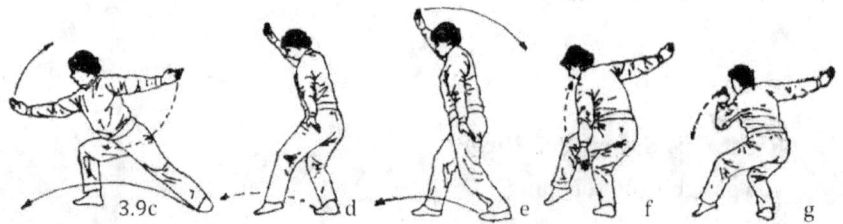

10. Right Empty Stance Tuck   yòu xūbù yǎnzhǎng   右虚步掩掌

Land the right foot to the rear left, turning it out, and turn left. Then take three steps, right, left, then right, to the forward left, stopping in a right T stance. Swing the left straight arm up and to the rear left to hold it out level. Swing the right arm down, forward, then right and up, then bend the elbow to place the hand in a vertical palm at the left ear. Look to the forward right.

THIRD FORM HUAQUAN (B)

(images 3.10a, 10b, 10c, 10d, 10e, 10f)

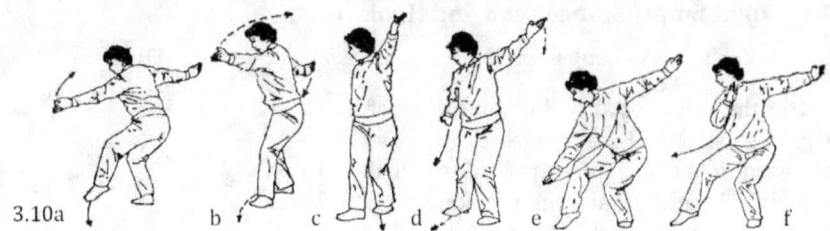

11. Left Empty Stance Tuck   zuǒ xūbù yǎnzhǎng   左虚步掩掌

This is the same as move 10, just transposing right and left. (images 3.11a, 11b, 11c, 11d)

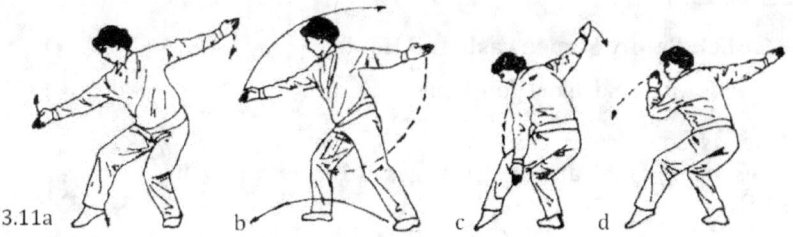

12. Jumping Turn, Left Empty Stance Lash And Hook
tiàozhuàn zuǒ xūbù bǎizhǎng gōushǒu   跳转左虚步摆掌勾手

Land on the left foot and shift forward, leaning the torso slightly forward. Raise the left arm, straightening it, and lash it flat out to the rear left. Lower the right hand then lash it forward and up to level, then medially rotate the forearm to turn the palm out. Look at the right hand. (image 3.12a, 12b, 12c) Push off with the left foot to jump up, swinging the right leg up. Turn around to the right one-eighty degrees whilst airborne. Land on the right foot, then touch the left foot down into a left empty stance. Swing the left hand up and over, forward, then down, forming a hook in front of the body at shoulder height, hook pointing down. Swing the right hand up and over, forward, then down to take a vertical palm by the left elbow. Look at the left hook. (images 12d, 12e, 12f)

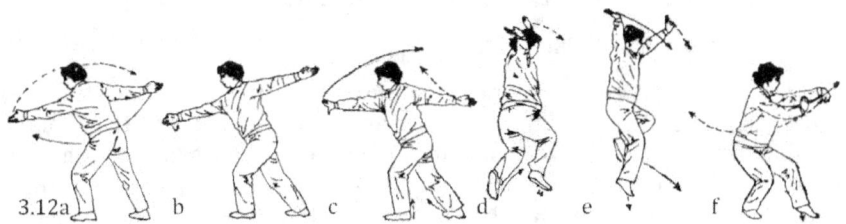

Section Two

13. Right Empty Stance Lash And Hook

yòu xūbù bǎizhǎng gōushǒu

右虚步摆掌勾手

Settle the left foot and shift onto the left leg, squatting and stepping the right foot forward to take a right empty stance. Push the right hand forward then make a hook and hook down at shoulder height, hook pointing down. Unhook the left hand and swing it down, back, up, forward, and down to take a vertical palm by the right elbow. Look at the right hook. (image 3.13a, 13b)

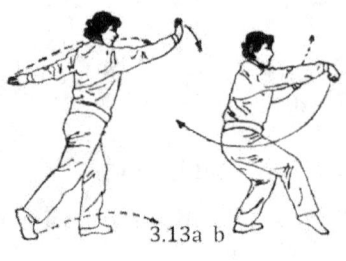

14. Left Empty Stance Lash And Hook

zuǒ xūbù bǎizhǎng gōushǒu

左虚步摆掌勾手

This is the same as move 13, just transposing right and left. (images 3.14a, 14b)

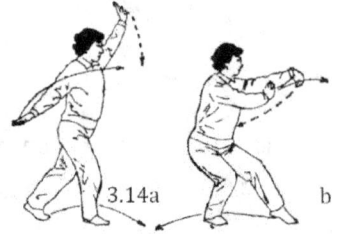

15. Withdraw, Bow Stance Cut

chè gōngbù qiēzhǎng

撤弓步切掌

Withdraw the left foot to take right bow stance. Cut with the right hand across in front, palm down. Clench the left fist and bring it to the waist, fist heart up. Look at the right hand. (image 3.15)

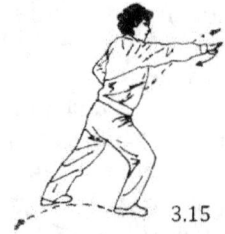

16. Turn Around, Open Bow Stance Elbow Butt

zhuànshēn hénggōngbù dǐngzhǒu

转身横弓步顶肘

Turn to the right and withdraw the right foot, bending the left knee. Unclench the left hand and thread it forward over the back of the right hand to shoulder height, palm up. Look at the left hand. (image 3.16a) Continue to turn to the right and shift to the right leg into a right open bow stance. Laterally rotate the right hand to turn the palm up, then swing it down, right, back, up, forward, and finally left, clenching the fist and bending the elbow to place the fist in front of the right side of the chest, arm and forearm tucked together, fist heart down. Look at the left hand. (images 16b, 16c)

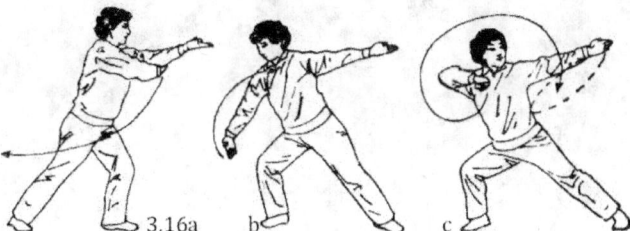

17. Turn Around, Open Bow Stance Elbow Butt

zhuànshēn hénggōngbù dǐngzhǒu　　　　　　转身横弓步顶肘

Turn to the left and shift to the left leg into a left bow stance. Unclench the right hand and circle the straight arm down, right, up, forward, then down again with a covering palm. Circle the left hand right and down to the left waist, then stab straight out to the forward left, at shoulder height, palm up, bringing the right hand to under the left arm. Look at the left hand. (image 3.17a) Continue to turn to the left and withdraw the left foot to the rear, shifting to the left leg to take a left open bow stance. Laterally rotate the left hand to turn the palm up, then swing down, left, up to the rear, then forward at the left, clenching the fist and bending the elbow to bring the fist to in front of the left side of the chest, upper arm and forearm tucked together, fist heart down. Laterally rotate the right arm to turn it over and stab forward with a vertical palm. Look at the right hand. (images 17b, 17c)

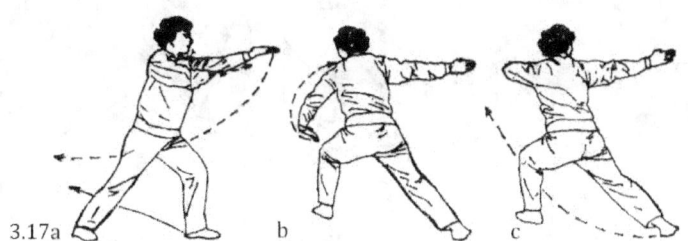

18. Snap Kick, Bow Stance Double Punch

tántuǐ gōngbù shuāng chōngquán　　　　　　弹腿弓步双冲拳

Shift to the left leg and straighten it, snapping the right leg out with a snap kick to belly height. Land the right foot and lift the left foot, turn right and take three steps forward, left, right, and left to the rear right, then shift to the right into a right bow stance. Bend the right elbow, clench the fist, and bring it up then down on the left to cover in front of the chest so that the fists are facing each other. Look to the forward left. (images 3.18a, 18b, 18c, 18d) Turn the torso to the left and straighten the right leg, shifting forward into a left bow stance. Separate the fists out to either side, forward and back to punch level with the fists at shoulder height, fist hearts down. Look at the right fist. (images 18e)

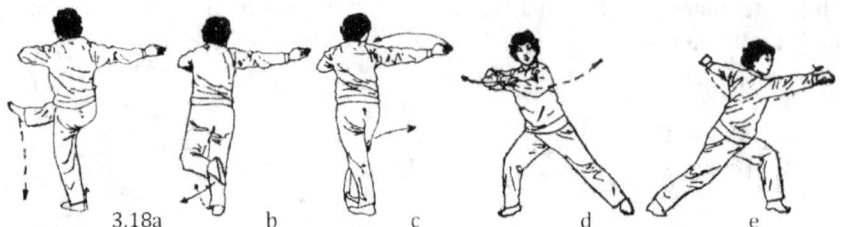

19. Turn Around, Open Bow Stance Elbow Butt

zhuànshēn héng gōngbù dǐngzhǒu 转身横弓步顶肘

Turn the torso slightly to the right and unclench the hands, right palm facing down and left palm flipping to face up. Bring the left hand down to the waist then stab it forward over the right forearm. Look at the left hand. (image 3.19a) Continue to turn to the right and shift to the right into a right open bow stance. Laterally rotate the right hand to flip the palm up, then circle it down, right, back and up to the front, then left, clenching the fist and bending the elbow to place the fist in front of the right side of the chest, upper arm and forearm tucked together fist heart down. Continue to stab the left hand forward with a vertical palm. Look at the left hand. (images 19b, 19c)

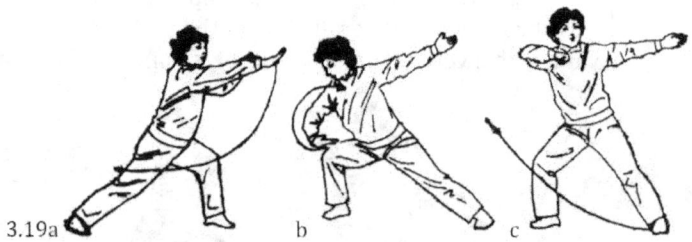

20. Snap Kick, Bow Stance Elbow Butt

tántuǐ gōngbù dǐngzhǒu 弹腿弓步顶肘

Shift to the right leg, bending it and doing a left snap kick to the forward left foot to belly height. (image 3.20a) Land the left foot in front of the right foot and shift forward, bending the right knee to swing the right leg up in front. Land the right foot forward and bend the left leg, lifting the left foot (images 20b, 20c, 20d) Land the left foot in front of the right, with a stamp, and shift forward, turning the torso around one-eighty degrees to the left. Step the right foot around past the left foot to the forward left and take a right bow stance. Bend the left arm slightly and lift it to do a framing block above the head, palm angled upwards. Point the right elbow forward. Look forward. (images 20e, 20f)

THIRD FORM HUAQUAN (B)

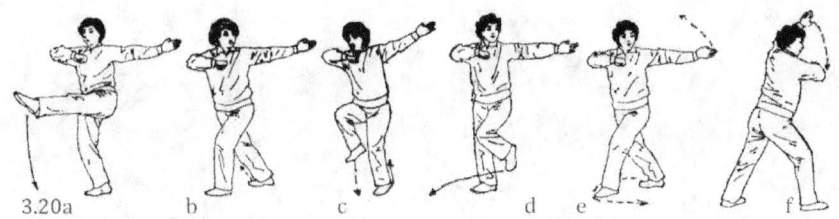

21. Bow Stance Hook And Punch

gōngbù guà chōngquán　　　　　　　　弓步挂冲拳

Lower the left hand down the front to the chest, palm out. Laterally rotate the right forearm to turn the fist up, and bring it forward and down to cover and chop at head height, fist heart angled up. Tuck the left hand into the right armpit, palm down. Look at the right fist. (images 3.21a, 21b) Lean forward and lower the right fist to hook back on the right side, fist heart down. Straighten up, clench the left fist and punch forward to shoulder height, fist heart down. Look at the left fist. (images 21c, 21d, 21e)

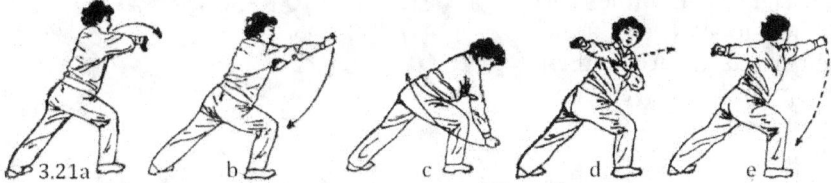

22.　Right Empty Stance Tuck　　yòu xūbù yǎnzhǎng　　右虚步掩掌

Lean forward, unclench the left hand and swing it down, then hook back. (image 3.22a) Shift back, bending the left leg to take a right empty stance. Continue to swing the left hand back, passing by the outside of the right knee then up to in front of the ear. The left arm is slightly bent, the fingers point to the upper rear, the palm is angled up. Look forward, to the left. (image 22b)

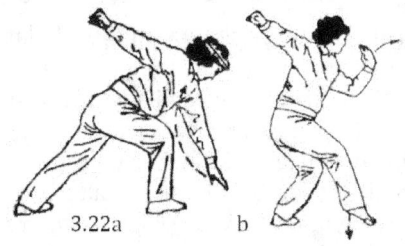

23.　Jump To Horse Stance Chop　　tiào mǎbù pīzhǎng　　跳马步劈掌

Settle the right foot and shift to the right leg, bending the left knee and lifting the left foot. Then swing the left foot forward and push off with the right foot to jump up, bending the right knee and lifting the right foot to take a long step forward, landing with the knees bent in a horse stance. Swing the left arm forward, keeping it straight, then down, to the rear, then up to raise it level. Lift the right fist and unclench the hand, to lower it with a chop, also level. Look at the right hand. (images 3.23a, 23b, 23c, 23d)

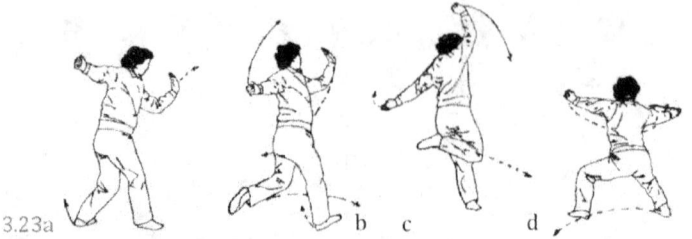

24. Turn Around, Bow Stance Chop

zhuànshēn gōngbù pīquán 转身弓步劈掌

Shift to the left leg and turn right, withdrawing the right foot one step to the rear to take a left bow stance. Bend the left elbow and laterally rotate, bringing the left hand to the waist then stabbing it out over the right arm to throat height, palm up. Medially rotate the right forearm to turn the palm down, and place it under the left upper arm. Look at the left hand. (image 3.24a) Turn rightward and shift to the right leg to a right bow stance. Swing the right hand down, to the right, then to the rear to hold it out level. Lift the left hand in front then chop down to level. Look at the left hand. (images 24b, 24c)

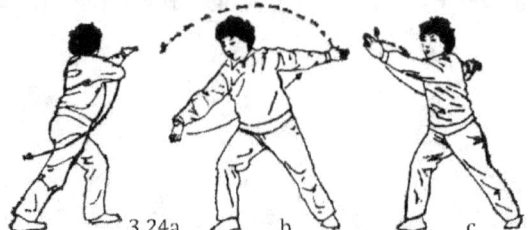

25. Turn Around, Open Bow Stance Elbow Butt

zhuànshēn hénggōngbù dǐngzhǒu 转身横弓步顶肘

Turn the torso slightly to the left, laterally rotate the right hand and bring it down to the waist, then stab it forward over the left forearm to throat height, palm up. Medially rotate the left forearm and bend the elbow, turning the palm down and tucking it under the right arm. Look at the right hand. (image 3.25a) Turn left and push into the right leg, straightening it and shifting to the left to take a left open bow stance. Laterally rotate the left hand to turn the palm up, then swing it down to the left, up to the rear, forward to the right, then clench the fist, bend the elbow and place the fist in front of the left chest, upper arm and forearm tucked together, fist heart down. Medially rotate the right hand to a vertical palm. Look at the right hand. (images 25b, 25c)

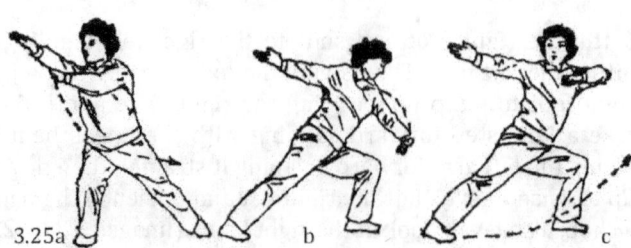

THIRD FORM HUAQUAN (B)

26. Snap Kick, Bow Stance Double Punch
tántuǐ gōngbù shuāng chōngquán 弹腿弓步双冲拳

This is the same as move 18, just in the opposite direction. (images 3.26a, 26b, 26c, 26d, 26e, 26f, 26g)

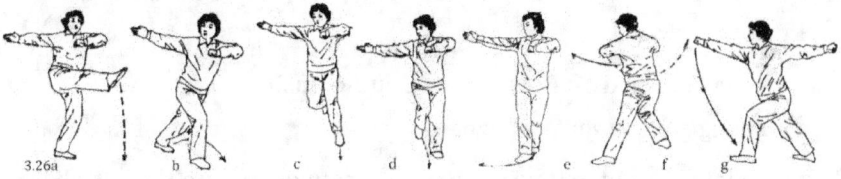

27. Left Empty Stance Tuck zuǒ xūbù yǎnzhǎng 左虚步掩掌

Unclench the hands and lean the torso forward. Medially rotate the right hand and lower the hand with a lashing hook outside the left shin. (image 3.27a) Shift back, bending the right knee and sitting down to take a left empty stance. Continue to swing the right hand to the left, back, up, and then down on the right, bending the arm to place the palm in front of the left ear, fingers pointing to the upper rear, palm out. Look to the forward right. (image 27b)

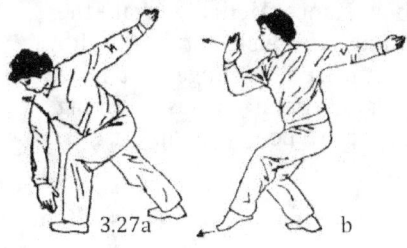

28. Jump To Horse Stance Chop tiào mǎbù pīzhǎng 跳马步劈掌

This is the same as move 23, just transposing right and left and moving in the opposite direction. (images 3.28a, 28b, 28c)

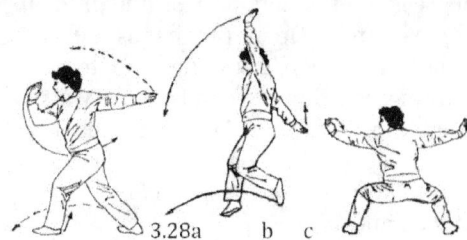

29. Turn Around, Horse Stance Double Push
zhuànshēn mǎbù shuāng tuīzhǎng 转身马步双推掌

Shift to the left leg, bending it slightly, and turn the torso leftward, turning the left foot out, then bending the right knee and lifting the right foot. Laterally rotate the hands and bring them to the waist, palms up. Step across with the right foot and squat into both legs in a horse stance. Push forward with both hands in vertical palms, fingers at nose height. Look forward. (images 3.29a, 29b, 29c)

CHAQUAN, VOLUME II

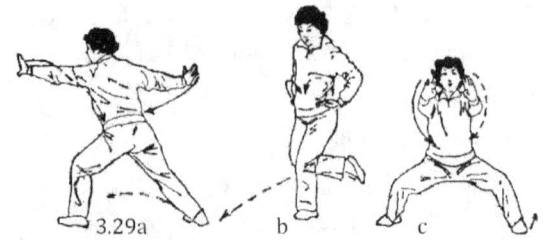

30. Step Forward To Bow Stance Double Push

shàng gōngbù shuāng tuīzhǎng   上弓步双推掌

Turn the left foot out and turn the body ninety degrees to the left, shifting onto the left leg. Open the hands out to either side, then circle them down, laterally rotating the palms to face up. (image 3.30a) Step the right foot forward into a right bow stance. Medially rotate the hands to push forward with vertical palms, fingers at nose height, palm edges striking forward. Look at the hands. (image 30b)

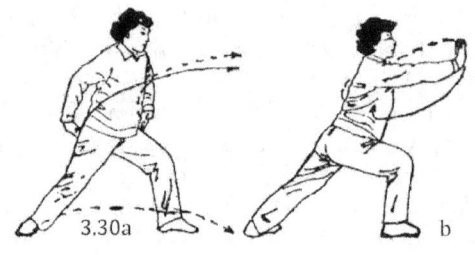

31. Turn Around, Horse Stance Double Push

zhuànshēn mǎbù shuāng tuīzhǎng   转身马步双推掌

Turn the left foot out and tuck the right foot in, turning the body ninety degrees to the left and sitting into a horse stance. Open the hands out to either side, then circle down, laterally rotating, to bring the hands to the waist, palms up. (image 3.31a) Then medially rotate the forearms and push forward, fingers to nose height, palms out. Look at the hands. (images 31b)

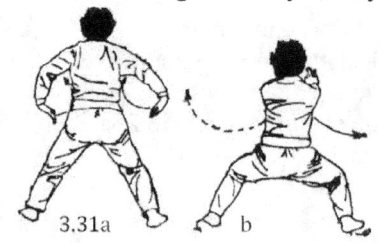

32. T Stance Framing Block And Hook

dīngbù jiàzhǎng gōushǒu   丁步架掌勾手

Turn the left foot out and turn the body left into a left bow stance. (image 3.32a) Separate the hands down at either side, swinging up to extend level to the front and the rear, left arm forward and right arm back. Take three steps forward, right, left, then right, then bend the knees and squat to take a right T stance. Circle the left arm up then back to above the left side of the head. Circle the right hand down, forward, and up, then hook it and swing it forward outside the right knee, hook facing back. Look forward. (images 32b, 32c, 32d, 32e, and 32e from the side)

52

THIRD FORM HUAQUAN (B)

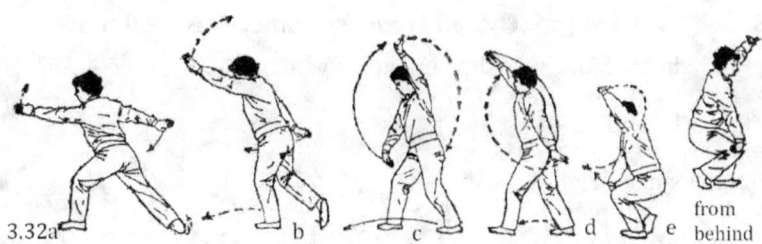

Section Three

33. Turn Around, Thread To Horse Stance Flash Palm

zhuànshēn chuānshǒu mǎbù liàngzhǎng   转身穿手马步亮掌

Stand up slightly. Swing the left hand back on the left, then down, and then forward, laterally rotating to bring the palm up in front of the belly. Swing the right hook forward and up. The forearms are now crossed in front of the belly, left arm above the right. (image 3.33a) Retreat the right foot one step and turn right, bending the knees to take a horse stance. Thread the left hand forward to level, palm forward. Unhook the right hand, laterally rotate it to turn the palm up, then circle it down, right, up, then left to flash above the head at the right, palm angled up. Look at the left hand. (images 33b, 33c)

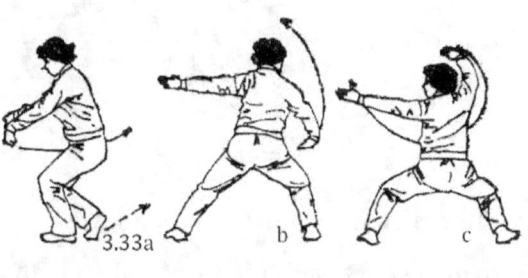

34. Turn Around, Thread To Horse Stance Flash Palm

zhuànshēn chuānshǒu mǎbù liàngzhǎng   转身穿手马步亮掌

Turn the left foot out and turn left. Laterally rotate the right hand and circle it to the right and down past the side of the waist, then thread it out over the left forearm. (image 3.34a) Withdraw the left foot, turn left, and sit into a horse stance. Continue to thread the right hand forward to level, palm up. Laterally rotate the left hand, turning the palm up, and circle it down, left, up, then right to flash above the head at the left, palm angled up. Look at the right hand. (images 34b, 34c)

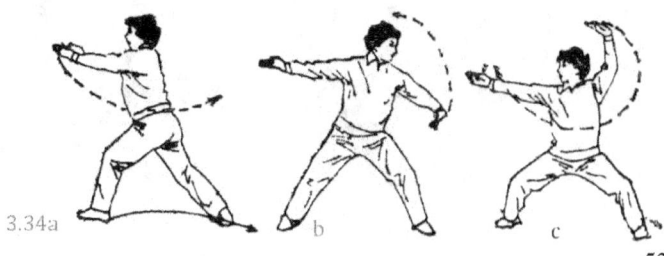

35. Turn Around, Thread To Horse Stance Flash Palm
zhuànshēn chuānshǒu mǎbù liàngzhǎng　　转身穿手马步亮掌

This is the same as move 34, just transposing right and left. (images 3.35a, 35b, 35c)

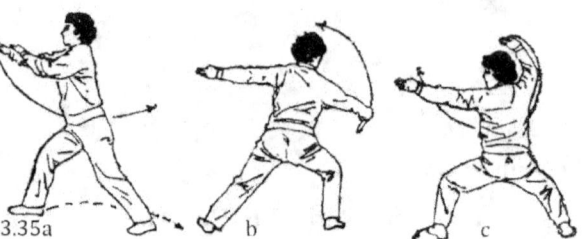

36. Turn Around, Thread To Horse Stance Flash Palm
zhuànshēn chuānshǒu mǎbù liàngzhǎng　　转身穿手马步亮掌

This is the same as move 34. (images 3.36a, 36b, 36c)

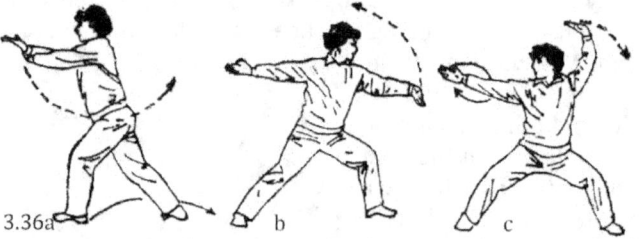

37. Jump To Insertion Stance Stab　tiào chābù chuānzhǎng　跳插步穿掌

Turn to the right and shift back to take a right empty stance. Lower the left palm with a vertical palm, holding it out to the side, palm angled outward. Medially rotate the right hand and draw a small circle right, back, and down, then laterally rotate to turn the palm up, and thread it up to the right with the elbow bent, fingers up, palm facing back and up. Look at the right hand. (image 3.37a) Take a step forward with the right foot and settle it, shifting forward. Thread the right hand forward and up, then shift completely onto the right leg and push off to jump up, swinging the left foot forward. Land forward on the left foot, then the right. Look to the forward right. (images 37b, 37c, 37d)

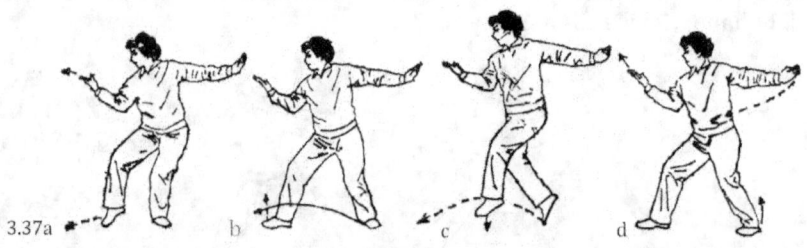

THIRD FORM HUAQUAN (B)

Shift to the right leg and bend the left knee to lift it, threading the right hand forward and bending the left elbow to bring the hand to the waist. Push off with the right foot to jump, swinging the left leg forward, turning to the right. Land on the left foot firmly, then bend the right knee and land the foot behind with an insertion step. Thread the left hand up over the right forearm to a level stab, palm forward. Medially rotate the right forearm to turn the palm down and tuck it into the left armpit. Look at the left hand. (images 37e, 37f, 37g, and 37g from behind)

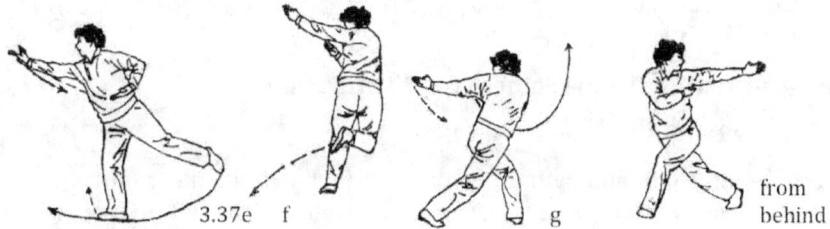

38. Turn Around, T Stance Framing Block And Planting Punch
zhuànshēn dīngbù jià zāiquán   转身丁步架载拳

Turn slightly to the right and separate and spread the arms out to either side, the right circling up and the left circling down. (image 3.38a) Continue to turn around to the right, then take two steps, first with the left, then the right foot. Continue to draw a full circle with the right arm up, right, forward and down to the rear to beside the right knee, palm in. Continue to draw a full circle with the left arm down, left, forward and up, clenching the fist and holding it above head. (images 38b, 38c, 38d, 38e) Take another step forward with the left foot and squat on both legs into a left T stance. Continue to circle the right hand down, back, then up, doing a framing block above the head, palm up. Punch straight down with the left fist beside the left knee, fist eye in, knuckles down. Look to the lower front. (image 38f)

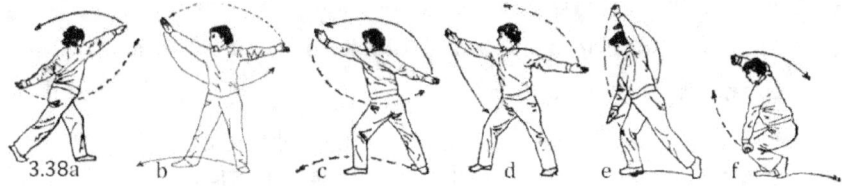

39. Turn Around, Horse Stance Chop
zhuànshēn mǎbù pīzhǎng   转身马步劈掌

Retreat the left foot back a step and swing the arms, the right going up and back on the right and the left going forward and up, so that the arms are level. (image 3.39a) Turn around to the right, turning out the left foot then

55

taking a long step forward with the right foot, landing with the foot hooked in and sitting into a horse stance. Continue to circle the left fist up until it is raised, then unclench the hand and continue to circle forward, down, back and up to finish extended out to the side, fingers pointing left, palm forward.

Circle the right arm down, right, back, up and over, forward to complete a chop, fingers pointing right, palm forward. Look at the right hand. (images 39b, 39c)

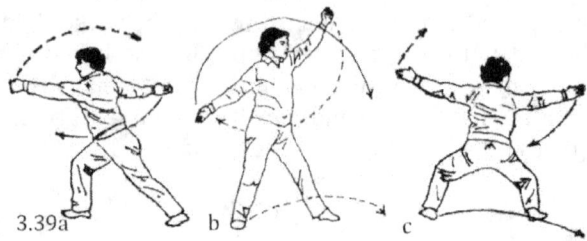

40. Turn Around, Bow Stance Low Planting Punch

zhuànshēn gōngbù xià zāiquán　　　　　　转身弓步下载拳

Turn slightly left and withdraw the left foot behind the right with an insertion step. Swing the left arm up to raise it on the left and swing the right arm down to lower it on the right. (image 3.40a) Turn one-eighty degrees to the left and place the left foot, turning it out and tucking in the right foot. As the body turns around, continue to swing the arms, the left going up, forward, and down to be raised on the left, and the right going down, right and back to be angled down on the right. (image 40b) Step the left foot across a half-step to the rear leg and bend the knee to take a left bow stance. Turn left and lean forward, swinging the arms. The left arm continues forward and down, then back and up to be raised with the fingers up. The right hand continues to the upper rear, the front, then clenches and punches down in front of the left foot, fist eye in, knuckles on the ground. Look at the right fist. (image 40c)

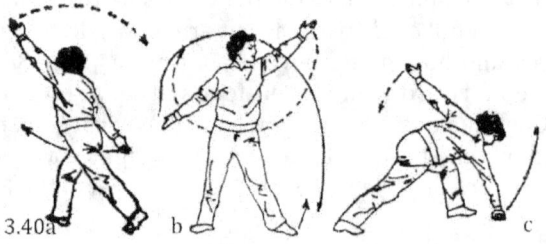

41. Turn Around, T Stance Framing Block And Planting Punch

zhuànshēn dīngbù jià zāiquán　　　　　　转身丁步架载拳

Straighten the torso and swing the arms, the right going up and the left going down so that they are level, slightly angled, the right fist a bit higher than the left hand. (image 3.41a) Turn around to the right, hooking the left foot in and the right foot out, straightening both legs. Continue to swing the right fist up, forward, and down in front of the body. Continue to swing the left hand down, then up at the side. (image 41b) Take two steps, left, then right. Continue to swing the arms, the left going up, forward, and down to finish raised in front, the right fist going down, back, then up to the lower right. Step the left foot forward and bend both knees to take a left T stance.

THIRD FORM HUAQUAN (B)

Bend the left elbow and raise the hand over the head, palm angled up. Bring the right fist up, forward, then punch down outside the right knee, fist eye in, knuckles down. Look to the lower right. (images 41c, 41d, 41e)

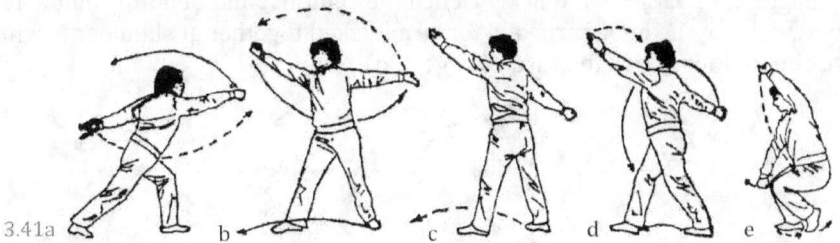

42. Squat And Pounce dūnshēn pūzhǎng 蹲身扑掌

Turn to the left and squat into a right T stance, left foot flat and right heel raised. Unclench the right hand and turn the palm down with a pressing pounce. Pounce forward and down with the left hand, palm down. The fingers point to the right. Look at the right hand. (image 3.42)

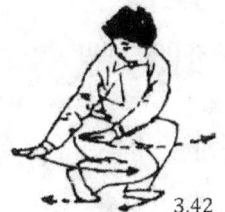

43. Squat And Pounce dūnshēn pūzhǎng 蹲身扑掌

Turn the stance to the right and the torso to the left into a left T stance, right foot flat and left heel raised. Bring the hands to press down, pouncing to the rear left, palms down, fingers pointing to the rear left. Look at the left hand. (image 3.43)

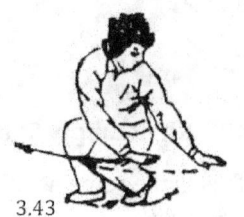

44. Squat And Pounce dūnshēn pūzhǎng 蹲身扑掌

Turn the stance to the left and the torso to the right, into a left T stance. Press down to the rear right. Look at the right hand. (image 3.44)

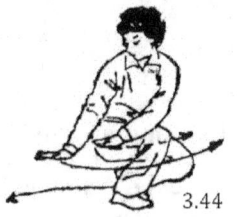

45. Turn Back, Bow Stance Elbow Butt

huíshēn gōngbù dǐngzhǒu 回身弓步顶肘

Turn slightly to the left and retreat the right foot back to take a right bow stance. (image 3.45a) Lift the left hand up in front of the knee then swing it to the rear, to finish level at the upper left, fingers pointing back, palm facing the forward left. Bring the right hand up past the knee then swing it back and up to the left, then forward and down to level in front of the body. (images 45b, 45c) Then quickly clench the right fist and bend the elbow to butt, holding the upper arm and forearm tucked together at shoulder height, fist heart down. Look forward. (image 45d)

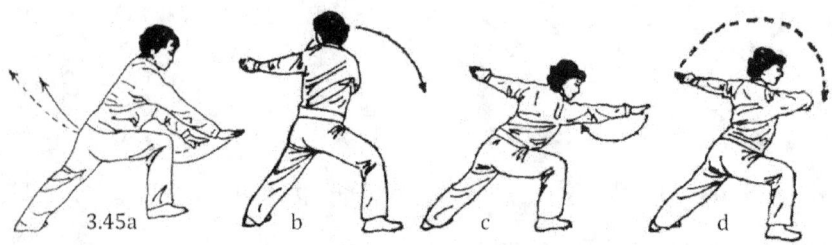

Section Four

46. Bow Stance Hook And Punch   gōngbù guà chōngquán   弓步挂冲拳

This is the same as move 21. (images 3.46a, 46b, 46c, 46d)

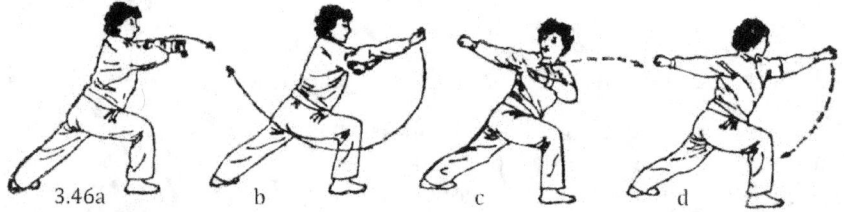

47. Right Empty Stance Tuck   yòu xūbù yǎnzhǎng   右虚步掩掌

This is the same as move 22. (images 3.47a, 47b)

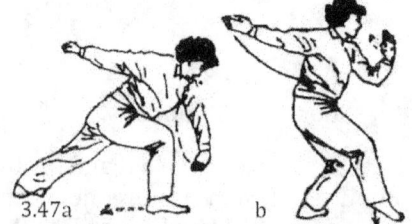

48. Empty Stance Brace   xūbù chēngzhǎng   虚步撑掌

Settle the right foot and turn the torso to the right, shifting to the right leg. Clench the right hand and bring the fist to the waist, fist heart up. Laterally rotate the left forearm to turn the palm up. (image 3.48a) Step the left foot forward, then the right, to take a right empty stance. Circle the left hand down, right, then forward, the back of the hand passing outside the right thigh to circle up to the forward left, then medially rotate, snap the wrist,

THIRD FORM HUAQUAN (B)

and snap the palm out, fingers pointing to the forward right. Look to the forward right. (images 48b, 48c)

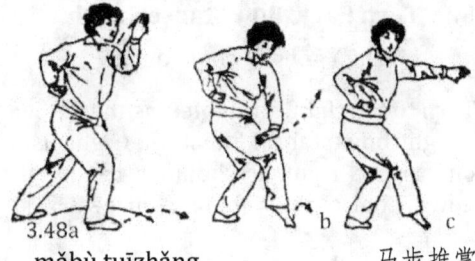

49. Horse Stance Push   mǎbù tuīzhǎng   马步推掌

Turn the right foot out and settle it, turning to the right and taking a long step forward with the left foot, feet parallel, weight more on the right leg. Laterally rotate the left hand and circle it back, down, then forward to the waist. (images 3.49a, 49b) Sit into a horse stance. Medially rotate the left hand and push forward, palm forward, fingers at hose height. Look at the left hand. (image 49c)

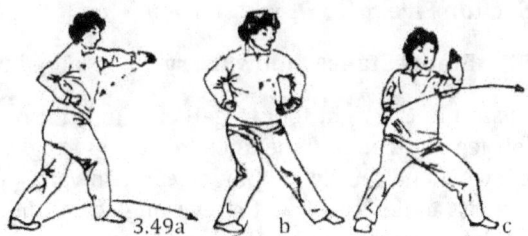

50. Bow Stance Punch   gōngbù chōngquán   弓步冲拳

Turn left and straighten the right leg to take a left bow stance. Punch the right fist forward with an upright fist to shoulder height. Pull the left hand in to the right elbow. Look at the right fist. (image 3.50)

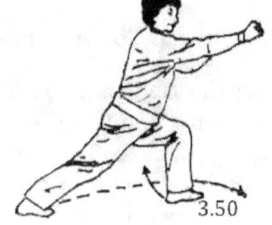

51. Jump To Horse Stance Push   tiào mǎbù tuīzhǎng   跳马步推掌

Shift to the left leg and push off to jump with a bent knee, swinging the right foot forward and up, then landing on it. Turn to the right and land forward on the left foot, tucked in. Sit into the legs in a horse stance. Bring the right fist to the waist, fist heart up. Push the left hand out to the left side, fingers up at nose height, palm angled forward. Look at the left hand. (images 3.51a, 51b)

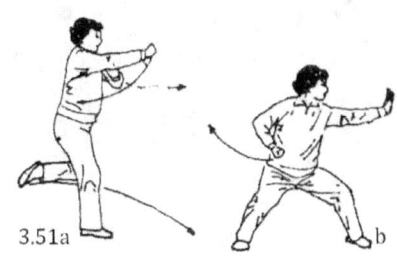

52. Turn Back, Bow Stance Punch

huíshēn gōngbù chōngquán　　　　回身弓步冲拳

Turn to the right, straightening the left leg to take a right bow stance. Punch the right fist straight out to the right at shoulder height, fist heart down. Look at the right fist. (image 3.52)

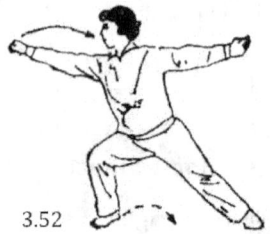

3.52

Section Five

53. Empty Stance Elbow Carry   xūbù kuàzhǒu　　虚步挎肘

Push into the right foot to gather it in, shifting to the left leg and bending the knee to sit into a right empty stance. Bend the right elbow to carry inwards, placing the fist under the jaw, fist eye angled in and down. Look to the lower front. (image 3.53)

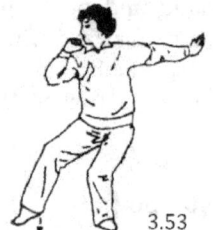

3.53

54. Jump To Bow Stance Chop   tiào gōngbù pīzhǎng　　跳马步劈掌

Set the right heel on the ground and shift to the right leg, pushing off to jump up, bending the knee and lifting it. Swing the left leg forward and up. (images 3.54a, 54b) Land on the left foot, then the right, touching it down in front in a right empty stance. Look to the lower front. (images 54c, 54d) Settle the right foot and shift forward, turning right into a right bow stance. Laterally rotate the right fist and bring it to the waist. Bring the left arm up then chop forward and down in front of the body at shoulder height, fingers forward, palm facing right. Look at the left hand. (image 54e)

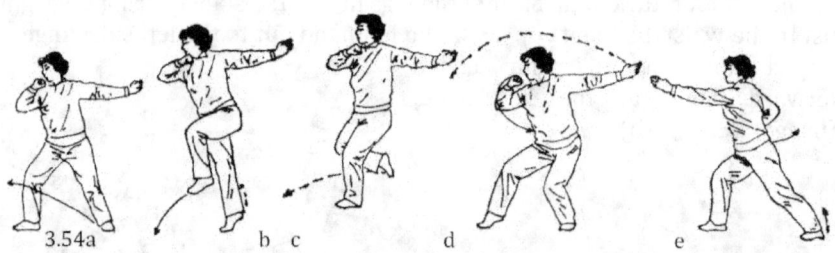

3.54a　　b　c　　　d　　　　e

THIRD FORM HUAQUAN (B)

55. Two Rising Kicks   èrqǐjiǎo   二起脚

Shift fully onto the right leg and lift the left knee, bending it. Unclench the right hand and swing it down and back, palm angled up. Medially rotate the left arm and swing the hand up in front, palm angled down. Look at the left hand. (image 3.55a) Swing the bent left knee up, swinging the right arm down, then forward and up, slapping the back of the hand into the left palm in front of the head. (image 55b) Push off with the right leg and jump up to complete a high snap kick. Slap the right foot with the right hand in front of the chest, swinging the left arm up and back. (image 55c) Land, first the left foot, then the right foot, and take a high empty stance. Lower the hands out level, the right arm in front, and the left arm to the side, palms down. Look at the right hand. (image 55d)

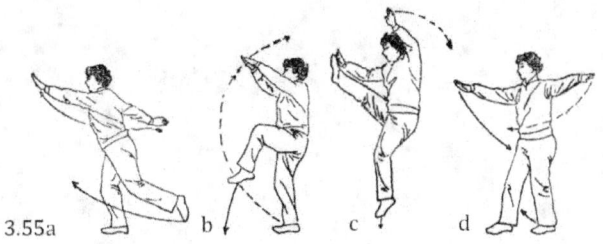

56. Wheel Over, Drop Stance Reverse Slap

     fānshēn pūbù fān pāizhǎng   翻身仆步翻拍掌

Set the right foot into the ground and shift onto the right leg, bending the knee and turning slightly to the right. Bend the left knee and lift it. Swing the arms down, then to the lower right at the right of the body. (image 3.56a) Push off with the right leg to jump up, turning one-eighty degrees in the air, landing the left foot, then the right, and dropping into a right drop stance. Swing the arms to the right, up and over, forward, and down to slap downwards. The back of the left hand, the little finger side, touches the ground. Look at the right hand. (images 56b, 56c)

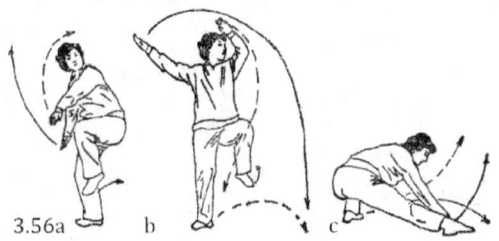

57. Step Forward, Drop Stance Reverse Slap

     shàng pūbù fān pāizhǎng   上仆步翻拍掌

Straighten the left leg and stand up, then bring the left foot up to step forward to the right. Extend the arms forward, medially rotating the left hand to turn the palm out and laterally rotating the right hand to turn the palm up. Step the right foot forward and drop into a right drop stance, leaning forward. Drop down with the hands, the back of the left hand near the ground and the little finger side of the right hand on the ground. Look at the right hand. (images 3.57a, 57b)

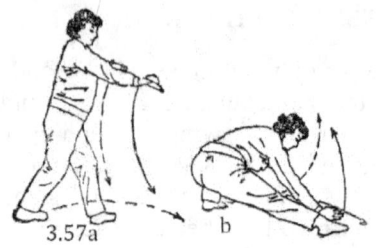

58. Step Forward, Drop Stance Reverse Slap

shàng pūbù fān pāizhǎng   上仆步翻拍掌

This is the same as move 57. (images 3.58a, 58b)

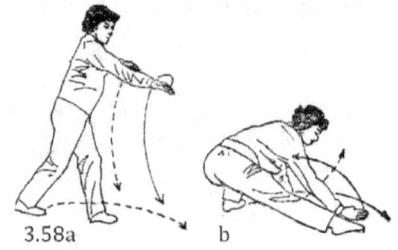

59. Back Sweep Kick   hòu sǎotuǐ   后扫腿

Push into the left leg and step forward with the foot hooked in, straightening the torso. Swing the hands to the rear right and place them on the ground, leaning forward. Squat on the left leg, lifting the heel, to pivot on the ball of the foot. Straighten the right leg and do a rear sweep kick a half-circle to the right, scraping the sole of the foot on the ground. Look to the lower front. (images 3.59a, 59b, 59c)

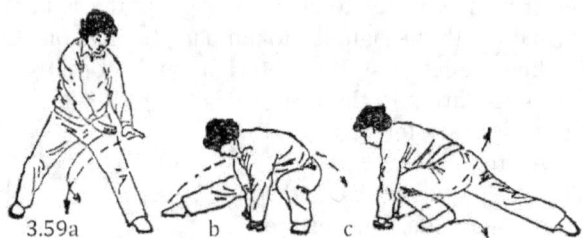

Section Six

60. Raised Knee Double Hooks   tíxī shuāng gōushǒu   提膝双勾手

Push into the left leg to bring it in and stand up, shifting back to take a left empty stance. Laterally rotate the hands to turn the palms up and separate them down and back, circling by their respective hips. Bend the left knee and lift it, foot pointing down, and extend the right leg to stand up in a raised knee stance. Continue to circle the hands at their respective sides, bringing them back and up to hook above the head. Look forward. (images 3.60a, 60b)

THIRD FORM HUAQUAN (B)

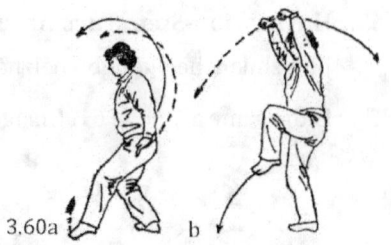

61. Hitting Hop-Step, Turn Around, Bow Stance Lash And Hook

jībù zhuànshēn gōngbù bǎizhǎng gōushǒu 击步转身弓步摆掌勾手

Settle the left foot forward, bending the knee slightly, pushing into the right foot to shift forward, and leaning forward. Unhook the hands and circle them to extend level, the left hand goes forward and down, the right hand goes back and down. (image 3.61a) Step the right foot forward and lift the bent left knee, then step the left foot forward, turning the foot out and turning ninety-degrees to the left. (images 61b, 61c) Step the right foot forward again and turn into a left bow stance. Laterally rotate the left hand and hook it, hooking left then back and down, hook pointing back. Swing the right hand forward and left to inside the left arm, palm out. Look at the right hand. (image 61d)

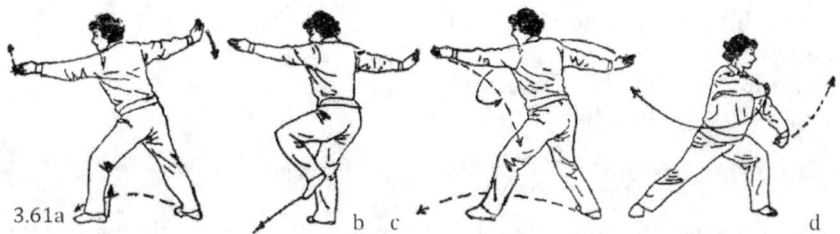

62. Hitting Hop-Step, Turn Around, Bow Stance Lash And Hook

jībù zhuànshēn gōngbù bǎizhǎng gōushǒu 击步转身弓步摆掌勾手

This is the same as move 61, just transposing left and right. (images 3.62a, 62b, 62c, 62d)

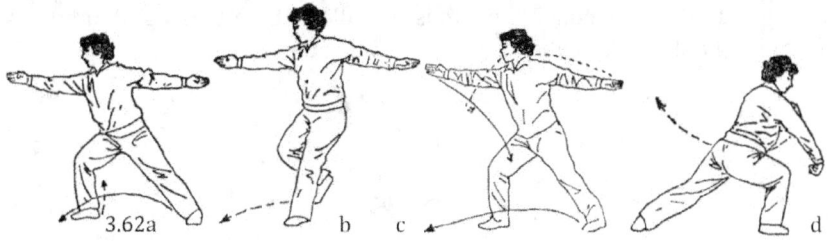

63. Hitting Hop-Step, Turn Around, Bow Stance Lash And Hook

jībù zhuànshēn gōngbù bǎizhǎng gōushǒu   击步转身弓步摆掌勾手

This is the same as move 61. (images 3.63a, 63b, 63c, 63d)

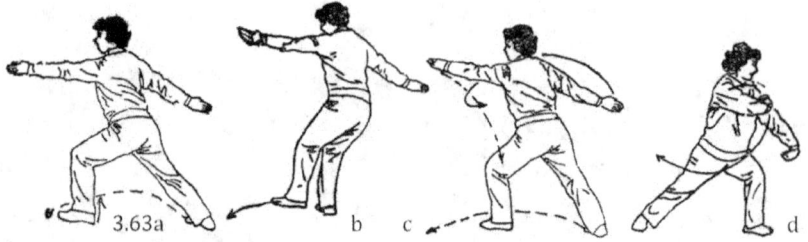

64. Whisk Hand, Closed Stance Flash Palm

dǎnshǒu bīngbù liàngzhǎng   掸手并步亮掌

Turn the torso to the right and shift right into a right bow stance. Laterally rotate the right hand and whisk the right thigh with the back of the hand, continuing on to the right, up, then left to flash above the head, a bit forward and right. Bring the left foot in beside the right and stand up. Look to the forward left. (images 3.64a, 64b, 64c)

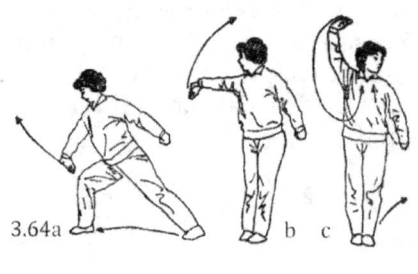

65. Closing Posture   shōu shì   收势

Retreat the left foot to take a right bow stance. Circle the right hand to the right, back, and down. Unhook the left hand and laterally rotate. These actions bring both hands in to the waist, then stab them both forward to chest height, shoulder width, palms up. Look at the hands. (image 3.65a) Withdraw the right foot to take a left bow stance. Clench both hands and bring the fists to in front of the chest. (image 65b) Bring the left foot in beside the right. Medially rotate both fists and gather them at the hips, looking to the left. Unclench the hands and allow them to hang naturally by the thighs. Look straight ahead. (images 65c, 65d)

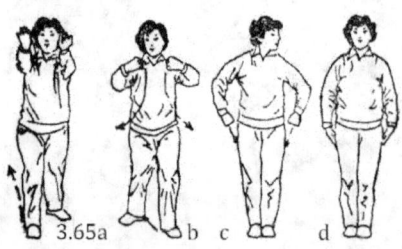

THIRD FORM HUAQUAN (A) (IMAGES ONLY)
三路滑拳（甲）

0. **Position Of Preparation**
   yùbèi shì
   预备势

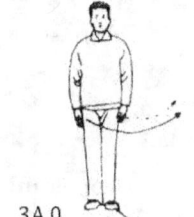

Section One
1. **Step Forward Closed Stance Facing Fists**
   shàngbù bīngbù duìquán
   上步并步对拳

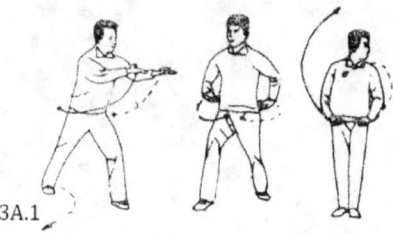

2. **Closed Stance Upper Lashing Fist**
   bīngbù shàng bǎiquán
   并步上摆拳

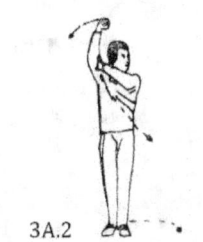

3. **Drop Stance Forearm Lift**　　pūbù chāozhǎng　　仆步抄掌

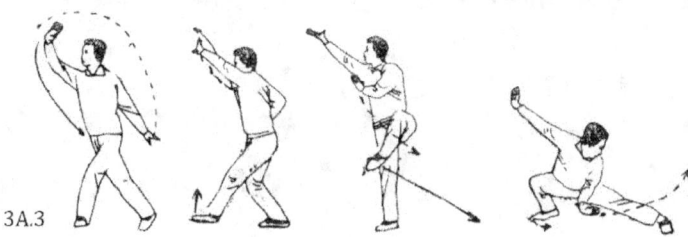

4. **Bow Stance Crossed Hands**
   gōngbù shízìzhǎng
   弓步十字掌

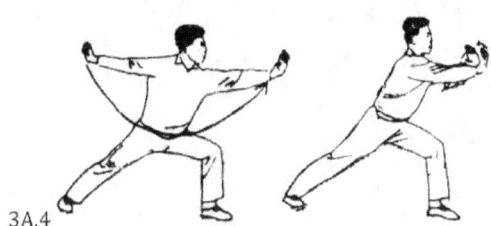

5. **Bow Stance Brush Aside, Press Down, And Stab**
   gōngbù lōu àn chāzhǎng 弓步搂按插掌

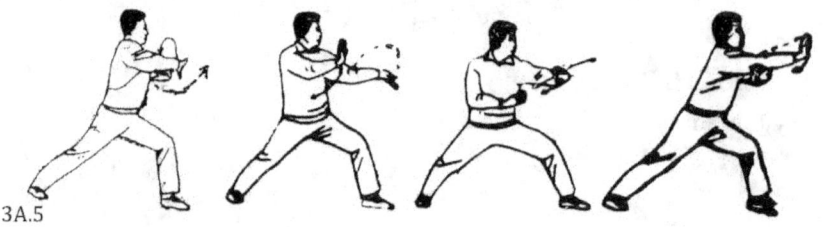

6. **Drop Stance Forearm Lift**　　pūbù chāozhǎng　　仆步抄掌

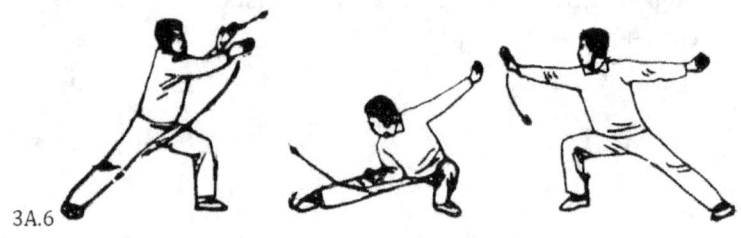

7. **Raised Knee Press Down**
   tíxī ànzhǎng
   提膝按掌

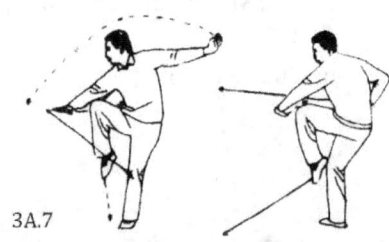

8. **Bow Stance Cut**
   gōngbù qiēzhǎng
   弓步切掌

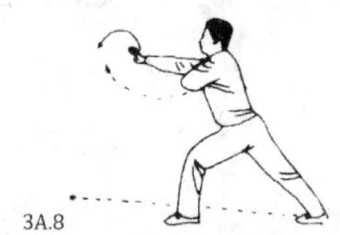

9. **Bow Stance Sideways Strike**
   gōngbù héng jīzhǎng
   弓步横击掌

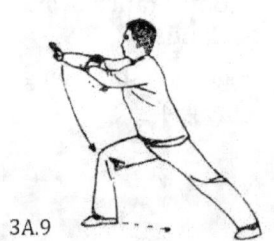

THIRD FORM HUAQUAN (A) (IMAGES ONLY)

10. Bow Stance Brush Aside, Press Down, And Punch

gōngbù lōu àn chōngquán 弓步搂按冲拳

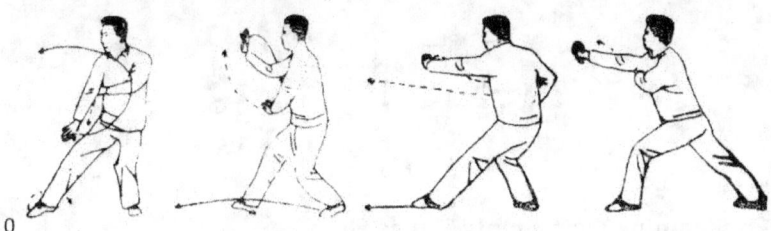

11. Drop Stance Forearm Lift pūbù chāozhǎng 仆步抄掌

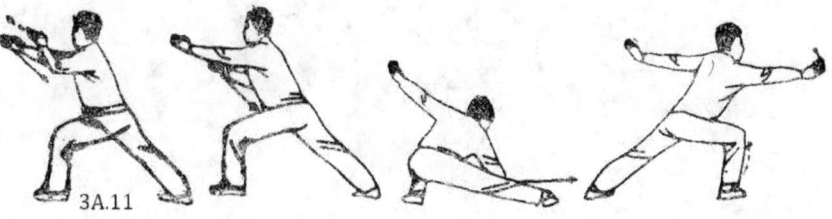

12. Raised Knee Scooping Snap

tíxī tiǎozhǎng
提膝挑掌

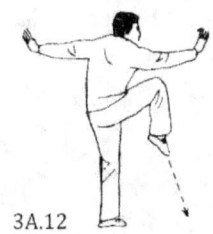

13. Walk To Empty Stance Scooping Snap

xíngbù xūbù tiǎozhǎng 行步虚步挑掌

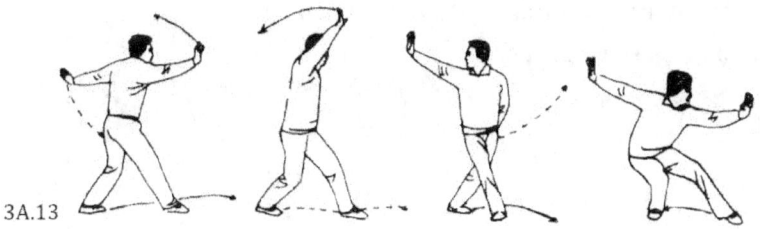

CHAQUAN, VOLUME II

14. Bow Stance Stab gōngbù chāzhǎng 弓步插掌

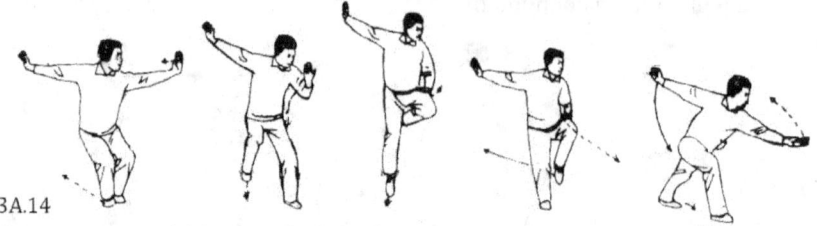

15. Jumping Turn, Empty Stance Chop
tiào zhuànshēn xūbù pīzhǎng 跳转身虚步劈掌

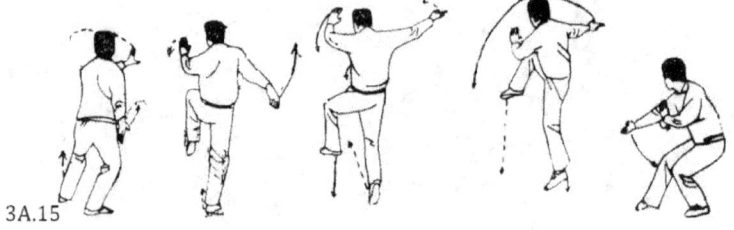

16. Jump Switch-Step Bow Stance Brush Aside, Press Down, And Punch huàntiàobù gōngbù lōu àn chōngquán 换跳步弓步搂按冲拳

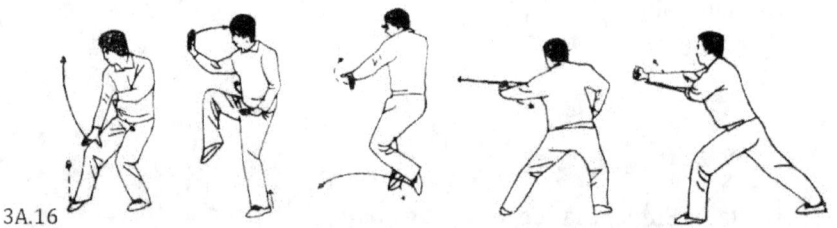

17. Bow Stance Framing Block And Punch
gōngbù jià chōngquán
弓步架冲拳

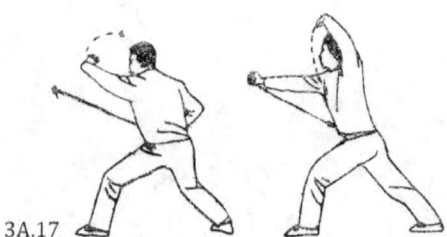

THIRD FORM HUAQUAN (A) (IMAGES ONLY)

18. **Hook, Back Sweep, Open Bow Stance Flash Palm**   guàzhǎng
    hòusǎo héngdāngbù liàngzhǎng   挂掌后扫横裆步亮掌

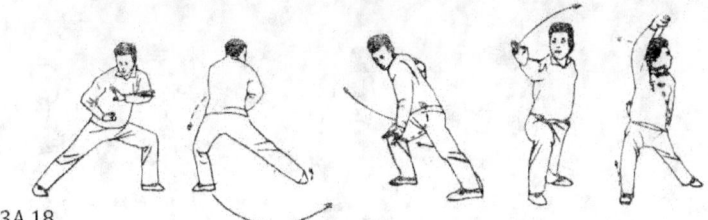

3A.18

19. **Drop Stance Forearm Lift**   pūbù chāozhǎng   仆步抄掌

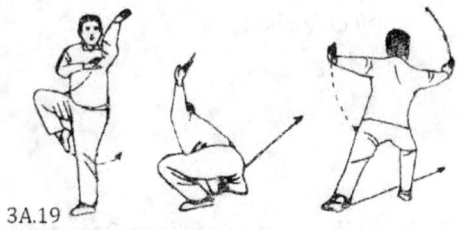

3A.19

20. **Walk To Empty Stance Scooping Snap**
    xíngbù xūbù tiǎozhǎng   行步虚步挑掌

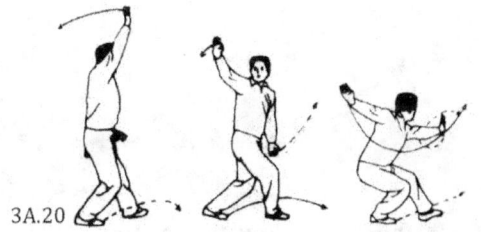

3A.20

21. **Bow Stance Sideways Strike**
    gōngbù héngjīzhǎng
    弓步横击掌

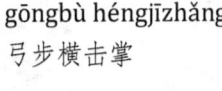
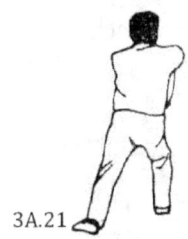

3A.21

22. **Bow Stance Stab**
    gōngbù chāzhǎng
    弓步插掌

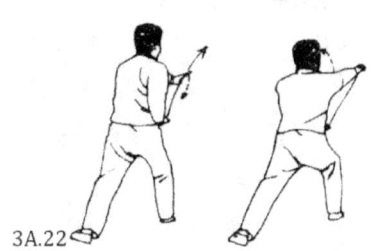

3A.22

CHAQUAN, VOLUME II

23. Horse Stance Framing Block And Cut
mǎbù shàngjià qiēzhǎng   马步上架切掌

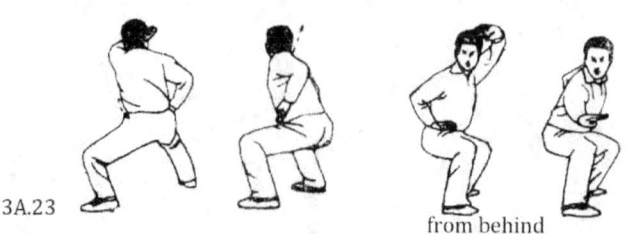

24. Drop Stance Forearm Lift
pūbù chāozhǎng
仆步抄掌

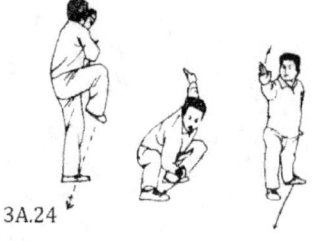

25. Walk To Empty Stance Scooping Snap
xíngbù xūbù tiǎozhǎng
行步虚步挑掌

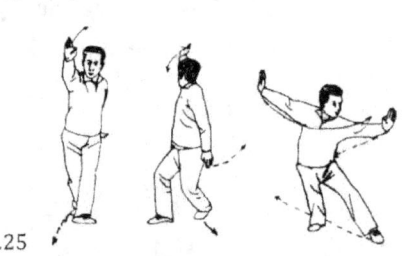

26. Withdraw To Bow Stance Hack
chèbù gōngbù kǎnzhǎng
撤步弓步砍掌

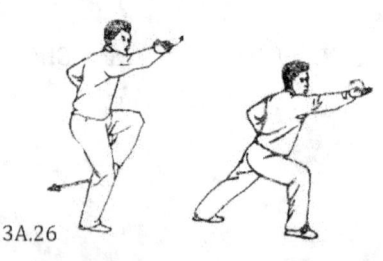

27. Drop Stance Forearm Lift   pūbù chāozhǎng   仆步抄掌

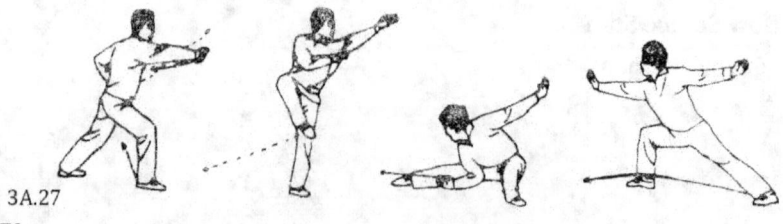

THIRD FORM HUAQUAN (A) (IMAGES ONLY)

28. Walk To Empty Stance Scooping Snap

xíngbù xūbù tiǎozhǎng 行步虚步挑掌

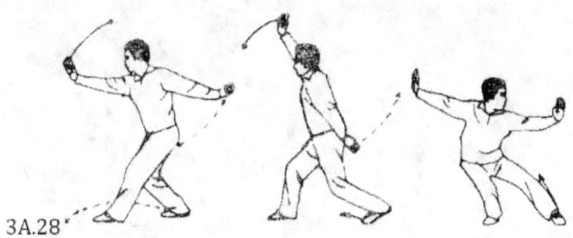

29. Raised Knee Scooping Snap

tíxī tiǎozhǎng
提膝挑掌

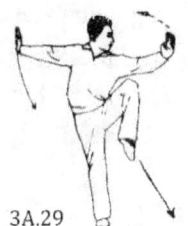

30. Walk To Empty Stance Scooping Snap

xíngbù xūbù tiǎozhǎng 行步虚步挑掌

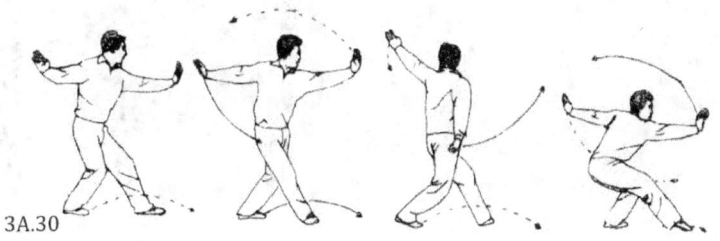

31. Flying Slap Kick　　　téngkōng fēijiǎo　　　腾空飞脚

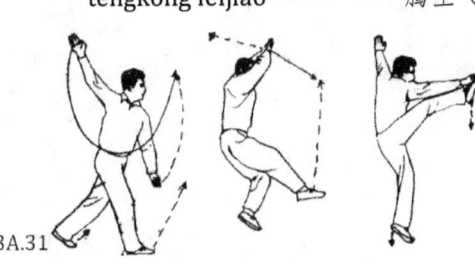

71

32. Horse Stance Chop

mǎbù pīzhǎng 马步劈掌

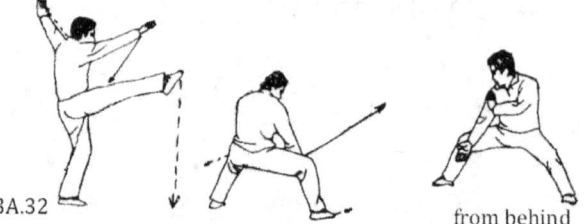

33. Bow Stance Lean

gōngbù kàoshēnzhǎng
弓步靠身掌

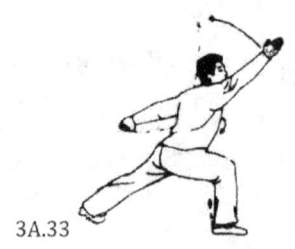

34. Turn Back, Bow Stance Double Stabs

huíshēn gōngbù shuāng chāzhǎng 回身弓步双插掌

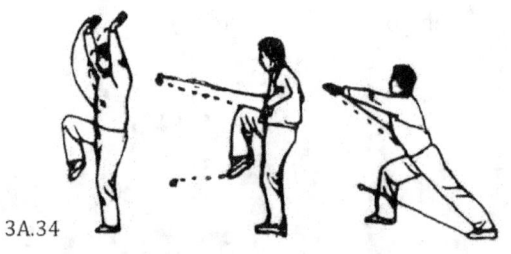

35. Left Bow Stance Double Stabs

zuǒ gōngbù shuāng chāzhǎng 左弓步双插掌

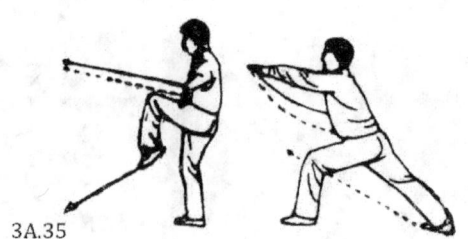

THIRD FORM HUAQUAN (A) (IMAGES ONLY)

36. Jumping Stride To Bow Stance Double Stabs

kuàtiàobù gōngbù shuāng chāzhǎng   跨跳步弓步双插掌

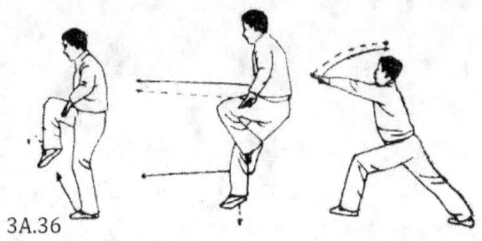

37. Bow Stance Carry And Strike

gōngbù tuōzhǎng jīzhǎng   弓步托掌击掌

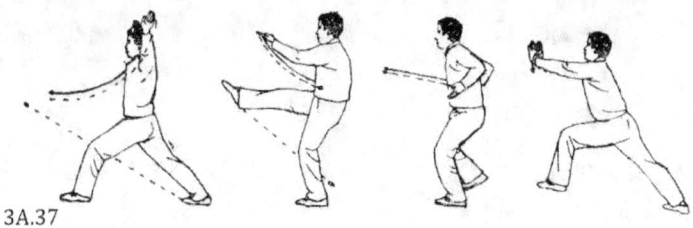

38. Bow Stance Brush Aside, Press Down, And Stab

gōngbù lōu yā chāzhǎng   弓步搂按插掌

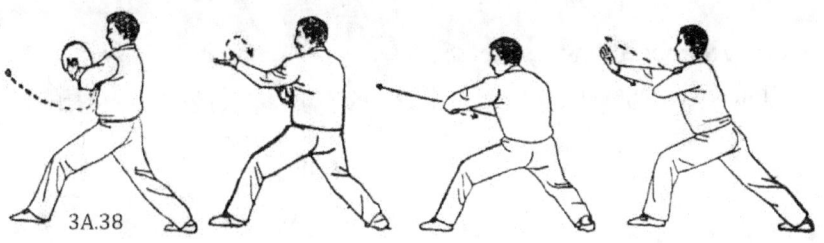

39. Drop Stance Forearm Lift   pūbù chāozhǎng   仆步抄掌

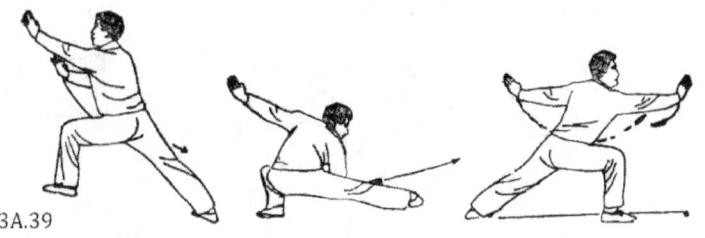

CHAQUAN, VOLUME II

40. Resting Stance Cut, Flash Palm
xūbù qiēzhǎng, liàng zhǎng 虚步切掌，亮掌

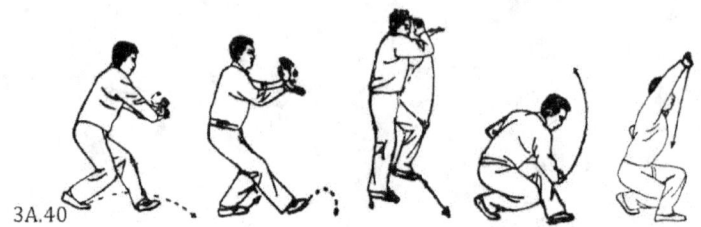

41. Raised Knee Press Down
tíxī ànzhǎng
提膝按掌

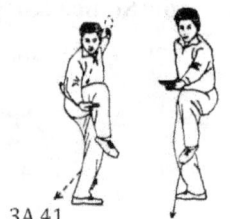

42. Bow Stance Cut
gōngbù qiēzhǎng
弓步切掌

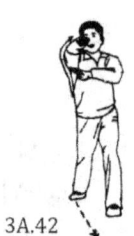

43. Bow Stance Sideways Strike
gōngbù héngjīzhǎng
弓步横击掌

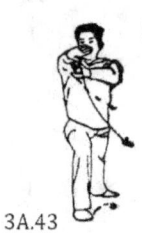

44. Left Bow Stance Brush Aside, Press Down, And Punch
zuǒ gōngbù lōu àn chōngquán 左弓步搂按冲拳

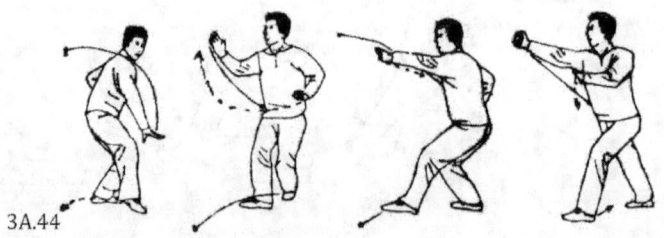

THIRD FORM HUAQUAN (A) (IMAGES ONLY)

45. Right Bow Stance Brush Aside, Press Down, And Punch

yòu gōngbù lōu àn chōngquán 　　　　　　右弓步搂按冲拳

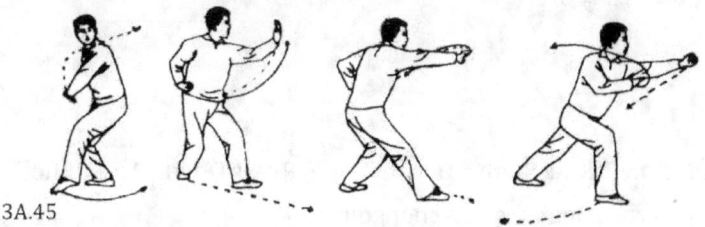

46. Left Bow Stance Brush Aside, Press Down, And Punch

zuǒ gōngbù lōu àn chōngquán 　　　　　　左弓步搂按冲拳

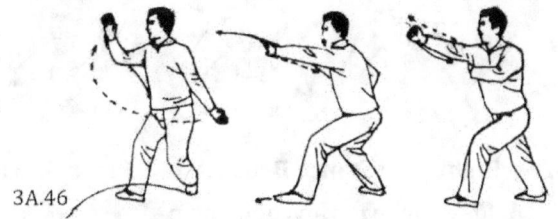

47. Drop Stance Forearm Lift　　　pūbù chāozhǎng　　　　仆步抄掌

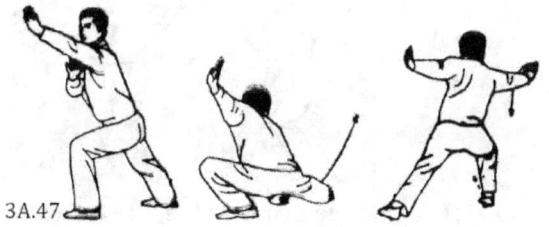

48. Raised Knee Press Down
tíxī ànzhǎng
提膝按掌

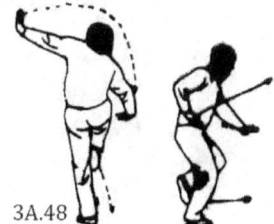

49. Bow Stance Cut
gōngbù qiēzhǎng
弓步切掌

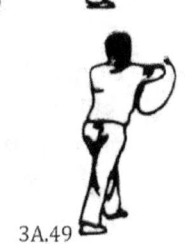

CHAQUAN, VOLUME II

50. **Bow Stance Sideways Strike**
gōngbù héngjīzhǎng
弓步横击掌

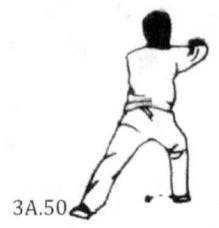

51. **Left Bow Stance Brush Aside, Press Down, And Punch**
zuǒ gōngbù lōu àn chōngquán   左弓步搂按冲拳

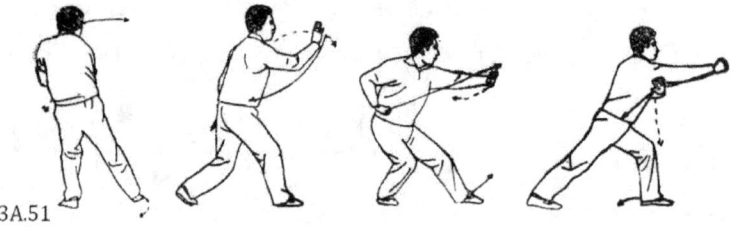

52. **Right Bow Stance Brush Aside, Press Down, And Punch**
yòu gōngbù lōu àn chōngquán   右弓步搂按冲拳

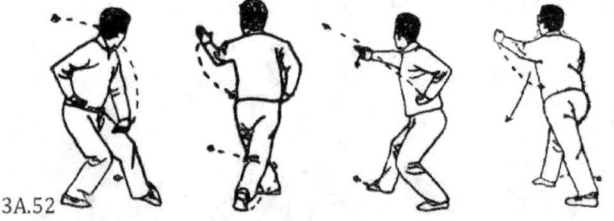

53. **Left Bow Stance Brush Aside, Press Down, And Punch**
zuǒ gōngbù lōu àn chōngquán   左弓步搂按冲拳

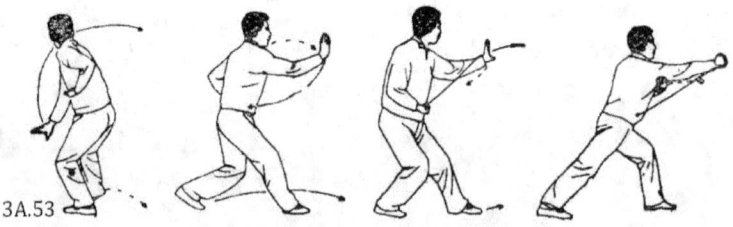

54. **Horse Stance Scoop Up And Punch**
mǎbù tiǎozhǎng chōngquán
马步挑掌冲拳

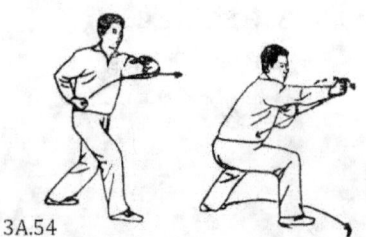

THIRD FORM HUAQUAN (A) (IMAGES ONLY)

55. **Resting Stance Press Down And Punch**
    xiēbù ànzhǎng chōngquán
    歇步按掌冲拳

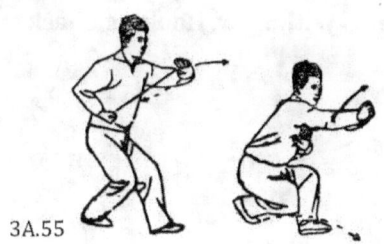

56. **Right Bow Stance Brush Aside, Press Down, And Punch**
    yòu gōngbù lōu àn chōngquán   右弓步搂按冲拳

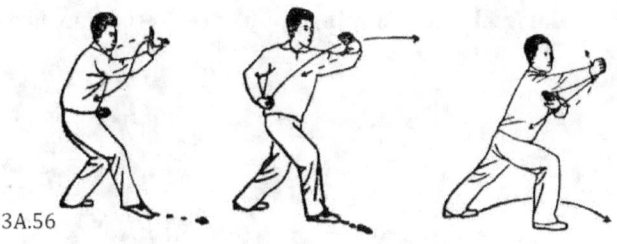

57. **Left Bow Stance Brush Aside, Press Down, And Punch**
    zuǒ gōngbù lōu àn chōngquán   左弓步搂按冲拳

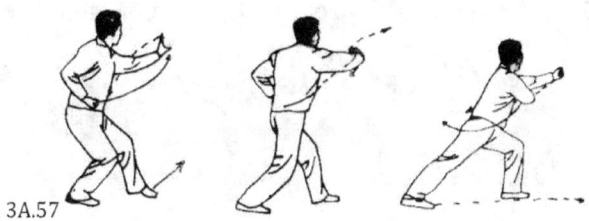

58. **Closed Stance Whisk And Roundhouse Punch**
    bīngbù dǎnzhǎng guànquán
    并步掸掌贯拳

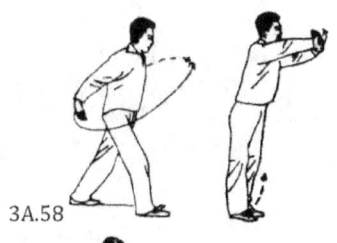

59. **Empty Stance Cut**
    xūbù qiēzhǎng
    虚步切掌

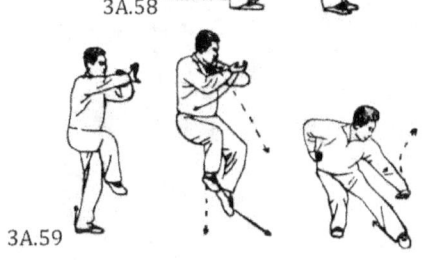

77

CHAQUAN, VOLUME II

Section Two

60. Withdraw, Hooking Check   chèbù gōubō   撤步勾拨

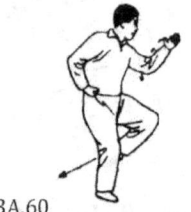
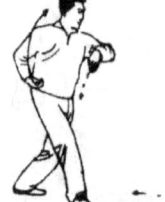
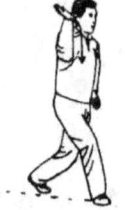
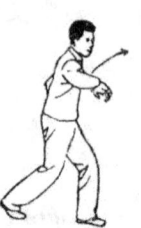

61. Raised Knee Scooping Snap   tíxī tiǎozhǎng   提膝挑掌

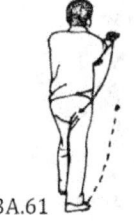
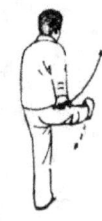
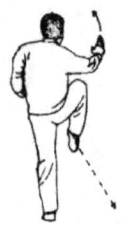

62. Curving Walk, Forearm Lift   húxíngbù chāozhǎng   弧形步抄掌

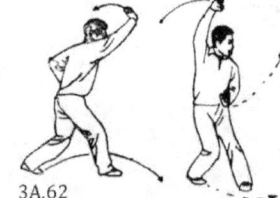
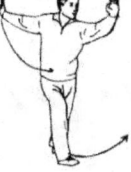
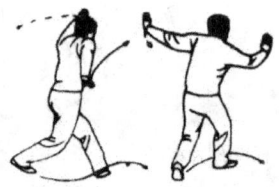
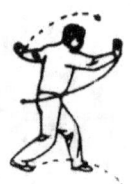

63. Turn Back, Left Bow Stance Hook And Strike

huíshēn zuǒ gōngbù gōuguà jīzhǎng   回身左弓步勾挂击掌

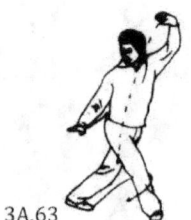
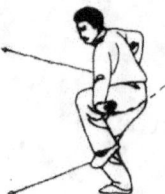
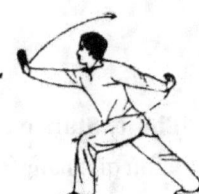

THIRD FORM HUAQUAN (A) (IMAGES ONLY)

64. Raised Knee Scooping Snap   tíxī tiǎozhǎng   提膝挑掌

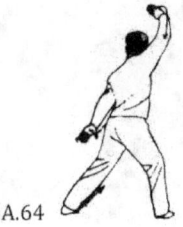
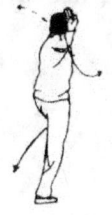
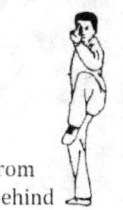

65. Curving Walk, Forearm Lift   húxíngbù chāozhǎng   弧形步抄掌

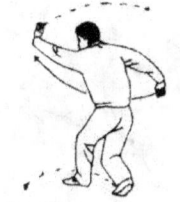
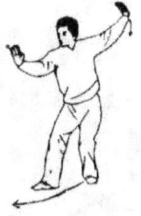
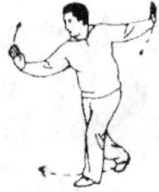
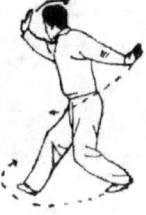
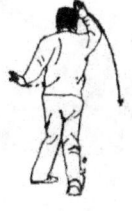

66. Turn Back, Right Bow Stance Hook And Strike
huíshēn yòu gōngbù gōuguà jīzhǎng
回身右弓步勾挂击掌

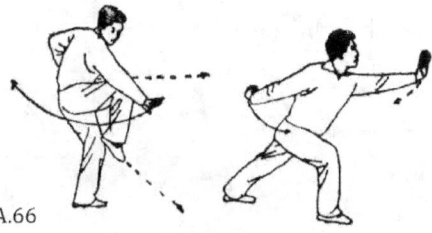

Section Three

67. Bow Stance Sideways Strike
gōngbù héngjīzhǎng
弓步横击掌

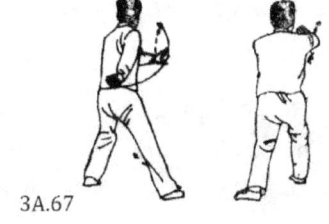

68. Bow Stance Stab
gōngbù chāzhǎng
弓步插掌

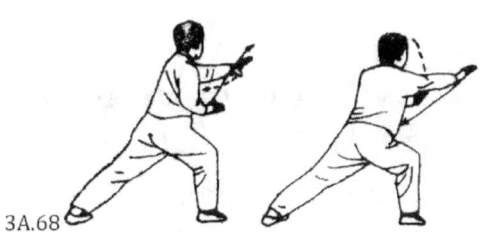

69. Horse Stance Framing Block And Cut
mǎbù shàngjià qiēzhǎng

马步上架切掌

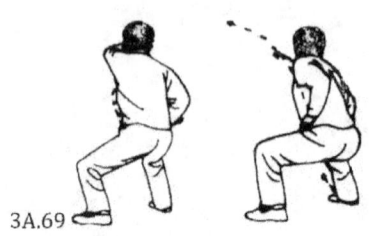

70. Drop Stance Forearm Lift   pūbù qiēzhǎng   仆步抄掌

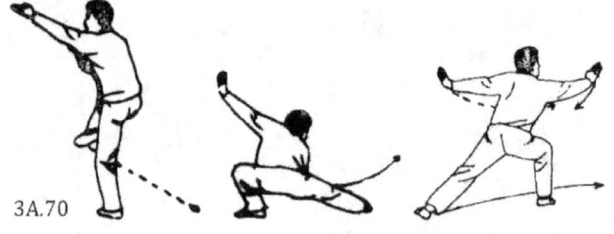

71. Step Forward, Brush Aside, Press Down, Flying Slap Kick
shàngbù lōu àn fēijiǎo   上步搂按飞脚

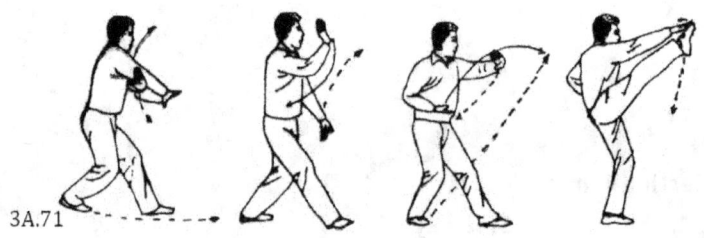

72. Horse Stance Cut
mǎbù qiēzhǎng

马步切掌

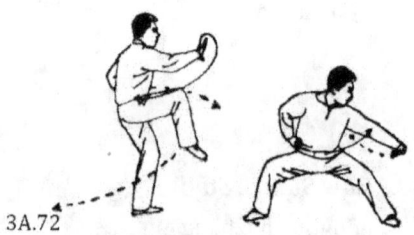

73. Bow Stance Brush Aside, Press Down, Right Stab
gōngbù lōu àn yòu chāzhǎng   弓步搂按右插掌

THIRD FORM HUAQUAN (A) (IMAGES ONLY)

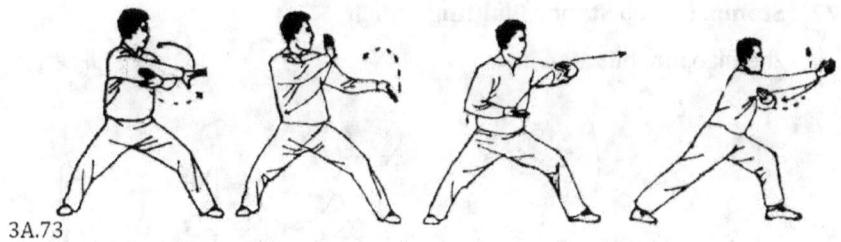

3A.73

74. Bow Stance Brush Aside, Press Down, Left Stab

gōngbù lōu àn zuǒ chāzhǎng   弓步搂按左插掌

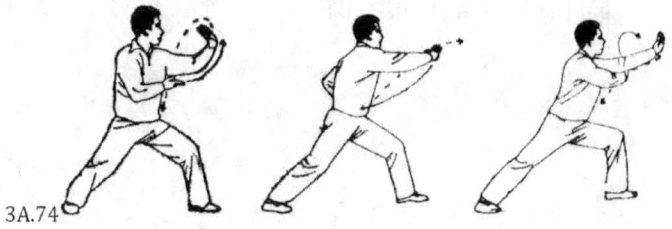

3A.74

75. Withdraw, Bow Stance Brush Aside, Press Down, Stab

chèbù gōngbù lōu àn zuǒ chāzhǎng   撤步弓步搂按插掌

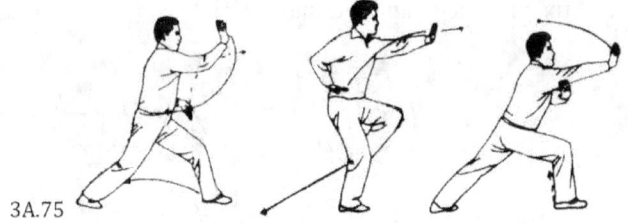

3A.75

76. Turn Back, Bow Stance Framing Block And Push

huíshēn gōngbù jià tuīzhǎng   回身弓步架推掌

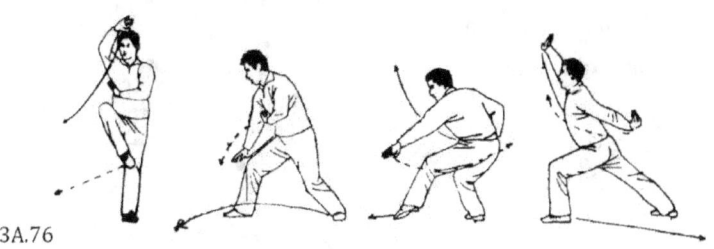

3A.76

77. Stomp, Closed Stance Planting Punch
zhēnjiǎo bīngbù zāiquán　　　　　　　　震脚并步栽拳

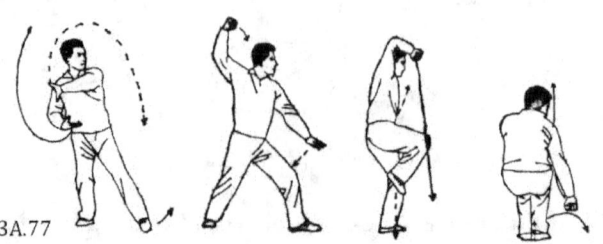

78. Covering Jump To Bow Stance Framing Block And Push
gài tiàobù gōngbù jià tuīzhǎng　　　　　　盖跳步弓步架推掌

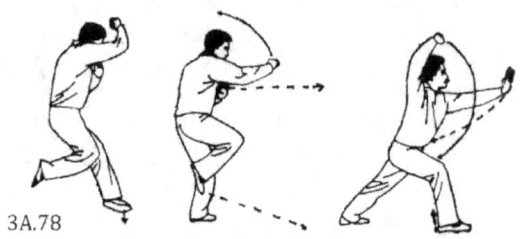

79. Raised Knee, Hook Down, Bow Stance Pounce On The Face
tíxī xià guà gōngbù pūmiànzhǎng　　　　　提膝下挂弓步扑面掌

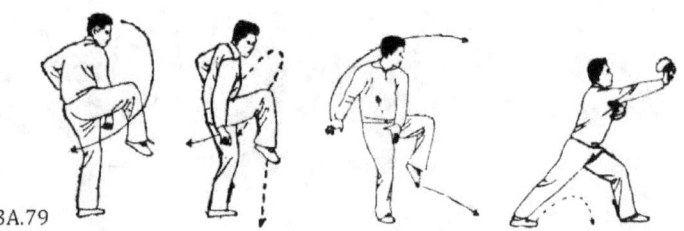

80. Empty Stance Cut
xūbù qiēzhǎng
虚步切掌

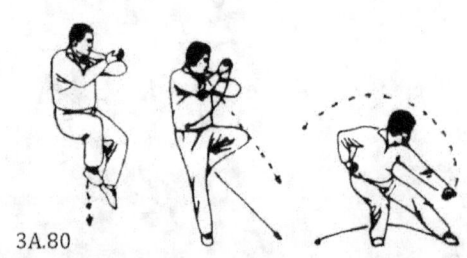

THIRD FORM HUAQUAN (A) (IMAGES ONLY)

Section Four

81. Stomp, Closed Stance Planting Punch

zhēnjiǎo bīngbù zāiquán

震脚并步栽拳

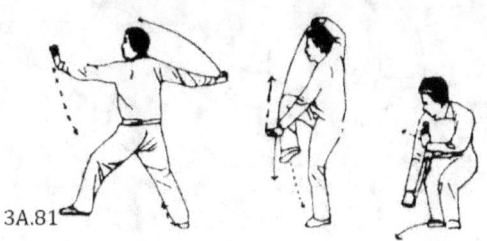

82. Resting Stance Press Down And Punch

xiēbù àn chōngquán

歇步按冲拳

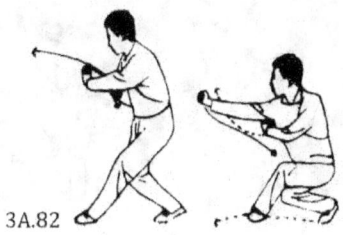

83. Horse Stance Scoop And Punch

mǎbù tiǎozhǎng chōngquán

马步挑掌冲拳

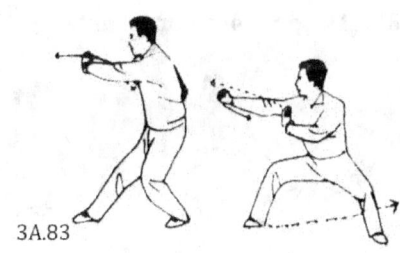

84. Drop Stance Forearm Lift

pūbù chāozhǎng

仆步抄掌

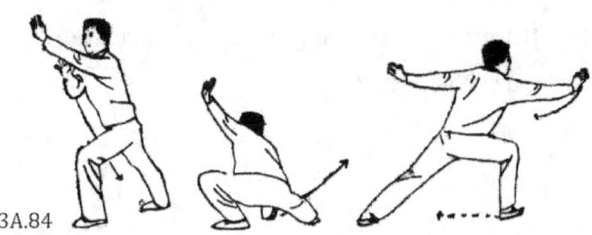

85. Hitting Hop-Step To Insertion Stance Stab
jībù chābù chāzhǎng   击步插步插掌

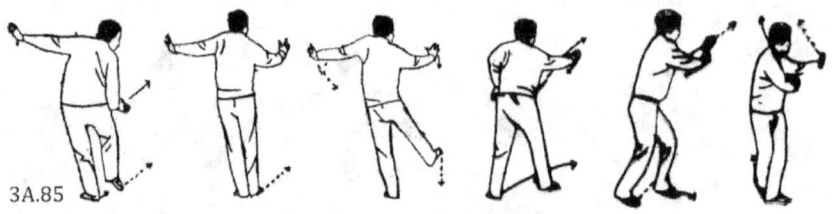

86. Turn Around To Bow Stance Double Strikes
zhuànshēn gōngbù shuāng jīzhǎng   转身弓步双击掌

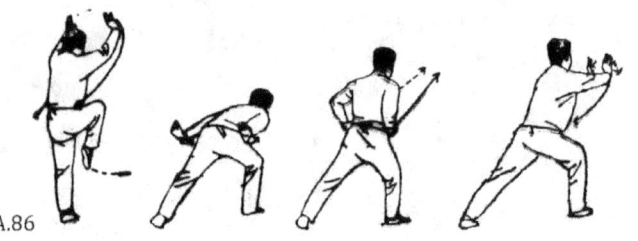

87. Drop Stance Forearm Lift   pūbù chāozhǎng   仆步抄掌

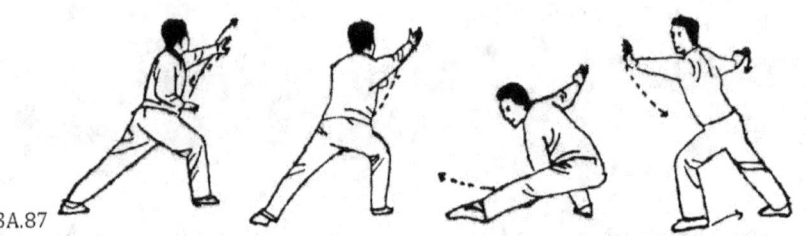

88. Hitting Hop-Step To Insertion Stance Stab
jībù chābù chāzhǎng   击步插步插掌

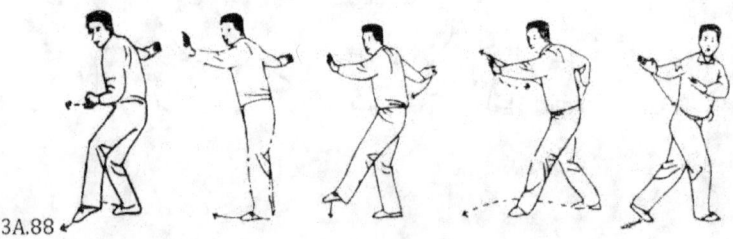

THIRD FORM HUAQUAN (A) (IMAGES ONLY)

89. Turn Around To Closed Stance Double Strikes
zhuànshēn bīngbù shuāng jīzhǎng
转身并步双击掌

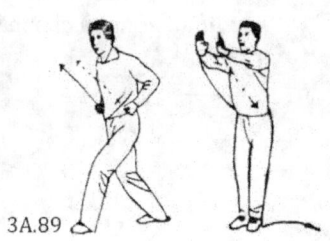

90. Withdraw To Closed Stance Double Strikes
chèbù bīngbù shuāng jīzhǎng
撤步并步双击掌

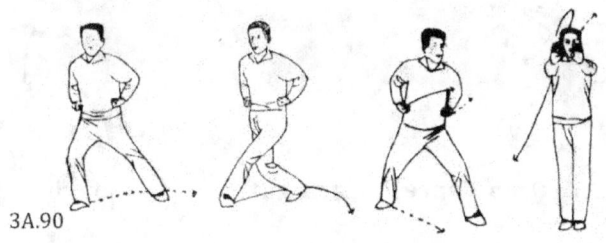

91. Empty Stance Elbow Carry
xūbù kuàzhǒu
虚步挎肘

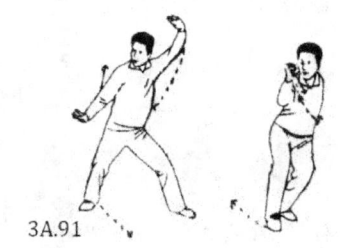

Section Five

92. Whisk And Snap Kick
dǎnzhǎng tántuǐ
撣掌弹腿

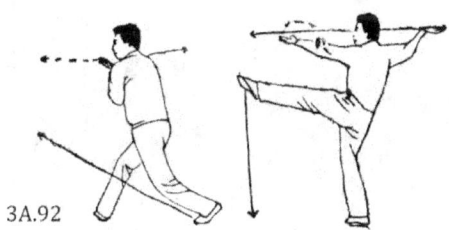

93. Bow Stance Stab
gōngbù chāzhǎng
弓步插掌

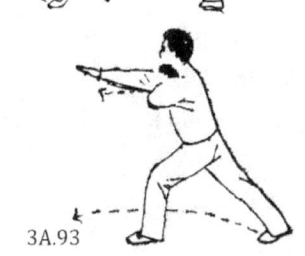

94. Turning Jump To Bow Stance Stab
tiàozhuàn gōngbù chāzhǎng   跳转弓步插掌

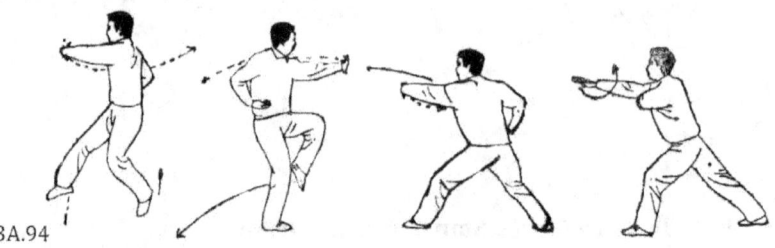

95. Bow Stance Hack
gōngbù kǎnzhǎng
弓步砍掌

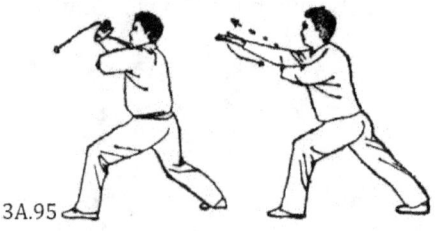

96. Drop Stance Forearm Lift
pūbù chāozhǎng   仆步抄掌

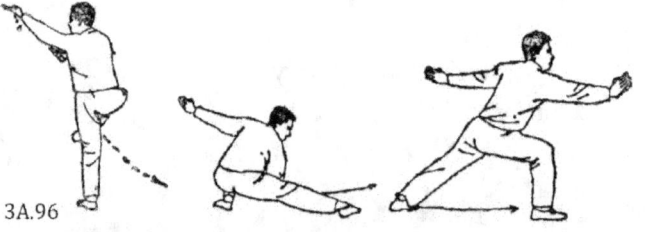

97. Empty Stance Scooping Snap
xūbù tiǎozhǎng   虚步挑掌

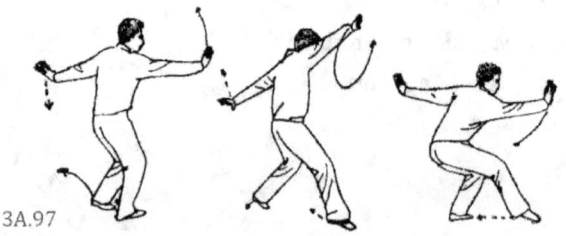

Section Six
98. Hitting Hop-Step To Insertion Stance Stab
jībù chābù chāzhǎng   击步插步插掌

THIRD FORM HUAQUAN (A) (IMAGES ONLY)

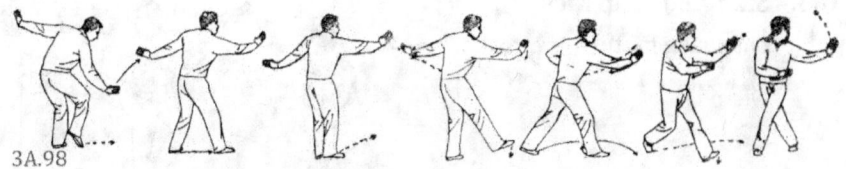

99. Turn Around To Bow Stance Stab
zhuànshēn gōngbù chāzhǎng

转身弓步插掌

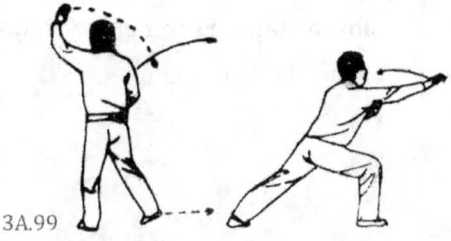

100. Drop Stance Brush Aside With A Hook   pūbù lōuguà   仆步搂挂

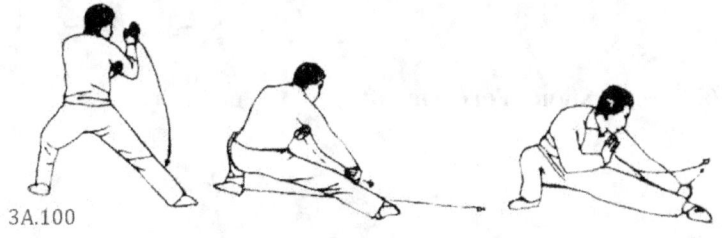

101. Bow Stance Roundhouse Punch   gōngbù guànquán   弓步贯拳

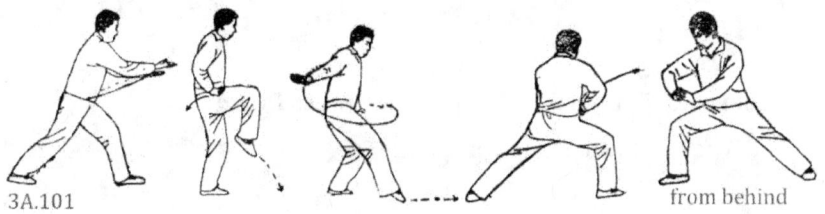

102. Bow Stance Stab
gōngbù chāzhǎng

弓步插掌

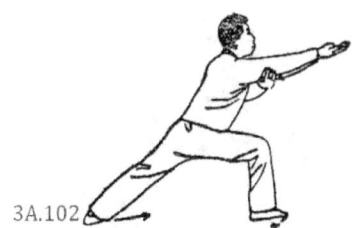

87

103. Stab And Snap Kick
chāzhǎng tántuǐ

插掌弹腿

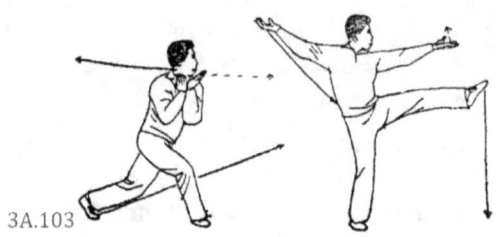

104. Closed Stance Framing Block And Punch
bīngbù jià chōngquán 并步架冲拳

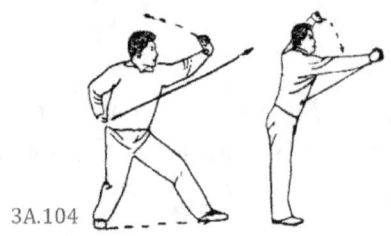

105. Drop Stance Forearm Lift
pūbù chāozhǎng 仆步抄掌

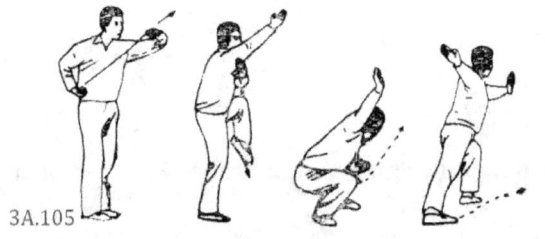

106. Big Leap Forward To Drop Stance Press Down
dàyuèbù qiáncuàn pūbù ànzhǎng 大跃步前窜仆步按掌

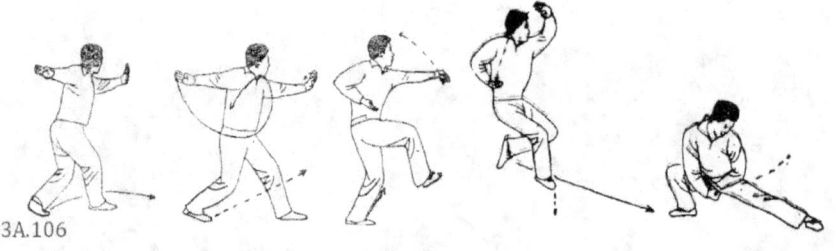

THIRD FORM HUAQUAN (A) (IMAGES ONLY)

107. Closed Stance Framing Block And Punch

bīngbù jià chōngquán 并步架冲拳

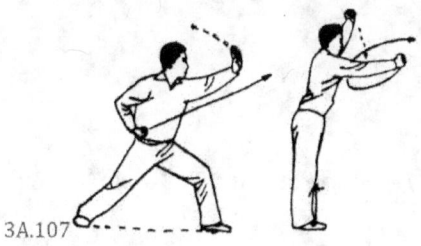

Section Seven

108. Drop Stance Forearm Lift pūbù chāozhǎng 仆步抄掌

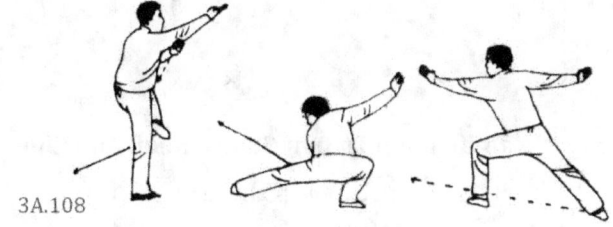

109. Walk, Brush Aside, Closed Stance Double Lash

xíngbù lōushǒu bīngbù shuāng bǎizhǎng 行步搂手并步双摆掌

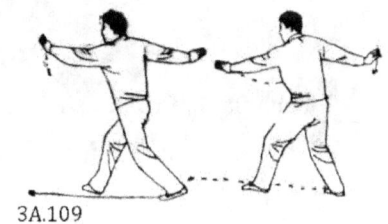

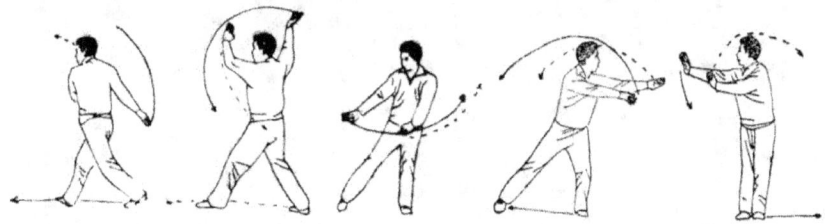

110. **Turn Back, Closed Stance Chop**
 huíshēn bīngbù pīzhǎng
 回身并步劈掌

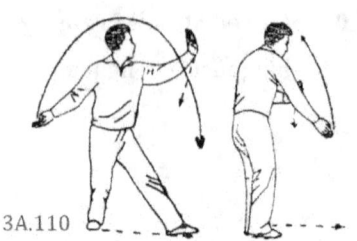

111. **Step Forward To Hook And Chop** shàngbù guà pīzhǎng 上步挂劈掌

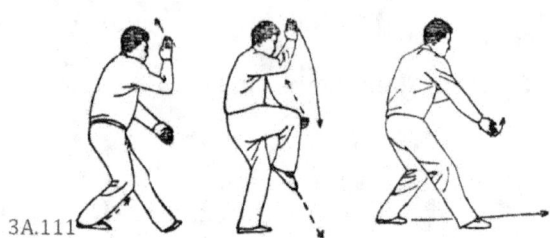

112. **Straddle Jump To Bow Stance Hook And Chop**
 kuà tiàobù gōngbù guà pīzhǎng   跨跳步弓步挂劈掌

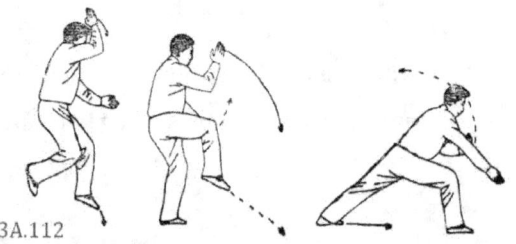

113. **Turn Back, Brush Aside, Hitting Hop-Step, Lean**
 huíshēn lōushǒu jībù kàoshēnzhǎng   回身搂手击步靠身掌

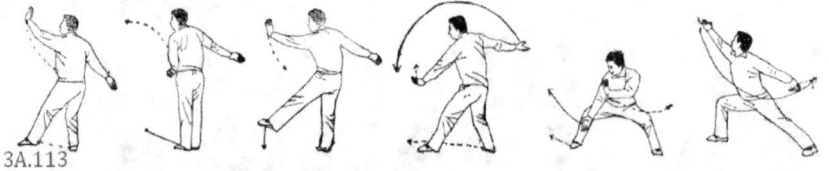

114. **Turn Back, Bow Stance Crossed Hands**
 huíshēn gōngbù shízìzhǎng
 回身弓步十字掌

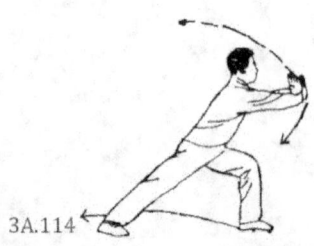

THIRD FORM HUAQUAN (A) (IMAGES ONLY)

115. Turn Back, Brush Aside And Lean

huíshēn lōushǒu jībù kàoshēnzhǎng　　回身搂手靠身掌

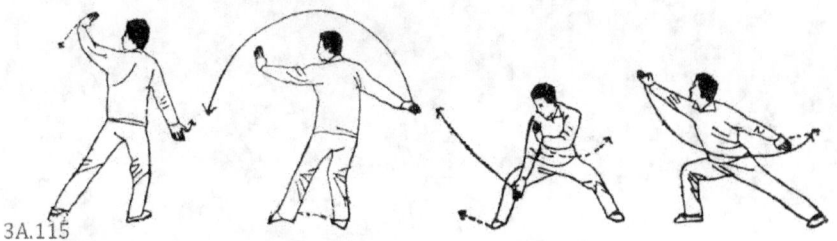

116. Turn Back, Bow Stance Crossed Hands

huíshēn gōngbù shízìzhǎng

回身弓步十字掌

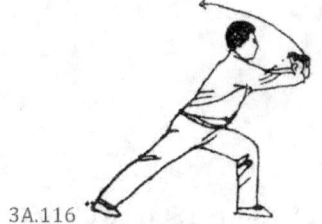

117. Turn Back, Brush Aside, Press Down, Right Bow Stance Punch

huíshēn lōu àn yòu gōngbù chōngquán　　回身搂按右弓步冲拳

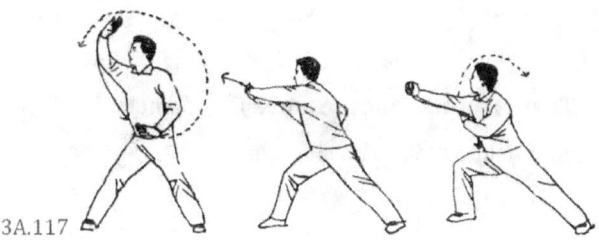

118. Turn Back, Brush Aside, Press Down, Left Bow Stance Punch

huíshēn lōu àn zuǒ gōngbù chōngquán　　回身搂按左弓步冲拳

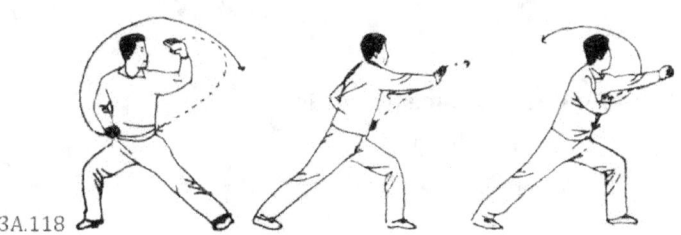

119. Jumping Turn, Brush Aside, Press Down, Left Bow Stance Punch
tiàozhuàn lōu àn zuǒ gōngbù chōngquán　　跳转搂按左弓步冲拳

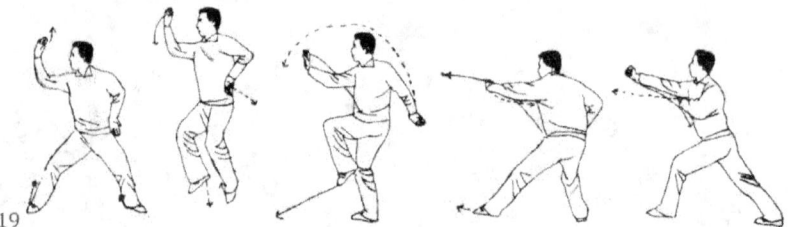

120. Horse Stance Left Punch
mǎbù zuǒ chōngquán

马步左冲拳

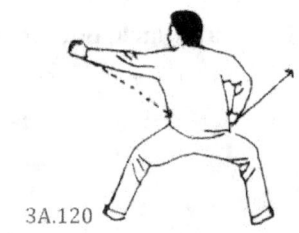

121. Horse Stance Right Punch
mǎbù yòu chōngquán

马步右冲拳

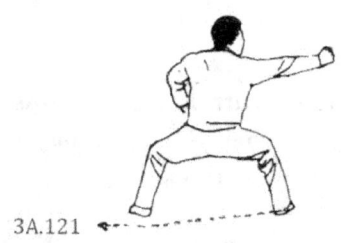

122. Turn Around, Horse Stance Left Punch
zhuànshēn mǎbù zuǒ chōngquán　　转身马步左冲拳

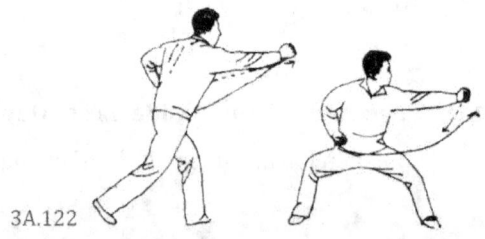

123. Bow Stance Slice Upwards
gōngbù liāozhǎng

弓步撩掌

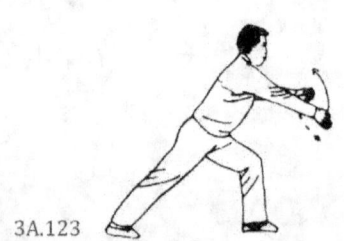

THIRD FORM HUAQUAN (A) (IMAGES ONLY)

124. Bow Stance Scoop And Punch

gōngbù tiǎozhǎng chōngquán   弓步挑掌冲拳

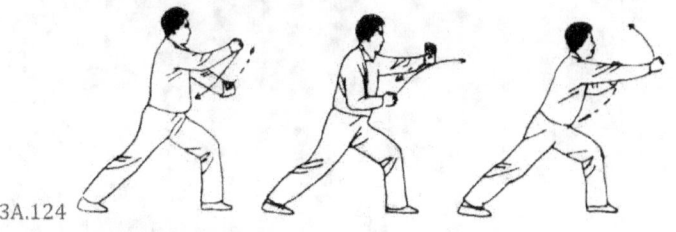

125. Closed Stance Punch Upwards

bīngbù shàng chōngquán   并步上冲拳

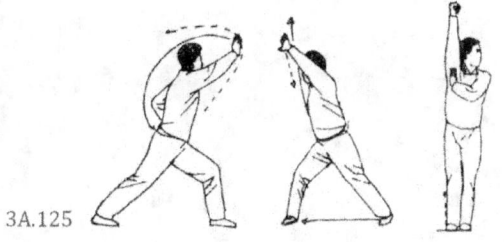

126. Stomp, Tucked Leg Balance

zhēnjiǎo kòutuǐ pínghéng

震脚扣腿平横

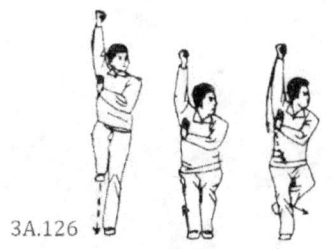

127. Closing Posture

shōu shì

收势

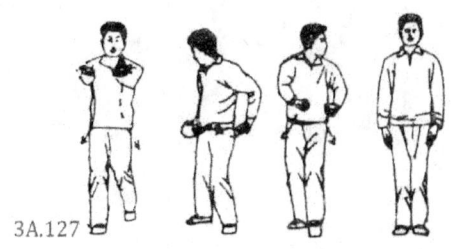

THIRD FORM PAOQUAN

三路炮拳

Names Of The Movements

Position Of Preparation
Section One
1. Facing Fists
2. Step Forward, Facing Fists
3. Bow Stance Push
4. Empty Stance Slice Upwards
5. Raised Knee Elbow Bend
6. Bow Stance Sideways Strike
7. Shifting Step, Snap Kick
8. Jump, Punch
9. Horse Stance Hammerfist
10. Left And Right Punches
11. Horse Stance Double Pushes
12. Single Whip Posture
13. Sliding Step, Sideways Hit
14. Snap Kick
15. Hastening Step, Push
16. Step Forward, Push

Section Two
17. Turn Around, Flowers
18. Framing Block And Snap Kick
19. Arrow Kick
20. Bow Stance Chops
21. Drop Stance, Framing Block And Hit
22. Front Cross-Over Step, Press Down And Hit
23. Resting Stance Crossed Hands
24. Side Thrust Kick
25. Bow Stance Push
26. Drop Stance Thread The Hand
27. Empty Stance Flash Palm
28. Jump Step, Chop
29. Bow Stance Push
30. Insertion Step, Flowers
31. Snap Kick
32. Squat, Double Pushes

Section Three

33. Squat, Double Pushes
34. Squat, Framing Block And Push
35. Horse Stance Hammerfist
36. Bow Stance Scoop And Hit
37. Drop Stance Thread The Hand
38. Empty Stance Flash Palm
39. Step Forward To Slap Kick
40. Empty Stance Slice Upwards
41. Bow Stance And Hit With A Chop
42. Snap Kick
43. Raised Knee Punch
44. Turn Around, Planting Punch
45. Turn Around, Bow Stance Punch

Section Four

46. Turn Around, Aligned Stance Punch
47. Insertion Step Stab
48. Turn Around, Cover And Hit
49. Resting Stance Flash Palm
50. Turn Around, Stab
51. Jump Step, Chop
52. Jump Kick
53. Bow Stance Hooking Fist
54. Bow Stance Reverse Palm Strike
55. Snap Kick, Punch
56. Bow Stance Scoop And Punch
57. Drop Stance Thread The Hand
58. Empty Stance Flash Palm
59. Step Forward, Stab
60. Turn Around, Smear
61. Closed Stance Raise The Hand
62. Stomp, Drop Stance Thread The Hand
63. Bow Stance Slicing Hook
64. Empty Stance Flash Palm
65. Withdraw, Press Down
66. Closing Posture

THIRD FORM PAOQUAN

0. Position Of Preparation   yùbèi shì   预备势

Stand at attention with the legs together, the feet turned out. Let the arms hang naturally by the body. Look straight ahead. (image P3.0)

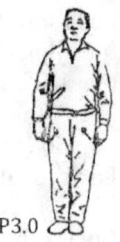

P3.0

Section One

1. Facing Fists   duìquán   对拳

Circle the hands to in front of the belly, clenching the fists with the fist hearts down, about two fist-widths between them. (image P3.1)

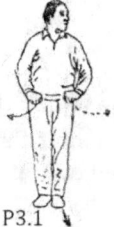

P3.1

2. Step Forward, Facing Fists   shàngbù duìquán   上步对拳

Push into the right foot to shift forward, stepping the left foot a half-step forward, leaving the ball of the right foot on the ground, the heel raised. Unclench the hands and circle them out to either side until the arms are angled down, the palms facing forward. Look to the left. (image P3.2a) Step the right foot up to the left foot to take a closed stance. Clench the fists and circle them to in front of the belly, fist hearts down, two fist widths between them. Look to the left. (image 2b)

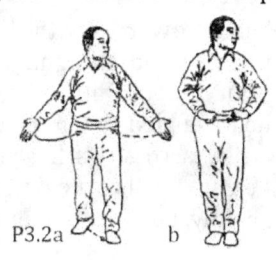

P3.2a   b

3. Bow Stance Push   gongbu tuīzhǎng   弓步推掌

Sit down into the legs, turning to the left. Punch the right fist into the left hand. Look to the left. (image P3.3a) Step the right foot across to the right side and turn left, taking a left bow stance. Clench the left fist and bring it to the waist, fist heart up. Unclench the right hand and push it forwards with a straight arm to shoulder height, fingers up, edge of palm forward. Look forward. (image 3b)

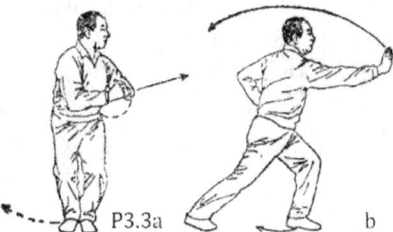

P3.3a   b

97

4. Empty Stance Slice Upwards   xūbù liāozhǎng   虚步撩掌

Push into the left foot and shift back, then retreat the left foot a half-step, touching down the ball of the foot with the heel raised. Turn to the right and circle the right hand up over the head then back on the right side, fingers up. Look to the forward right. (image P3.4a) Sit down into a left empty stance. Unclench the left hand and slice upwards in front, fingers up. Look forward. (image 4b)

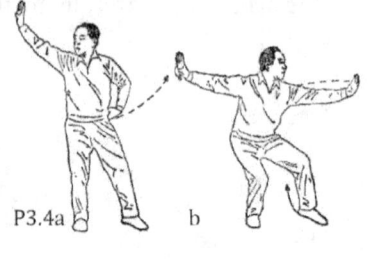

5. Raised Knee Elbow Bend   tíxī qūzhǒu   提膝屈肘

Push into the left foot and shift to the right leg, bending the left knee to raise it with the ankle plantar-flexed. Clench both hands. Bend the left elbow tightly and hold the arm at shoulder height, fist heart down. Hold the right arm out to the rear, arm straight at shoulder height, fist eye up. Look forward. (image P3.5)

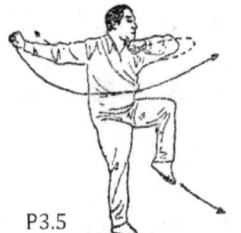

6. Bow Stance Sideways Strike   gōngbù héngdǎ   弓步横打

Land forward on the left foot, bending the knee forward and straightening the right leg, lifting the right heel slightly. Circle the left fist behind, fist heart angled down. Circle the right fist forward to strike across. Both arms are straight at shoulder height, fist hearts down. The body leans forward slightly. Look at the right fist. (image P3.6)

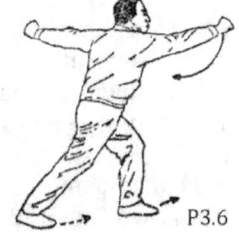

7. Shifting Step, Snap Kick   yíbù tántuǐ   移步弹腿

Push the right foot into the ground and do a moving step with the left foot, bending the left knee and straightening the right, sliding the right foot forward. Laterally rotate the right arm and bring it in, bending the elbow, fist heart up. Look forward. (image P3.7a) Bend the right knee and lift it, then quickly do a snap kick forward, ankle plantar-flexed. Stand firmly on the left leg. Look forward. (image 7b)

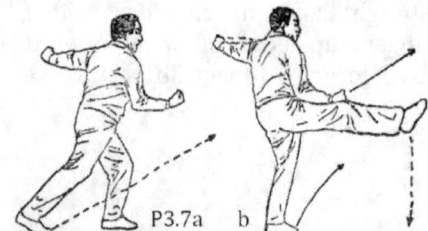

THIRD FORM PAOQUAN

8. Jump Step, Punch   tiàobù chōngquán   跳步冲拳

Push into the left leg to jump up, landing on the right leg and standing firmly on it, bending the left knee and lifting it, ankle plantar-flexed. Punch the right fist forward to shoulder height, arm straight, fist eye up. Bend the left arm and bring the fist to in front of the chest, fist eye down. Look at the right fist. (image P3.8a) Without changing the stance, turn left. Lift the right fist above the head, bending the arm. Cut the left fist across to the left side, the arm curved, fist eye up. Look forward to the left. (image 8b)

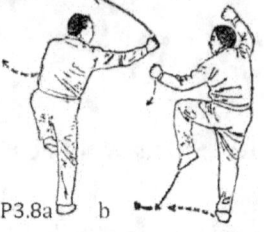

9. Horse Stance Hammerfist   mǎbù záquán   马步砸拳

Land forward on the left foot, then do a bumping step with the right foot into the left foot, moving the left foot forward, bending the left leg and straightening the right leg. Bring the left fist in slightly. Look forward. (image P3.9a) Push the right foot into the ground and shift forward, pivoting on the left foot, stepping the right foot forward and turning left into a horse stance. Do a hammerfist down in front with the right fist, forearm horizontal, fist eye up. Bring the left fist to the waist, fist heart up. Look to the right. (image 9b)

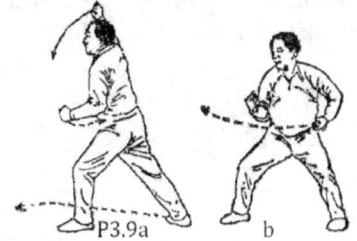

10. Left And Right Punches   zuǒ yòu chōngquán   左右冲拳

Push into the left leg and turn right, taking a right bow stance. Punch the left fist out to the right side at shoulder height, arm straight, fist eye up. Bring the right fist to the waist, fist heart up. Look to the right side. (image P3.10a) Turn left, sitting into a horse stance. Punch the right fist out to the right side to shoulder height, arm straight, fist eye up. Bring the left fist to the waist, fist heart up. Look to the right side. (image 10b)

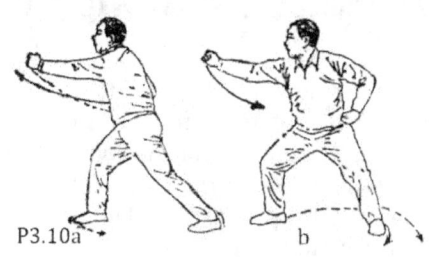

11. Horse Stance Double Pushes   mǎbù shuāng tuīzhǎng   马步双推掌

Push into the right leg and shift left, pivoting on the left foot turn around to the right, retreating the right foot back one step. Stand up with the feet apart, legs slightly bent. Bring the right fist to the waist, fist heart up. Look forward. (image P3.11a) Sit down into a horse stance. Unclench both hands

99

and push forward with both hands to shoulder height, arms straight, fingers up. Look forward. (image 11b)

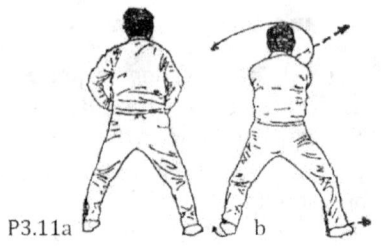

12. Single Whip Posture   dānbiān shì   单鞭势

Push into the left leg and shift right, bending the right leg forward and straightening the left leg. Bring the fists up, then separate them to the left and right, fingers up. Look forward. (image P3.12a) Step the left foot forward into a left bow stance. Clench both hands and circle the fists at their sides to in front of the chest, arms bent, fist hearts up. Lean forward slightly. Look forward. (image 12b) Without changing the stance, tuck the fists into the chest, fist hearts in. Look forward. (image 12c) Punch the fists to shoulder height, front and back simultaneously, arms straight, fist eyes up. Look forward. (image 12d)

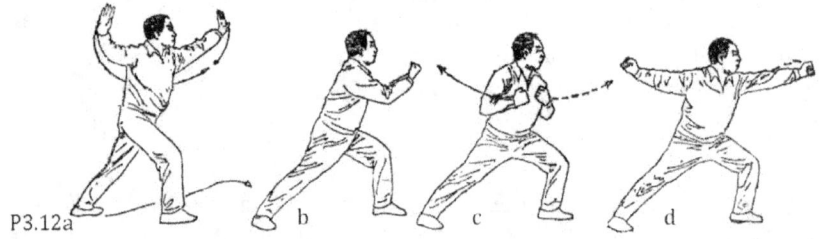

13. Sliding Step, Sideways Hit   huàbù héngdǎ   滑步横打

Without changing the bow stance, bend the left elbow, holding it at shoulder height, fist heart down. Look forward. (image P3.13a) Push into the right foot to shift forward, then slide it forward along the ground, landing on the ball of the foot with the heel lifted. Circle the left fist flat forward, left, then right. Circle the right fist forward to strike sideways in front. Both arms are straight at shoulder height, fist hearts down. Look forward. (image 13b)

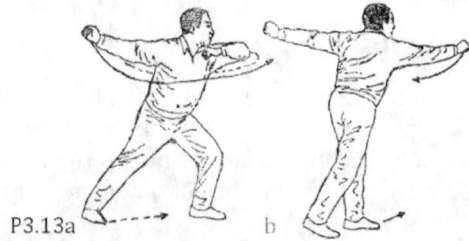

THIRD FORM PAOQUAN

14. Snap Kick   tántuǐ   弹腿

Move the left foot forward and shift forward. Laterally rotate the right forearm and bend the elbow, turning the fist heart up. Look forward. (image P3.14a) Bend the right knee and lift it, then do a snap kick forward with the ankle plantar-flexed. Stand firmly on the left leg. Look forward. (image 14b)

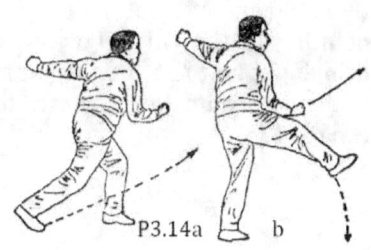

15. Hastening Step, Push   qūbù tuīzhǎng   趋步推掌

Land the right foot forward, bending the knee forward. Punch the right fist forward, fist eye up. Look forward. (image P3.15a) Lean forward. Unclench the left hand and bring it to the chest. Look forward. (image 15b) Step the left foot forward, then bump the right foot into the left to take a little hop-jump, landing the feet right, then left, landing forward with the knees bent. Slide the left hand along inside the right arm to push forward, palm forward, fingers up. Laterally rotate the right arm and bring the fist to the waist, fist heart up. Look forward. (image 15c)

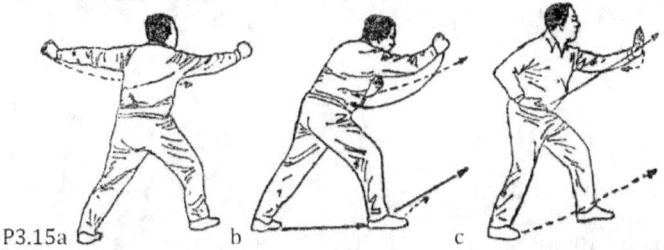

16. Step Forward, Push   shàngbù tuīzhǎng   上步推掌

Step the right foot forward, turning left and bending both legs. Unclench the right hand and slide it forward on top of the left arm, arm straight at shoulder height, palm forward, fingers up. Clench the left hand and place the fist under the right elbow. Look forward. (image P3.16)

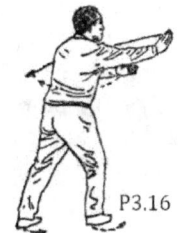

Section Two

17. Turn Around, Flowers   zhuànshēn wǔhuāshǒu   转身舞花手

Pivot on the balls of both feet to turn around to the left, bending the knees. Bring the arms around with the body, holding them flat to the left, right hand on top of the left, both palms down. Look forward. (image P3.17a)

Shift forward, bending the left leg and straightening the right. Circle the hands with a flower action, doing a full circle on either side, then separate them down and out to their respective sides, palms forward, fingers pointing to the sides. Look forward. (image 17b) Stomp the right foot, bringing it up to beside the left foot, and bend both knees. Circle the hands at their sides up, then forward to cross in front of the belly. Look forward. (image 17c)

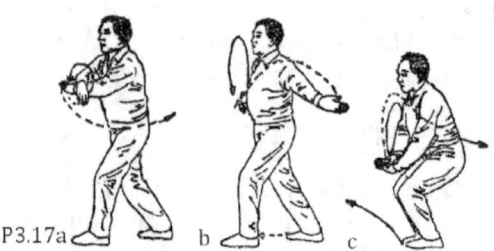

18.　　Framing Block And Snap Kick　　jià tántuǐ　　架弹腿

Circle the hands up, then out, to hold them out at their respective sides, arms angled slightly down, hands holding hooks. Bend and lift the left knee, then quickly do a snap kick forward, ankle plantar-flexed. Bend the right leg slightly. Look forward. (image P3.18)

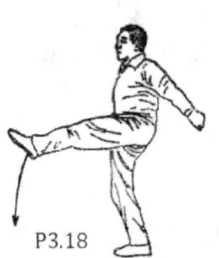

19.　　Arrow Kick　　　　　　jiàntántuǐ　　箭弹腿

Land forward on the left foot, bending the knee forward. Look forward. (image P3.19a) Step the right foot forward, bending the knee forward and bending the left leg slightly, lifting the left heel. Bring the hook hands forward, starting to lift them, palms down. Look forward. (image 19b) Push off with the left, then the right foot, to jump up. Swing the hook hands up in front, the back of the hands leading. Look forward. (image 19c) Land on the left foot, supporting the weight, and doing a snap kick with the right leg, ankle plantar-flexed. Unhook the hands. Lift the right hand above the head and lift the left in front. Look forward. (image 19d)

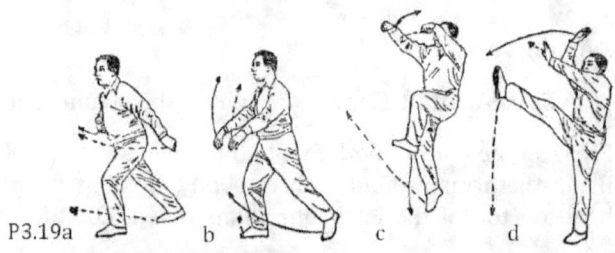

20.   Bow Stance Chops   gōngbù pīzhǎng   弓步劈掌

Land the right foot and take a right bow stance. Chop down to level with the right hand, using the edge of the palm, fingers forward. Place the left hand at the right elbow, fingers up. Look at the right hand. (image P3.20a) Without changing the stance, hook up the right hand, lifting it beside the right ear, fingers back. Chop forward with the left hand to shoulder height, hitting with the palm edge, arm straight, fingers up. Look at the left hand. (image 20b) Do another level chop with the right hand, bringing the left hand to the inside of the right upper arm. Look at the right hand. (image 20c)

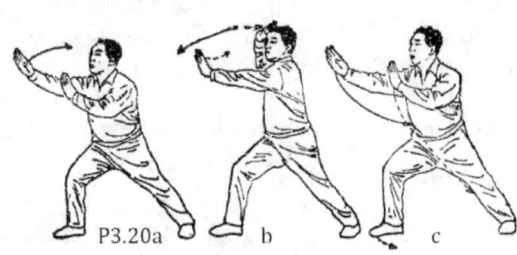

21.   Drop Stance, Framing Block And Hit   pūbù jiàdǎ   仆步架打

Turn left and sit down into a left drop stance. Clench the right hand and bring the fist to the waist, fist heart up. Thread the left hand along the inside of the left leg. Look to the lower left. (image P3.21a) Push into the right leg and shift to the left, turning left, into a left bow stance. Circle the left hand forward to do a framing block above the head, palm forward, fingers pointing right. Punch the right fist forward to the left to shoulder height, arm straight, fist eye up. Look forward, to the left. (image 21b)

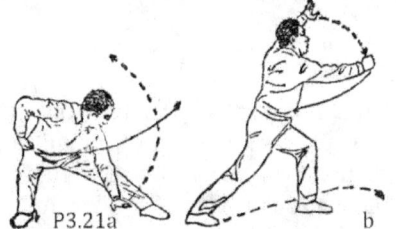

22.   Front Cross-Over Step, Press Down And Hit   gàibù àndǎ   盖步按打

Push into the right leg, shifting forward, then step the right foot forward with the foot turned out, lifting the left heel, so that the legs are crossed and bent. Bring the right fist to the waist, fist heart up. Bring the left hand forward to press down, palm down, fingers pointing right. Look forward, to the left. (image P3.22a) Without changing the stance, punch the right fist forward over the left arm, angling downwards, fist eye on top. Bring the left hand to under the right elbow. Lean forward slightly. Look forward, to the left. (image 22b)

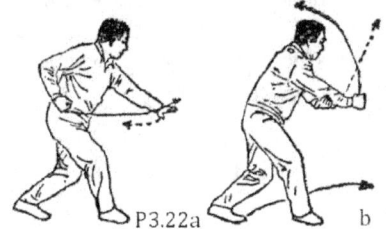

23. Resting Stance Crossed Hands   xiēbù shízìshǒu   歇步十字手

Step the left foot to the forward left, turning right so that the feet are parallel. Unclench the right hand and cross the hands, then raise them in front, the right hand lifting out to the rear right and the left hand lifting to the front, to the left. Look forward, to the left. (image P3.23a) Insert the right foot behind the left leg to take a resting stance. Circle the hands down from each side, bringing them to cross in front of the chest, the left hand inside the right. Look forward, to the left. (image 23b)

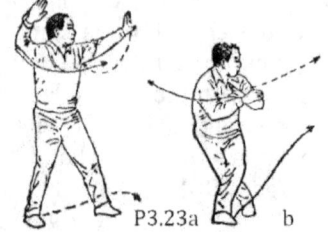

24. Side Thrust Kick   cèchuāituǐ   侧踹腿

Stand up on the right leg and lift the left knee, then do a heel kick with the left foot forward, to the left. Brace to either side with the hands, arms straight at shoulder height. Look forward, to the left. (image P3.24)

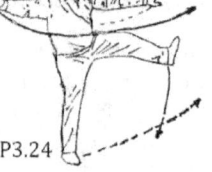

25. Bow Stance Push   gōngbù tuīzhǎng   弓步推掌

Land forward on the left foot then take a step forward with the right foot and turn left, taking a right bow stance. Clench the left hand and bring the fist to the waist, fist heart up. Push forward, to the left, with the right hand, to shoulder height, arm straight and fingers up. Look forward. (image P3.25)

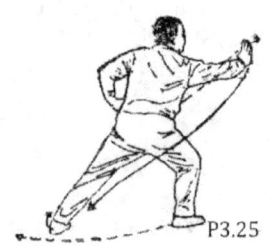

26. Drop Stance Thread The Hand   pūbù chuānzhǎng   仆步穿掌

Push into the right foot to shift back, turning around to the right, pivoting on the left foot, then stepping the right foot back to take a right drop stance. Unclench the left hand and thread it forward along the inside of the right arm, fingers up. Bend the right arm, then thread the right hand down along the inside of the right leg, fingers forward. Look to the lower front. (image P3.26)

THIRD FORM PAOQUAN

27. Empty Stance Flash Palm   xūbù liàngzhǎng   虚步亮掌

Push into the left foot and shift forward, standing up. Retreat the right foot a half-step to take a right empty stance. Circle the right hand forward and up in front, to the right, the arm slightly bent, fingers up. Look forward, to the right. (image P3.27)

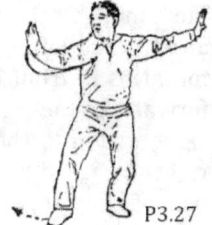

P3.27

28. Jump Step, Chop   tiàobù pīzhǎng   跳步劈掌

Push into the left foot and shift forward, stepping the right foot forward a half-step and bending the knee forward, straightening the left leg. Bend the right arm flat at the shoulder, palm down. Look forward, to the right. (image P3.28a) Step the left foot forward, bending the knee forward and straightening the right leg, lifting the heel. Lift the right hand to in front of the face, fingers up. Look forward, to the right. (image 28b) Push off with both feet, first right, then left, to jump up, then land the feet, first right, then left, with the legs bent, turning right. Circle the right hand forward and down, lifting it out to the right, behind. Circle the left hand up then chop forward. The arms are straight at shoulder height, fingers up. Look forward, to the left. (image 28c)

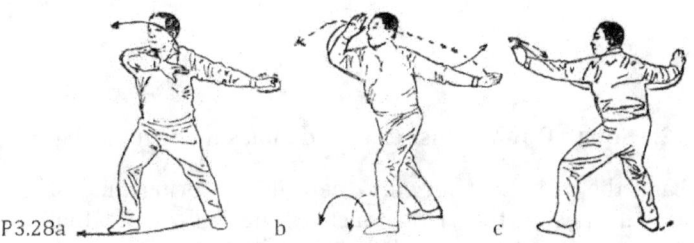

P3.28a   b   c

29. Bow Stance Push   gōngbù tuīzhǎng   弓步推掌

Push into the right foot and turn left into a left bow stance. Bring the right fist to the waist then push out along the left arm forward, to the left, arm slightly bent, palm forward, fingers up. Medially rotate the left arm and bring the hand in to press down, palm down, fingers pointing right. Look forward, to the left. (image P3.29)

P3.29

30. Insertion Step, Flowers   chābù wǔhuāshǒu   叉步舞花手

Push into the right foot and shift forward, stepping the right foot forward and turning left. Lean towards the left and shift onto the left leg. Cross the forearms in front of the belly, right arm above the left, palms down. Look forward, to the right. (image P3.30a) Push into the left foot and shift to the right, crossing the left foot behind the right toward the right side, touching the ball of the foot down, heel raised. The legs are crossed and bent. Circle the hands to the left and up towards the right, turning over a complete circle until the right hand is below the left. The right palm faces up and the left palm faces down. Look forward, to the right. (image 30b)

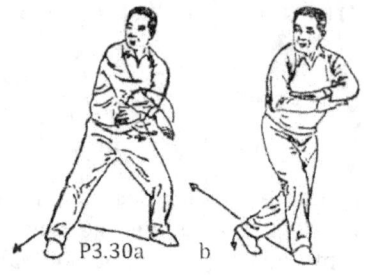

31. Snap Kick   tántuǐ   弹腿

Shift to the left leg and raise the bent right knee, then quickly do a snap kick to the front, ankle plantar-flexed. Look forward, to the right. (image P3.31)

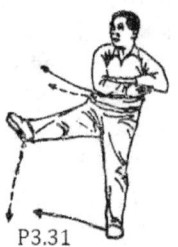

32. Squat, Double Pushes   dūnbù shuāng tuīzhǎng   蹲步双推掌

Land the right foot forward then quickly bring the left foot up beside the right, touching the ball of the foot down, heel raised, and half-squat on both legs. Push forward, to the right, with both hands, striking with the edge of the palms, the arms slightly bent, fingers up. Look forward, to the right. (image P3.32)

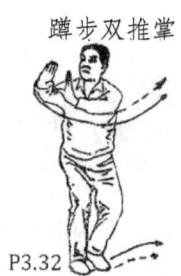

Section Three

33. Squat, Double Pushes   dūnbù shuāng tuīzhǎng   蹲步双推掌

Turn leftward and step the left foot forward towards the left side, then quickly bring the right foot in beside the left, touching the ball of the foot down, heel raised, both legs in a half-squat. Push forward, to the left, with both hands, striking with the edge of the palms, the arms slightly bent, fingers up. Look forward, to the left. (image P3.33)

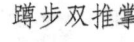
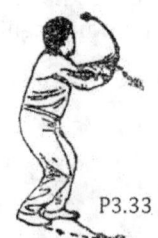

THIRD FORM PAOQUAN

34. Squat, Framing Block And Push   dūnbù jià tuīzhǎng   蹲步架推掌

Turn rightward and step the right foot forward to the right side, then quickly bring the left foot in beside the right, touching the ball of the foot down, heel raised, both legs half-squatting. Do a framing block above the head at the right with the right hand, palm forward, fingers pointing to the upper left. Push the left hand forward to the right, arm slightly bent, palm forward, fingers up. Look forward, to the right. (image P3.34)

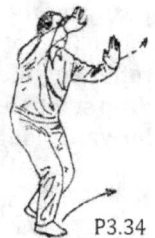

P3.34

35. Horse Stance Hammerfist   mǎbù záquán   马步砸拳

Turn leftward and step the left foot forward to the left, bending both legs. Cut the left hand across in front, to the left side, fingers up. Lower the right hand. Look forward, to the left. (image P3.35a) Bring the right foot up to bump the back of the left foot, taking a half-step forward with the left foot. Then step forward with the right foot and turn left into a horse stance. Clench the right hand and circle up then do a hammerfist down in front, the elbow bent and the fist heart up. Clench the left hand and bring the fist to the waist, fist heart up. Look forward, to the right. (image 35b)

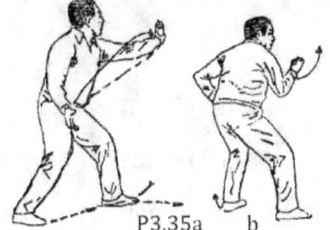

P3.35a   b

36. Bow Stance Scoop And Hit   gōngbù tiǎodǎ   弓步挑打

Push into the left foot and shift right, turn right and bend the right knee forward and straighten the left knee. Circle the right fist up at the right to do a framing block, fist heart down, arm curved. Look forward, to the right. (image P3.36a) Turn right and step the left foot in front of the right, lifting the right heel, pressing the ball of the foot down. Circle the right fist up over the head to the rear, at the right side, fist heart down. Do a framing block upwards with the left fist, fist heart down, arm curved. Look forward, to the right. (image 36b) Step the right foot forward, to the right, into a right bow stance. Bring the right fist past the waist to punch forward to the right, arm straight at shoulder height, fist eye up. Bring the left fist to the waist. Look forward, to the right. (image 36c)

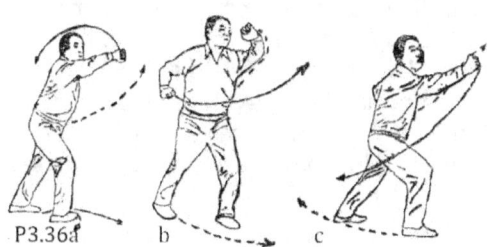

P3.36a   b   c

37. Drop Stance Thread The Hand   pūbù chuānzhǎng   仆步穿掌

Push into the right foot and shift back, pivoting on the left foot and turning around to the right, retreating the right foot one step to sit into a right drop stance. Unclench the hands. Slide the left hand forward along inside the right arm, then thread the right hand down and back along the inside of the right leg. Look down to the right. (image P3.37)

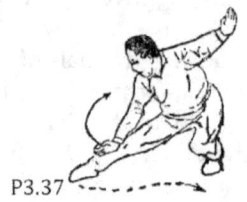

38. Empty Stance Flash Palm   xūbù liàngzhǎng   虚步亮掌

Stand up and bring the right foot in a half-step, to take a right empty stance. Circle the right hand up and cock both wrists to point the fingers up. Look forward, to the right. (image P3.38)

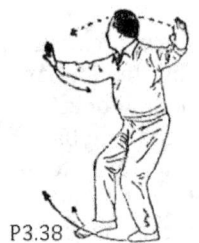

39. Step Forward To Slap Kick   shàngbù pāizhǎng   上步拍脚

Step the right foot forward, to the right, a half-step, then step the left foot in the same direction, straightening both legs slightly. Circle the left hand over the head to press down in front, palm down, fingers pointing right. Bring the right hand to in front of the chest, palm down, fingers pointing left. Look forward. (image P3.39a) Shift forward and swing the right leg up in front. Clench the left hand and bring the fist to the waist, fist heart up. Circle the right hand over and forward to slap the foot. Look forward, to the right. (image 39b)

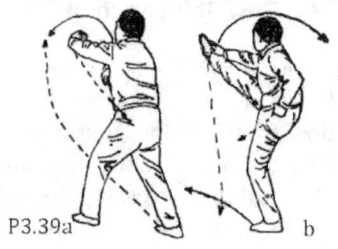

40. Empty Stance Slice Upwards   xūbù liāozhǎng   虚步撩掌

Land the right foot forward then step the left foot forward a half-step, touching down the ball of the foot. Turn the torso rightward and circle the right hand up and over to the rear right, fingers up. Unclench the left hand and move the arm forward and down. Look at the right hand. (image P3.40a) Sit down into a left empty stance. Slice the left hand forward and up, fingers up. Look at the left hand. (image 40b)

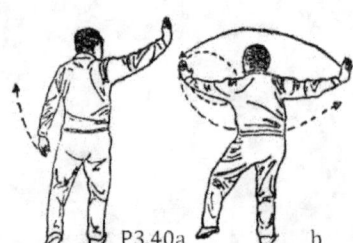

THIRD FORM PAOQUAN

41. Bow Stance Hit With A Chop   gōngbù pīdǎ   弓步劈打

Step the left foot forward to take a left bow stance. Circle the left hand down, then up, a full circle, then circle it down and back, clenching the fist and holding it out at shoulder height to the rear left, arm straight, fist eye up. Clench the right hand and circle it over the head to chop down in front, fist eye up. The body is turned leftward. Look at the right fist. (image P3.41)

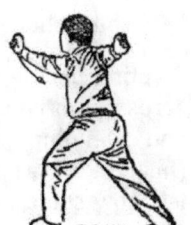

42. Snap Kick   tántuǐ   弹腿

Without changing the bow stance, laterally rotate the right forearm to turn the back of the fist to strike flat down, fist heart up. Look forward. (image P3.42a) Shift forward and bend the right knee, lifting it, then doing a snap kick with the ankle plantar-flexed. Bring the right fist to the waist, fist heart up. Look forward. (image 42b)

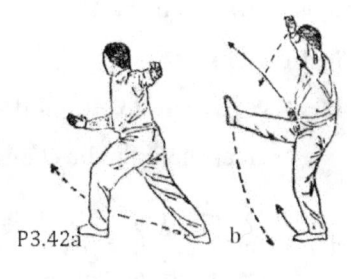

43. Raised Knee Punch   tíxī chōngquán   提膝冲拳

Land the right foot forward and lift the bent left knee, turning slightly leftward. Circle the left fist forward to inside the right arm and punch forward with the right fist, arm straight at shoulder height, fist eye up. Look at the right fist. (image P3.43)

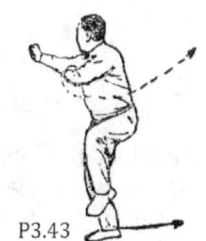

44. Turn Around, Planting Punch   zhuànshēn zāiquán   转身载拳

Turn to the left and land the left foot behind to the left, bending both legs. Unclench the left hand and circle it to lash to the rear at the left, fingers up. Look at the left hand. (image P3.44a) Pivot on the left foot to turn around to the left and land the right foot forward. Then step the left foot again, bringing it in to the right foot to take a closed stance with the legs bent. Circle the right fist up and over to plant a punch down at the left, fist eye in. Smear the left hand to the right side of the chest. Look to the right. (image 44b)

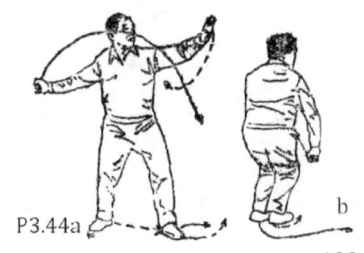

45. Turn Around, Bow Stance Punch

zhuànshēn gōngbù chōngquán 转身弓步冲拳

Pivoting on the right foot, turn around to the left and step the left foot across from behind the right foot to the right side, bending the right knee and extending the left. Bring the right fist to the waist. Look to the left side. (image P3.45a) Turn to the left into a left bow stance. Circle the left hand to the left, clench it, and bring the fist to the waist, fist heart up. Punch the right fist forward to the left side, arm straight at shoulder height, fist heart up. Look forward. (image 45b)

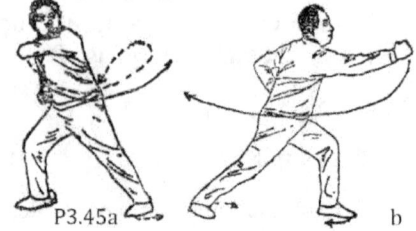

Section Four

46. Turn Around, Aligned Stance Punch

zhuànshēn shùnbù chōngquán 转身顺步冲拳

Push into the left foot and turn right into a right bow stance. Bring the right fist to the waist, then punch to the right, arm straight at shoulder height, fist eye up. Look at the right fist. (image P3.46)

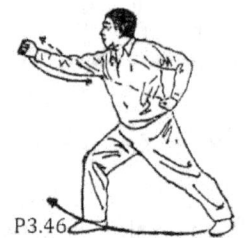

47. Insertion Step Stab   chābù chuānzhǎng   叉步穿掌

Push into the left foot and shift right, then step the left foot forward and turn right, both legs bent. Unclench both hands and slide the left hand along on top of the right arm to stab forward, arm straight at shoulder height, fingers forward. Bring the right hand to the left side of the chest. Look at the left hand. (image P3.47a) Step the right foot behind the left foot out to the left side with an insertion step, touching the ball of the foot down. The legs are crossed and slightly bent. Look at the left hand. (image 47b)

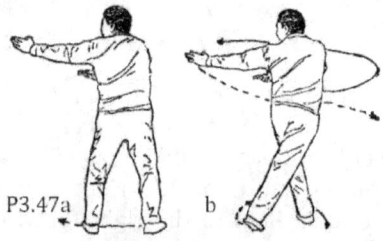

48. Turn Around, Cover And Hit   zhuànshēn gàidǎ   转身盖打

Pivoting on both feet, turn around to the right. Smear the right hand flat across to the right and back with a straight arm, palm down, fingers pointing forward. Hold the left arm angled downwards. Look at the right hand. (image P3.48a) Turn right, lifting the left heel and bending both legs

THIRD FORM PAOQUAN

slightly. Circle the left hand over the head to press down in front, palm down, fingers pointing right. Clench the right hand and bring the fist to the waist, fist heart up. Look forward. (image 48b) Step the left foot forward into a left bow stance. Punch the right fist out to the front, passing over the left forearm, arm straight at shoulder height, fist eye up. Bring the left hand to under the right arm, palm down. Look forward. (image 48c)

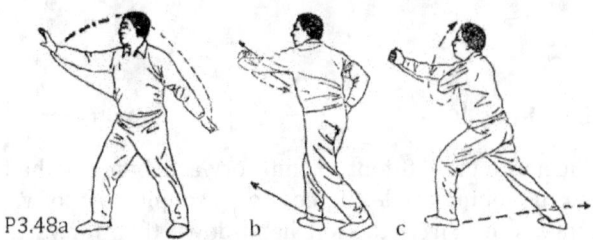

49. Resting Stance Flash Palm   xiēbù liàngzhǎng   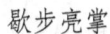

Push into the left foot to shift back, turning right, then step the left foot behind the right foot to the right with an insertion step, into a resting stance. Bring the right fist to the waist, fist heart up. Circle the left hand to flash it in front above the head, palm forward, fingers pointing right. Look to the right side. (image P3.49)

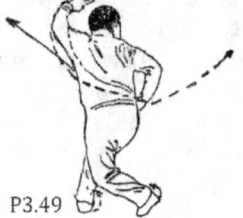

50. Turn Around, Stab   zhuànshēn chuānzhǎng   转身穿掌

Pivoting on both feet, turn around to the left and stand up with the feet parallel. Thread the right hand along the inside of the left arm to the left. Bring the left hand around and down to slice upwards. Both arms are straight at shoulder height, fingers pointing up. Look at the left hand (image P3.50)

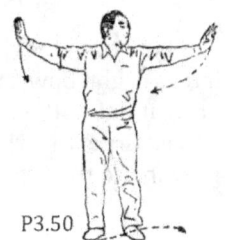

51. Jump Step, Chop   tiàobù pīzhǎng   跳步劈掌

Turn left and step the right foot forward, bending the right knee forward and bending the left knee slightly, lifting the left heel. Bend the left arm to bring the hand in, palm down. Hold the right arm angled downwards. Look forward. (image P3.51a) Push into the right foot to jump up, landing the left, then the right foot forward in a right drop stance. Circle the left hand up, forward, then down to the rear at the left, fingers pointing back. Circle the right hand up then chop forward and down inside the right leg. Look forward to the right. (image 51b)

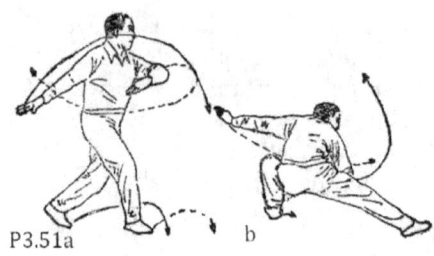

P3.51a   b

52. Jump Kick   tiàotī   跳踢

Push into the left foot to shift forward, bending the right knee forward and straightening the left knee. Do a scooping lift forward with the right hand, fingers up. Circle the left hand down then forward. Look forward. (image P3.52a) Push into the right foot to jump up. Land on the left foot, standing firmly. Do a snap kick with the right leg, leaving the leg suspended, ankle plantar-flexed. Circle the right hand to the rear at the right. Slice the left hand forward, fingers pointing forward. Look at the left hand. (image 52b)

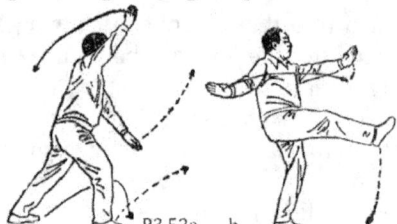

P3.52a   b

53. Bow Stance Hooking Fist   gōngbù gōuquán   弓步勾拳

Land the right foot forward and turn slightly to the left into a right bow stance. Clench the right hand and bring it flat to the front then hook the wrist, fist heart down. Grab the right fist with the left hand. Look forward, to the right. (image P3.53)

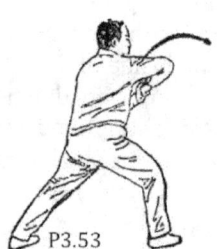

P3.53

54. Bow Stance Reverse Palm Strike   gōngbù fǎnzhǎng   弓步反掌

Without changing the right bow stance, unclench the right hand and circle it over to strike forward with the back of the hand, palm up, fingers forward. Bring the left hand to under the right arm, palm down, finger to the right. Look forward. (image P3.54)

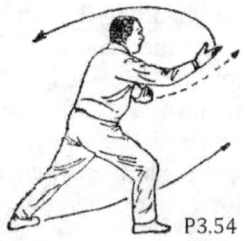

P3.54

THIRD FORM PAOQUAN

55. Snap Kick, Punch   tántuǐ chōngquán   弹腿冲拳

Push into the left foot and shift forward, standing up on the right leg and lifting the bent left knee. Then quickly do a snap kick forward with the left leg, ankle plantar-flexed. Circle the right hand over the head to hold it out to the right, fingers up. Stab the left hand forward to shoulder height, arm straight, fingers pointing forward. Look forward. (image P3.55a) Land forward on the left foot into a left bow stance, clenching the right hand and bringing it past the waist to punch forward to shoulder height, arm straight, fist eye up. Bring the left hand in by the right arm. Lean forward slightly. Look forward. (image 55b)

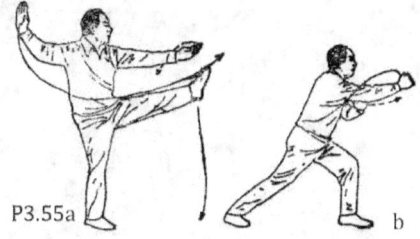

56. Bow Stance Scoop And Punch   gōngbù tiǎo chōngquán   弓步挑冲拳

Without changing the bow stance, raise the right fist slightly and bring it in in to the chest, fist heart in. Circle the left hand down slightly then scoop forward, fingers up. Look forward. (image P3.56a) Punch the right fist forward to shoulder height, arm straight, fist eye up. Place the left hand inside the right arm. Look forward. (image 56b)

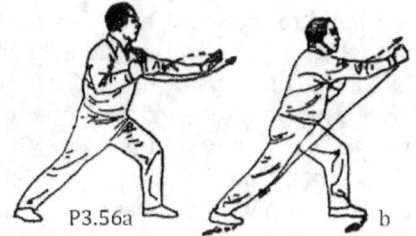

57. Drop Stance Thread The Hand   pūbù chuānzhǎng   仆步穿掌

Turn right and sit down into a right drop stance. Thread the left hand out above the right arm to the left, fingers up, then unclench the right hand and slide it down and along inside the right leg to the lower right, fingers forward. Look to the lower right. (image P3.57)

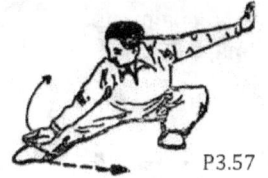

58. Empty Stance Flash Palm   xūbù liàngzhǎng   虚步亮掌

Push into the left foot and stand up, bringing the right foot back a half-step to take a right empty stance. Circle the right hand forward with a scooping lift, fingers up. Look forward. (image P3.58)

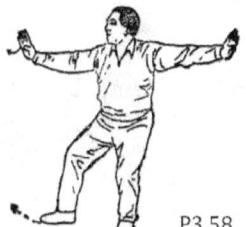

59. Step Forward, Stab   shàngbù chuānzhǎng   上步穿掌

Step the right foot forward a half-step, turning the right hand over, palm up. Look at the right hand. (image P59a) Step the left foot forward, still looking at the right hand. (image 59b) Step the right foot forward, keeping both legs bent, still looking at the right hand. (image 59c)

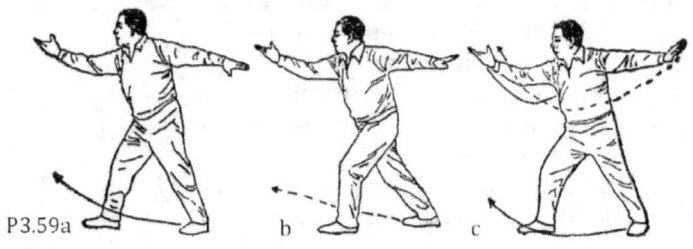

60. Turn Around, Smear   zhuànshēn mōzhǎng   转身抹掌

Push into the left foot and shift forward, then step the left foot forward and turn around to the right, stepping to an upright parallel stance. Bring the left hand to the waist then thread it out to the right along the right arm, straightening the arm at shoulder height, fingers forward. Bring the right hand in to the left side of the chest, fingers up. Look at the left hand. (image P3.60a) Push into the right foot and shift to the left, then pivot on the left foot to turn around to the right. Move the right foot to the left behind the left foot and stand up with the feet parallel. Smear around with the right hand to the right and back, arm straight at shoulder height, palm down. Bring the left hand to the waist, palm up. Look at the right hand. (image 60b)

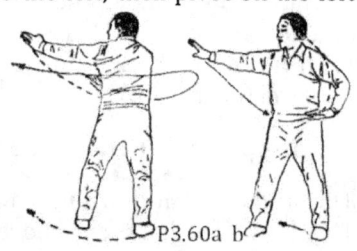

61. Closed Stance Raise The Hand   bīngbù jūzhǎng   并步举掌

Quickly step the left foot up to the right foot and stand straight up with the feet together. Bring the right hand to the waist, palm up. Circle the left hand to lift it up above the head, palm up, fingers pointing back. Look to the right side. (image P3.61)

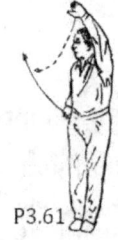

62. Stomp, Drop Stance Thread The Hand
tà pūbù chuānzhǎng   踏仆步穿掌

Without changing the stance, thread the right hand out to the right side at shoulder height, arm straight, fingers up. Press the left hand down inside the right arm, fingers up. Look to the right side. (image P3.62a) Bend the right knee and lift it with the ankle plantar-flexed. Keep looking to the right side (image 62b) Land the right foot with a stomp and bend both legs. Keep looking to the right side. (image 62c) Take a straddle step with the left foot to the left side, turning slightly rightward to take a right bow stance. Keep looking to the right side. (image 62d) Turn leftward and sit down into a left drop stance. Thread the left hand along inside the left leg to the lower left, fingers pointing left. Look to the lower left. (image 62e)

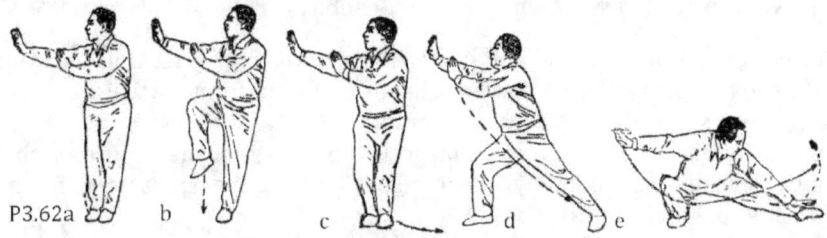

63. Bow Stance Slicing Hook   gōngbù liāogōu   弓步撩勾

Push into the right foot and shift left into a left bow stance. Circle the left hand forward to level, fingers up. Hook the right hand and circle it down then to the left to slice up, the hook setting under the left hand, hook pointing down. Look forward. (image P3.63)

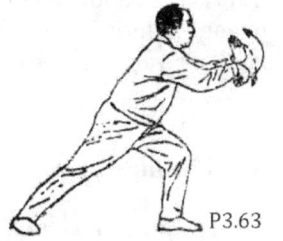

64. Empty Stance Flash Palm   xūbù liàngzhǎng   虚步亮掌

Without changing the bow stance, unhook the right hand so that the palms are facing each other. Then pivot around the wrists to circle the hands, flipping over at the left, until the right hand is above with the palm down and the left hand is below with the palm up. Turn slightly rightward. Look to the left side. (image P3.64a) Push into the left foot and turn right, moving the left foot to the right into a left empty stance. Keeping the hands together, place them at the left side of the chest. Look to the lower front. (image 64b) Clench the left hand and bring it to the waist, fist heart up. Slide the right hand down along the front of the left leg to the foot to slice with the fingers pointing down. Lean forward. Look at the right hand. (image 64c) Circle the right hand forward and up to flash above the head, palm forward, fingers pointing left. Straighten the torso. Look to the left. (image 64d)

CHAQUAN, VOLUME II

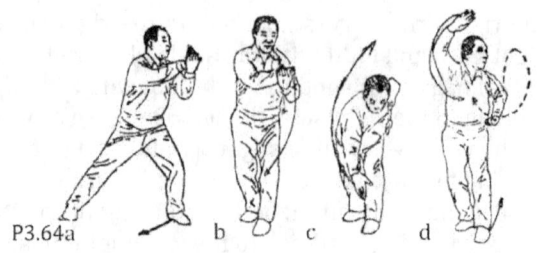

P3.64a   b   c   d

65. Withdraw, Press Down   chèbù ànzhǎng   撤步按掌

Retreat the left foot behind and bend the right knee forward. Unclench the left hand and bring it up so that both hands come out from the waist at their respective sides to arrive with simultaneous stabs forward, palms up, fingers forward. Look forward. (image P3.65a) Retreat the right foot and touch the ball of the foot down, heel raised. Separate the hands down out to the side, palms forward. Look forward. (image 65b) Bring the left foot in beside the right foot and stand up straight. Circle the hands to press down in front of the body, palms down, fingers pointing to each other. Look forward. (image 65c)

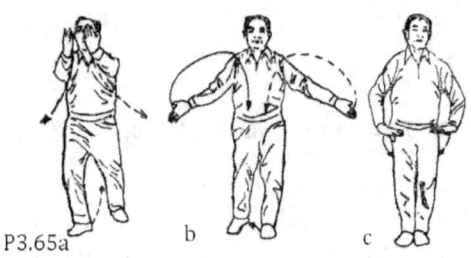

P3.65a   b   c

66. Closing Posture   shōu shì   收势

Lower the hands and stand to attention. Look forward. (image P3.66)

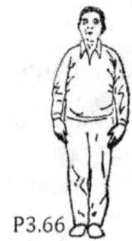

P3.66

SIXTH FORM PAOQUAN

六路炮拳

0. Position Of Preparation

Section One
1. Closed Stance Facing Fists
2. Closed Stance Embrace With Fists
3. Raised Knee Lash
4. Left Bow Stance Framing Block And Punch
5. Left Empty Stance Palm Edge Strike
6. Switchover Palms
7. Left Empty Stance Flash Palm
8. Left Empty Stance Stab
9. Left Empty Stance Embrace
10. Step Forward, Separate The Hands
11. Right Snap Kick
12. Right Bow Stance Palm Edge Strike
13. Hitting Hop-Step Palm Edge Strike
14. Left Bow Stance Palm Edge Strike
15. Raised Knee Punch To The Side

Section Two
16. Left Drop Stance Thread The Hand
17. Left Bow Stance Scooping Snap
18. Step Forward, Snap Kick
19. Left Bow Stance Palm Edge Strike
20. Jump To Resting Stance Double Carry
21. Palm Edge Strike To The Side, Side Kick
22. Raised Knee Scooping Snap

Section Three
23. Step Forward Slice Up
24. Jumping Snap Kick
25. Horse Stance Left And Right Hammerfist
26. Horse Stance Scooping Snap
27. Right Bow Stance Punch
28. Horse Stance Framing Block And Punch
29. Horse Stance Left Brush Aside
30. Horse Stance Right Brush Aside
31. Turn Around, Snap Kick
32. Horse Stance Left And Right Hammerfist
33. Horse Stance Scoop

34. Left Bow Stance Punch
35. Horse Stance Punch
36. Right Empty Stance Block
37. Left Bow Stance Punch
38. Left Empty Stance Block
39. Right Bow Stance Punch

Section Four

40. Horse Stance Left Brush Aside
41. Horse Stance Right Brush Aside
42. Raised Knee Reverse Hook
43. Left Bow Stance Punch
44. Jumping Two Rising Kicks
45. Horse Stance Double Lash

Section Five

46. Left Bow Stance Strike
47. Forward Jump To Strike
48. Raised Knee Punch To The Side

Section Six

49. Left Drop Stance Brush Aside
50. Raised Knee Scooping Snap
51. Curving Walk, Slice Up
52. Aerial Outside Crescent Kick
53. Jump Switch-Step To Bow Stance Punch

Section Seven

54. Right Drop Stance Thread The Hand
55. Jumping Two Rising Kicks
56. Left Empty Stance Scooping Snap
57. Left Bow Stance Chop With The Fist
58. Right Snap Kick
59. Raised Knee Punch To The Side

Section Eight

60. Right Bow Stance Hack
61. Left Bow Stance Hack
62. Horse Stance Stab
63. Turn Around, Front Sweep Kick
64. Jumping Two Rising Kicks
65. Strike To The Side, Side Thrust Kick
66. Left Bow Stance Scooping Snap
67. Left Bow Stance Punch

Section Nine

68. Right Drop Stance Thread The Hand
69. Right Empty Stance Scooping Snap

70. Raised Knee Scooping Snap
71. Step Forward, Left And Right Stabs
72. Jump To Closed Stance Double Press Down
73. Closed Stance Separate The Hands
74. Closed Stance, Left And Right Press Down
75. Raised Knee Roundhouse Punch
76. Horse Stance Elbow Press
77. Turn Around, Resting Stance Press Down
78. Left Snap Kick
79. Left Bow Stance Punch
80. Right Drop Stance Thread The Hand
81. Left Empty Stance Strike
82. Left Bow Stance Strike
83. Step Forward, Left Snap Kick
84. Hitting Hop-Step, Slice Up
85. Stomp, Planting Punch
86. Left Drop Stance Brush Aside
87. Right Drop Stance Brush Aside
88. Turn Around, Snap Kick
89. Jump To Bow Stance Punch

Section Ten

90. Right Drop Stance Thread The Hand
91. Raised Knee Scooping Snap
92. Curving Walk, Left And Right Scoop Up
93. Jump To Resting Stance Double Lashes

Section Eleven

94. Hitting Hop-Step Slice Up
95. Right Bow Stance Scooping Snap
96. Right Bow Stance Chop With The Fist
97. Raised Knee Scooping Snap

Section Twelve

98. Left And Right Retreating Back Insertion Step
99. Raised Knee Block
100. Right Bow Stance Framing Block And Strike
101. Closed Stance Facing Fists
102. Closing Posture

CHAQUAN, VOLUME II

0. Position Of Preparation   yùbèi shì   预备势

Stand at attention. (imageP6.0a) Staying in place, look to the left. (image 0b)

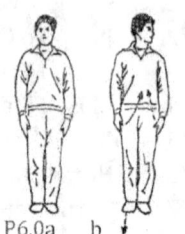

P6.0a   b

Section One

1. Closed Stance Facing Fists   bīngbù duìquán   并步对拳

Step the right foot forward to the right. Stab the hands to chest height towards the forward left, palms up. Look at the hands. (image P6.1a) Step the left foot forward then bring the right foot up to meet it in a closed stance. Bring the hands down to their respective sides at the waist, then medially rotate the arms and circle the hands forward and up, swinging in to make facing fists in front of the chest with the arms straight. The fist eyes are facing each other at shoulder height and width. Look forward. (image 1b)

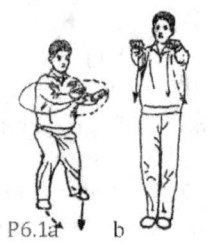

P6.1a   b

2. Closed Stance Embrace With Fists   bīngbù bàoquán   并步抱拳

Without changing the stance, lower the fists to either side of the waist, fist hearts up. Look to the left. (image P6.2)

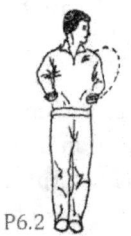

P6.2

3. Raised Knee Lash   tíxī bǎizhǎng   提膝摆掌

Unclench the left hand and circle it back and around the outside until it is in front, palm up and level. Look forward. (image P6.3a) Bend the left knee and raise it. Medially rotate the left arm and drop the wrist and elbow so that the fingers point up. Look to the left side. (image 3b)

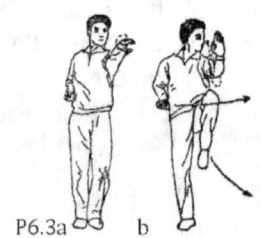

P6.3a   b

SIXTH FORM PAOQUAN

4. **Left Bow Stance Framing Block And Punch**

   zuǒ gōngbù jià chōngquán   左弓步架冲拳

Land the left foot to the forward left, bending the knee and straightening the right leg, to take a left bow stance. Lower the left hand down the front and swing out to the left side with an upward framing block, palm angled upward. Punch the right fist forward with a standing fist to shoulder height. Look forward. (image P6.4)

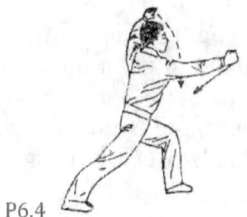

5. **Left Empty Stance Palm Edge Strike**   zuǒ xūbù jīzhǎng   左虚步击掌

Unclench the right hand and medially rotate it, lowering it on the left side, fingers pointing down by the left knee. Stab the left hand in to tuck into the right armpit, palm down. (image P6.5a) Turn the torso rightward and laterally rotate the right hand, clenching it with the fist heart up. Set the left hand on top of the right elbow crease. Look forward. (image 5b) Place the left foot in front of the right foot, touching down the ball of the foot and bending the right knee to take a left empty stance. Bring the right fist to the waist. Strike forward and level with the left hand, fingers up. Look at the left hand. (image 5c)

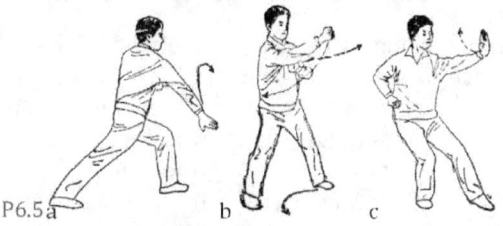

6. **Switchover Palms**   huàn jīzhǎng   换击掌

Without changing the stance, turn the left palm over, palm down, and swing it level out to the left side. (image P6.6a) When it arrives at the side, turn the palm up and chop across towards the right, stopping in front. (image 6b) Unclench the right hand and strike it forward and level, fingers up. Medially rotate the left arm and tuck the hand into the right armpit. Look forward. (image 6c)

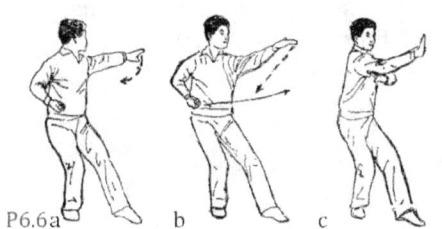

7. Left Empty Stance Flash Palm   zuǒ xūbù liàngzhǎng   左虚步亮掌

Without changing the stance, turn the right hand palm down and sweep it out to the right side, keeping it level. (image P6.7a) Turn the right hand to palm up and chop it across the front to under the left armpit. Flash the left hand, first bringing it down, then up at the left, palm up. Look forward. (image 7b)

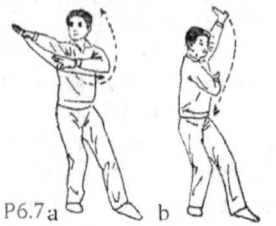

8. Left Empty Stance Stab   zuǒ xūbù chuānzhǎng   左虚步穿掌

Still without changing the stance, lean forward, hook the left hand, and do a hooking action down outside the left leg, hook pointing up. (image P6.8a) Straighten the torso and stab the right hand straight up past the ear, fingers pointing up, palm turned out. Look forward. (image 8b).

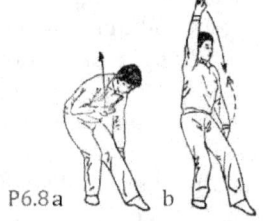

9. Left Empty Stance Embrace   zuǒ xūbù hézhǎng   左虚步合掌

Without changing the stance, hook the left hand and circle it out and up past the face to the chest, palm out. Lower the right hand down past the face to the chest, crossing the arms with the left on top and the right below it. Both palms face out. Look forward. (image P6.9a) Still without changing the stance, separate the palms, circling them down and out, then up and back past the face to cross again in front of the chest, the same as before. (image 9b)

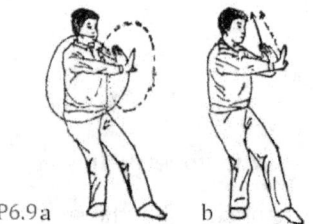

10. Step Forward, Separate The Hands   shàngbù fēnzhǎng   上步分掌

Advance the left foot and do framing blocks with both hands up past the chest to above the head. (image P6.10a) Step the right foot forward, and continue on to step the left foot forward. Separate the hands out to either side to stretch out level, palms out. Look forward. (image 10b)

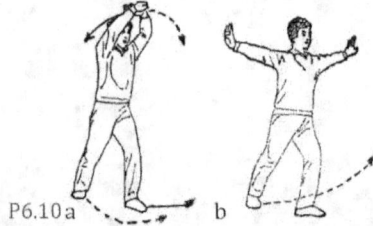

SIXTH FORM PAOQUAN

11. Right Snap Kick   yòu tántuǐ   右弹腿

Bend the right knee and lift it, snapping forcefully forward with the lower leg to kick with the ankle plantar flexed. Look forward. (image P6.11)

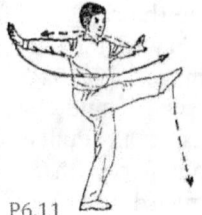

12. Right Bow Stance Palm Edge Strike yòu gōngbù jīzhǎng 右弓步击掌

Land the right foot and bend the knee, extending the left leg to take a right bow stance. Bend the right elbow and bring the hand past the waist then strike out to the front, fingers up. Lash the left hand out at the rear left, fingers up, arm level. Look forward. (image P6.12)

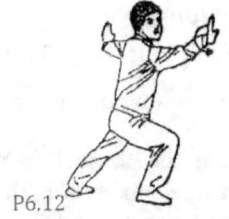

13. Hitting Hop-Step Palm Edge Strike   jībù jī zhǎng   击步击掌

Shift forward. Brush aside with the right hand, grabbing outwards, then clenching and turning the fist heart up. (image P6.13a) Step the left foot forward and push off with it, swinging the right foot forward, to jump up and forward, tapping the feet together whilst airborne. Bring the left hand in to the waist then strike forward, fingers up, arm level. Bring the right fist to the waist. Look forward. (image 13b)

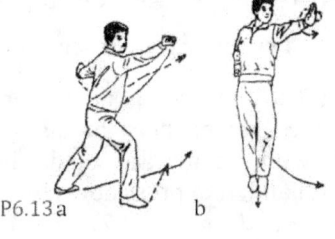

14. Left Bow Stance Palm Edge Strike

zuǒ gōngbù jī zhǎng   左弓步击掌

Land the right foot where it is, then land the left foot forward, bending both knees to take a half horse stance. Circle the left hand out and up, drawing a small circle, then press down, fingers pointing right, palm forward. Look forward. (image (P6.14a) Push the right heel out and extend the knee to take a left bow stance. Unclench the right hand and strike straight forward, fingers up. Turn the left palm over to palm down, and place it under the right elbow, fingers pointing right. Look forward. (image 14b)

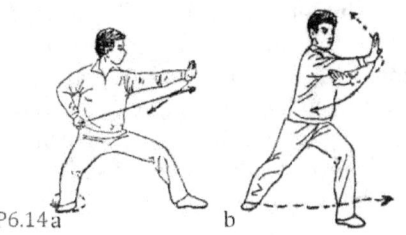

15. Raised Knee Punch To The Side   tíxī cè chōngquán   提膝侧冲拳

Step the right foot forward, doing a framing block across and up above the head with the left hand. Clench the right hand and bring the fist to the waist. (image P6.15a) Turn the torso leftward and bend the left knee, raising it. Punch forward with the right fist, with an upright fist. Press forward and down with the left hand by the right shoulder. Look to the left after punching. (image 15b)

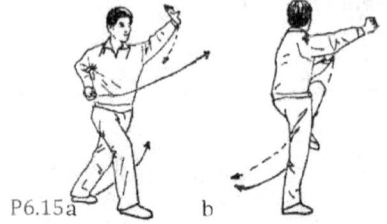

P6.15a   b

Section Two
16. Left Drop Stance Thread The Hand

     zuǒ pūbù chuānzhǎng   左仆步穿掌

Turn the torso leftward and squat fully on the right leg, extending the left foot out to the left side along the ground. Thread the left hand down and out along inside the left leg. Unclench the right hand and hold it up to the right side. Both palms face forward, and the arms form an angled line. Look at the left hand. (image P6.16)

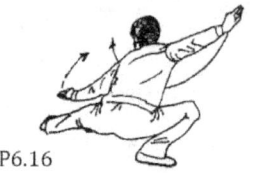

P6.16

17. Left Bow Stance Scooping Snap   zuǒ gōngbù tiǎozhǎng   左弓步挑掌

Shift to the left leg, bending the knee to take a left bow stance. Lower the right hand, circling it forward to scoop up with the arm at shoulder height, fingers up. Circle the left hand in to press down by the right elbow crease. Look forward. (image P6.17)

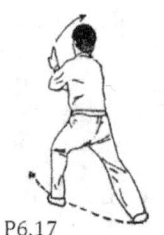

P6.17

18. Step Forward, Snap Kick   shàngbù tántuǐ   上步弹腿

Step the right foot forward with the foot turned out, lifting the left heel on the spot. Do a framing block with the right hand up above the head with the fingers pointing forward. (image P6.18a) Lift the left leg with the knee bent, then snap the lower leg to kick forcefully forward with the ankle plantar-flexed. Strike the left hand directly forward with the fingers up. Swing the right hand out to the right side, fingers also up. Look at the left hand. (image 18b)

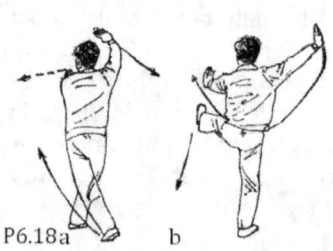

P6.18a   b

SIXTH FORM PAOQUAN

19. Left Bow Stance Palm Edge Strike   zuǒ gōngbù jīzhǎng   左弓步击掌

Land the left foot and bend the knee, extending the right leg to take a left bow stance. Bend the right elbow to bring the hand to the waist, then strike directly forward, fingers up. Press the left hand in and down inside the right elbow, fingers up. Look forward. (image P6.19)

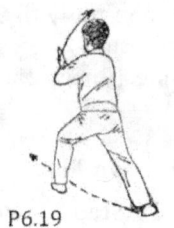

P6.19

20. Jump To Resting Stance Double Carry

tiào xiēbù shuāng tuōzhǎng   跳歇步双托掌

Shift forward and step the right foot forward with the foot turned out, lifting the left heel on the spot. Do a framing block with the right hand up above the head. (image P6.20a) Push off with the right leg and turn the torso to the right, swinging the left leg forward to jump up. Separate the hands up and out to the sides, palms up. (image 20b) Land the left foot first, pointed forward. Then land the right foot, inserting it behind the left leg, and squat fully into a resting stance. Continue to circle the hands so that they come down then do a lifting action in front of the chest, palms up at chest height. The palm edges – the little fingers – stick together. Look to the left side. (image 20c)

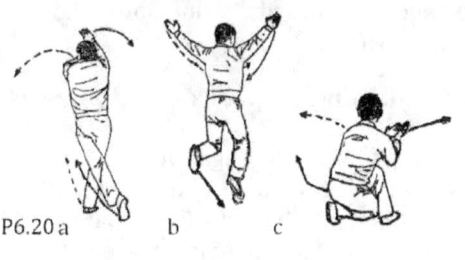

P6.20 a   b   c

21. Palm Edge Strike To The Side, Side Kick

cè jīzhǎng chuāituǐ   侧击掌踹腿

Stand up, straightening the right leg. Bend and lift the left knee then do a side thrust kick to the left side. Separate the hands out to either side so that the arms are level, just below shoulder height, the fingers pointing forward. Look to the left side. (image P6.21)

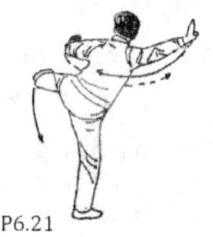

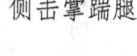

P6.21

22. Raised Knee Scooping Snap   tiàobù tiǎozhǎng   跳步挑掌

Turn the torso rightward and land the left foot to the forward right with the foot turned in. Lower the left hand in order to scoop up to the front. Cut the right hand flat across to the right. Look at the left hand. (image P6.22a) Bend and raise the right knee. Continue to scoop the left hand up in front, then hook the hand and continue on to the rear left, hook pointing down. Scoop up with the right hand to level with the fingers up. Look to the right side. (image 22b)

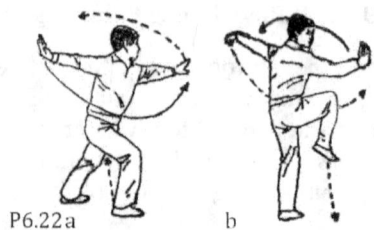

P6.22a   b

Section Three

23. **Step Forward Slice Up**   shàngbù liāozhǎng   上步撩掌

Turn the torso rightward and land the right foot to the front right with the foot turned out, shifting forward so that the left heel is raised. Lower the left hand to slice up in front. Swing the right hand up and over to the rear, continuing on to the upper right. (image P6.23a) Step the left foot forward, and then the right. Continue to circle the left hand forward and up in front, palm forward. Continue to circle the right hand back and down so that the arm is angled downwards, palm down. Look forward. (image 23b)

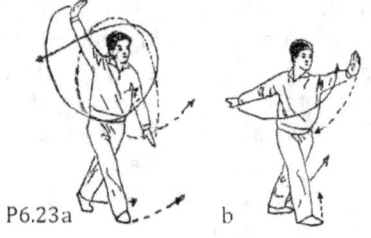

P6.23a   b

24. **Jumping Snap Kick**   téngkōng tántuǐ   腾空弹腿

Push off with the right leg to jump up, swinging the bent left knee up in front. Hook the right hand forward and up to in front of the face, bending the elbow with the fingers up. Clench the left hand and bring the fist to the waist. (image P6.24a) Quickly kick with the right leg, snapping the lower leg out with the ankle plantar-flexed. Look forward. (image 24b)

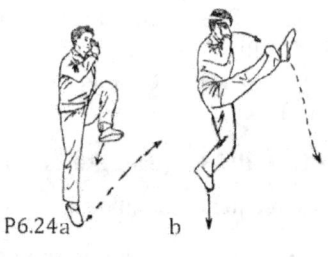

P6.24a   b

25. **Horse Stance Left And Right Hammerfist**
    mǎbù zuǒ yòu záquán   马步左右砸拳

Land on the left foot and turn the torso leftward, then land the right foot to the right side with the foot turned in. Bend both knees to sit into a horse stance. Lower the right hand in front with the fingers pointing up at nose height. Look forward. (image P6.25a) Stay in stance, clench the right hand and bring it to the waist. Do a hammerfist punch with the left fist to shoulder height, going up, then forward with the elbow slightly bent and fist eye up. Look forward. (image 25b) Still in stance, bring the left fist to the waist and do a hammerfist punch with the right fist in the same manner. (image 25c) Repeat again on the left. (image 25d)

SIXTH FORM PAOQUAN

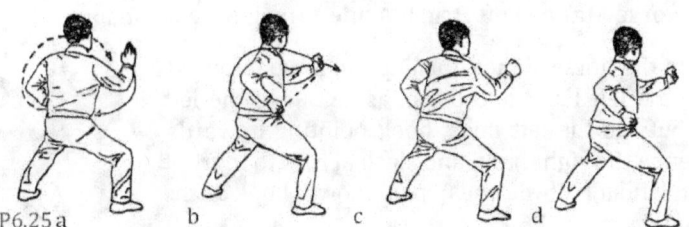

P6.25 a   b   c   d

26. Horse Stance Scooping Snap mǎbù tiǎozhǎng 马步挑掌

Stay in the horse stance and unclench the left hand, pressing down by the right shoulder. Raise the right fist to scoop up with a straight arm, fist eye facing back when it gets to the top. Look to the right side. (image P6.26)

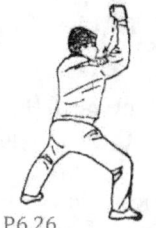

P6.26

27. Right Bow Stance Punch yòu gōngbù chōngquán 右弓步冲拳

Stay in the horse stance and turn the torso slightly leftward. Laterally rotate the right arm and do an intercepting block inwards in front of the chest, fist heart up, forearm level. Press the left hand on the right forearm. Look at the right fist. (image P6.27a) Turn the torso rightward, pushing the left heel out and straightening the leg. Twist the right heel in and bend the knee to take a right bow stance. Clench the left hand and punch forward to shoulder height. Medially rotate the right fist and place it under the left elbow, fist heart down. Look forward. (image 27b)

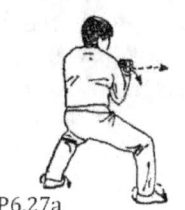 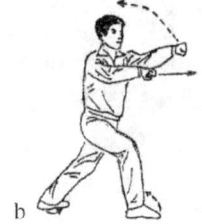

P6.27a   b

28. Horse Stance Framing Block And Punch

mǎbù jià chōngquán 马步架冲拳

Turn the torso leftward. Hook in the right foot and twist the left heel inwards, sitting into a horse stance. Do a framing block with the left fist upwards on the left side above the head, fist eye angled down. Punch the right fist directly to the right side to shoulder height with a flat fist. Look at the right fist. (image P6.28)

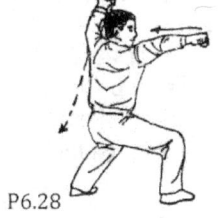

P6.28

127

29. Horse Stance Left Brush Aside   mǎbù zuǒ lōushǒu   马步左搂手

Stay in the horse stance, turning the torso leftward. Hook the left hand and brush aside out to the left side outside the left knee, hook pointing upwards. Unclench the right hand and slash across to in front of the left side of the chest, palm down. Look at the left hand. (image P6.29)

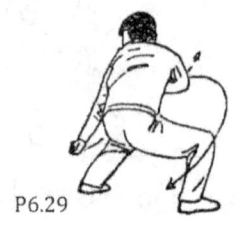

P6.29

30. Horse Stance Right Brush Aside   mǎbù yòu lōushǒu   马步右搂手

Stay in the horse stance, turning the torso rightward. Hook the right hand and brush aside out to the right and down to outside the right knee, hook pointing up. Unhook the left hand and bring the hand across in front of the body, lashing at an angle to the right side of the chest, palm down. Look at the right hand. (image P6.30)

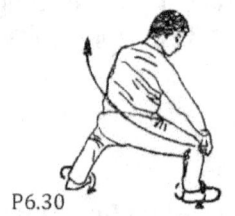

P6.30

31. Turn Around, Snap Kick   zhuànshēn tántuǐ   转身弹腿

Turn to the right and stand up, turning the right foot out and the left foot in, and shifting forward, lifting the left heel. Swing the right hook so that it circles back, then up to level at the right side, hook pointing down. (image P6.31a) Lift the left bent knee then do a strong snap kick with the ankle plantar flexed. Look forward. (image 31b)

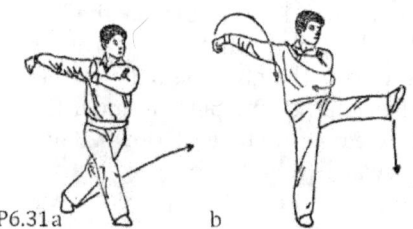

P6.31a   b

32. Horse Stance Left And Right Hammerfist

mǎbù zuǒ yòu záquán   马步左右砸拳

Turn the torso rightward and land the left foot to the left side with the foot hooked in. Sit into a horse stance. Unhook the right hand and lower it past the face to in front of the right side of the chest, with the arm slightly bent and fingers pointing up at nose height. The left hand remains in front of the right side of the chest. Look forward. (image P6.32a) Stay in stance and do three hammerfist punches, starting with the left fist. This is the same as move 25, just facing in the opposite direction. (images 32b, 32c, 32d)

SIXTH FORM PAOQUAN

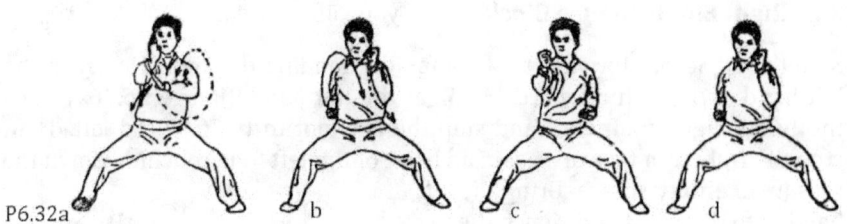

P6.32a b c d

33. Horse Stance Scoop   mǎbù tiǎoquán   马步挑拳

Remain in the horse stance. Unclench the right hand and press down at the left shoulder. Scoop up with the left fist with a straight arm above, fist eye facing the rear. Look to the left side. (image P6.33)

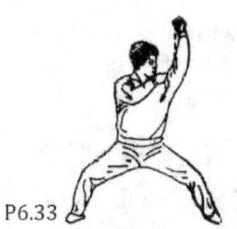

P6.33

34. Left Bow Stance Punch   zuǒ gōngbù chōngquán   左弓步冲拳

Stay in the horse stance, turning the torso rightward. Laterally rotate the left arm and bring it inward and down to do an intercepting block in front of the chest, forearm flat, fist heart up. Keep the right hand on the left forearm. Look at the left fist. (image P6.34a) Turn the torso leftward, turn the right heel out and straighten the leg, bending the left knee to take a bow stance. Clench the right hand and punch forward to shoulder height with a flat fist. Medially rotate the left arm and place it under the right elbow, fist heart down. Look forward. (image 34b)

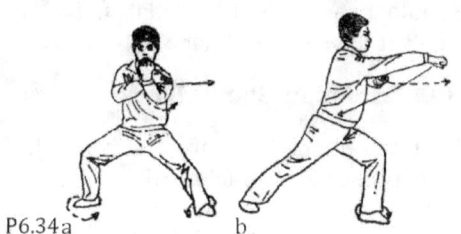

P6.34a b

35. Horse Stance Punch   mǎbù chōngquán   马步冲拳

Turn the torso rightward and press the left heel outwards, sitting into a horse stance. Bring the right fist to the waist. Punch the left fist out to the left side to shoulder height, fist flat. Look at the left fist. (image P6.35)

P6.35

36. Right Empty Stance Block yòu xūbù gēquán 右虚步格拳

Step the right foot forward to the left side, bending the knee. Unclench the left hand and brush outwards. Look at the left hand. (image P6.36a) Turn the torso slightly leftward and step the left foot to the forward left. Then step the right foot forward again, in front of the left foot, touching down the toes in an empty stance. Bring the left hand in to the waist and clench the fist. Do an elbow block with the right fist, circling out and up to in front of the body, fist eye angled up at nose height. The right forearm is cutting inwards with a bent elbow, the elbow on line with the right knee. Look at the right fist. (image 36b)

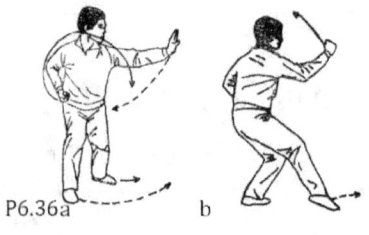

37. Left Bow Stance Punch zuǒ gōngbù chōngquán 左弓步冲拳

Turn the torso rightward. Step the right foot forward and bend the knee to take a right bow stance. Medially rotate the right arm and bend the elbow to do a framing block upwards above the head. Look forward. (image P6.37a) Step the left foot forward and bend the knee to take a left bow stance. Bring the right fist back, then in to the waist. Punch forward with the left fist to shoulder height with a flat fist. Look at the left fist. (image 37b)

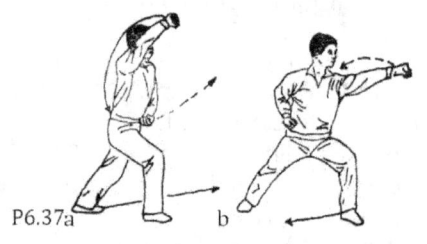

38. Left Empty Stance Block zuǒ xūbù gēquán 左虚步格拳

Turn the torso rightward and bring the left foot over in front of the right, touching the toes down and sitting into a left empty stance. Laterally rotate the left fist and cut it across inwards to in front of the body with the arm bent, elbow above the left knee, fist eye angled up in front of the nose. Look at the left fist. (image P6.38)

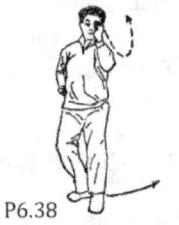

39. Right Bow Stance Punch yòu gōngbù chōngquán 右弓步冲拳

Turn the torso leftward and advance the left foot, bending the knee. Do a framing block up above the head with the left fist, fist eye down. (image P6.39a) Step the right foot forward and bend the knee, straightening the left leg to take a right bow stance. Punch directly forward with the right fist to

SIXTH FORM PAOQUAN

shoulder height. Bring the left fist in to the waist. Look at the right fist. (image 39b)

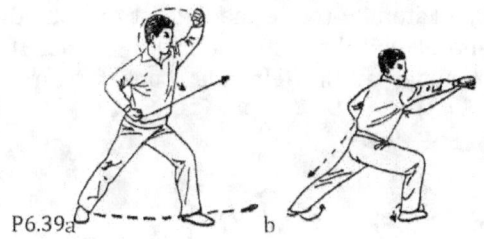

P6.39a — — — b

Section Four

40. Horse Stance Left Brush Aside   mǎbù zuǒ lōushǒu   马步左搂手

Turn the torso leftward, turning the right foot inwards and sitting into a horse stance. Unclench the left hand, make a hook, and brush aside to the left side to outside the left knee, hook pointing up. Unclench the right hand and cut it across to in front of the left side of the chest, palm facing left. Look at the left hand. (image P6.40)

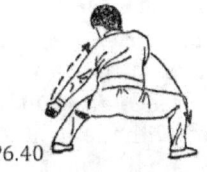

P6.40

41. Horse Stance Right Brush Aside   mǎbù yòu lōushǒu   马步右搂手

Stay in stance, turning the torso rightward. Hook the right hand and do a brushing action down to the right side to outside the right knee, hook facing up. Unhook the left hand and cut across to in front of the right side of the chest, palm facing right. Look at the right hand. (image P6.41)

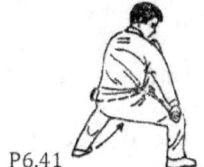

P6.41

42. Raised Knee Reverse Hook   tíxī fǎn guàquán   提膝反挂拳

Turn the torso leftward and stand up on the right leg, straightening it. Lift the bent left knee. Clench the left hand and do a hooking action forward and down with the arm inverted, towards the rear left, fist heart down. Clench the right hand and bring the fist to the waist. Look to the lower left side. (image P6.42)

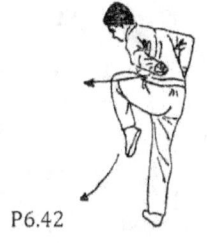

P6.42

43. Left Bow Stance Punch

   zuǒ gōngbù chōngquán   左弓步冲拳

Land the left foot forward and bend the knee, straightening the right leg to take a left bow stance. Punch the right fist directly forward with a standing fist. Laterally rotate the left fist to a standing fist and extend the arm out slightly higher than the shoulder at the left side. Look forward. image P6.43)

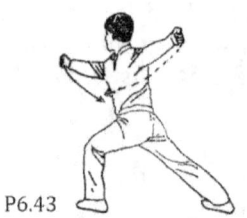

P6.43

44. Jumping Two Rising Kicks   téngkōng èrqǐjiǎo   腾空二起脚

Shift forward, lifting the right heel. Unclench the right hand and medially rotate the arm, hooking downwards with a straight arm, palm facing the rear. Unclench the left hand and bend the arm to stab under the right armpit, palm down. Look at the right hand. (image P6.44a) Step the right foot forward. Circle the right hand left and up, passing in front to go out level at the rear right. Circle the left hand down and left, passing up to go out level in front. Both palms face down. Look forward. (image 44b) Push off with the right leg to jump up, swinging the bent left knee up and forward to aid the jump. Swing the right hand down to go up in front to slap the back of the hand into the left palm above and in front of the head. Look forward. (image 44c) Quickly extend the right leg to kick with the ankle plantar-flexed. Slap the right foot with the right hand in front of the chest. Swing the left hand over to the left side. Look forward. (image 44d)

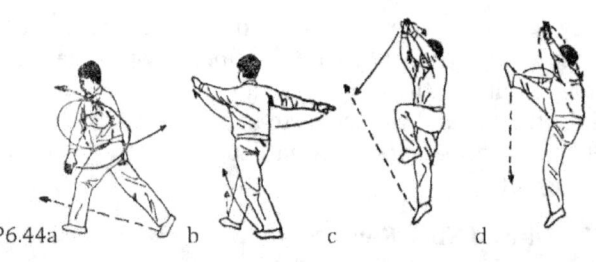

P6.44a   b   c   d

45. Horse Stance Double Lash   mǎbù shuāng bǎizhǎng   马步双摆掌

Land on the left foot, turning to the left. Land the right foot, hooked in, to the right side, to stand up in an open parallel stance. Lower the left hand to level, palm facing left. Circle the right hand in front of the body to the left side of the chest, palm facing left. Look to the left side. (image P6.45a) Step the right foot across to the right a half-step and bend both knees to sit into a horse stance. Lower both hands with the arms straight, to swing down on the right, then past the body to the left. Finish with the hands in standing palms, both facing left. Look at the left hand. (image 45b)

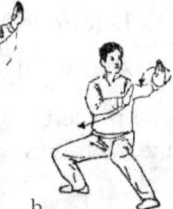

P6.45a   b

132

SIXTH FORM PAOQUAN

Section Five

46. Left Bow Stance Strike   zuǒ gōngbù jīzhǎng   左弓步击掌

Without changing the stance, make a small circle with the left hand out and in to press down, fingers pointing up. Bring the right fist to the waist. Look at the left hand. (image P6.46a) Turn the torso leftward and push the right heel out, straightening the knee to push the left knee into a left bow stance. Unclench the right hand and strike forward, fingers up. Bring the left hand in to tuck under the right elbow, palm down. Look forward. (image 46b)

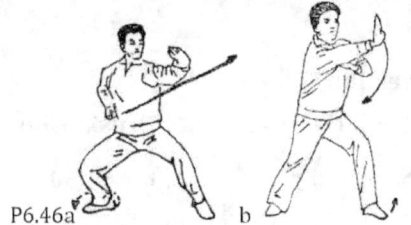

47. Forward Jump To Strike   qián tiàobù jīzhǎng   前跳步击掌

Turn the torso leftward and shift forward, turning the left foot outward and lifting the right heel. Medially rotate the right arm and lower it to outside the left knee, palm facing the rear. (image P6.47a) Bend the right knee and lift it. Circle the right hand in, then forward to brush across with the palm facing forward. Swing the left hand down, then to the rear left, palm down. (image 47b) Push off with the left leg to jump up, tucking the lower leg up with a natural back swing kick whilst airborne. Continue to circle the left hand up and over to press down in front at shoulder height, palm forward. Clench the right hand and bring the fist to the waist. (image 47c) Land on the right leg, then land the left foot forward, foot pointing forward. Turn rightward and bend both legs to sit into a half horse stance. (image 47d) Turn the torso leftward and turn the right heel out, straightening the right leg and bending the left to take a left bow stance. Unclench the right hand and strike directly forward with the fingers up. Tuck the left hand inside the right elbow, fingers up. Look at the right hand. (image 47e)

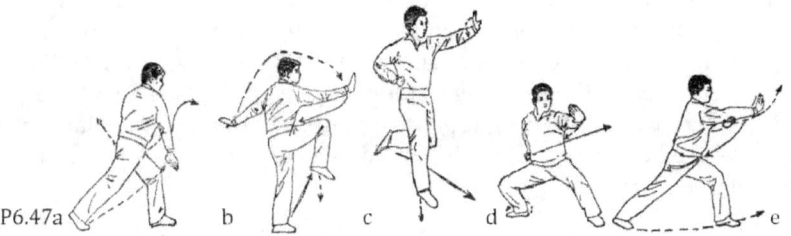

48. Raised Knee Punch To The Side   tíxī cè chōngquán   提膝侧冲拳

Step the right foot forward. Clench the right hand and bring the fist to the waist. Do a framing block up with the left hand, palm edge up. (image P6.48a) Turn the torso leftward and raise the bent left knee. Punch the right fist directly forward with a standing fist. Bring the left hand in to in front of the right side of the chest with a standing palm, palm facing right. Look to the left side. (image 48b)

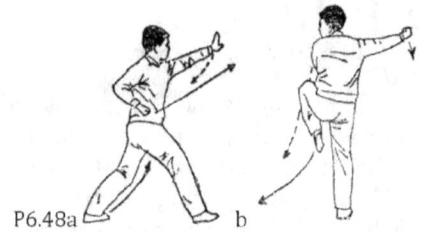

P6.48a   b

Section Six

49. Left Drop Stance Brush Aside   zuǒ pūbù lōushǒu   左仆步搂手

Squat fully on the right leg and lower the left leg out to the left side, extending it straight with the foot tucked in, to take a left drop stance. Turn the torso slightly leftward. Hook the left hand and bring it down the body to brush outwards at the left knee, hook pointing up. Unclench the right hand and hold it level out to the right side, palm down. Look to the left side. (image P6.49)

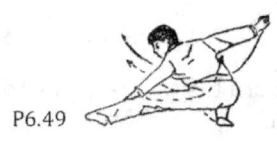

P6.49

50. Raised Knee Scooping Snap   tíxī tiǎozhǎng   提膝挑掌

Shift to the left leg and stand up, raising the right knee. Turn the torso leftward. Lower the right hand in order to scoop up in front to shoulder height, fingers up. Circle the left hook-hand up and back to the left side, hook pointing down on arrival. Look at the right hand. (image P6.50)

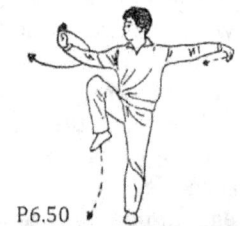

P6.50

51. Curving Walk, Slice Up   húxíngbù liāozhǎng   弧行步撩掌

Land the right foot to the left front with the foot turned out. Medially rotate the right hand, moving it out, down, and up, then forward to stab out with the palm up. Unhook the left hand and turn the palm down. (image P6.51a) Step the left foot to the front right, then step the right foot forward again. Make a full circle with the right hand up and back to the same place, palm up. Make a full circle with the left hand down and forward, and back to the same place, palm down. (image 51b) Step the left foot forward, then the right foot again. Slice the left hand forward, passing down then

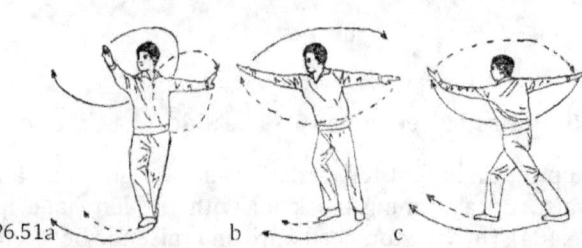

P6.51a   b   c

forward to level, palm up. Swing the right hand up and over to the rear, palm down. Look at the left hand. (image 51c)

52. Aerial Outside Crescent Kick   téngkōng wàibǎilián   腾空外摆莲

Step the left foot forward, then step the right foot again, with the foot turned out. Swing the right hand down to lift in front to level, fingers up. Swing the left hand up and over to the rear to level, fingers up. (image P6.52a) Swing the left knee up and to the right, turning the body rightward. Quickly push off with the right leg to jump up. Swing the right hand across to the right and the left hand up to the right, so that the left hand slaps the back of the right hand in front of the head. (image 52b) Extend the right leg to swing it straight from inside to up and out with the foot held firmly and slightly tucked in. Lower the hands to slap the foot with a sharp sound in front of the body, first the left, then the right. Look at the hands. (image 52c)

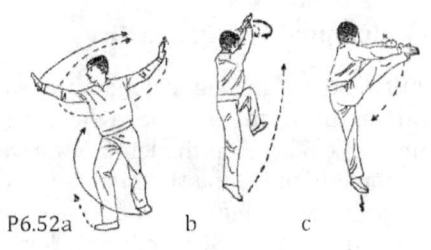

P6.52a   b   c

53. Jump Switch-Step To Bow Stance Punch

    huàntiàobù chōngquán   换跳弓步冲拳

Land on the left foot and swing the right leg outward with the knee still up (do not touch down). Swing the hands over to the left side, holding the left hand extended level out to the left side and the right hand in front of the left side of the chest. Both palms face left. Look at the left hand. (image P6.53a) Turn the torso rightward and brush the right hand up and to the right side, palm out. Look at the right hand. (image 53b) Continue to turn rightward and push off with the left leg to jump up, tucking the lower leg up with a natural back kick, letting the right leg hang naturally (but not yet touching down). Bring the left hand over at the left to press down in front, palm forward, fingers pointing right. Clench the right hand and bring the fist to the waist. (image 53c) Land on the right foot and straighten the leg, landing the left foot forward into a left bow stance. Punch the right fist forward to shoulder height with a standing fist. Bring the left hand in to tuck under the right elbow, palm down. Look at the right fist. (image 53d)

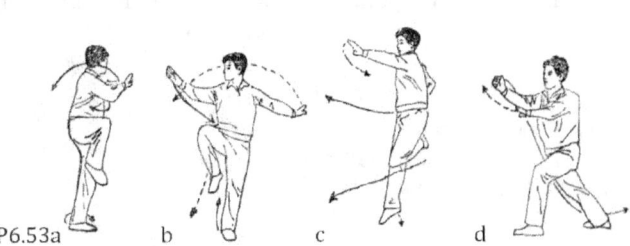

P6.53a   b   c   d

Section Seven

54. Right Drop Stance Thread The Hand

yòu pūbù chuānzhǎng   右仆步穿掌

Turn the torso rightward and squat fully on the left leg, extending the right leg along the ground. Laterally rotate the left hand and extend it out under the right arm, thumb up. Unclench the right hand and thread it along inside the right leg, thumb up. Look at the right hand. (image P6.54)

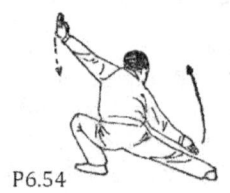

P6.54

55. Jumping Two Rising Kicks   téngkōng èrqǐjiǎo   腾空二起脚

Shift to the right leg, extending the left leg and bending the right. Do a framing bock up with the right hand, palm forward. Lower the left arm. (image P6.55a) Step the left foot forward, then step the right foot forward. Continue to move the right hand up, swinging it over and down to the rear, palm down. Swing the left hand down to come forward and up, palm forward. (image 55b) Bend the left knee and swing it forward and up, quickly pushing off with the right leg to jump up. Continue to swing the right hand so that it moves down then forward and up, slapping the back of the hand into the left palm in front of, and a bit higher than, the head. (image 55c) Quickly swing the right foot up with the leg straight, to kick with the ankle plantar-flexed. Lower the right hand to slap the foot. Lash the left hand across to the left side, holding it level with the palm down. Look at the right hand. (image 55d)

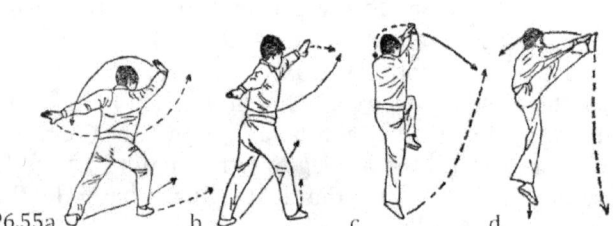

P6.55a   b   c   d

56. Left Empty Stance Scooping Snap   zuǒ xūbù tiǎozhǎng   左虚步挑掌

Land on the left leg then land the right foot, shifting forward to the right leg and lifting the left heel. Lash the right hand across to the rear and hook it to the rear right, hook pointing down, arm at shoulder height. Lower the left hand down the left side to the hip, palm in. Look at the right hand. (image P6.56a) Step the left foot forward, touching down the toes and half-squatting on the right leg. Scoop the left hand forward to shoulder height, fingers up. Lower the right

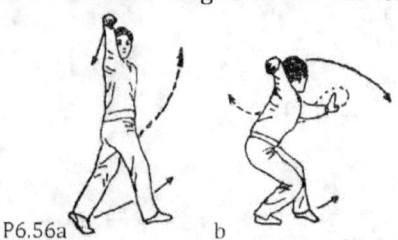

P6.56a   b

hook-hand slightly at the rear right, so that the top of the hook is higher than the shoulder. Look at the left hand. (image 56b)

57. Left Bow Stance Chop With The Fist

zuǒ gōngbù pīquán 左弓步劈拳

Step the left foot forward a half-step and bend the knee, straightening the right leg to take a left bow stance. Move the left hand in, then out to brush aside, clench to a fist, then swing down and back to level at the left side, fist eye up. Clench the right hand and bring the fist up and over to chop down in front at shoulder height, fist eye up. Look at the right fist. (image P6.57)

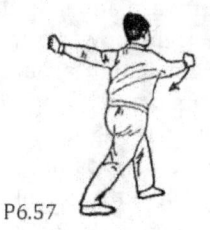

P6.57

58. Right Snap Kick

yòu tántuǐ 右弹腿

Laterally rotate the right arm to turn the fist heart up, and bend the elbow to press down with the forearm level. (image P6.58a) Shift forward to the left leg and straighten it to stand up. Bend and lift the right knee then forcefully kick forward with the foot plantar-flexed. Bring the right elbow in tight to the right flank. Look forward. (image 58b)

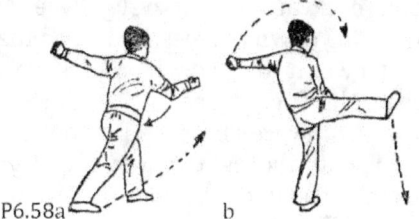

P6.58a   b

59. Raised Knee Punch To The Side

tíxī cè chōngquán 提膝侧冲拳

Land the right foot forward, bending the knee. Unclench the left hand and bring it over to press down in front, thumb side down. Bring the right fist in to the waist. (image P6.59a) Turn the torso leftward and raise the left knee, ankle plantar-flexed to point the foot down. Straighten the right leg to stand firmly. Punch the right fist forward. Tuck the left hand in front of the right side of the chest, palm facing right. Look to the left after the punch. (image 59b)

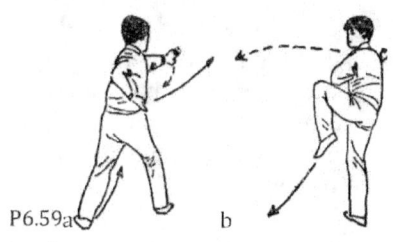

P6.59a   b

Section Eight

60. Right Bow Stance Hack　　yòu gōngbù kǎnzhǎng　　右弓步砍掌

Land the left foot forward with the foot turned out. Circle the left hand forward and out to the left side, palm out. Unclench the right hand and turn the palm forward. Look at the left hand. (image P6.60a) Turn the torso leftward and step the right foot in front of the left, bending the knee to take a right bow stance. Bring the right hand around from the outside to hack forward with the arm slightly higher than the shoulder, palm up. Bring the left hand in to the right elbow crease. Look at the right hand. (image 60b)

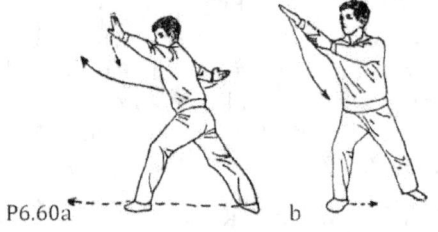

P6.60a　　b

61. Left Bow Stance Hack　　zuǒ gōngbù kǎnzhǎng　　左弓步砍掌

Shift back, turn the torso slightly leftward, bring the right foot in a half-step, touching down the toes, and sit on the left leg. Medially rotate the right arm and lower it to beside the right knee, palm facing the rear. Look forward, to the right side. (image P6.61a) Step the right foot around in an arcing step, passing inwards past the left foot, landing with the foot turned out. Brush aside with the right hand, out and to the right side, palm back. Lower the left hand behind. (image 61b) Turn to the right and take an arcing step with the left foot, passing by close to the right foot and bending the knee on landing, to take a left bow stance. Bring the left hand out and forward to hack upwards just above shoulder height, palm up. Bring the right hand in to the left elbow crease. Look at the left hand. (image 61c)

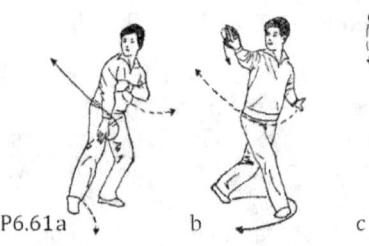

P6.61a　　b　　c

62. Horse Stance Stab　　mǎbù chuānzhǎng　　马步穿掌

Shift back to the right leg and bring the left foot back a half-step, touching the ball of the foot down. Medially rotate the left hand and bend the elbow to press down and in, palm forward. Clench the right hand and bring the fist to the waist. (image P6.62a) Settle on the left foot, then step the right foot forward and turn left, tucking in the right foot and pushing the left foot outwards to sit into a horse stance. Unclench the right

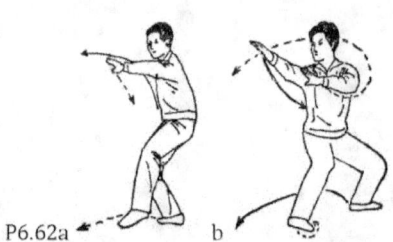

P6.62a　　b

SIXTH FORM PAOQUAN

hand and stab it forward, threading over the back of the left hand, fingers at nose height. Bring the left hand in to sit on the right upper arm, palm down. Look at the right hand. (image 62b)

63. Turn Around, Front Sweep Kick zhuànshēn qián sǎotuǐ 转身前扫腿

Turn around one-eighty degrees to the left so that the torso faces in the opposite direction, pivoting on the ball of the right foot and withdrawing the left foot to the rear. Sit again with the knees bent. Sweep the left straight arm around to with the rearward turn to the left, palm out, thumb down. Clench the right hand and bring the fist to the waist. Look at the left hand (image P6.63a) Turn the torso leftward, turning the left foot out and shifting to the left leg, extending the right leg. Unclench the right hand and thread the hand out over the left hand so that the arms cross, palms out. (image 63b) Squat fully on the left leg, lifting the heel, and extend the right leg to sweep forward with the foot hooked in. Swing the arms out to their respective sides, swinging the left hand up to flash at the upper left with the palm up, and swinging the right hand down to hook at the lower right, hook pointing up. Look at the right leg. (image 63c) Continue to turn three-sixty degrees around to the left so that the right foot does a full-circle scraping front sweep. Look forward. (image 63d)

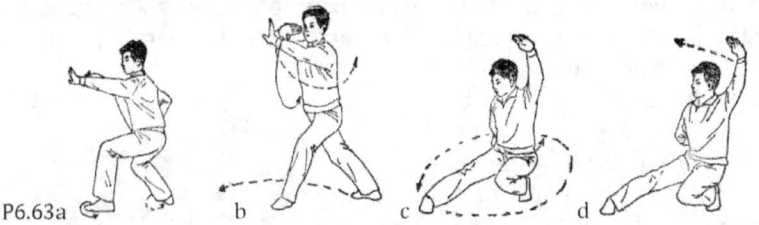

64. Jumping Two Rising Kicks téngkōng èrqǐjiǎo 腾空二起脚

Shift forward and stand up, bending the right knee and straightening the left. Swing the left hand across to above the head with the palm up. (image P6.64a) Bend the left knee and swing it forward and up, unhooking the right hand and swinging it forward and up. Lower the left hand in front so that the back of the right hand slaps into the left palm in front of the head. (image 64b) Quickly push off with the right leg and swing it straight up in front with the foot plantar-flexed. Lower the right hand to slap the right foot in front of the chest with a sharp sound. Swing the left hand across to the rear left, palm out. Look forward. (image 64c)

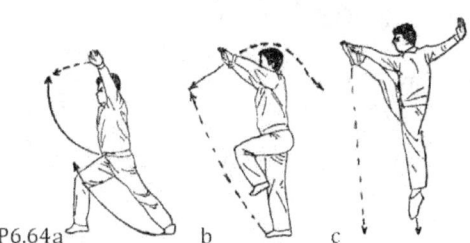

65. Strike To The Side, Side Thrust Kick cèjīzhǎng chuāituǐ 侧击掌踹腿

Land on the left leg then land the right foot forward, turning right and turning out the right foot, lifting the left heel and bending both knees. Laterally rotate the right arm to turn the palm up, swinging it flat across to the right. Laterally rotate the left hand and swing the straight arm across to the right to cross with the right hand in front of the chest, palm up. The little finger sides touch. Look to the left side. (image P6.65a, 65b) Straighten the right leg and stand on it, lifting the left knee bent, then forcefully kick with the heel to the left side. Separate the hands out level to either side. The fingers and left foot all point forward. Look at the left foot. (image 65c)

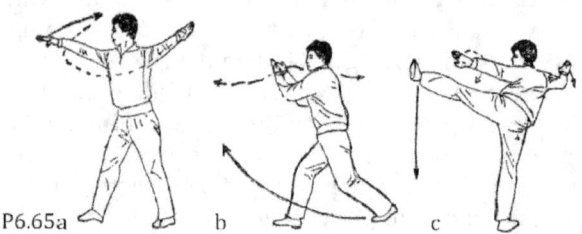

66. Left Bow Stance Scooping Snap zuǒ gōngbù tiǎozhǎng 左弓步挑掌

Land the left foot to the left side and bend both knees. Press down and in with the left hand, palm out. Look at the left hand. (image P6.66a) Turn the torso leftward and straighten the right leg to take a left bow stance. Circle the right hand down and through to scoop up in front at shoulder height, fingers up. Place the left hand on top of the right forearm. Look forward. (image 66b)

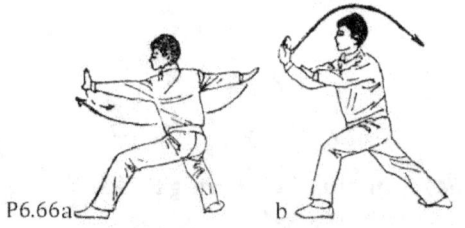

67. Left Bow Stance Punch zuǒ gōngbù chōngquán 左弓步冲拳

Shift back without moving the feet, turning the torso rightward and bending the right knee. Swing the right hand up and over to the rear to hold it out level, fingers up. Look at the right hand. (image P6.67a) Turn the torso leftward and straighten the right leg to take a left bow stance. Clench the right hand and bring the fist to the waist, then punch directly forward with a standing fist. Place the left hand on top of the right forearm. Look forward. (image 67b)

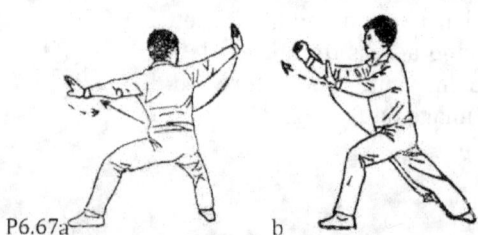

SIXTH FORM PAOQUAN

Section Nine

68. Right Drop Stance Thread The Hand

yòu pūbù chuānzhǎng　　　　　　　　右仆步穿掌

Turn the torso rightward and squat fully on the left leg, extending the right leg along the ground to take a right drop stance. Unclench the right hand and thread it down and along inside the right leg. Hold the left arm out, angled upwards. Both palms face forward. Look at the right hand. (image P6.68)

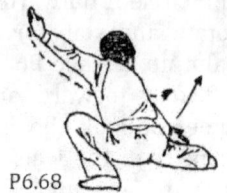

P6.68

69. Right Empty Stance Scooping Snap

yòu xūbù tiǎozhǎng　　　　　　　　右虚步挑掌

Shift to the right and turn the torso rightward, bending the right leg and extending the left. Lift the right arm to level and clench the fist, fist eye up. Bend the left arm and bring the hand to the waist, then thread to tuck into the right armpit, palm down. (image P6.69a) Step the left foot forward and bend the knee. Extend the left hand forward and up with a framing block, palm forward. Bring the right hand to the waist. (image 69b) Step the right foot forward and touch the toes down in a right empty stance. Continue to swing the left hand up and over, hooking as it moves to the rear, hook pointing down. Dig the right hand down to scoop up in front to shoulder height, fingers up. Look at the right hand. (image 69c)

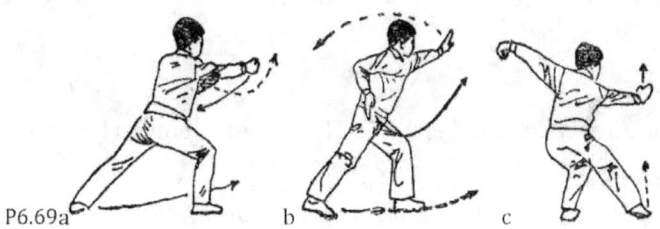

P6.69a　　　b　　　c

70. Raised Knee Scooping Snap　　tíxī tiǎozhǎng　　提膝挑掌

Stand up, straightening the left leg to stand on it, and raising the bent right knee. Look forward. (image P6.70)

P6.70

71. Step Forward, Left And Right Stabs

shàngbù zuǒ yòu chuānzhǎng   上步左右穿掌

Land the right foot forward, bending the knee. Medially rotate the right arm and circle it outwards, then bring the hand to the waist, and then laterally rotate and stab forward and up, palm up. (image P6.71a) Step the left foot forward and bend the knee. Unhook the left hand and bring it to the waist, then thread forward and up, palm up. Bring the right hand back to set under to the left elbow, palm up. Look forward. (image 71b)

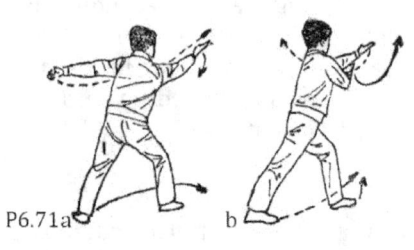

72. Jump To Closed Stance Double Press Down

tiào bīngbù shuāng ànzhǎng   跳并步双按掌

Push into the left leg to jump up, swinging the bent right knee forward as you jump. Medially rotate the arms and open them down and out, swinging out to the sides angled upwards, palms out. Look forward. (image P6.72a) Land the left foot, then the right, to a closed stance, sitting down into a half-squat. Bring the hands in past the face and down to press down at the kneecaps, fingers pointing to each other. Look at the hands. (images 72b and from behind)

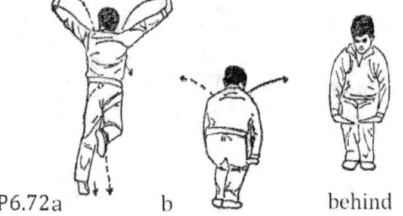

73. Closed Stance Separate The Hands   bīngbù fēnzhǎng   并步分掌

Stand up. Separate the hands upwards out to level at either side, palms up. Look forward. (image P6.73)

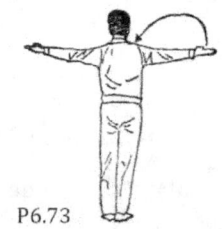

74. Closed Stance, Left And Right Press Down

bīngbù zuǒ yòu ànzhǎng   并步左右按掌

Bend the right arm and bring the hand in to the face then press down to the belly, palm down. Look at the right hand. (image P6.74a) Bend the left arm and bring the hand in to the face then press down to the belly, palm down.

SIXTH FORM PAOQUAN

Clench the right hand and swing it down at the right, fist heart out. Look at the left hand. (image 74b)

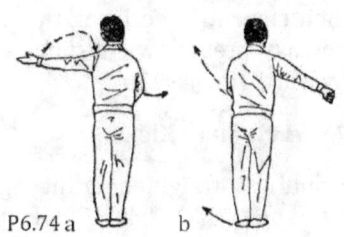

P6.74 a   b

75. Raised Knee Roundhouse Punch   tíxī guànquán   提膝贯拳

Stride the left foot across to the left. Slice the left hand up at the left side, palm out. Look at the left hand. (image P6.75a) Turn the torso leftward and turn the left foot out. Bend the right knee inward, then raise it. Swing the right fist from the right to the left, angled up, to strike the knuckles into the left palm in front of the face. Both arms are bent, forming a circle. The fist is at eye height, fist heart facing out. Look at the right fist. (image 75b)

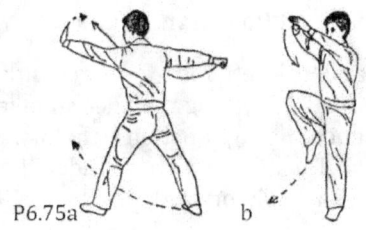

P6.75a   b

76. Horse Stance Elbow Press   mǎbù yāzhǒu   马步压肘

Land the right foot to the right side and bend both knees to sit into a horse stance. Laterally rotate the right arm and bend the elbow to press down, fist heart inwards at nose height, elbow down. Slide the left hand down the right arm to stop on top of the forearm. Look at the right fist. (image P6.76)

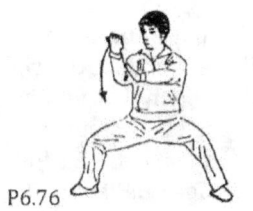

P6.76

77. Turn Around, Resting Stance Press Down
zhuànshēn xiēbù ànzhǎng   转身歇步按掌

Without changing the stance, reach the torso slightly to the left. Unclench the right hand, medially rotate and lower it, turning the thumb down. Slide the left hand along the right arm. Look to the right side. (image P6.77a) Turn the torso rightward and turn the right foot out. Bring the left leg in a half-step towards the right leg. Bend both knees, tucking the left knee into the right knee depression, lifting the heel. The legs are now crossed. Brush the right hand out to the right side

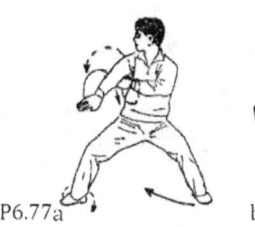 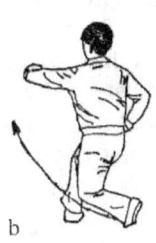

P6.77a   b

then clench it and bring the fist to the waist. Circle the left hand up and down to press down at shoulder height in front, fingers pointing back. Look forward. (image 77b)

78. Left Snap Kick   zuǒ tántuǐ   左弹腿

Stand up, straightening the right leg. Bend and lift the left knee, then snap the lower leg to kick strongly forward, ankle plantar-flexed. Look forward. (image P6.78)

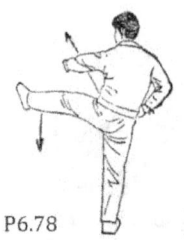

P6.78

79. Left Bow Stance Punch   zuǒ gōngbù chōngquán   左弓步冲拳

Land the left foot forward with the foot pointing forward, bending the knee to take a left bow stance. Punch the right fist directly forward with a standing fist. Tuck the left hand under the right elbow, palm down. Look forward. (image P6.79)

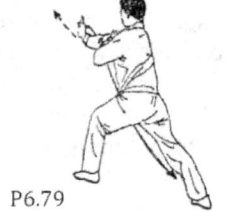

P6.79

80. Right Drop Stance Thread The Hand
yòu pūbù chuānzhǎng   右仆步穿掌

Turn around to the right and squat fully on the left leg, extending the right leg into a right drop stance. Unclench the right hand and slide it along inside the right leg. Extend the left hand out to the left side. Both palms face forward. Look at the right hand. (image P6.80)

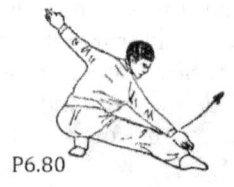

P6.80

81. Left Empty Stance Strike   zuǒ xūbù jīzhǎng   左虚步击掌

Shift to the right leg and stand up, straightening the torso, extending the left leg and bending the right knee. Slice up to level with the right arm. (image P6.81a) Step the left foot forward with the foot turned out. Medially rotate the right arm and lower the straight arm outside the left thigh, palm facing right. Stab the left hand under the right armpit, palm down. (image 81b) Step the right foot forward. Brush the right hand across in front then clench the fist, fist heart up at shoulder height. Place the left hand inside the right upper arm. (image 81c) Step the left foot forward, touching down the toes to take a left empty stance. Strike forward with the left hand, fingers up. Bring the right fist in to the waist. Look at the left hand. (image 81.d)

SIXTH FORM PAOQUAN

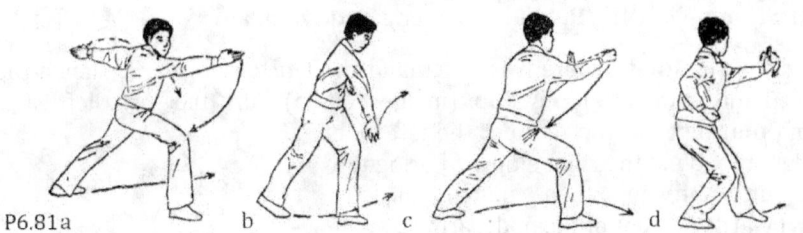

P6.81a   b   c   d

82. Left Bow Stance Strike   zuǒ gōngbù jīzhǎng   左弓步击掌

Advance the left foot a half-step and bend both knees to take a half horse stance. Draw a small circle outwards then inwards with the left hand to press down, palm out. (image P6.82a)
Turn the torso leftward and extend the right leg to take a left bow stance. Unclench the right hand and strike directly forward, fingers up. Bring the left hand in to tuck under the right upper arm, palm down. Look forward. (image 82b)

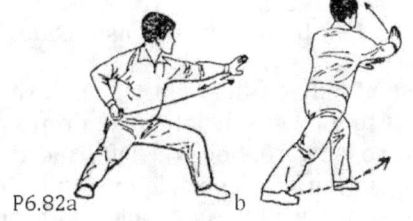

P6.82a   b

83. Step Forward, Left Snap Kick   shàngbù zuǒ tántuǐ   上步左弹腿

Step the right foot forward with the foot turned out, lifting the left heel. Do a framing block with the right arm above the head. (image P6.83a) Stand up on the right leg, lifting the bent left knee, then quickly snap the lower leg out to kick with the foot plantar-flexed. Strike directly forward with the left hand, fingers up. Swing the right hand further to the upper right, palm facing the rear. Look at the left foot. (image 83)

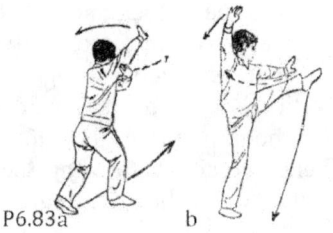

P6.83a   b

84. Hitting Hop-Step, Slice Up   jībù liāozhǎng   击步撩掌

Land the left foot forward. Cut the left hand inward across in front of the chest. Lower the right hand to level at the right side. Look at the right hand. (image P6.84a) Push off with the left foot to jump forward, tapping the right foot in behind the heel whilst airborne. Lower the left hand to slice upwards and forward. The arms extend in a level straight line with the thumbs up. Look at the left hand. (image 84b)

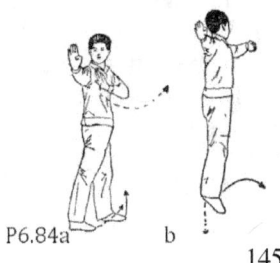

P6.84a   b

85. Stomp, Planting Punch   zhēnjiǎo xià zāiquán   震脚下栽拳

Land the right foot where it is, then land the left foot forward. Clench the right hand with the fist eye up. (image P6.85a) Turn the torso leftward, bring the right foot up to meet the left foot, and stomp. Bend the right elbow to bring the fist up and in, then punch directly downwards in front of the body, arm straight, fist heart in. Cut the left hand inwards to the right side of the chest, palm facing right. Look to the right side. (image 85b)

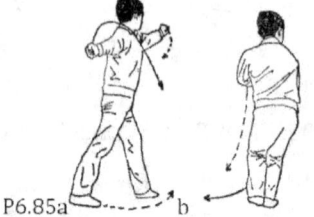

86. Left Drop Stance Brush Aside   zuǒ pūbù lōushǒu   左仆步搂手

Squat fully on the right leg and extend the left leg out to the left side into a left drop stance. Turn the torso leftward. Hook the left hand and brush out to the lower left to outside the left leg, hook pointing up. Unclench the right hand and bend the elbow to swing to the left side of the chest, palm facing left. Look at the left hook-hand. (image P6.86)

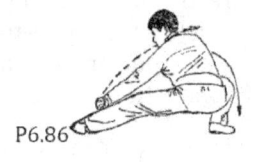

87. Right Drop Stance Brush Aside   yòu pūbù lōushǒu   右仆步搂手

Shift to the left leg and squat on it, extending the right leg in a right drop stance. Turn the torso rightward. Hook the right hand and swing the straight arm forward then out to brush aside to the lower right above the right leg, hook pointing up. Unhook the left hand and bend the elbow to bring the hand across to the right side of the chest, palm facing right. Look at the right hook-hand. (image P6.87)

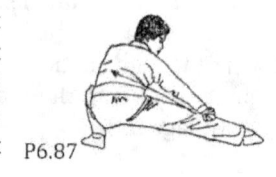

88. Turn Around, Snap Kick   zhuànshēn tántuǐ   转身弹腿

Shift to the right leg, bending the knee and straightening the left leg, lifting the heel. Turn the torso rightward. Lift the right hook-hand up behind to hold it out level at the right side, hook pointing down. (image P6.88a) Bend and lift the left knee, then snap the lower leg forcefully to kick with the ankle plantar-flexed. Look at the left foot. (image 88b)

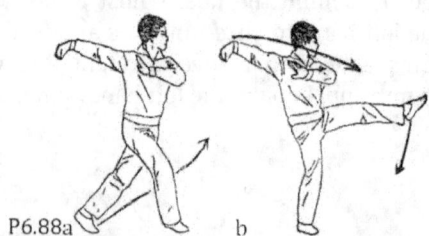

SIXTH FORM PAOQUAN

89. Jump To Bow Stance Punch   tiào gōngbù chōngquán   跳弓步冲拳

Land the left foot to the forward left, turning the foot out and turning the torso to the left. Unhook the right hand and bring it forward and down to outside the left thigh, thumb side in. Slide the left hand along to tuck into the right armpit. Look at the right hand. (image P6.89a) Bend and raise the right knee. Bring the right hand in to brush across in front, palm out. Swing the left hand out to the rear left, angled downwards, palm down. Look forward. (image 89b) Push off with the left leg, swinging the lower leg up with a natural rear kick up whilst airborne. Bring the left hand up and over to press down in front at shoulder height, fingers pointing right. Clench the right hand and bring the fist to the waist. (image 89c) Turn the torso rightward and land on the right foot. Land the left foot with the foot pointing forward and bend both knees to take a half horse stance. (image 89d) Straighten the right leg and bend the left to take a left bow stance. Punch directly forward with the right fist to shoulder height, with an upright fist. Bring the left hand in to support under the right elbow, fingers up. Look forward. (image 89e)

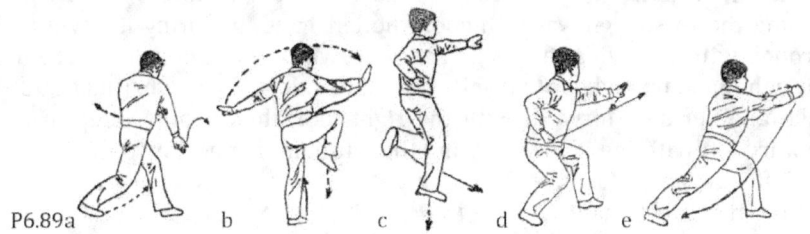

Section Ten

90. Right Drop Stance Thread The Hand

  yòu pūbù chuānzhǎng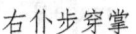

Turn around to the right and squat on the left leg, extending the right leg to take a right drop stance. Unclench the right hand and thread it down along inside the right leg. Extend the left hand out to the left side. Both palms face left. Look at the right hand. (image P6.90)

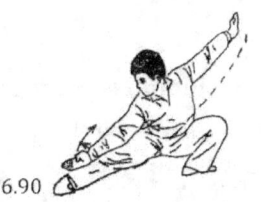

91. Raised Knee Scooping Snap   tíxī tiǎozhǎng   提膝挑掌

Shift to the right leg, bending the right knee and straightening the body. Bring the left hand down, to come through and slice up in front with a straight arm, thumb side on top. Bring the right hand in to the left elbow crease. (image P6.91a) Step the left foot forward, turning the foot out. Continue to slice the left hand upward with a straight arm, palm turned out. Straighten the right arm down to place the hand at the right hip, palm in.

(image 91b) Bend the right knee and raise it, standing up on the left leg. Scoop up in front with the right hand to shoulder height, fingers up.

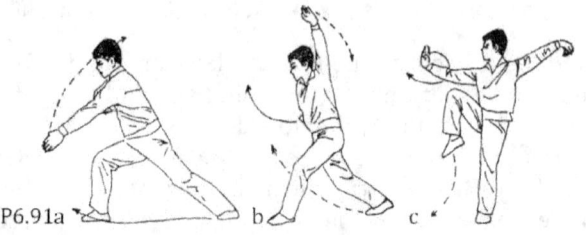

Continue to swing the left hand to the rear, hooking as it moves out to the left side. The peak of the hook is slightly higher than the shoulder. Look forward. (image 91c)

92. Curving Walk, Left And Right Scoop Up

húxíngbù zuǒ yòu liāozhǎng   弧行步左右撩掌

Land the right foot forward to the left with the foot turned out. Medially rotate the right hand and move it out, down, and then in and forward in a circular threading palm, palm up. (image P6.92a) Take an arcing step with the left foot, passing by in front of the right foot to the forward right, turning the torso rightward. Unhook the left hand and bring it down and through with a curving threading action forward with the palm up. Swing the right hand up and out to level at the right side, palm down. (image 92b) Take another step forward with the right foot, then another step to the forward left with the left foot. Swing the left hand flat across to the rear at the left side, palm down. Lower the right hand, bring it forward, then swing up with the palm angled up. Look forward. (image 92c)

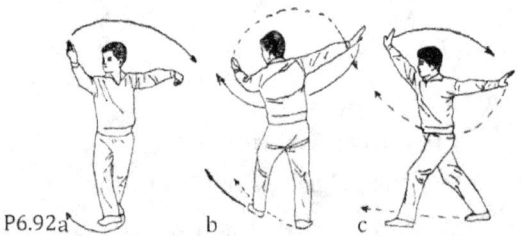

93. Jump To Resting Stance Double Lashes

tiào xiēbù shuāng bǎizhǎng   跳歇步双摆掌

Step the right foot to the forward left with the foot turned in. Continue to swing the left hand so that it circles down and through forward, raising it to level with the fingers up. Continue to swing the right hand back to level, palm down. (image P6.93a) Step the left foot forward with the foot turned out, turning the torso leftward. Swing the right hand up and over to level in front, palm down. Bring the left hand to the right elbow crease, palm facing right. Look at the right hand. (image 93b) Without a pause, push into the left foot to jump up, tucking the lower leg up behind with a natural swinging kick. Swing the right leg behind the left leg to the right side. Swing the hands to the left and up with the palms forward. (image 93c) Land the right

SIXTH FORM PAOQUAN

foot on the spot then land the left foot, passing behind the right leg, crossing and sitting into both legs to take a resting stance. Continue to swing the arms from above over to the right side, fingers pointing up. Look at the right hand. (image 93d)

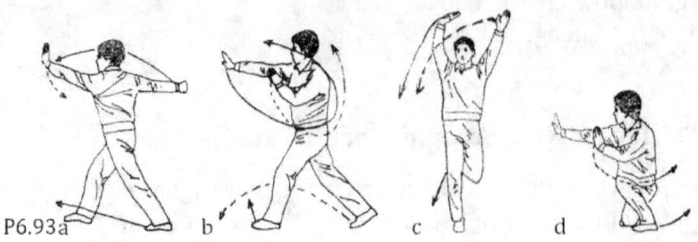

Section Eleven
94. Hitting Hop-Step Slice Up   jībù liāozhǎng   击步撩掌

Turn around to the left and step the left foot forward in the new direction. Lower the left hand through to slice up to the front, thumb side up. Look at the left hand. (image P6.94a) Push off with the left leg to jump forward and up, bumping the right foot in behind the left whilst airborne. Continue to slice the left hand up until it is level. Both palms face forward relative to the body. Look at the left hand. (image 94b)

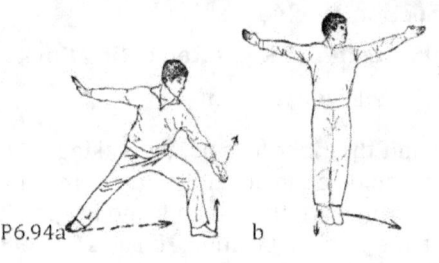

95. Right Bow Stance Scooping Snap
   yòu gōngbù tiǎozhǎng   右弓步挑掌

Land the right foot where it is, land the left foot forward, then step the right foot forward, bending the knee to take a right bow stance. (image P6.95a) Bring the right hand down and through to scoop up level in front, fingers forward. Bring the left hand in to the right forearm. Look at the right hand. (image 95b)

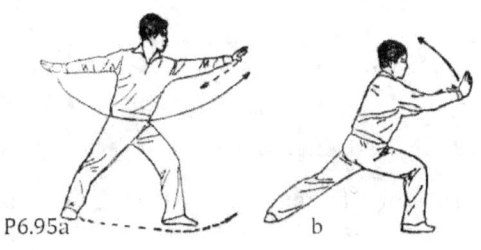

96. Right Bow Stance Chop With The Fist
   yòu gōngbù pīzhǎng   右弓步劈掌

Without changing the stance, clench the right hand and slice up with a straight arm over the head. Extend the left hand straight forward, fingers up.

149

CHAQUAN, VOLUME II

(image P6.96a) Chop the right fist down with a straight arm until it is level, fist eye up. Bring the left hand into the right elbow crease. Look at the right fist. (image 96b)

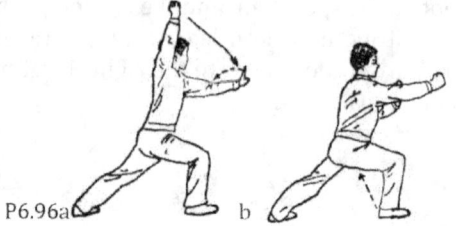

97. Raised Knee Scooping Snap   tíxī tiǎozhǎng   提膝挑掌

Shift back to the left leg and raise the bent right knee, foot pointing down. Scoop up with the right arm, tucking the elbow in so that the fist eye is angled inwards towards the nose. Look at the right fist. (image P6.97)

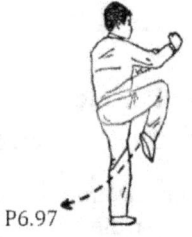

Section Twelve

98. Left And Right Retreating Back Insertion Step
    zuǒ yòu tuìchābù   左右退叉步

Land the right foot behind, taking an insertion step behind the left leg. Do not change the position of the arms. (image P6.98a) Retreat four more steps, starting with the left foot, and keeping the arms in the same position. Finish in the original position. (images 98b, 98c, 98d, 98e)

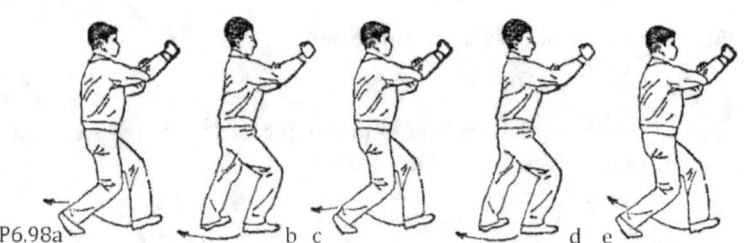

99. Raised Knee Block   tíxī gēquán   提膝格拳

Stride the left foot across to the left side, then lift the bent right knee. Block the right fist across inwards, fist eye staying on top. Keep the left hand at the right elbow crease. Look at the right fist. (images P6.99a, 99b)

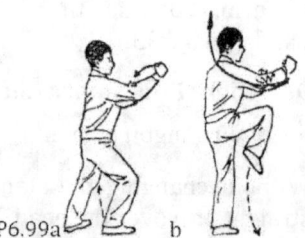

SIXTH FORM PAOQUAN

100.   Right Bow Stance Framing Block And Strike

yòu gōngbù jià jīzhǎng   右弓步架击掌

Land the right foot to the right front, bending the knee to take a right bow stance. Medially rotate the right arm and do a framing block out above the head, fist heart angled up. Keep the left hand at the right elbow crease. Look to the right side. (image P6.100a) Strike the left hand directly forward to level, fingers up. Look at the left hand. (image 100b)

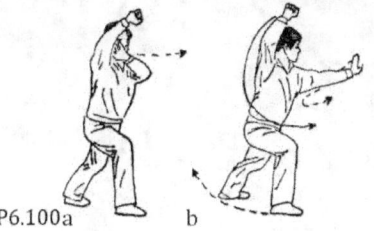

101.   Closed Stance Facing Fists   bīngbù duìquán   并步对拳

Shift to the left leg and withdraw the right foot. Unclench the right hand and lower it. Bring the hands to the waist then stab them forward, palms up. (image P6.101a) Settle into the right foot and bring the hands again to the waist, then circle them outwards at either side and forward, clenching fists. (image 101b) Shift to the right leg and withdraw the left foot to beside it, standing up. Turn the fists in to face each other in front of the belly, fist eyes facing in. Look to the left side. (image 101c)

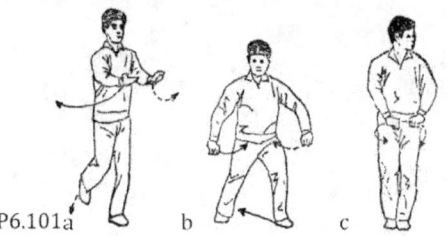

102.   Closing Posture   shōu shì   收势

Unclench the hands and lower them at either side to stand to attention. Look forward. (image P6.102)

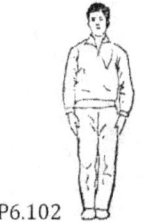

151

NINTH FORM PAOQUAN

九路炮拳

Names Of The Movements

Position Of Preparation
Section One
1. Closed Stance Facing Fists
2. Left Flat Stab
3. Right Thread
4. Left Thread
5. Elbow Carry
6. Resting Stance Flash Palm
7. Bow Stance Sideways Hit
8. Horse Stance Low Cut
9. Back Insertion Stance Thread Up
10. Horse Stance Low Cut
11. Jumping Heel Kick
12. Bow Stance Chop With Fist
13. Scoop And Hit
14. Empty Stance Framing Block And Planting Punch
15. Bow Stance Swinging Chop With Fist
16. Backfist Hammerfist
17. Snap Kick
18. Jumping Snap Kick
19. Jump To Drop Stance Double Cut
20. Snap Kick, Backfist
21. Bow Stance Press Down And Hit
22. Restrain The Horse Posture
23. Horse Stance Double Hooks
24. Snap Kick
25. Bow Stance Push

Section Two
26. Drop Stance Thread The Hand
27. Empty Stance Scooping Snap
28. Raised Knee Scooping Snap
29. Walking Threading Hand
30. Back Insertion Stance Lash
31. Raised Knee Scooping Snap

Section Three
32. Walking Threading Hand

Section Four
33. Empty Stance Low Chop
34. Jump, Stab Up
35. Drop Stance Slice
36. Two Rising Kicks
37. Bow Stance Slap Elbow
38. Bow Stance Chop
39. Empty Stance Slice Upwards With Palm Up
40. Bow Stance Flat Roundhouse Punch
41. Heel Kick, Punch
42. Bow Stance Punch

Section Five
43. Hitting Hop-Step, Lean On A Mountain
44. Stomp, Horse Stance Punch
45. Flowers
46. Left Bow Stance Scooping Snaps To The Sides
47. Right Bow Stance Scooping Snaps To The Sides
48. Closed Stance Planting Punch Down
49. Wheel Over, Horse Stance Chop
50. Back Insertion Stance Thread Up
51. Horse Stance Cut Down
52. Hook, Snap Kick
53. Bow Stance Push
54. Drop Stance Thread The Hand
55. Empty Stance Scooping Snap

Section Six
56. Hitting Hop-Step, Tornado Kick
57. Horse Stance Chop
58. Bow Stance Thread The Hand
59. Wheel Over, Closed Stance Punch
60. Stomp, Bow Stance Punch
61. Bow Stance Low Hammerfist
62. Drop Stance Low Hammerfist
63. Bow Stance Low Punch
64. Half Horse Stance Low Hammerfist
65. Empty Stance Framing Block And Planting Punch
66. Front Touch Stance Facing Fists
67. Closing Posture

NINTH FORM PAOQUAN

0. Position Of Preparation   yù bèi shì   预备势

Stand to attention with the feet together, the head and torso upright, and the arms hanging naturally at the sides. Look forward. (image P9.0)

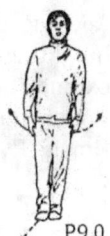

Section One

1. Closed Stance Facing Fists   bīngbù duìquán   并步对拳

Take a half-step forward with the right foot, towards the right. Circle the hands back and out to their respective sides, arms naturally bent, palms in. Look forward. (image P9.1a) Bring the left foot up beside the right foot to a closed stance. Clench both hands, medially rotate the arms, and circle the fists forward and in to face each other in front of the belly, fist hearts down, knuckles facing, about ten centimetres apart. Look to the forward left. (image 1b)

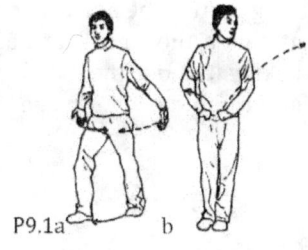

2. Left Flat Stab   zuǒ píng chāzhǎng   左平插掌

Pause for an instant, then unclench the left hand and bring it up past the left side of the chest, then extend it flat to the left, arm at shoulder height, palm down. Bring the right fist up to the waist. Look past the left hand. (image P9.2)

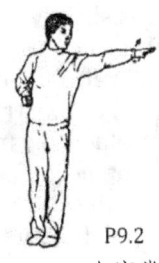

3. Right Thread   yòu chuānzhǎng   右穿掌

Laterally rotate the left hand to turn the palm up. Look at the left hand. (image P9.3a) Lash the left hand to the front with a straight arm. Unclench the right hand and thread it forward over the left arm to the elbow crease, palm down. Look forward. (image 3b) Bend the left elbow and open the elbow outwards, bringing the left hand to in front of the left side of the chest, palm up. Turn the right palm down then extend it forward and to the right, cutting across to the right side. Look at the right hand. (image 3c)

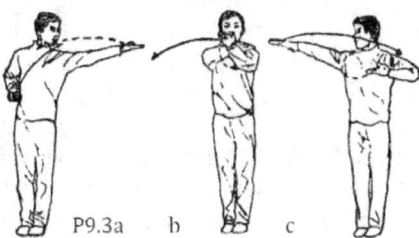

4. **Left Thread** zuǒ chuānshǒu 左穿手

Keeping the right palm facing down, lash it to the front then bend the elbow in front of the chest. Turn the left palm up and extend it out to the forward right underneath the right elbow. Watch the right hand in action, then look past the left hand. (image P9.4)

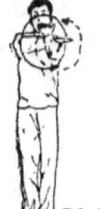

5. **Elbow Carry** tuōzhǒu shì 托肘势

Pivoting at the elbows, circle the left hand down and out, bringing it to beside the left ear, fingers pointing back, palm up. Circle the right hand up past the face then to the chest, tucking it under the left elbow, palm up. Look through the left forearm to the left. (image P9.5)

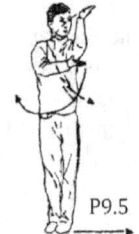

6. **Resting Stance Flash Palm** xiēbù liàngzhǎng 歇步亮掌

Stop for an instant, then step the left foot out to the left side, bending the legs slightly and shifting towards the right leg. Brush the left hand past the face and down in front of the belly, palm down. Bring the right hand past the belly and out behind the right hip, palm forward. Look at the left hand. (image P9.6a) Take an insertion step with the right foot, passing behind the left foot toward the left, and sit down with the right heel raised, so that the legs are folded together in a resting stance. Continue to brush the left hand down and back, then hook it behind the body, hook pointing up. Swing the right hand with a straight arm up at the side above the head, fingers pointing left, palm up, finishing with the arm curved. Look forward, to the left. (image 6b)

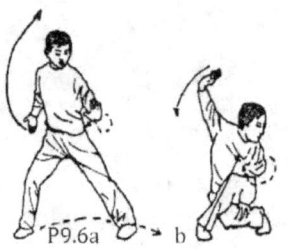

7. **Bow Stance Sideways Hit** gongbu héng dǎzhǎng 弓步横打掌

Shift to the left and stand up on the left leg, lifting the bent right knee with the foot hanging down naturally. Bring the left hand in to the left hip then scoop up in front, arm bent, fingers up at chest height. Extend the right hand down to the right rear, palm down, to balance. Look forward, to the left. (image P9.7a) Land the left foot into a left bow stance. Brush across to the left and back with the left hand, extending the arm out behind, palm back. Cut the right arm across in front, keeping it straight, to strike in front of the

NINTH FORM PAOQUAN

body, palm facing left, fingers forward. The arms are angled high and low, near shoulder height. Look past the right hand. (image 7b)

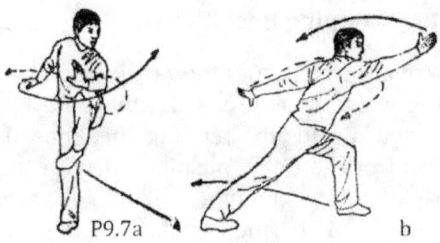

8. Horse Stance Low Cut   mǎbù xià qiēzhǎng   马步下切掌

Pause briefly, then turn the torso slightly to the right and shift back to the right. Step the left foot to the right behind the right leg, into a back insertion stance. Bend the right arm slightly and bring it around to the right with the body turn, to above and in front of the head, fingers up, palm facing left. Bring the left hand to the waist, across the belly to the right ribs, stabbing with the forearm tight to the belly, palm up. Look to the lower right. (image P9.8a) Shift to the right and step the right foot sideways to the front right, sitting into a horse stance. Do a framing block with the left hand, placing a sideways hand above the left side of the head, first passing outside the right hand. Cut the right hand down to outside the right knee, passing by the chest, fingers forward, palm angled down and in. Both arms are slightly bent. Look past the right hand. (image 8b)

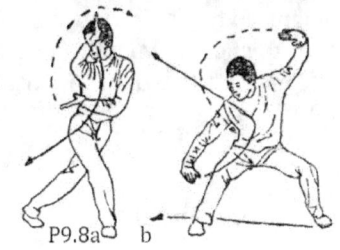

9. Back Insertion Stance Thread Up

chābù shàng chuānzhǎng   叉步上穿掌

Shift to the right and step the left foot to the right behind the right leg, taking a back insertion stance. Circle the left hand to the right, then down to press down under the right armpit, thumb tight to the ribs. Bring the right hand past the belly, chest, and right shoulder to stab up to the right with a straight arm, palm angled up and in. Look past the right hand. (image P9.9)

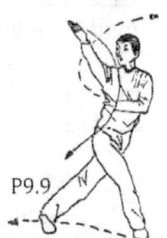

10. Horse Stance Low Cut

mǎbù xià qiēzhǎng   马步下切掌

This is the same as move 8. (image P9.10)

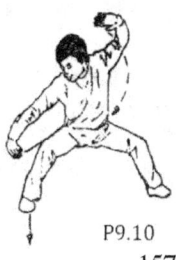

157

CHAQUAN, VOLUME II

11. Jumping Heel Kick   tiàoqǐ dēngjiǎo   跳起蹬脚

Move the right foot forward, clenching both hands and bringing the fists to the waist. Look forward. (image P9.11a) Push into the left foot to swing it forward and up, bending the knee in front of the belly, pushing off with the right foot to jump up. Look forward. (image 11b) Land forward on the left foot and tuck up the right foot, then do a right thrust kick up to the front with the leg straight and the ankle dorsiflexed. Look past the kick. (image 11c)

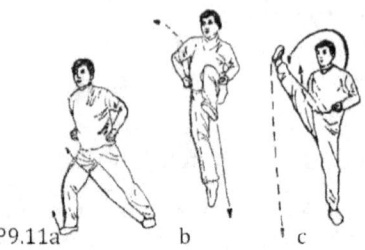

12. Bow Stance Chop With Fist   gōngbù pīzhǎng   弓步劈拳

Land forward on the right foot, into a right bow stance. Unclench the left hand and extend it forward, palm up, to chest height. Extend the right fist to the back, then swing it up and over to chop down in front to chest height, fist eye up. Place the left hand at the right forearm. Look past the right fist. (image P9.12)

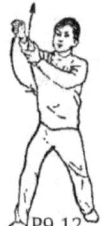

13. Scoop And Hit   tiǎodǎ   挑打

Bring the right fist to the waist. Scoop up with the left hand, tiger's mouth leading, to in front of the head, arm slightly bent. Look past the left hand. (image P9.13a) Punch the right fist forward to shoulder height, bringing the left hand in to in front of the right shoulder, palm tight to the right upper arm near the shoulder, fingers up. Look past the right fist. (image 13b)

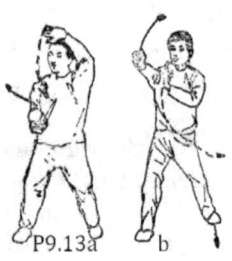

14. Empty Stance Framing Block And Planting Punch
     xūbù jià zāiquán   虚步架栽拳

Advance the left foot to the forward left, parallel to the right foot, with the toes touching down. Turn the torso leftward and take an empty stance. Clench the left hand and bring it down, past the belly, then out to just above the left knee, medially rotating so that the tiger's mouth is in, the knuckles down. Do a framing block with the right fist above the head, fist heart angled forward and up. Look to the left. (image P9.14)

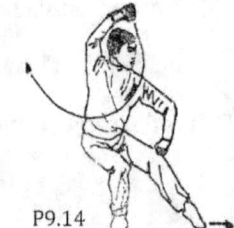

NINTH FORM PAOQUAN

15. Bow Stance Swinging Chop With Fist gōngbù lūnpīquàn 弓步抡劈拳

Move the left foot forward and shift to the right leg. Bring the left fist in, past the belly, and up to in front of the right shoulder, fist eye in. Circle the right hand down the left side of the chest, belly, then to the rear, holding it level with the fist eye up. Look to the left. (image P9.15a) Shift forward into a left bow stance. Turn the torso leftward, bringing the left fist up, over the head, then left, down, and back, holding it flat to the rear with the fist eye up. Keep the right arm straight and bring it up over the head to the front, to chop level in front with the fist eye up. The arms draw a straight line through the shoulders. Look past the right fist. (image 15b)

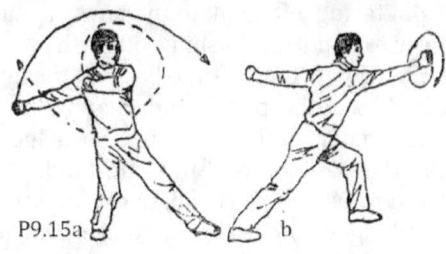

16. Backfist Hammerfist fǎnbèi záquán 反背砸拳

Medially rotate the right fist and, pivoting it around the elbow, circle it over and down, drawing a half-circle, laterally rotating to do a strong backfist down in front at waist height, the elbow bent so that the forearm is flat, fist heart up. Look at the right fist. (image P9.16)

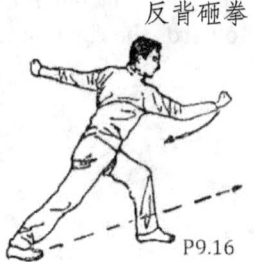

17. Snap Kick tántītuǐ 弹踢腿

Shift to the left leg and raise the right knee, then do a snap kick out level, snapping forcefully into the lower leg at waist height, ankle plantar-flexed. Bring the right forearm in so that the elbow is tight to the ribs, fist eye up. The forearm and thigh are level and parallel. Look forward. (image P9.17)

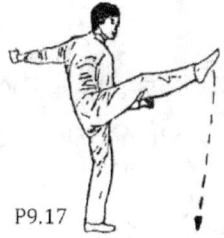

18. Jumping Snap Kick tiàoqǐ tántītuǐ 跳起弹踢腿

Land the right foot, pointing it forward. (image P9.18a) Swing the left knee, bending it to lift forward and up. Push off with the right foot to jump up. Bring the right hand in to the belly. Look forward. (image 18b) Land on the left foot, kicking the right leg up with a snap kick. Look at the right foot. (image 18c)

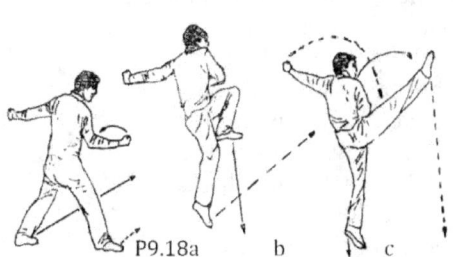

159

19. Jump To Drop Stance Double Cut

tiào pūbù shuāng duòzhǎng   跳仆步双剁掌

After the jump kick, land on the left foot, then land the right foot. Circle the left hand up and forward, going to the belly, fingers forward, palm facing right. Circle the right hand past the chest up and forward to level, fingers up, palm facing left. Look to the lower front. (image P9.19a) Swing the left foot forward and up, pushing off with the right foot to jump up. Circle both hands down, then up and back on the left side. The left hand goes up to level, tiger's mouth up. The right hand goes to the left shoulder, tiger's mouth down. Look to the lower front. (image 19b) Land on the left foot, keeping the right knee raised in front. Circle the hands upwards together, the left hand to behind the head, tiger's mouth up, the right hand to in front of the head, tiger's mouth back. (image 19c) Squat fully on the left leg and extend the right foot out along the ground into a drop stance, foot turned in. Chop down with the hands together, hitting the ground inside the right leg. The right hand is ahead of the left hand, both palm edges hit the ground. Look towards the right hand. (image 19d)

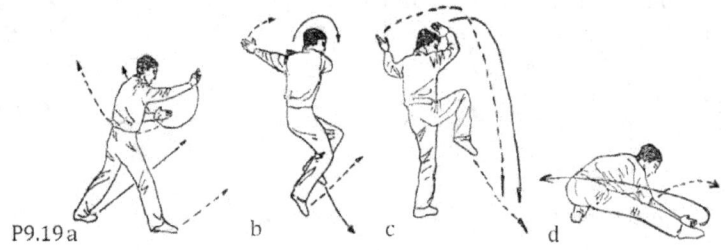

P9.19a   b   c   d

20. Snap Kick, Backfist   tántuǐ fǎnbèiquán   弹腿反背拳

Push into the left leg and shift forward, turning the torso rightward. Extend the left hand forward with an upright palm, to shoulder height. Bring the right hand along above the right foot, then brush aside to the rear right to behind the body, tiger's mouth down. Look towards the right hand. (image P9.20a) Turn the right foot out and straighten the left leg, turn slightly to the right, lifting the bent left knee to the belly, shin tucked in, sole of the foot tucked in to the thigh. Bring the left hand in past the face to press down in front of the chest, with the elbow bent and the palm down. Clench the right hand and bring it in to the hip then up to the chest, bending the elbow to tuck in beside the left forearm, fist heart down. Look past the left hand. (image 20b) Land on the left foot, pushing off the

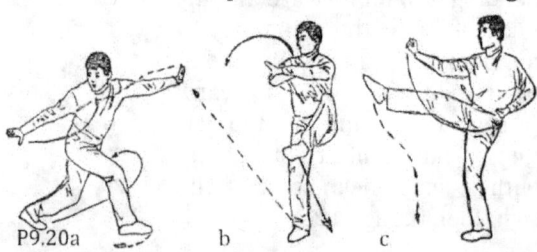

P9.20a   b   c

NINTH FORM PAOQUAN

right foot to do a snap kick to the front right. Clench the left hand and bring the fist to the waist. Circle the right fist up to flip over with a backfist, fist at shoulder height, arm slightly bent, fist heart angled up and in. Look to the right side. (image 20c)

21. Bow Stance Press Down And Hit   gōngbù yādǎ   弓步压打

Land the right foot forward and shift to stand between the legs. Unclench the right hand and medially rotate it, lowering it to the left hip, palm down. Unclench the left hand and bring it past the belly to stab under the right armpit, palm down. Look to the lower front. (image P9.21a) Turn the right foot out. Bend the right elbow upward, bringing the hand to the left shoulder then out to the front right at eye height, tiger's mouth left, fingers forward. Balance the action with the left hand, bringing it down to the left hip, tiger's mouth out, palm forward. Look to the lower front. (image 21b) Step the left foot forward then sit into a half horse stance. Circle the left hand up the side to the upper front. When it arrives at shoulder height, medially rotate the wrist to press down with a sideways palm, palm down. Circle the right hand to the right then clench it and bring the fist to the waist, fist heart up. Look past the left hand. (image 21c) Shift forward into a left bow stance. Continue to press down with the left hand, bending the elbow to tuck the hand into the right armpit, fingers up, palm out. Slide the right fist out over the left wrist to punch forward and down, fist heart down. Look past the right fist. (image 21d)

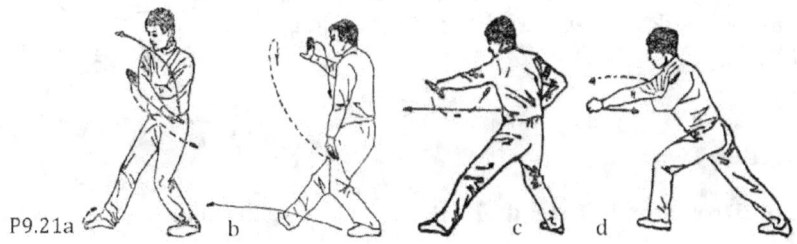

P9.21a   b   c   d

22. Restrain The Horse Posture   lēimǎ shì   勒马势

Sit back into a left half horse stance. Clench the left hand and snap it forward from under the right arm with a bent elbow, the fist at eye height, fist heart facing right. Laterally rotate the right fist and bring it in to under the left elbow, also with a bent elbow, fist heart facing left. Look in the direction of the left hand. (image P9.22)

23. Horse Stance Double Hooks   mǎbù shuāng gōushǒu   马步双勾手

Pause for an instant, then tuck in the left foot to take a horse stance. Hook both hands and circle them down and back at their respective sides, with a brushing action, extending straight arms to the back with the hooks up. Turn the head right. Look to the right. (image P9.23)

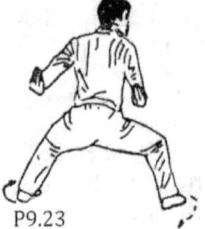

24. Snap Kick   tántītuǐ   弹踢腿

Turn the right foot out and push into the left heel to turn to the right into a right bow stance. Keep the hands in place. Look forward. (image P9.24a) Shift forward and stand up on the right leg. Do a snap kick with the left leg. Look forward. (image 24b)

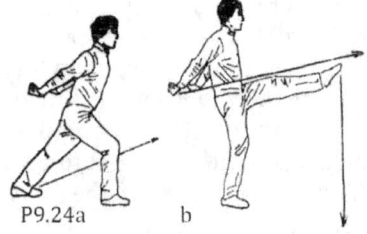

25. Bow Stance Push   gōngbù tuīzhǎng   弓步推掌

Land the left foot and press forward into a left bow stance. Unhook the right hand and bring it past the waist to push directly forward, fingers up, palm edge forward. Look forward. (image P9.25)

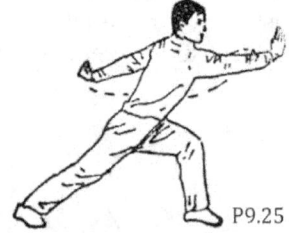

Section Two

26. Drop Stance Thread The Hand   pūbù chuānzhǎng   仆步穿掌

Laterally rotate the right hand to turn the palm up, bending the elbow slightly. Unhook the left hand and bring it to the waist, then extend it to the front over the right forearm, palm up, back of the hand on the right arm. Look forward. (image P9.26a) Drop down, squatting on the left leg and extending the right leg along the ground, leaning right slightly, in a drop stance. Continue to extend the left arm forward until it is straight, tiger's mouth up. Bend the right arm and bring the hand in to the belly, then slide it along the inside of the right leg to the foot, tiger's mouth up. Look past the right hand. (image 26b)

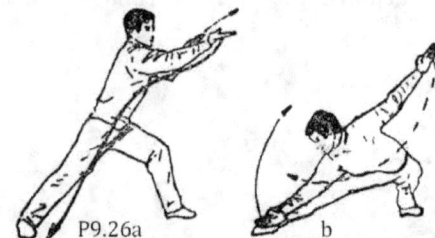

NINTH FORM PAOQUAN

27. Empty Stance Scooping Snap   xūbù tiǎozhǎng   虚步挑掌

Shift to the right leg. Straighten the right hand and lift the hand to above the head at the right, tiger's mouth facing left. Lower the straight left arm to in front of the body to knee height, tiger's mouth forward. Look to the front, to the left. (image P9.27a) Step the left foot forward, to the left. Circle the straight right arm back and down to the back on the right, palm down. Circle the straight left arm forward and up to scoop up above the head, palm forward. Look forward, to the right. (image 27b) Step the right foot forward to the left, touching down the toes and sitting on the left leg in a right empty stance. Scoop up with the right hand with a vertical palm, fingers at shoulder height. Lower the straight left arm behind to head height, tiger's mouth up. Look past the right hand. (image 27c)

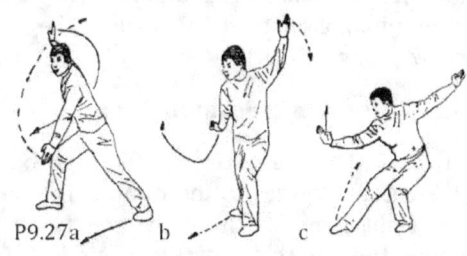

28.   Raised Knee Scooping Snap   tíxī tiǎozhǎng   提膝挑掌

Pause briefly, then stand up, straightening the left leg and raising the bent right knee, with the foot pointing down and tucked in. Do not change the position of the left hand. Continue to scoop up with the right hand until the fingers are at eye height. (image P9.28)

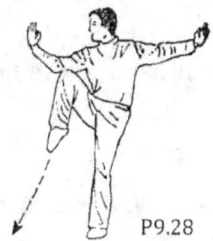

29.   Walking Threading Hand   xíngbù chuānzhǎng   行步穿掌

Shift forward and land the right foot, keeping both legs bent. Look forward. (image P9.29a) Stride the left foot forward. Laterally rotate the right hand to turn the palm up. Bend the left elbow to bring the left hand to the waist, palm up. Look past the right hand to the front. (image 29b) Step the right foot forward. Thread the left hand through with the palm up, to pass over the right forearm, sliding the back of the hand on the arm. Look forward. (image 29c) Stride the left foot forward. Bring the right hand to the waist, palm up. Extend the left hand to thread and stab forward until the arm is

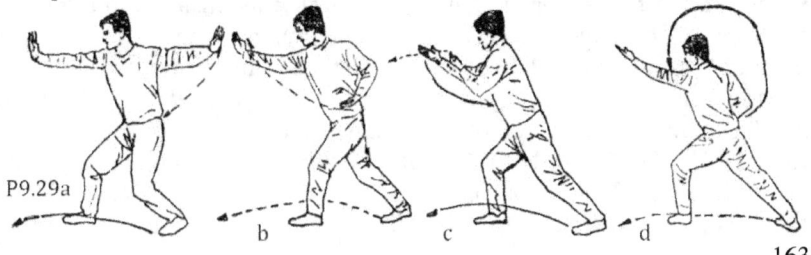

fully extended, palm up. Look past the left hand. (image 29d)

30. Back Insertion Stance Lash   chābù bǎizhǎng   叉步摆掌

Turn in the left foot and step the right foot behind it towards the left with an insertion step, touching the ball of the foot down in a back insertion stance. Medially rotate the left hand to a vertical palm. Circle the right hand to the right and back, then up over the head and down on the left to in front of the left shoulder with a vertical palm, tiger's mouth in. Follow the movement of the right hand with the head. (image P9.30)

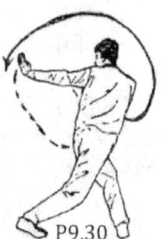

31. Raised Knee Scooping Snap   tíxī tiǎozhǎng   提膝挑掌

Pivot on the heel of the left foot and ball of the right foot to turn around one-eighty degrees to the right. Bring the left hand down to the hip. Stick the right hand to the belly and bring it down, then as the body turns, circle it up and back to chop down flat behind with a vertical palm. Look past the right hand. (image P9.31a) Turn the head to the left. Raise the bent left knee. Scoop up with the left hand to eye height. Look past the left hand. (image 31b)

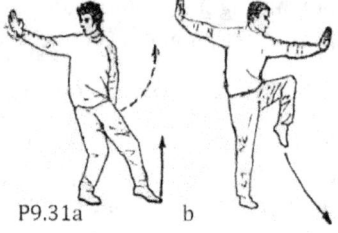

Section Three

32. Walking Threading Hand   xíngbù chuānzhǎng   行步穿掌

Land the left foot forward, bending both legs slightly. Look forward. (image P9.32a) Stride the right foot out in front of the left. Medially rotate the left hand and circle it up and over the head to the left. Medially rotate the right hand and circle it down to the rear right, a bit lower than the waist, palm down. Look forward. (image 32b)

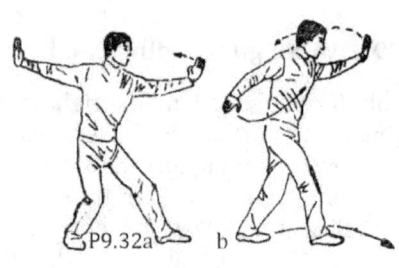

Stride the left foot forward. Continue to circle the left hand to the rear, to shoulder height at the left side. Bring the right hand to the waist, heel of the palm tight to the waist. Look forward. (image 32c) Stride the right foot to the front right, turning the foot out. Continue to circle the left hand down and back. Stab the right hand forward, palm up. Look past the right hand. (image 32d) Stride the left foot to the forward right, hooking the foot in, knee slightly pushing forward. Laterally rotate the left hand and bring it to the waist, then thread it out above the right forearm, palm up. Look forward.

NINTH FORM PAOQUAN

(image 32e) Sit down to a left bow stance. Clench the right hand and bring it to the waist, fist heart up. Stab the left hand forward, extending the arm, palm up. Snap the head to look behind to the right. Look to the rear right. (image 32f)

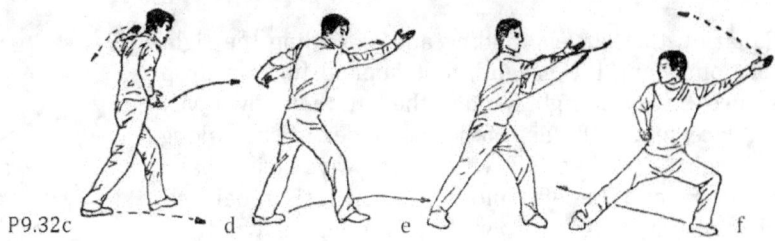

Section Four

33. Empty Stance Low Chop   xūbù xià pīzhǎng   虚步下劈掌

Pause briefly, then shift back and withdraw the left foot back, turning in the right foot and turning one-fifty degrees to the left. Bring the left hand around with the turn, keeping the arm straight and circling it up then back to finish raised with the tiger's mouth back. Do not change the position of the right fist. Turn the head with the turn of the body. Look forward, to the left. (image P9.33a) Shift left and turn the body slightly left. With the body turn, circle the left hand, keeping the arm straight, down to behind the left hip. Unclench the right hand and raise it behind the body at the right, tiger's mouth facing left. Look forward and down. (image 33b) Sit down, half-squatting on the left leg and placing the toes of the right foot forward in a right empty stance. Chop forward and down with the right hand to inside the right shin, tiger's mouth forward. Balance the action with the left hand, bending the elbow to place the hand in front of the right shoulder, tiger's mouth in. Look past the right hand. (image 33c)

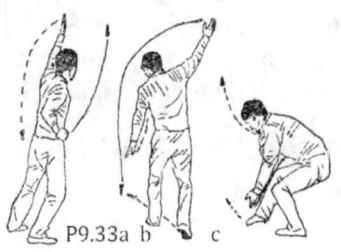

34. Jump, Stab Up   tiàoqǐ shàng chuānzhǎng   跳起上穿掌

Pause briefly, then move the right foot forward and stand up. Extend the left hand up past the face to the front and up, bending the arm slightly, palm down. Bring the right hand in to the belly, palm up. Look in the direction of the left hand. (image P9.34a) Swing the left leg up in front, pushing into the right leg to jump up, raising the right knee. Press down with the left hand, tucking it into the right armpit.

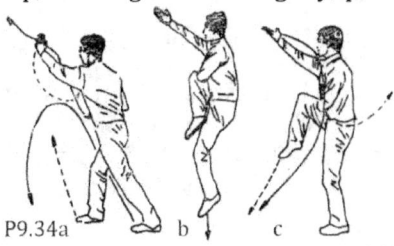

Thread the right hand out above the left forearm and up, arm straight, palm up. Look at the right hand. (image 34b) First land on the left foot, standing up, keeping the right knee bent and raised. (image 34c)

35. Drop Stance Slice   pūbù xiāozhǎng   仆步削掌

Squat on the left leg, landing and extending the right foot out along the ground, foot hooked in, in a drop stance. Circle the right hand to the left, then down past the face, and then past the left shoulder to slide along the right leg to the foot with a sideways strike, palm down. Extend the left hand out to the back to balance, also with a sideways palm, tiger's mouth down. Look past the right hand. (image P9.35)

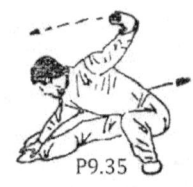

36. Two Rising Kicks   èrqǐjiǎo   二起脚

Shift to the right leg and push into the left leg, extending it. Lift the left hand above the head and lower the right hand back to behind the right hip. Look forward. (image P9.36a) Swing the left knee up in front and push off with the right leg to jump. Swing the right straight arm up to slap the back of the hand into the left palm, with a clear sound, above the head. Look forward and up. (image 36b) Land on the left foot and swing up the right foot with the leg straight, ankle plantar-flexed. Swing the left hand back with a vertical palm, fingers level with the head. Lower the right hand to slap the right foot. Look past the right hand. (image 36c)

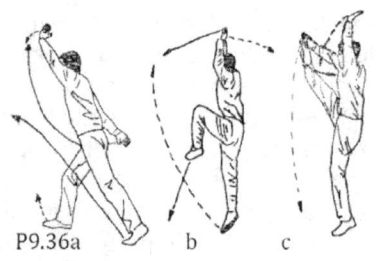

37. Bow Stance Slap Elbow   gōngbù pāizhǒu   弓步拍肘

Land forward on the right foot, to the right, into a right bow stance. Clench the right hand and bring it in front of the chest, forearm close to the chest, fist heart down. Circle the left hand up, forward, then down to slap on top of the right elbow. The forearms are folded in front of the chest. Look at the right elbow. (image P9.37)

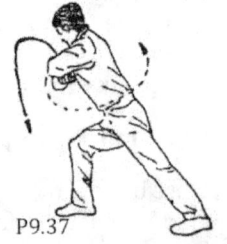

38. Bow Stance Chop   gōngbù pīzhǎng   弓步劈掌

Unclench the right hand and bring it inside the left arm, up past the face, then circle down to the front with a chop. Lower the left hand then scoop up behind to head height. Both tiger's mouths face up, and the arms form a straight, angled, line. Look past the right hand. (image P9.38)

NINTH FORM PAOQUAN

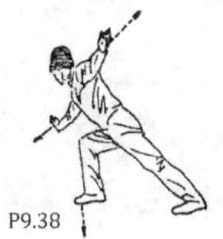

P9.38

39. Empty Stance Slice Upwards With Palm Up

xūbù liāoyīnzhǎng   虚步撩阴掌

Pause briefly, then shift back, turning left and bringing the right foot in to an empty stance placement. Bring the left hand up and the right hand down with the movement. Look forward, to the lower right. (image P9.39a) Shift forward and step the left foot forward to the left side, turning the torso and circling the arms along with the movement. The left hand circles back and down and the right hand circles forward and up. Both arms remain straight, and the hands follow the opposite sides of the circle simultaneously. Look down to the right. (image 39b) Step the right foot forward to the left, touching the toes down in a right empty stance. Bring the right hand down then in to the right hip, and then slice up to hip height, palm up. Clench the left hand and bring the fist to the waist. Look past the right hand. (image 39c)

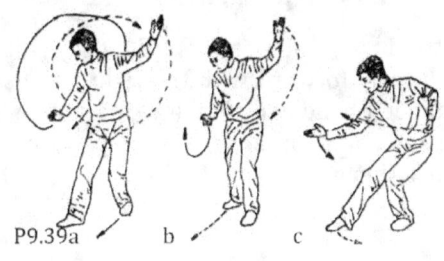

P9.39a   b   c

40. Bow Stance Flat Roundhouse Punch

gōngbù héngguànquán   弓步横贯拳

Turn the right foot in. Medially rotate the right hand and clench it. Medially rotate the left hand and extend it, setting the wrist on top of the right forearm. Look by the left hand. (image P9.40a) Step the left foot behind the right leg with a back insertion step to the right, with the heel lifted. Turn to the left and bring the left hand around to the left to brush flat aside, tiger's mouth down, palm out. Bring the right fist in to the waist. Look at the left hand. (image 40b) Pivot on the ball of the left foot and the heel of the right foot to continue to turn to the left, continuing also to bring the left hand around to brush flat aside to the rear. Look at the left hand as it turns. (image 40c) Set both feet firmly in a left bow stance, twisting the torso leftward. Clench the left hand, laterally rotating, and bring the fist to the waist. Do a roundhouse punch with the right fist forward and to the left, medially rotating, to hit with a bent arm and cocked wrist in front of the chest, fist eye down and fist heart forward at chest height. Look in the direction of the right fist. (image 40d)

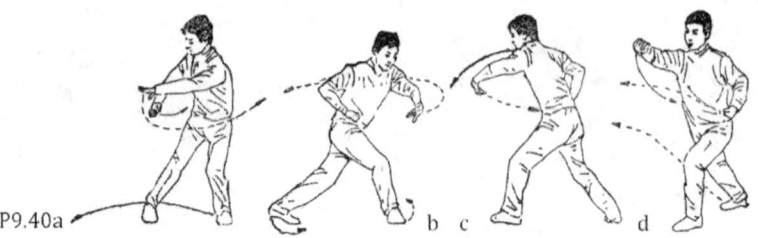

P9.40a   b   c   d

41. Heel Kick, Punch   dēngtuǐ chōngquán   蹬腿冲拳

Shift forward and do a heel kick forward to belly height with the right leg, ankle dorsi-flexed. Bring the right fist to the waist. Punch forward with the left fist to shoulder height, fist eye up. Look at the left fist. (image P9.41)

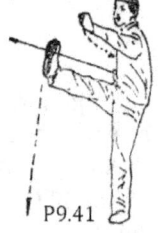

P9.41

42. Bow Stance Punch   gōngbù chōngquán   弓步冲拳

Land the right foot forward into a right bow stance. Punch directly forward with the right fist, fist eye up. Unclench the left hand and place a vertical palm in front of the right shoulder, palm tight to the upper arm. Look past the right fist. (image P9.42)

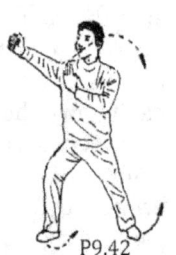

P9.42

Section Five

43. Hitting Hop-Step, Lean On A Mountain
jībù kàoshānzhǎng   击步靠山掌

Turn in the right foot and turn out the left foot, standing up and turning left. Do not change the placement of the right fist. Bring the left hand up past the face then circle flat out to the left side, tiger's mouth up. Look past the left hand. (image P9.43a) Shift forward, taking a shifting step forward with the left foot, pushing off the right foot to jump forward, causing the left foot to jump forward. When both feet are in the air, the right leg bumps into the left. The body is upright. (image 43b) Land both feet simultaneously in an open parallel stance. Scoop up naturally with the left hand and allow the right hand to lower naturally. Look forward, to the left. (image 43c) Step the right foot forward and turn left, sitting into a horse stance. Unclench the right hand and lift the straight arm up over the head to chop down in front to the left knee, palm forward. Bend the left elbow to bring the hand to the right shoulder, palm in. Look at the right hand. (image 43d) Jump up with both feet to turn to a bow stance. Do a lean with the right arm to the upper right, keeping it straight, the hand to shoulder height. Separate the left hand out to the lower rear. The arms are in a line, slightly angled up and down, both tiger's mouths up. Look past the right hand. (image 43e)

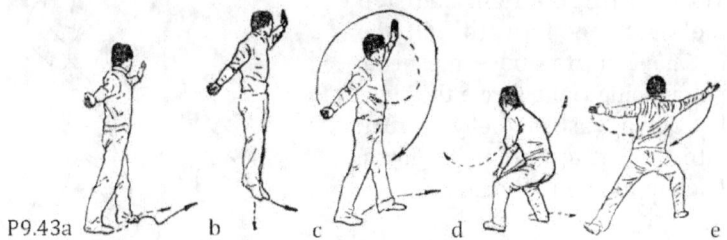

44. Stomp, Horse Stance Punch

zhēnjiǎo mǎbù chōngquán　　　　　　　　　　　　　震脚马步冲拳

Shift left and turn a bit to the left. Hook the straight right arm down until the hand is in front of the left knee, palm in. Bend the left elbow to tuck the hand into the right armpit, palm down. Look at the right hand. (image P9.44a) Lift the right foot with the foot turned out in front of the left shin, turning the body rightward. Bend the right elbow and medially rotate, bringing the hand up past the face, to stop in front of the right side of the head, palm forward, tiger's mouth down. Laterally rotate the left hand and bring it down to past the belly to beside the left hip, tiger's mouth out. Look forward. (image 44b) Stomp with the right foot, lifting the left foot. Laterally rotate the left hand and bring it up the side, over the head, then medially rotate and press down in front to shoulder height, palm down. Laterally rotate the right hand and clench the fist, bringing it to the waist. (image 44c) Land on the left foot at the left and sit into a horse stance. Press down the left hand, bending the elbow to place the hand in front of the right shoulder with a vertical palm. Punch straight forward with the right fist, fist eye up. Look forward. (image 44d)

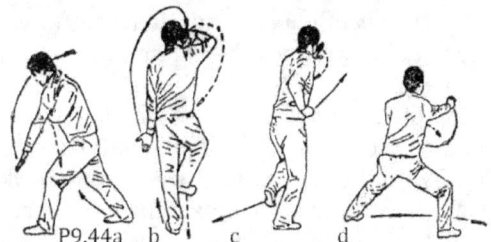

45. Flowers　　　　　　　wǔhuāshǒu　　　　　　　　舞花手

Pause briefly, then shift to the right, stepping the left foot forward to the right with a front cross-over step in front of the right leg, foot turned out, into a cross stance. Stab the left hand in under the right armpit. Medially rotate the right hand to hook down to in front of the left elbow. Look forward, to the right. (image P9.45a) Step the right foot to the right. Lower the left hand past the belly to behind the hip. Bring the right fist up, over the head, then to the right, to above the head at the right, fist eye facing the head. Look forward. (image 45b) Turn a bit to the right and step the right foot forward. Lift the left hand up to above the head, palm facing right. Circle the right fist down, past the belly, to tuck into the left armpit, palm down. Look to the right. (image 45c)

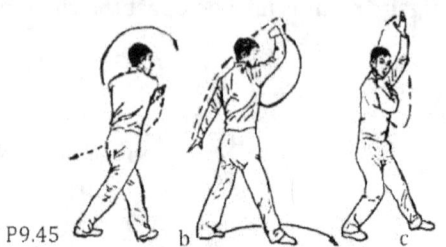

46. Left Bow Stance Scooping Snaps To The Sides

zuǒ gōngbù cè tiǎoquán 左弓步侧挑拳

Shift forward, pressing down into a left bow stance. Clench the left hand and bring it to the right, then down to in front of the right shoulder, then past the belly to scoop up to the left to shoulder height, fist eye up. Watch the movement of the left hand. (image P9.46a) Scoop the right fist up past the belly to the right, fist eye up. The arms are both out to the sides. Turn the head with the rightward turn. Look past the right hand. (image 46b)

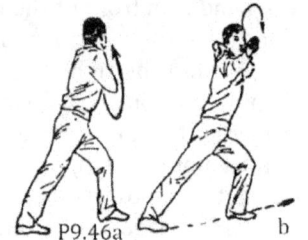

47. Right Bow Stance Scooping Snaps To The Sides

yòu gōngbù cè tiǎoquán 右弓步侧挑拳

Pause briefly, then step the right foot forward to a right bow stance. Bend the left elbow to tuck the fist into the right armpit. Bring the right fist up to above the head, fist eye facing back. Look forward, to the left. (image P9.47a) Bring the right fist to the left and down past the left shoulder, then past the belly to scoop up to the right side to shoulder height, fist eye up. Turn the head with the action of the right hand. Look past the right fist. (image 47b) Scoop the left fist down past the belly then forward to the left to shoulder height, fist eye up. Turn the head with the action of the left hand. Look past the left fist. (image 47c)

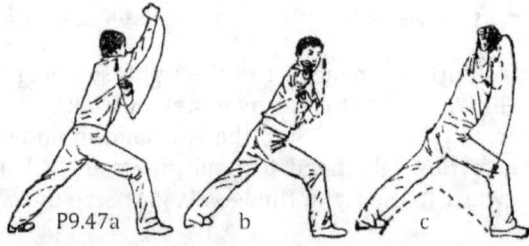

NINTH FORM PAOQUAN

48. Closed Stance Planting Punch Down

bīngbù xiàzāiquán   并步下栽拳

Pause briefly, then shift left and bring in the right foot to a closed stance, half-squatting. Bring the right fist in close the right side, and punch down just below the knee, fist heart back. Unclench the left hand and bring it to in front of the right shoulder with a vertical palm. Look past the right fist. (image P9.48)

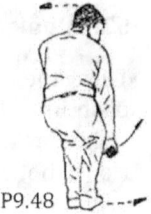
P9.48

49. Wheel Over, Horse Stance Chop

fānshēn mǎbù pīzhǎng   翻身马步劈掌

Pause briefly, then move the right foot to the right. Open the right hand a bit to the right and bring the left hand up past the face to above the head at the left. Look up to the left. (image P9.49a) Pivot on the ball of the right foot to turn one-eighty degrees to the left, then step the left foot behind the right with a back insertion step. Bring the arms around with the turn of the body. Watch the action of the left hand. (image 49b) Step the right foot forward to the left, turning into a horse stance. Continue to circle the arms in a full, vertical, circle, the left hand down and the right hand up, until the arms are level, palms forward. Look to the right. (image 49c)

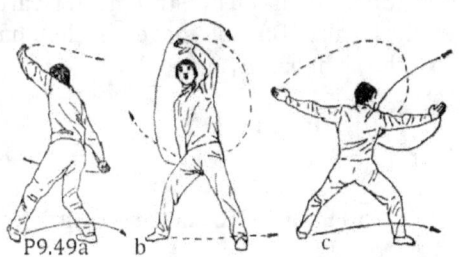
P9.49a   b   c

50. Back Insertion Stance Thread Up

chābù shàng chuānzhǎng   叉步上穿掌

Shift to the right and step the left foot behind the right leg with a back insertion step, heel lifted, taking a back insertion stance. Bring the left hand over the head then press down under the right armpit, palm down. Bring the right hand to in front of the chest then thread up on the right, palm forward. Look past the right hand.(image P9.50)

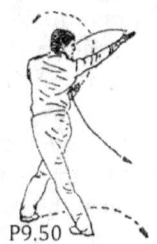
P9.50

51. Horse Stance Cut Down

mǎbù xiàqiēzhǎng   马步下切掌

Shift to the right and step the right foot sideways to the front right, sitting into a horse stance. Do a framing block with the left hand, placing a sideways hand above the left side of the head, first passing

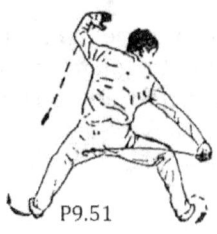
P9.51

171

outside the right hand. Cut the right hand down to outside the right knee, passing by the chest, fingers forward, palm angled down and in. Both arms are slightly bent. Look past the right hand. (image P9.51)

52. Hook, Snap Kick gōushǒu tántītuǐ 勾手弹踢腿

Turn the right foot out and push into the left heel, turning right into a right bow stance. Hook both hands and brush aside to the rear, hooks pointing up. Look forward. (image P9.52a) Do a snap kick with the left foot. (image 52b)

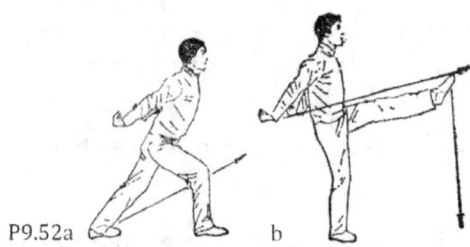

53. Bow Stance Push pūbù tuīzhǎng 仆步推掌

Land forward on the left foot into a left bow stance. Unhook the right hand and bring it in to the waist, then push straight forward with a vertical palm. Do not move the left hand. Look past the right hand. (image P9.53)

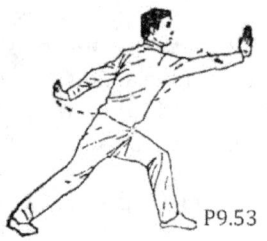

54. Drop Stance Thread The Hand pūbù chuānzhǎng 仆步穿掌

Laterally rotate the right hand, turning the palm up. Unhook the left hand and bring it in to the waist, then extend it out above the right forearm, palm up. (image P9.54a) Squat fully on the left leg and extend the right leg out along the ground. Continue to extend the left hand in front, then medially rotate it to turn the tiger's mouth up. Bring the right hand in to the belly, then thread it out along the inside of the right leg to the foot, tiger's mouth up. Look at the right hand. (image 54b)

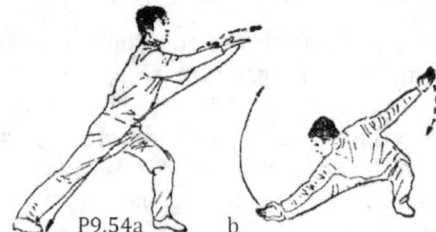

55. Empty Stance Scooping Snap xūbù tiǎozhǎng 虚步挑掌

Shift to the right leg and stand up. Raise the straight right arm up and lower the straight left arm so that the arms make a straight line, the right higher than the left. Look forward and down. (image P9.55a) Retreat the right foot behind the left. Continue to circle the hands, the right up and the left to the left side of the hip. Look forward. (image 55b) Sit down to a half-squat, touching the toes of the left foot down in a left empty stance. Scoop up in front with the left hand, fingers at eye height. Drop the right hand down at the back to balance, fingers at head height in a vertical palm. Look past the left hand. (image 55c)

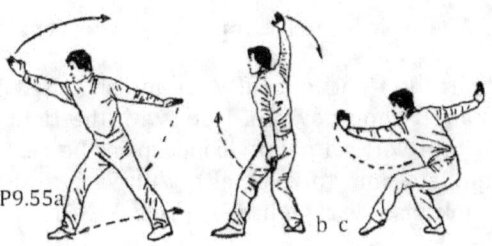

Section Six

56. Hitting Hop-Step, Tornado Kick   jībù xuánfēngjiǎo   击步旋风脚

Pause briefly, then stand up. Bring the left hand in to the left ribs, palm up. Look forward. (image P9.56a) Shift the left foot forward, pushing into the right foot to jump up, causing the left foot to also leave the ground, so that the right leg bumps into the left leg whilst airborne. Extend the left arm straight in front. (image 56b) Land the feet in a front to back open parallel stance. (image 56c) Step the right foot forward with the legs slightly bent, shifting more to the right leg. Clench the right hand and raise it in front, tucking the left hand into the right armpit. Look forward. (image 56d)

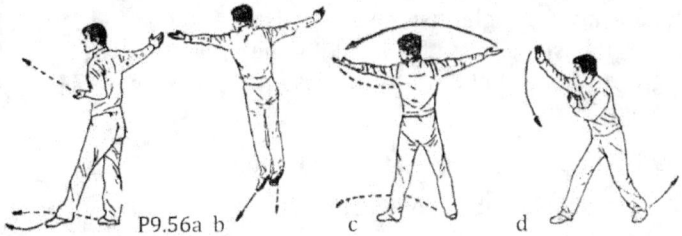

Lower the right hand. Look to the left. Swing the left leg up behind, swinging in a half-circle, pushing into the right leg to jump up and turning the waist around to the left to wheel around. Swing both arms up to aid the transfer of power into the jump. (images 56e, 56f) Jumping, land on the left foot and continue to swing the right leg up with an inside crescent kick. Slap the right foot with the left hand when they are in front of the face. (image 56g) After the slap, land the right foot in a circular path to the left. Extend the arms level in a straight line. Look down to the left. (image 56h)

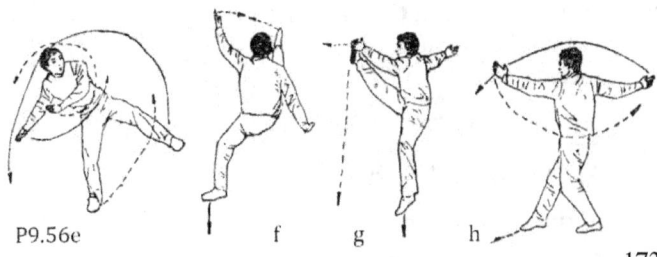

57. Horse Stance Chop   mǎbù pīzhǎng   马步劈掌

Shift the right foot forward and sit into a horse stance. Chop down in front with the right hand with a vertical palm. Scoop up in the rear with the left hand to level, also with a vertical palm. Look past the right hand. (image P9.57)

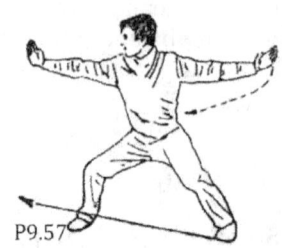

58. Bow Stance Thread The Hand   gōngbù chuānzhǎng   弓步穿掌

Turn slightly to the right and step the left foot forward to the right with the foot hooked in. Clench the right hand and laterally rotate it. Bring the left hand to the waist. Look in the direction of the right hand. (image P9.58a) Bend into the left leg to take a left bow stance. Thread the left hand out along on top of the right arm, palm up. Bring the right fist to the waist. After the stab, turn the head to the right to look behind, to the right. (image 58b)

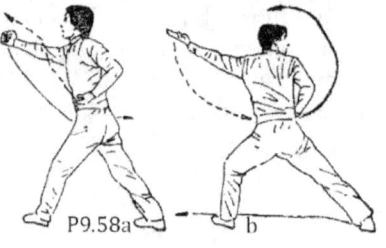

59. Wheel Over, Closed Stance Punch

fānshēn bīngbù chōngquán   翻身并步冲拳

Turn to the right and step the right foot past the left leg, withdrawing to the left. Clench the left hand and bring it to the waist. Circle the right fist to the right and up over the head towards the front. (image P9.59a) Turn the torso to the right, bring the right hand to the right and down to the waist. Unclench the left hand and circle it up and to the right to above and in front of the head in a sideways palm. Look forward, to the right. (image 59b) Step the left foot in beside the right foot and stand up. Press the left hand down in front of the right shoulder with a vertical palm. Bring the right fist to the left forearm then punch to the right side to shoulder height, fist eye up. Look past the right fist. (image 59c)

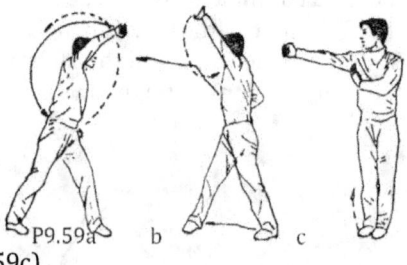

60. Stomp, Bow Stance Punch

zhēnjiǎo gōngbù chōngquán   震脚弓步冲拳

Lift the right foot straight up. (image P9.60a) Stomp with the right foot, half-

NINTH FORM PAOQUAN

squatting into both legs. Turn the head to the left. (image 60b) Step the left foot out to the left into a left bow stance. Clench the left hand, bring it to the waist, then punch out to the left at shoulder height, fist eye up. Look forward. (image 60c)

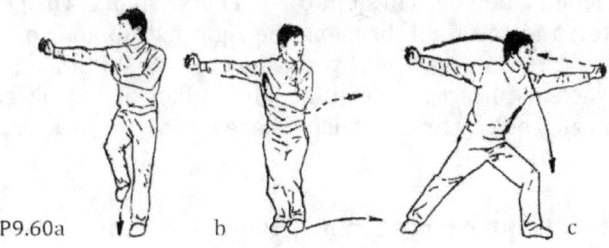

P9.60a   b   c

61. Bow Stance Low Hammerfist   gōngbù xià záquán   弓步下砸拳

Bend the left elbow to hook the fist up by the left ear, fist heart in. Bend the right elbow to bring the fist up, then past the right ear to do a hammerfist downwards to the front, in front of the left knee, arm slightly bent, fist heart up. Look at the right fist. (image P9.61)

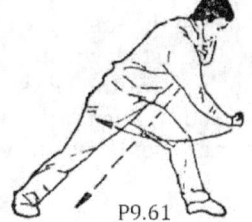

P9.61

62. Drop Stance Low Hammerfist   pūbù xià záquán   仆步下砸拳

Sit back into a left drop stance. Bring the right fist in to the waist. Bring the left fist across with the rightward turn of the waist to do a hammerfist down in front of the groin, about twenty centimeters off the ground, elbow bent with the fist heart up. Look at the left fist. (image P9.62)

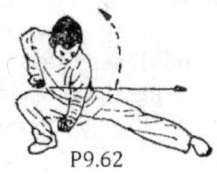

P9.62

63. Bow Stance Low Punch   gōngbù xià chōngquán   弓步下冲拳

Push into the right leg, extending it to turn into a left bow stance. Bring the left fist past the face to do a framing block above the head. Punch forward and down with the right hand to knee height. Look to the right. (image P9.63)

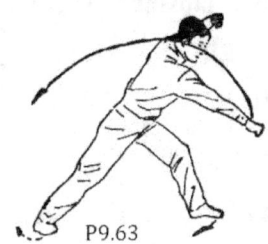

P9.63

64. Half Horse Stance Low Hammerfist

bànmǎbù xià záquán   半马步下砸拳

Shift back, turning the right foot out and the left foot in, bending both legs to sit into a half horse stance. Turn the torso to the right, bringing the right fist up and to the right to do a hammerfist downwards outside the right knee, fist heart up. Keep the left fist blocking above the head. Look by the right fist. (image P9.64)

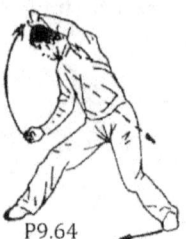
P9.64

65. Empty Stance Framing Block And Planting Punch

xūbù jià zāiquán   虚步架栽拳

Shift to the right and bring the left foot in a half-step, touching the toes down to take a left empty stance. Bring the left fist down in front of the face to do a planting punch above the left knee, fist eye in. Raise the right fist to do a framing block above the head, fist eye down. Both arms are bent. Look forward, to the left. (image P9.65)

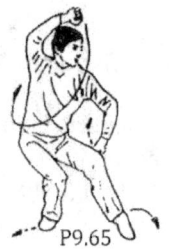
P9.65

66. Front Touch Stance Facing Fists   qiándiǎnbù duìquán   前点步对拳

Shift to the right, turning the right foot out and pushing the left heel to the left to turn. Unclench both hands. Lower the right hand, circling both hands at their respective sides to the hips, the arms naturally bent, palms forward. Look forward, to the left. (image P9.66a) Step the left foot a half-step to the forward left, touching the toes down and standing straight on both legs, turning the body slightly leftward. Clench both hands, medially rotate, and circle them forward to face each other in front of the belly, fist hearts down, about ten centimeters apart. Turn the head to the left. (image 66b)

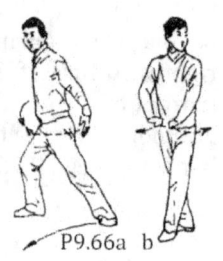
P9.66a b

67. Closing Posture   shōu shì   收势

Pause briefly, then move the left foot forward and bring the right foot up beside it. Unclench the hands and let them hang naturally at the sides. Turn the head straight. Look forward. (image P9.67)

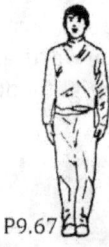
P9.67

FIRST FORM HONGQUAN
头路洪拳

Names Of The Movements

Position Of Preparation

Section One
1. Closed Stance Facing Fists
2. Empty Stance Press Down, Scooping Fist
3. Bow Stance Framing Block And Punch
4. Bow Stance Brush Aside, Press Down, Punch
5. Bow Stance Brush Aside, Press With Palm, Stab
6. Open Bow Stance Flash Palm
7. Bow Stance Brush Aside, Press Down, Stab
8. Horse Stance Stab
9. Resting Stance Press
10. Step Forward, Brush Aside, Press Down, Right Flying Slap Kick
11. Left Flying Slap Kick
12. Turn Back, Aerial Flying Slap Kick
13. Empty Stance Scooping Snap

Section Two
14. Step Forward, Aerial Flying Slap Kick
15. Bow Stance Framing Block And Punch
16. Bow Stance Brush Aside, Press With Palm, Stab
17. Horse Stance Stab
18. Turn Back, Bow Stance Palm Edge Strike
19. Empty Stance Hook And Press Down
20. Raised Knee Hook And Scoop

Section Three
21. Curving Steps Forearm Lift
22. Aerial Turn Back, Outside Crescent Kick
23. Empty Stance Scooping Snap

Section Four
24. Hitting Hop-Step, Tornado Kick
25. Horse Stance Chop
26. Stomp, Planting Punch
27. Bow Stance Brush Aside, Press With Palm, Stab
28. Horse Stance Stab
29. Resting Stance Press With Palm
30. Bow Stance Stab

31. Bow Stance Brush, Press, Punch
32. Bow Stance Cut And Punch
33. Raised Knee Stab
34. Drop Stance Forearm Lift
35. Aerial Arrow Kick
36. Back Insertion Stance Framing Block And Punch

Section Five
37. Bow Stance Brush Aside, Press, Punch
38. Turn Back, Bow Stance Hack
39. Drop Stance Forearm Lift
40. Bow Stance Roundhouse Punch
41. Stomp, Planting Punch
42. Bow Stance Brush Aside, Press With Palm, Stab
43. Horse Stance Stab
44. Resting Stance Hook, Press With Palm
45. Bow Stance Stab
46. Bow Stance Brush Aside, Press With Palm, Punch
47. Raised Knee Stab
48. Drop Stance Forearm Lift
49. Aerial Arrow Kick
50. Resting Stance Framing Block And Punch
51. Bow Stance Brush Aside, Press, Punch
52. Empty Stance Stab
53. Raised Knee Carry
54. Curving Walk, Closed Stance Carry

Section Six
55. Drop Stance Forearm Lift
56. Hitting Hop-Step, Guiding Hand, Tornado Kick
57. Horse Stance Chop
58. Bow Stance Brush Aside, Press With Palm, Stab
59. Turn Back, Bow Stance Slice Upwards
60. Tucked Leg Slice Upwards
61. Empty Stance Scooping Snap
62. Closing Posture

FIRST FORM HONGQUAN

0. **Position Of Preparation** yùbèi shì 预备势

Stand to attention. (image H1.0)

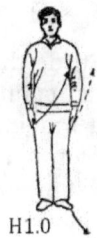

H1.0

Section One

1. **Closed Stance Facing Fists** bīngbù duìquán 并步对拳

Stride the left foot to the forward left, turning slightly leftward. Swing the arms forward to in front of the chest, palms up. Look at the hands. (image H1.1a) Stride the right foot to the forward right, turning slightly rightward. Swing the arms back in, slapping the backs of the hands on the outside of the thighs, then circling them behind and out. (image 1b) Bring the left foot in beside the right foot, to a closed stance. Continue to circle the arms forward and in, clenching fists in front of the belly. Medially rotate the arms and tuck the wrists, turning the fist eyes inward. The fists are about ten to fifteen centimeters apart. Snap the head to the left. Look forward, to the left. (image 1c)

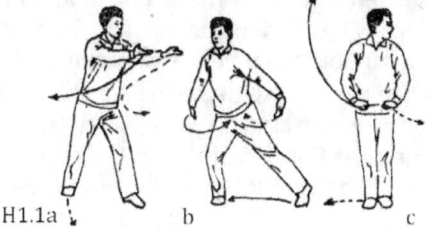

H1.1a b c

2. **Empty Stance Press Down, Scooping Fist**

xūbù ànzhǎng tiǎoquán 虚步按掌挑拳

Take a straddle step to the right with the right foot and shift to the right leg. Unclench the fists. Swing the right arm rightward and up with a straight arm to the upper right, turning the torso slightly rightward. Swing the left arm down at the left. Look at the right hand (image H1.2a) Turn the torso slightly leftward and squat deeply on the right leg into a left empty stance. Scoop up at the left with the left hand, clenching it with the fist eye up and the elbow slightly bent, fist just under jaw height. Swing the straight right arm up over the head and down to the left, stopping the hand in the left elbow crease. Turn the head sharply to the left. Look past the scooping fist. (image 2b)

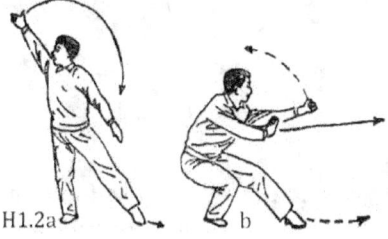

H1.2a b

179

3. Bow Stance Framing Block And Punch

gōngbù jià chōngquán 弓步架冲拳

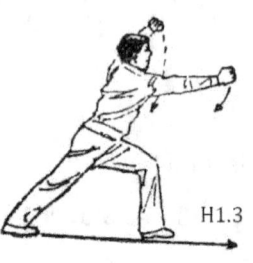

Stride the left foot forward and extend the right leg, taking a bow stance. Bend the left elbow to do a framing block above and in front of the head. Clench the right hand and quickly extend the elbow to punch forward with an upright fist to shoulder height, using the push of the right leg, the snap of the hips, the turn of the waist, and the extension of the shoulder. Look past the punch. (image H1.3)

4. Bow Stance Brush Aside, Press Down, Punch

gōngbù lōu yā chōngquán 弓步搂压冲拳

Step the right foot forward. Unclench the right hand and swing it down to the left. Unclench the left hand and lower it to stab under the right armpit. Look at the right hand. (image H1.4a) Press forward into the right leg, continuing to circle the right hand to the left and up to in front of the head, then clench it with the fist heart forward. Swing the left hand down in front, on the left side. Look forward. (image 4b) Step the left foot a big step forward. Continue to circle the right fist to the right and down in front of the belly, then circle in to tuck into the right armpit. Swing the left hand up, left, then in to in front of the head at the left, elbow bent to press down, fist heart in at eyebrow height. Look at the left elbow. (image 4c) Push into the right leg to take a left bow stance. Punch the right fist directly forward to shoulder height. Press down with the left elbow, then swing the arm at the side out to the rear until the fist is upright, fist eye up, at shoulder height. Look past the right fist. (image 4d)

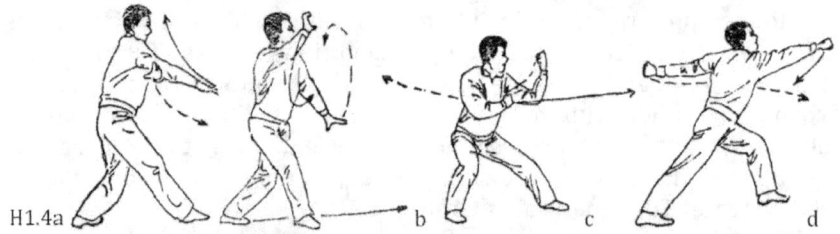

5. Bow Stance Brush Aside, Press With Palm, Stab

gōngbù lōu àn chāzhǎng 弓步搂按插掌

Unclench the right hand and swing it down to the left. Unclench the left hand and bend the elbow to bring the fist in front past the chest, then stab under the right arm. The arms are crossed, right palm down, left palm tight under the right elbow. Look at the right hand. (image H1.5a) Continue to circle the right hand to the left and up past the face to brush aside at the forward right, palm forward. Swing the left hand down past the belly to the lower front at the left, palm down. (image 5b) Continue to circle the right hand out, down, then in to beside the right ribs, bending the elbow and turning the palm up. Continue to swing the left hand out, up, then in to in front of the face. Look forward. (image 5c) Turn the left palm down, bend the elbow and press down in front of the chest. Medially rotate the right arm to turn the right hand palm in, fingers forward and up, stabbing it forward over the back of the left hand. The left hand is tight under the right elbow. Look at the right hand. (image 5d)

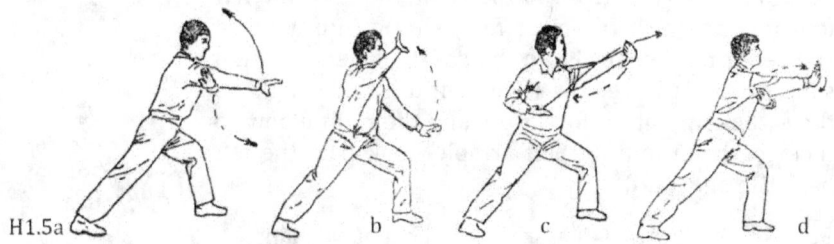

6. **Open Bow Stance Flash Palm**   héngdāngbù liàngzhǎng   横裆步亮掌

Laterally rotate the left arm to turn the fingers forward, palm in, and thread it forward over the right arm. Turn the right hand to a vertical palm and bring it in. Look at the left hand. (image H1.6a) Sit back, turning ninety degrees to the right, turning the right knee out and extending the left leg, turning the left toes in, to take an open bow stance. Continue to thread the left hand forward to full extension. Continue to bring the right hand down at the side to the right then circle up. When it arrives above the head, bend the elbow and snap the wrist with a flash palm. Simultaneous with the flash palm, snap the left hand to a vertical palm. Watch the right hand as it circles, then snap the head sharply to the left as the palm flashes. Look forward, to the left. (image 6b)

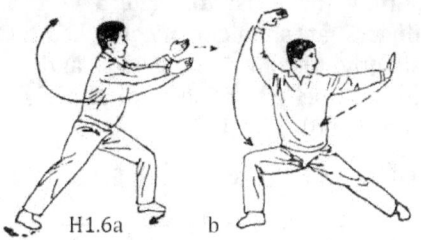

7. **Bow Stance Brush Aside, Press Down, Stab**

    gōngbù lōu yā chāzhǎng   弓步搂压插掌

Push into the right leg and shift to the left leg, raising the right knee and leaning the torso slightly to the right. Brush aside with the right hand rightward and down, palm down. Bend the left elbow and clench the fist to bring the fist to the waist. Look at the right hand. (image H1.7a) Take a long straddle step with the right foot to the right, bending the knee to a right bow stance. Stab the right hand up to the right to throat height, fingers forward. Look at the right hand. (image 7b)

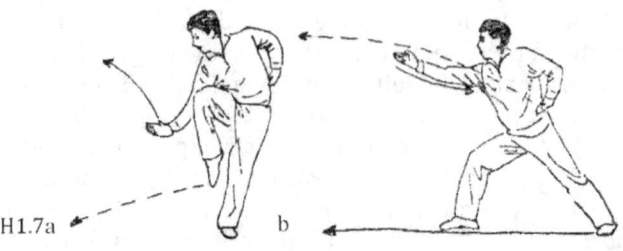

8. Horse Stance Stab   mǎbù chāzhǎng   马步插掌

Turn one-eighty degrees to the right and step the left foot forward past the right foot, sitting into a horse stance. Bring the left fist to the chest, unclench it, and slide it forward over the right arm to stab straight to throat height, fingers forward. Bend the right elbow to tuck the hand into the left armpit. Look past the left hand. (image H1.8)

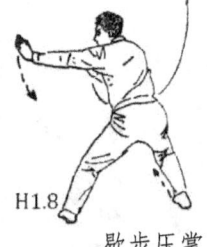

9. Resting Stance Press   xiēbù yāzhǎng   歇步压掌

Turn ninety degrees to the right and shift to stand up on the left leg, lifting the right leg up behind with the knee bent. Bring the right hand down past the belly then straighten the arm and scoop up to the right, palm in. Hook the left hand and lower it slightly. Look forward. (image H1.9a) Land the right leg behind the body, with the thighs crossed, squatting fully into a resting stance with the thighs pressed together. Continue to bend the right elbow and press down, setting the wrist to make a vertical palm, fingers at shoulder height. Lean forward slightly. Clench the left hand and bring the fist to the waist. Look at the right hand. (image 9b)

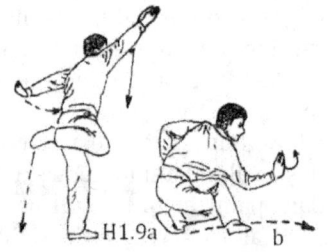

10. Step Forward, Brush Aside, Press Down, Right Flying Slap Kick
shàngbù lōu àn yòu fēijiǎo   上步搂按右飞脚

Step the right foot forward. Extend the right arm and swing it straight to the left, palm down. Unclench the left hand and bring it past the chest to stab under the right armpit. Look at the right hand. (image H1.10a) Step the left foot forward. Continue to circle the right hand up past the face, then to the right and down, brushing aside in front of the belly. Continue to swing the left hand down in past the belly to the left and up in front of the head. Look forward. (image 10b) Shift to the left leg and stand up on it, kicking the right leg up in front with a straight leg, ankle plantar-flexed, to chest height. Bend the left elbow and press down in front of the chest, then clench the fist and bring it to the waist. Bring the right hand up past the chest, out over the left hand, then extend it forward to slap the right foot. Look at the right hand. (image 10c)

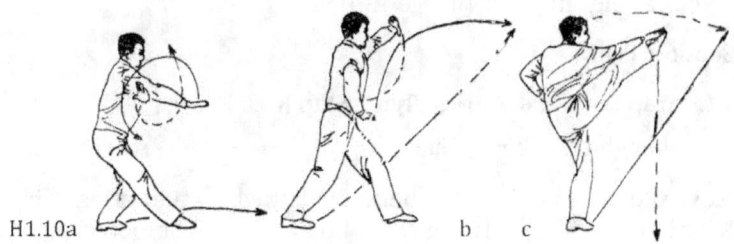

11. Left Flying Slap Kick   zuǒ fēijiǎo   左飞脚

Land the right foot and stand on it, then extend the left leg and do a straight kick forward with the ankle plantar-flexed. Unclench the left hand and extend it up and forward to slap the left foot. Clench the right hand and bend the elbow to bring the fist to the waist. Look at the left hand. (image H1.11)

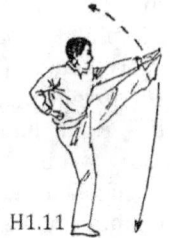

12. Turn Back, Aerial Flying Slap Kick

huíshēn téngkōng fēijiǎo   回身腾空飞脚

Bend the left knee then land with the foot turned in, turning around one-eighty degrees to the right. Raise the left arm. Look straight forward. (image H1.12a) As soon as the left foot lands, immediately push into it to jump, lifting the left bent knee up. Unclench the right hand and swing it forward and up. Lower the left hand slightly, to slap the back of the right hand in front of the head. (image 12b) Kick with the right foot, slapping it with the right hand. Extend the left arm up to the rear. Look forward. (image 12c)

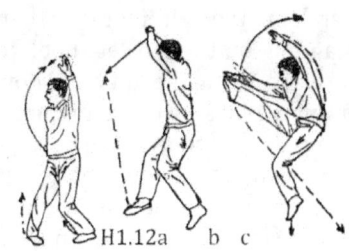

13. Empty Stance Scooping Snap   xūbù tiǎozhǎng   虚步挑掌

Land on the left foot, touching the ball of the foot down and bending the knee, then land the right foot behind the body, settling onto it and turning ninety degrees to the right. Swing the right arm up and back to the upper rear. Lower the left arm down to the lower left. Look at the right hand. (image H1.13a) Squat on the right leg into a left empty stance. Scoop up in front with the left hand,

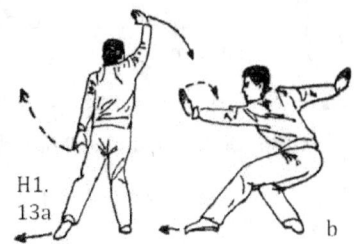

fingers at nose height. Lower the right hand to extend the arm level, fingers at head height. As you complete the scoop, sharply turn the head to the left to look at the left hand. (image 13b)

Section Two

14. Step Forward, Aerial Flying Slap Kick

shàngbù téngkōng fēijiǎo   上步腾空飞脚

Move the left foot forward. Bend the left elbow and bring it in and down. Look at the left hand. (image H1.14a) Step the right foot forward to the left. Circle the left hand down then forward to level. Look at the left hand. (image 14b) Bend the right knee as the foot lands, to immediately push off to jump. Swing the right hand down beside the body then up in front, slapping the back of the hand into the left palm in front of the head with a sharp sound. (image 14c) Do a right kick and slap the right hand on the foot whilst airborne. Swing the left arm up behind on the left. Look forward. (image 14d)

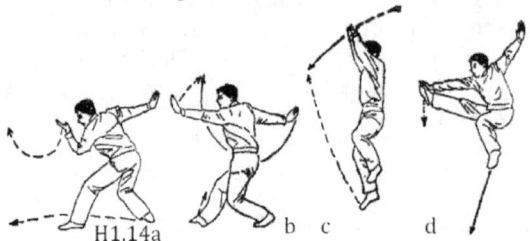

15. Bow Stance Framing Block And Punch

gōngbù jià chōngquán   弓步架冲拳

Land on the left foot and bend the knee slightly to absorb the shock, standing on the left leg. Look forward. (image H1.15a) Land the right foot forward. Bring the left hand down past the side, then bend the elbow to do a framing block forward and up. Clench the right hand and bend the elbow to bring the fist to the waist. Look at the left hand. (image 15b) Step the right foot forward another half-step and bend the knee to a right bow stance, turning ninety degrees to the left. Continue to do a framing block with the left hand, moving behind the head. Punch the right fist forward with an upright fist. Look past the right fist. (image 15c)

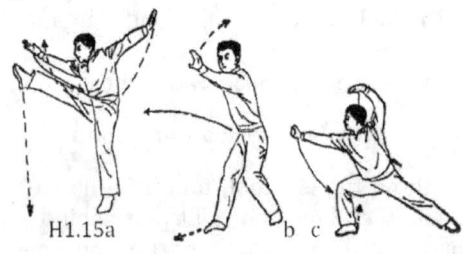

16. Bow Stance Brush Aside, Press With Palm, Stab

gōngbù lōu yā chāzhǎng   弓步搂压插掌

This is the same as move 7. (images H1.16a, 16b)

FIRST FORM HONGQUAN

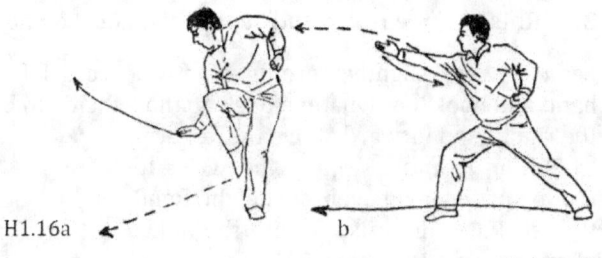

H1.16a   b

17. Horse Stance Stab mǎbù chāzhǎng 马步插掌

This is the same as move 8. (image H1.17)

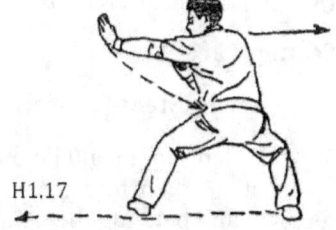

H1.17

18. Turn Back, Bow Stance Palm Edge Strike

huíshēn gōngbù jīzhǎng 回身弓步击掌

Turn ninety degrees to the right and withdraw the right foot, extending it and bending the left knee to take a left bow stance. Strike directly to the front with the right hand at eyebrow height, palm edge forward. Clench the left hand and bring it to the waist. Look at the right hand. (image H1.18)

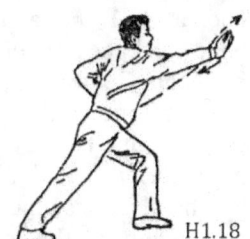

H1.18

19. Empty Stance Hook And Press Down

xūbù gōushǒu ànzhǎng 虚步勾手按掌

Unclench the left hand and extend it forward out above the right arm, holding it level, turning the torso ninety degrees rightward. (image H1.19a) Circle the right hand down, past the body, to the rear to level. Shift to the right leg and bend the knee for a transitional bow stance. Look at the right hand (image 19b) Sit on the right leg to take a left empty stance. Hook the left hand, bending the wrist. Turn ninety degrees leftward. Continue to circle the right arm up and over the head, and then down at the left, to press down at the left elbow crease. Look forward. (image 19c)

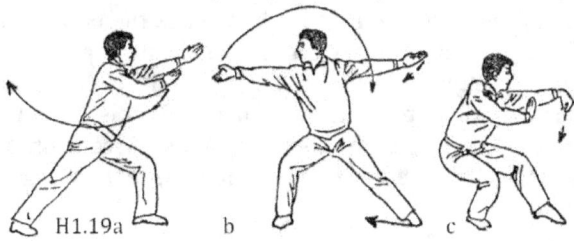

H1.19a   b   c

20. Raised Knee Hook And Scoop   tíxī gōushǒu tiǎozhǎng   提膝勾手挑掌

Lean forward slightly, turning ninety degrees leftward. Unhook the left hand and hook it down, then back on the left side to hold it out level. Extend the right hand forward above the left arm, extending it and snapping the wrist to scoop up, fingers at eyebrow height. Bend the left knee and raise it with the ankle plantar-flexed, the shin tucked in. Extend the right leg and stand up. Look at the right hand. (images H1.20a, 20b)

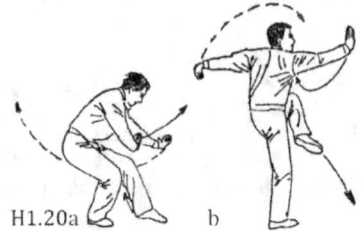

Section Three

21. Curving Steps Forearm Lift   húxíngbù chāozhǎng   弧形步抄掌

Turn the left foot in and land forward, to the left. Unhook the left hand and swing it up then forward to in front of the head, medially rotating the forearm and bending the elbow. Lower the right hand and bend the elbow to bring the hand to the belly. (image H1.21a) Step the right foot forward, turned out. Continue to swing the left hand down, bending the elbow. Thread the right hand up past the chest then cross it with the left forearm. Look at the right hand. (image 21b) As soon as the right foot touches down, bend the knee and jump up with a hop-step. Bend the left knee and lift it in front, to jump forward and up. Continue to lift with the right hand forward and up. Hook the left hand and swing the straight arm down at the side, to raise behind. Turn the head to the left to look to the left. (image 21c)

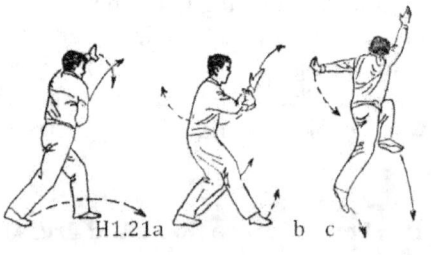

22. Aerial Turn Back, Outside Crescent Kick

   téngkōng huíshēn wàibǎilián   腾空回身外摆莲

As soon as the right foot lands, land on the left foot in front, hooked in, then step the right foot forward, turned out. (images H1.22a, 22b) Quickly push into the ground to jump up, turning around two-seventy degrees to the right. Unhook the left hand and swing it down, then up the side to the front. Continue to swing the right hand back then down at the side to swing up in front, slapping the back of the hand into the left palm in front of the head. (image 22c) Lash with both hands to the right and down, swinging the right leg up and out to the right with a straight leg, to do an outside crescent kick, hitting the left, then the right palms in front of the head with a slapping sound. Bend the left knee, bringing in and lifting it. Look forward. (image 22d)

FIRST FORM HONGQUAN

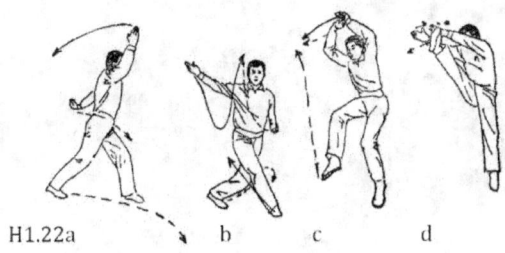

H1.22a   b   c   d

23. Empty Stance Scooping Snap   xūbù tiǎozhǎng   虚步挑掌

As the left foot lands, bend the knee to absorb the shock and continue to swing the right leg to the outside, to land it to the rear at the right. Then shift to the right leg, turning ninety degrees to the right. Lash the right arm up towards the back. Lash the left arm down to the left side. Look at the right hand. (images H1.23a, 23b) Bend the right knee to sit into a left empty stance. Lift the left straight arm up so the fingers are at eyebrow height, then snap the left wrist. Continue to lower the right arm to hold it level at the right side. As the left hand snaps, turn the head quickly to the left. Look past the left hand. (image 23c)

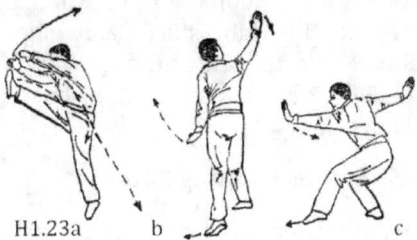

H1.23a   b   c

Section Four

24. Hitting Hop-Step, Tornado Kick   jībù xuànfēngjiǎo   击步旋风脚

Move the left foot forward, bending the left elbow and bringing it in. Push off with the right foot to jump forward, bumping the left heel with the instep of the right foot whilst airborne. (images H1.24a, 24b) When the right foot hits the ground, swing the left foot forward and extend the left hand directly forward. Look at the left hand. (image 24c) Land with the left foot turned out, turning ninety degrees leftward. Bend the right elbow and bring it to the ribs, then thread the hand forward over the left arm, bending the left elbow to bring the hand in. The arms are crossed. Look at the right hand. (image 24d) Step the right foot forward, turning ninety degrees leftward, continuing to thread the right hand forward, and bringing the left hand to tuck into the right armpit. (image 24e) Hook the right foot in then immediately push off strongly to jump up. Swing the arms down, past the belly to the rear left, then up, turning the head and waist to the left, so that the body spins a full two-seventy degrees around to the left. Bend the left knee, or swing the leg straight, up and out. After the right foot pushes off, swing the straight leg up and inwards with a quick closing kick, slapping the sole of the right foot with the left palm in front of the face. Look straight ahead. (image 24f)

CHAQUAN, VOLUME II

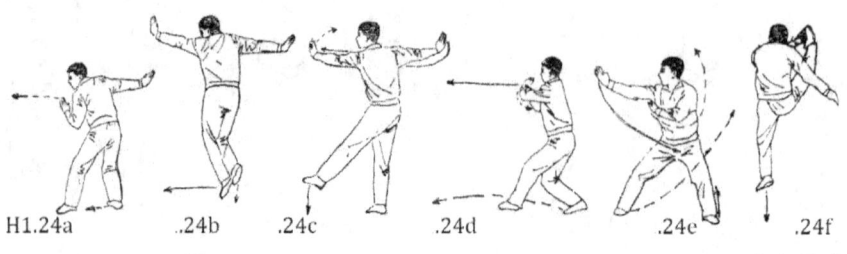

H1.24a   .24b   .24c   .24d   .24e   .24f

25. Horse Stance Chop   mǎbù pīzhǎng   马步劈掌

Land on the left foot first and bend the knee to absorb the impact. Lower the left arm and swing the right arm up behind. Look forward. (image H1.25a) Turn ninety degrees to the right and land the right foot into a horse stance. Chop the right arm out level to the right side, palm edge down. Hold the left arm out level to the left side. Look at the right hand. (image 25b)

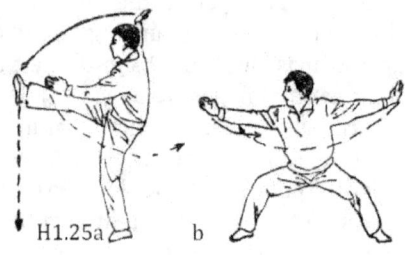

26. Stomp, Planting Punch   zhēnjiǎo zāiquán   震脚栽拳

Swing the left hand down past the belly to under the right arm, then slide the back of the hand tight outside the right arm to the front, extending it slightly. Laterally rotate the right arm and bend the elbow to bring the hand in. Look at the left hand. (image H1.26a) Clench the right fist and lower it past the ribs, then lift it at the rear right. Brush aside with the left hand past the belly. Look at the right fist. (image 26b) Stomp the right foot beside the left foot, hitting firmly with the whole foot, and squat to a closed stance. Bend the right elbow and medially rotate the fist to punch down past the belly, extending the elbow with a planting punch, knuckles down. Look at the right fist. (image 26c)

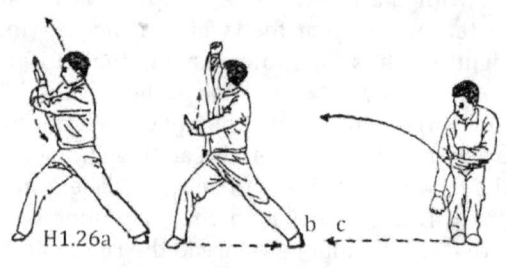

27. Bow Stance Brush Aside, Press With Palm, Stab

gōngbù lōu yā chāzhǎng   弓步搂压插掌

Straddle step the right foot a long step to the right into a right bow stance. Unclench the right hand and bring the hand in, up, and past the belly to chop levelly out to the right side. Look at the right hand. (image H1.27a) Continue on the same as move 7. (images 27b, 27c)

FIRST FORM HONGQUAN

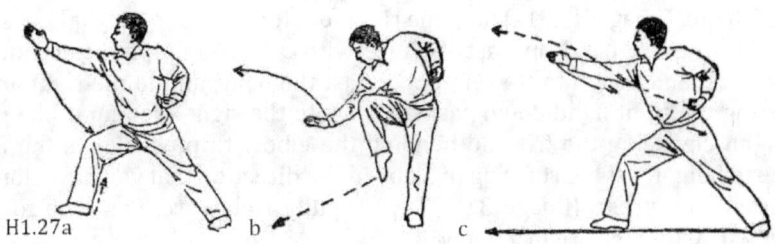

H1.27a   b   c

28. Horse Stance Stab   mǎbù chāzhǎng   马步插掌

This is the same as move 8. (image H1.28)

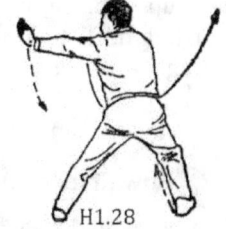

29. Resting Stance Press With Palm   xiēbù yāzhǎng   歇步压掌

This is essentially the same as move 9, except that in the resting stance the left arm is held behind in a reverse hook. (images H1.29a, 29b)

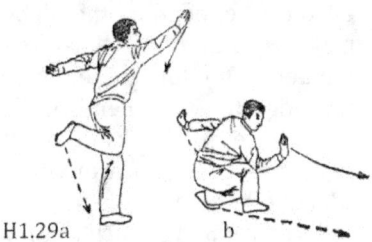

30. Bow Stance Stab   gōngbù chāzhǎng   弓步插掌

Take a long step forward with the right foot and set into a right bow stance. Laterally rotate the right hand to turn the palm up and stab levelly forward, to the right, to throat height. Look at the right hand. (image H1.30)

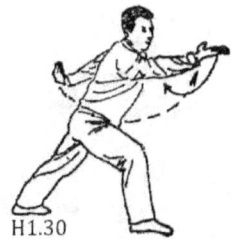

31. Bow Stance Brush Aside, Press, Punch

gōngbù lōu yā chōngquán   弓步搂压冲拳

Step the left foot forward, to the right. Unhook the left hand and swing it forward over the right arm, palm down. Medially rotate the right arm and bend the elbow to bring the hand in. The forearms are crossed. Look at the left hand. (image H1.31a) Step the right foot forward into a right bow stance. Bring the left hand up past the face with a brushing grab, clenching the hand, then circle it to the left, down past the belly, and to the right armpit. Bring the right hand down past the belly to the right, then up to the upper right, clenching the fist and bending the elbow to press down, the fist at head height, fist heart facing in. Look in the direction that you have done the brush and press. (image 31b) Turn slightly rightward. Continue to press down with the right elbow, bringing the fist down at the side, then swing the straight arm up to place the fist levelly out behind. Punch the left fist straight to the left with an upright fist. Look past the left fist. (image 31c)

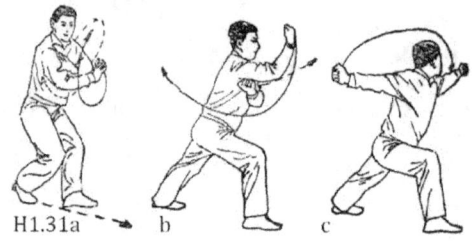

32. Bow Stance Cut And Punch

gōngbù qiēzhǎng chōngquán　　　　　　　　弓步切掌冲拳

Unclench the right hand and swing it up and over to the front, then down past the face, bending the elbow to press down at the left elbow crease. (image H1.32a) Turn the torso slightly leftward to send out the right shoulder, extending the elbow, to cut out over the left arm, palm down, palm edge forward. Bend the left elbow to bring the fist in, tucking the elbow to the ribs. Look at the right hand. (image 32b) Punch the left fist out levelly over the right arm with an upright fist. Bring the right hand in to under the left elbow. (image 32c) Do another cutting strike with the right hand. (image 32d) Punch again with the left fist. (image 32e) Do a framing block up at the right with the right hand. Bend the left elbow to bring the left fist in as the right hand blocks, then do another level punch. Look past the left fist. (image 32f)

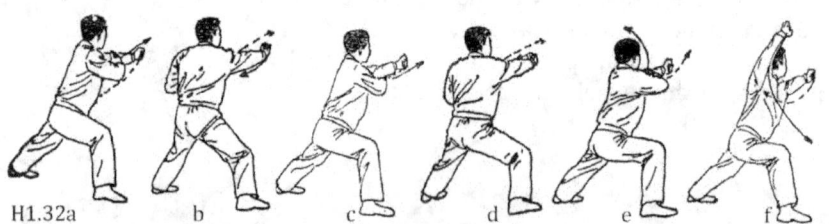

33. Raised Knee Stab　　　　　tíxī chāzhǎng　　　　　　提膝插掌

Swing the right hand out, then down past the belly. Unclench the left hand, bend the elbow, and bring the hand past the chest to stab under the right armpit. Look at the right hand. (image H1.33a) Turn the torso ninety degrees to the right. Circle the right hand to the left, then up in front of the head to do a circling brush aside, then bend the elbow to bring the hand to the waist. Lower the left hand past the belly to the left, then up, swinging up in front of the head. Look at the left hand. (image 33b) Turn the torso ninety degrees to the left. Turn the right palm up and thread it out over the back of the left hand to the upper right, to head height. Press down with the left hand, then tuck the hand into the right armpit. Shift to the right leg, extend the knee to stand up, and raise the bent left knee. Look at the right stabbing palm. (image 33c)

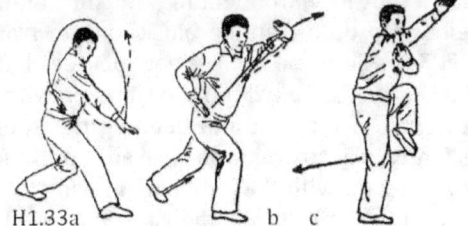

34. Drop Stance Forearm Lift   pūbù chāozhǎng   仆步抄掌

Bend the right knee and squat fully, extending the left leg out to the side, tucking in the foot. Medially rotate the left hand to turn the palm edge down. Turn the head to the left and look left. (image H1.34a) Slide the left hand past the belly and along the inside of the thigh, fingers forward, back of hand on the leg, to thread out to the forward left. Lean forward slightly, push into the right leg and press the left knee forward, shifting forward and standing up. Let the right hand drop to level. Look at the left hand. (image 34b)

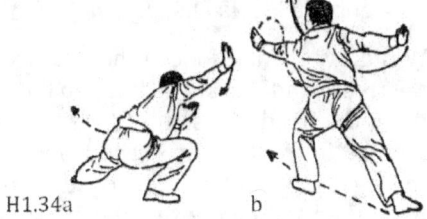

35. Aerial Arrow Kick   téngkōng jiàntán   腾空箭弹

Step the right foot forward and turn ninety degrees to the left. Scoop up with the left hand, then bend the elbow to bring the hand to the waist. Drop the right hand, bring it past at the side to scoop up in front to head height. Look at the right hand. (image H1.35a) Bend the right knee as the foot touches down, to jump up immediately, swinging the left knee up. Lift the right leg, first bending the knee then quickly extending it to snap out level. Strike the left hand straight forward. Clench the right hand and bend the elbow to bring the fist to the waist. Look past the kick. (images 35b, 35c)

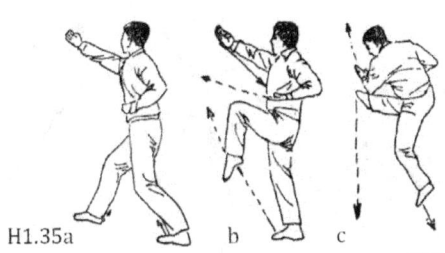

36. Back Insertion Stance Framing Block And Punch

chābù jià chōngquán　　　　　　　　　　插步架冲拳

Land on the left foot, bending the knee to absorb the shock, then step the right foot forward, bending the knee and turning in the foot. Bend the left elbow to do a framing block high in front of head. Look straight. (image H1.36a) Turn the torso ninety degrees leftward and step the left foot to the right side, going behind the right leg with an insertion step, touching down the ball of the foot and bending the knee slightly. The thighs are crossed. Continue to block up with the left hand, moving it to the upper left. Punch the right fist levelly to the right side with an upright fist. Turn the head right and look past the punch. (image 36b)

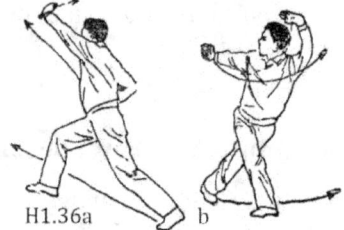

Section Five

37. Bow Stance Brush Aside, Press, Punch

gōngbù lōu yā chōngquán　　　　　　　　弓步搂压冲拳

Withdraw the left foot to the forward left with an outward turn. Unclench the right hand and swing it flat to the left, palm down. Bend the left elbow to bring the hand across the chest to stab under the right arm. The arms are crossed in front of the chest. Look at the right hand. (image H1.37a) Step the right foot to the left, hooked in, turning one-eighty degrees to the left. Bend the right elbow slightly and swing the hand to the upper left in front of the head, taking a spiraling line. Extend the left elbow and swing the hand forward and left in front of the chest. (image 37b) Continue to turn a further one-eighty degrees to the left. Swing the right hand to the left and back behind the head. Lower the left hand slightly. Look flat. (image 37c) Take a small straddling step with the left foot to the left. Continue to swing the right hand down, left, then across in front of the belly to clench a fist under the left armpit. Swing the left hand left and up to above the head at the left, then clench it and bend the elbow to press down. Look at the elbow. (image 37d) Press down a bit more with the left elbow, then bring the fist by the side to the rear, holding a flat fist to the side. Turn the torso ninety degrees to the left to take a left bow stance. Punch the right fist to the right side with a flat fist. Look past the right fist. (image 37e)

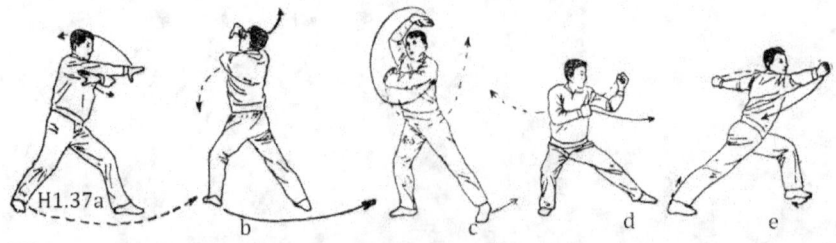

FIRST FORM HONGQUAN

38. Turn Back, Bow Stance Hack

huíshēn gōngbù kǎnzhǎng　　　　　　回身弓步砍掌

Lift the left heel to swivel on the ball of the foot, turning one-eighty degrees around to the right. Raise the bent right knee. Bring the right fist to the waist. Unclench the left hand and chop flat across to throat height. Look at the left hand. (image H1.38a) Bend the left knee and withdraw the right foot, pushing it straight into a left bow stance. (image 38b)

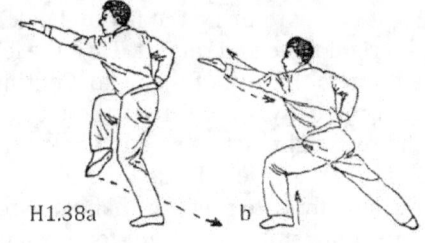

39. Drop Stance Forearm Lift　　pūbù chāozhǎng　　仆步抄掌

Push into the left foot, bending the knee and lifting it, shifting to the right leg and standing straight up on it, turning one-eighty degrees rightward. Flip over the left palm to palm down and bring it in. Turn the right palm up and bring it past the chest, passing over the back of the left palm and stabbing out to the upper left. Lean the torso slightly to the right. Look at the right hand. (image H1.39a) Bend the right leg fully to squat and extend the left leg out to the left side, foot tucked in, in a left drop stance. Flip the left hand over so that the tiger's mouth is up and the fingers point up, bring it past the belly then along the inside of the left leg, extending it to thread forward. Lean the torso slightly to the left. Look at the left hand. (image 39b)

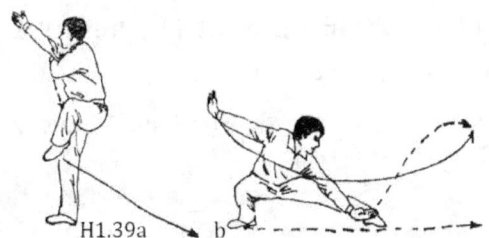

40. Bow Stance Roundhouse Punch　　gōngbù guànquán　　弓步贯拳

Push into the right foot and bend the left knee, shifting forward into a transitional left bow stance. Continue to thread the left hand forward and up, looking at the left hand. Then take a large step forward with the right foot into a right bow stance, turning the body ninety degrees to the left. Clench the right hand and tuck the wrist, medially rotating the arm and bending the elbow to lash across in front of the chest, punching with the knuckles into the left palm at throat height. Look at the right punch. (image H1.40)

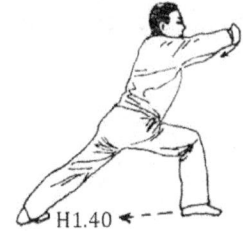

41. Stomp, Planting Punch   zhēnjiǎo zāiquán   震脚栽拳

Shift back to the left leg and bring in the right foot a half-step, touching down the ball of the foot. Bend the left elbow to stab the hand to under the right armpit, palm down. Then extend it to brush on the right arm. Bend the right elbow to bring the fist in. Look at the left hand. (image H1.41a) Bend the right knee and raise it. Turn the left palm to face out, and brush forward and up to in front of the head. Continue to bring the right fist down and in, past the belly, then extend the elbow and raise the arm straight to lash to the rear right, fist heart out. Look at the left hand. (image 41b) Turn ninety degrees to the left. Raise the right fist up to above the right shoulder. Bend the left elbow to press the hand down in front of the right knee. (image 41c) Forcefully stomp the right foot, placing the entire sole of the right foot on the ground beside the left foot, and fully bending both knees. Cock the right wrist and bend the elbow to bring the fist to the body, then extend the elbow to punch straight down outside the right thigh, knuckles down. Swing the left hand to tuck into the right armpit. Look at the right fist. (image 41d)

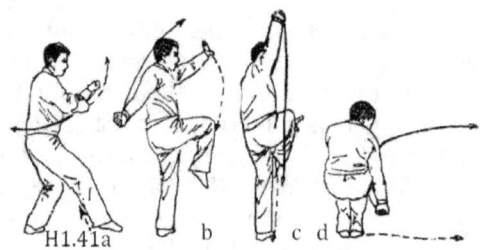

42. Bow Stance Brush Aside, Press With Palm, Stab

gōngbù lōu yā chāzhǎng   弓步搂压插掌

This is the same as moves 7 and 27, just in the opposite direction. (images H1.42a, 42b, 42c)

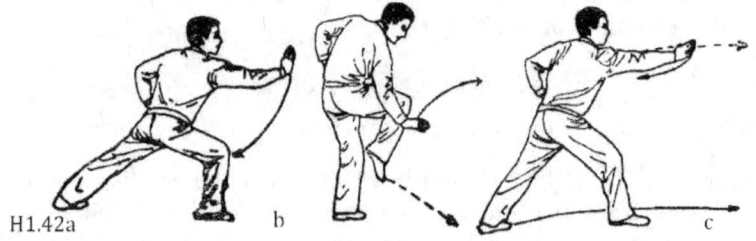

43. Horse Stance Stab   mǎbù chāzhǎng   马步插掌

This is the same as moves 8 and 28, just in the opposite direction. (image H1.43)

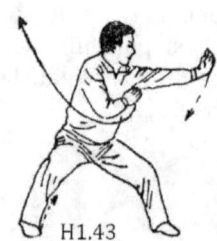

FIRST FORM HONGQUAN

44. Resting Stance Hook, Press With Palm

xiēbù gōushǒu yāzhǎng 歇步勾手压掌

This is similar to move 9 and the same as move 29, just in the opposite direction. (images H1.44a, 44b)

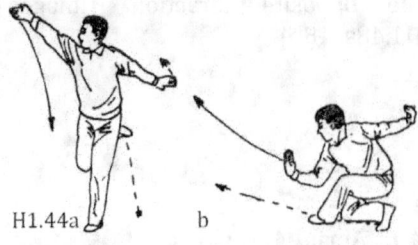

45. Bow Stance Stab   gōngbù chāzhǎng   弓步插掌

This is the same as move 30, just in the opposite direction. (image H1.45)

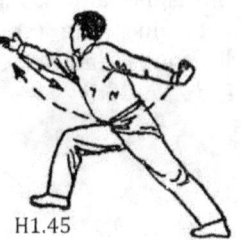

46. Bow Stance Brush Aside, Press With Palm, Punch

gōngbù lōu yā chōngquán 弓步搂压冲拳

This is the same as move 31, just in the opposite direction. (images H1.46a, 46b, 46c)

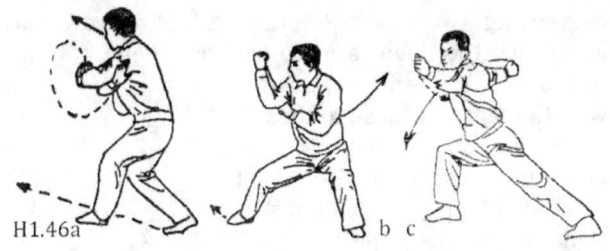

47. Raised Knee Stab   tíxī chāzhǎng   提膝插掌

This is the same as move 33, just in the opposite direction. (images H1.47a, 47b, 47c)

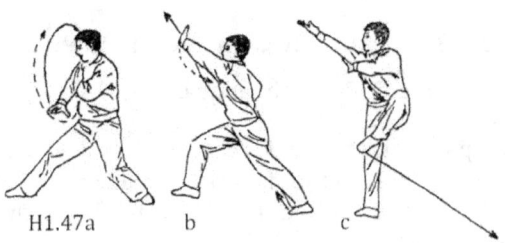

48. Drop Stance Forearm Lift   pūbù chāozhǎng   仆步抄掌

This is the same as move 34, just in the opposite direction. (images H1.48a, 48b)

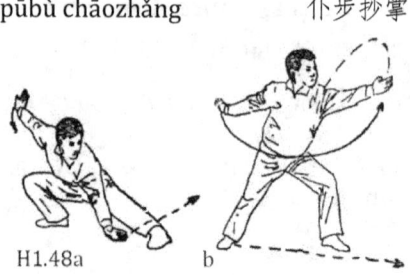

49. Aerial Arrow Kick   téngkōng jiàntán   腾空箭弹

This is the same as move 35, just in the opposite direction. (images H1.49a, 49b, 49c, 49d)

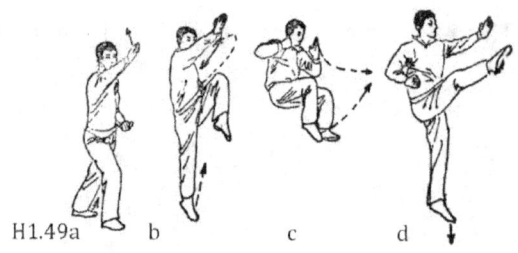

50. Resting Stance Framing Block And Punch

xiēbù jià chōngquán   歇步架冲拳

Land on the left foot, bending the knee to absorb the shock, then land the right foot, hooking it in. Bend the left elbow to block upwards in front of the head. Look straight forward. (images H1.50a, 50b) Turn the torso ninety degrees rightward and step the left foot forward, passing behind the right leg so that the thighs are crossed, then bend both knees to squat with the thighs one above the other, sitting with the buttocks close to the rear lower leg, in a resting stance. Continue to block up with the left hand at the upper left. Punch the right fist level to the right side with an upright fist. Turn the head right and look past the punching fist. (image 50c)

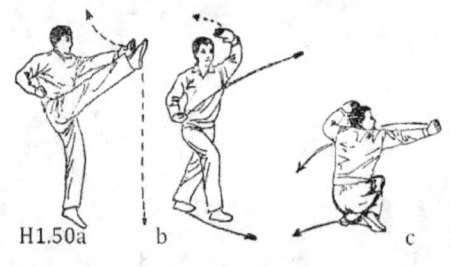

51. Bow Stance Brush Aside, Press, Punch

gōngbù lōu yā chōngquán   弓步搂压冲拳

Step the left foot forward, to the left side. Stand up and turn ninety degrees to the left. Turn the right fist flat, unclench it, and swing the arm across low to the left. Bend the left elbow and bring the hand in, palm down, to stab past the chest to under the right armpit. Look at the right hand. (image H1.51a) Step the right foot forward, to the left side. Continue to swing the right hand to the left and up, with the palm forward, to brush aside in front of the head. Extend the left elbow to bring the hand down past the belly towards the lower left. Look forward. (image 51b) Take a long step forward, to the left side, with the left foot. Clench the right fist and continue to circle to the right, then down to tuck into the left armpit. Continue to swing the left hand up and forward on the left. When it arrives high in front on the left, clench the fist and bend the elbow to press down. Look at the elbow. (image 51c) Turn the torso a further ninety degrees left. Continue to press down with the left elbow, keeping the fist tight to the side, then swing it down to the rear until it is extended on line with the leg with a flat fist. Punch forward with the right fist with an upright fist. Look past the punching fist. (image 51d)

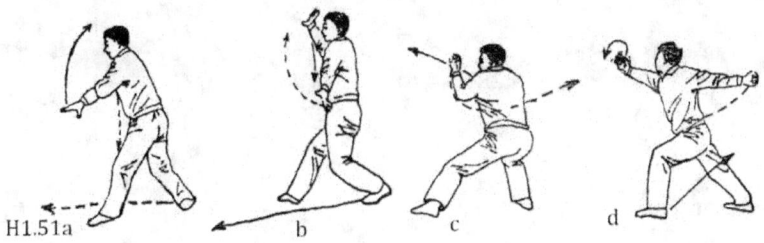

52. Empty Stance Stab　　　　xūbù chāzhǎng　　　　虚步插掌

Push into the left foot, bending the knee and lifting it, tucking the foot tight behind the right knee while shifting to the right leg and bending the right knee. Unclench the right hand and tuck it in, medially rotating the arm and bending the elbow. Unclench the left hand and bend the elbow to stab in by the belly. Look at the right hand. (image H1.52a) Turn the torso ninety degrees rightward and sit deeply into the right leg in a left empty stance. Stab the left hand forward over the back of the right hand to throat height. Press down with the right hand and bend the elbow to bring the hand to the waist. Look at the left hand. (image 52b)

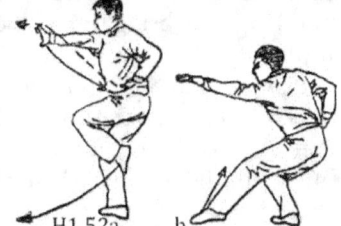

53. Raised Knee Carry

　　tíxī tuōzhǎng　　　　　　　　　提膝托掌

Stand up on the right leg, bending and raising the left knee to at least belly height, the foot tight to the lower leg and tucked in. Lift up with a carrying action with the left hand. Look at the left hand. (image H1.53)

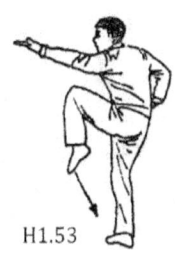

54. Curving Walk, Closed Stance Carry

húxíngbù bīngbù tuōzhǎng   弧形步并步托掌

Bend the right knee to a half-squat and turn in the left foot, landing it inwards. (image H1.54a) Turn the right foot out to step forward with an outwards swinging action. (image 54b) Step again, left and right, in a similar way. (images 54c, 54d) Keep the torso upright whilst walking, keeping the knees slightly bent. When stepping each foot, land on the heel first, then gradually settle the whole foot. Look at the left hand. When the left foot arrives at the fifth step, straighten the left knee and bring the right foot in beside the left foot in a closed stance. (images 54e, 54f)

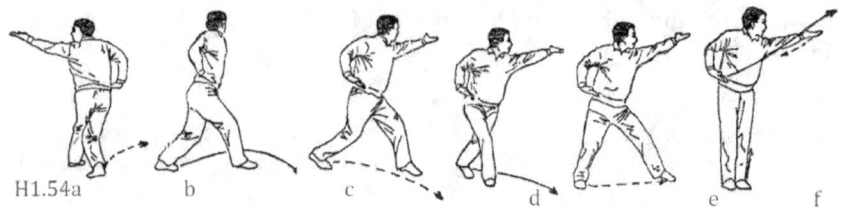

Section Six

55. Drop Stance Forearm Lift   pūbù chāozhǎng   仆步抄掌

Medially rotate the left arm, turning the palm in and tucking it, palm down. Turn one-eighty degrees to the left. Thread the right hand up past the chest and above the back of the left hand to head height at the left. Lean slightly to the right. Bend and raise the left knee. Look at the right hand. (image H1.55a) Bend the right knee to a full squat and extend the left foot out to the left side in a drop stance. Flip the left hand over, turning the tiger's mouth up, and bring it past the belly, sliding the back of the hand along the inside of the left leg to the left, stabbing forward quickly. Lean to the left. Medially rotate the right hand to turn the tiger's mouth up. Turn the head quickly to the left. Look at the left lifting hand. (image 55b) Extend the right knee and bend the left knee to take a bow stance. Extend both arms out to either side. Look forward, to the left side. (image 55c)

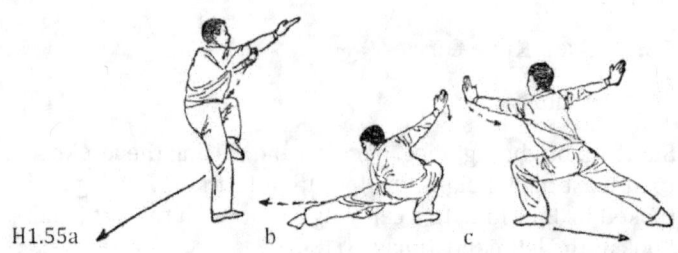

56. Hitting Hop-Step, Guiding Hand, Tornado Kick

jībù yǐnshǒu xuànfēngjǎio　　　　　击步引手旋风脚

Bend the right knee and bring in the left foot. Bend the left elbow and circle the hand in. Look at the left hand. (image H1.56a)

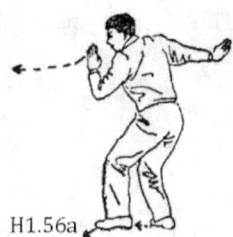

Move the left foot forward a bit and push into the right foot to jump, bumping the inside of the right foot into the left heel whilst airborne, so that the body leaps forward. Extend the left elbow to push straight forward. Look at the left hand. (image 56b) Land firmly on the right foot and swing the left foot, kicking up and forward. (image 56c) Land on the left foot and step the right foot forward, tucking it in, turning around one-eighty degrees to the left. Bend the right elbow and tuck it in, to bring the hand to the waist, then extend it forward to the right side, passing over the left arm. Continue to bend the left elbow to bring the hand in. Look at the right hand. (image 56d) Quickly and forcefully push into the right foot to jump up. Swing both arms down past the belly on the left side to swing up with force, turning the waist and head to the left, so that the body spins a full two-seventy degrees leftward. Swing the left leg up and back, keeping the knee bent or straight. After the right foot has pushed off, swing it up with a straight leg to do an inside crescent kick. Slap the right foot with the left hand in front of the face. Look level. (images 56e, 56f)

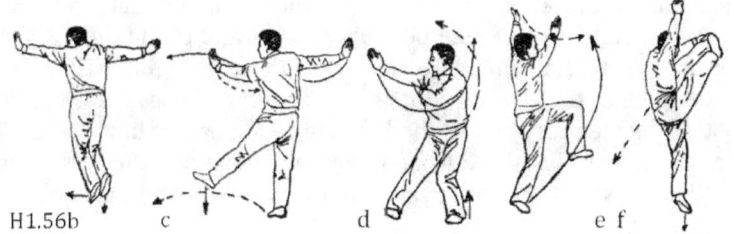

57. Horse Stance Chop　　　　　mǎbù pīzhǎng　　　　　马步劈掌

This is the same as move 25. (image H1.57a, 57b)

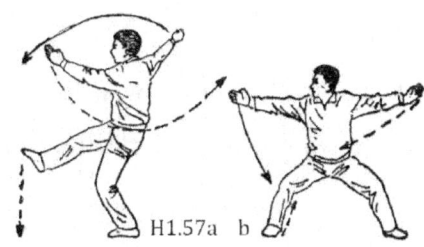

58. Bow Stance Brush Aside, Press With Palm, Stab

gōngbù lōu yā chāzhǎng 弓步搂压插掌

This is the same as move 27. (image H1.58a, 58b)

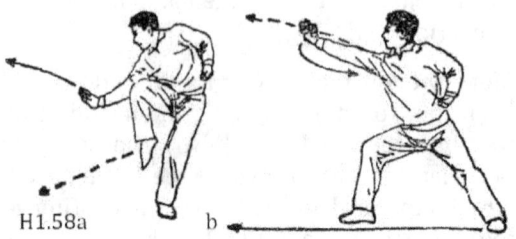

59. Turn Back, Bow Stance Slice Upwards

huíshēn gōngbù liāozhǎng 回身弓步撩掌

Step the left foot forward to the right side and turn around one-eighty degrees to the right. Unclench the left hand and turn the tiger's mouth up, palm in, and bring it past the chest then stab out to the left side above the right arm with a level palm. Medially rotate the right hand and bend the elbow to tuck the hand into the armpit, palm in. Look at the left hand. (image H1.59a) Do an insertion step with the right foot, passing behind the left foot to the left side. Turn the body around one-eighty degrees to the right, shifting onto the right leg and bending the right knee to a half-squat. Bend and lift the left knee with the foot tucked in tight behind the right knee. Swing the right arm as the body turns, down and to the right, then up, with a straight arm, finishing extended up to the rear right. Swing the left arm down outside the hip. Look at the right hand. (image 59b) Stride the left foot a long step forward to the left side to take a left bow stance. Lean the torso forward slightly. Slice forward and up with the left hand with a straight wrist. Lower the right arm a bit behind. Look past the left hand. (image 59c)

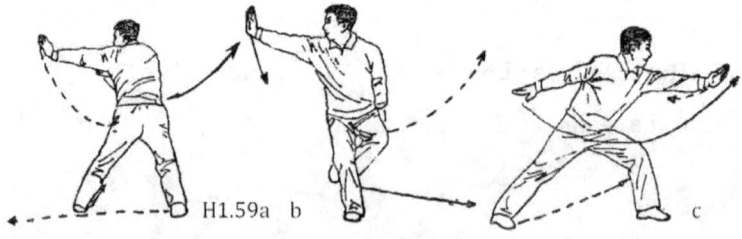

60. Tucked Leg Slice Upwards

kòutuǐ liāozhǎng 扣腿撩掌

Shift forward, bending the left leg and standing on it. Bend and lift the right knee to tuck the foot in behind the left knee. Turn the right palm in and slice it past the side and forward to level, cocking the wrist on arrival. Scoop up

FIRST FORM HONGQUAN

slightly with the left hand, then bend the elbow and bring the hand to the right ribs. Look at the right hand. (image H1.60)

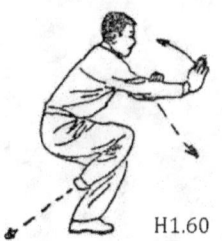

H1.60

61. Empty Stance Scooping Snap   xūbù tiǎozhǎng   虚步挑掌

Stand up and land the right foot behind, bending the knee to half-squat and touching the toes of the left foot down, turning the torso ninety-degrees to the right. Lower the left hand, keeping the arm straight. Bend the right elbow slightly and scoop up. Look at the left hand. (image H1.61a) Lean forward slightly and squat more fully into a left empty stance. Clench the left hand and bend the elbow slightly to scoop up to jaw height, fist eye up. Clench the right hand and bend the elbow to lower the fist to the left elbow. Look at the left fist. (image 61b)

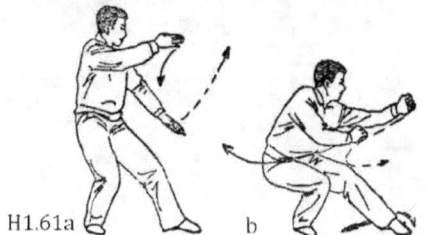

H1.61a

62. Closing Posture   shōu shì   收势

Turn ninety degrees to the right and withdraw the left foot to the rear left. Unclench the hands and bring them out to the sides, slapping the back of the hands on the outside of the thighs, then circling back and out. Look level. (image H1.62a) Bring the right foot in beside the left foot and stand with the feet together. Continue to circle the hands forward and in, clenching fists in front of the belly. Turn the head to look to the left. (image 62b) Then stand to attention. (image 62c)

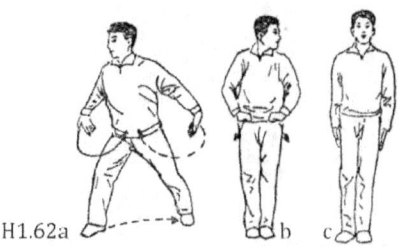

H1.62a   b   c

FOURTH FORM HONGQUAN

四路洪拳

Names Of The Movements

Position Of Preparation
Section One
1. Closed Stance Left Stab
2. Closed Stance Hack
3. Closed Stance Smear
4. Turn Around, Hack
5. Stomp, Snap Kick And Push
6. Jump To Bow Stance Punch To The Sides
7. Drop Stance Thread The Hand
8. Snap Kick And Push
9. Step Around, Bow Stance Punch To The Sides
10. Horse Stance Punch Upwards
11. Horse Stance Three Punches
12. Brush Aside, Bow Stance Fan The Hand
13. Driving Hop-Step, Arrow Kick Framing Block
14. Bow Stance Brace To The Side
15. Retreat, Bow Stance Brace
16. Drop Stance Thread The Hand, Arrow Kick
17. Closed Stance Framing Block And Punch

Section Two
18. Turn Around, Closed Stance Framing Block And Punch
19. Turn Back, Closed Stance, Squat, Hook And Stab
20. Turn Back, Closed Stance, Squat, Hook And Stab
21. Right Bow Stance Press Down And Stab
22. Angled Slap Kick
23. Left Bow Stance Punch
24. Drop Stance Thread The Hand
25. Step Forward, Three Reaching Hands
26. Slap Kick, Empty Stance Vertical Palm
27. Left Sweep Kick
28. Bow Stance Framing Block And Punch
29. Turn Around, Empty Stance Hook

Section Three
30. Raised Knee Scooping Snap
31. Jump To Insertion Step Stab

32. Turn Around, Bow Stance Double Lashes
33. Retreat, Three Fanning Hands
34. Raised Knee Scooping Snap
35. Walking Outside Crescent Kick
36. Closed Stance Chop
37. Double Flying Swallows
38. Horse Stance Double Chops
39. Bow Stance Scoop And Hook
40. Snap Kick, Bow Stance Double Braces
41. Empty Stance Double Framing Blocks

Section Four

42. Turn Around, Horse Stance Punch Upwards
43. Turn Around, Horse Stance Elbow Butt
44. Bow Stance Cover And Stab
45. Snap Kick, Separate The Hands
46. Jumping Turn Around, Close Stance Stab
47. Snap Kick, Separate The Hands
48. Hitting Hop-Step Stab
49. Raised Knee Right Punch
50. Hitting Hop-Step Stab
51. Tornado Kick, Horse Stance Chop
52. Jump To Insertion Stance Stab
53. Turn Around, Closed Stance Lash

Section Five

54. Jump To Bow Stance Chop
55. Hook, Turn Around, Stab
56. Closed Stance Stab
57. Snap Kick, Separate The Hands

Section Six

58. Closed Stance Framing Block And Punch
59. Open Bow Stance Hook And Flash The Hand
60. Drop Stance Thread The Hand
61. Bow Stance Framing Block And Push
62. Horse Stance Hack
63. Jumping Straddle Step, Horse Stance Hack
64. Jumping Turn Around, Bow Stance Hack
65. Straddle Step Lash
66. Empty Stance Slice Upwards Hook
67. Empty Stance Scoop And Push
68. Closing Posture

FOURTH FORM HONGQUAN

0.   Position Of Preparation   yùbèi shì   预备势

Stand with the legs straight, and together, with the arms handing naturally. Look forward. (image H4.0a) Open the elbows a bit to the outside and clench the fists, turning the fist eyes to face in (tiger's mouths facing the hips). Look to the left. (image 0b) Step the left foot forward. Unclench the hands and stab forward, palms up, to eye height. Look at the palms. (image 0c) Step the right foot forward. Whisk both hands at the sides, slapping the back of the hands at belly height. Then bring the left foot up to stand at attention with the feet together and separate the hands to either side, to circle up to chest height (clenching with fist eyes facing) holding the fists at shoulder height with the arms straight. Look forward. (images 0d, 0e)

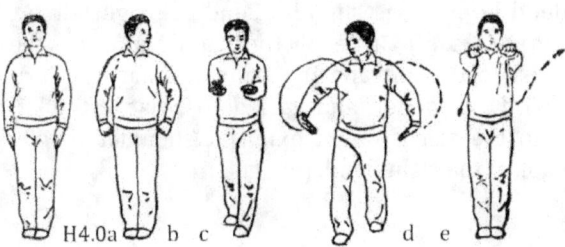

Section One

1.   Closed Stance Left Stab   bīngbù zuǒ chuānzhǎng   并步左穿掌

Gather the right fist at the waist. Unclench the left hand and stab out to the left, first passing by the waist. The arm is straight, at shoulder height, and the palm up. Look at the left hand. (image H4.1)

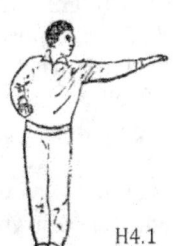

2.   Closed Stance Hack   bīngbù kǎnzhǎng   并步砍掌

Swing the left hand flat across to the right, turning the torso to the right. The palm still faces up, and the hand is still at shoulder height. Look at the left hand. (image H4.2)

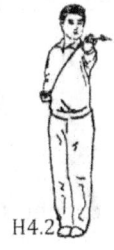

3.   Closed Stance Smear   bīngbù mōzhǎng   并步抹掌

Unclench the right hand and stab forward over the left palm, palm down, then turn the torso to the right and hack flat across to the right, so that the arm is extended out at the right side. Bend the left elbow and bring the hand to in front of the left side of the chest, palm up. Look at the right hand. (images H4.3a, 3b)

CHAQUAN, VOLUME II

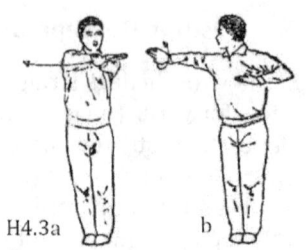

4. **Turn Around, Hack** zhuànshēn kǎnzhǎng 转身砍掌

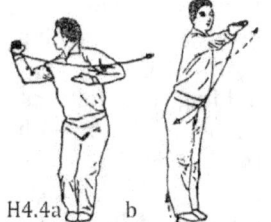

Bend both knees slightly. Bend the right elbow. (image H4.4a) Unclench the hand and circle the wrist to the left and up, palm turning up. Turn slightly to the left and hack across flat to the left with the arm straight, palm at shoulder height. Look at the right hand. (image 4b)

5. **Stomp, Snap Kick And Push** zhēnjiǎo tántuǐ tuīzhǎng 震脚弹腿推掌

Bend the right knee and lift it. Whisk the back of the right hand down on the right thigh. Push forward with the left hand with an upright palm. (image H4.5a) Stomp the right foot and lift the left foot. Hook the left hand and circle the right hand to the right, up, forward, then down, stopping in the left elbow crease. Look at the left hand. (image 5b) Do a snap kick with the left leg to waist height. Push forward with the right hand with an upright palm. Circle the left hook down, back, then up, holding the hook down. Look at the left foot. (image 5c)

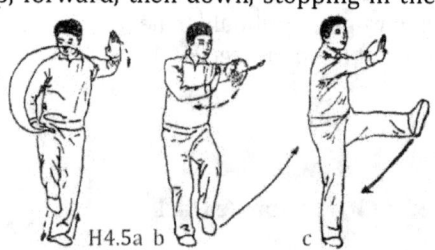

6. **Jump To Bow Stance Punch To The Sides**

   tiào gōngbù cè chōngquán 跳弓步侧冲拳

Bend the left knee to bring the foot back in. Bend the right elbow to bring the right hand in. Look at the right hand. (image H4.6a) Land the left foot in front and shift to the left leg. Stab the right hand forward, palm up. Step the right foot forward and shift to the right leg, lifting the left foot. Stab the left hand over the right. Look at the left hand. (images 6b, 6c) Push off the right foot to swing the left foot up in front, jumping forward. Separate the arms out to either side, raising them level. Land on the left foot, then land the right foot, into a right bow stance. Chop the right hand down in front, thumb up, elbow slightly bent. Bend the left elbow to tuck the hand into the right armpit, palm down. Look at the right hand. (images 6d, 6e)

FOURTH FORM HONGQUAN

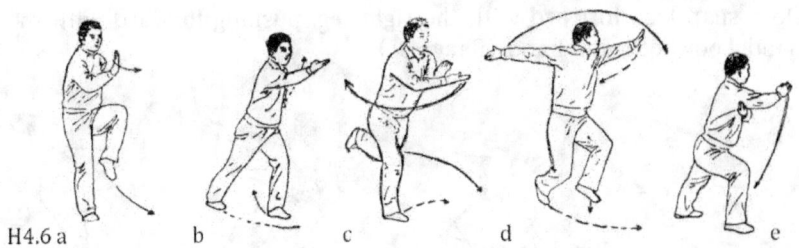

H4.6a　　b　　c　　d　　e

Lean forward slightly. Clench the right fist and bring it down, to the right, past in front of the right knee, then up to hold it level at the right side, turning the body rightward. Look at the right fist. (images 6f, 6g) Turn the torso to the left and bring the left fist to the left waist. (image 6h) Punch straight to the left side, fist eye up. Look at the left fist. (image 6i)

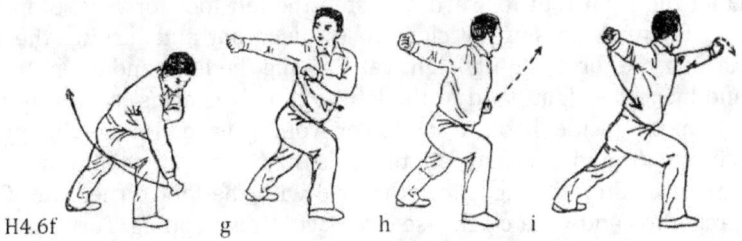

H4.6f　　g　　h　　i

7. Drop Stance Thread The Hand　　pūbù chuānzhǎng　　仆步穿掌

Turn the torso slightly rightward. Unclench the left hand and lower it to the right. Bring the right fist to the waist. (image H4.7a) Shift to the right leg and lift the left foot, turning the torso leftward. Unclench the right hand and stab it forward over the left hand, arm straight, hand at shoulder height. Look at the right hand. (image 7b) Land the left foot to the rear left, turning rightward and squatting completely on the right leg, into a left drop stance. Thread the left hand to inside of the thigh, palm upright. Look at the left hand. (image 7c and from behind)

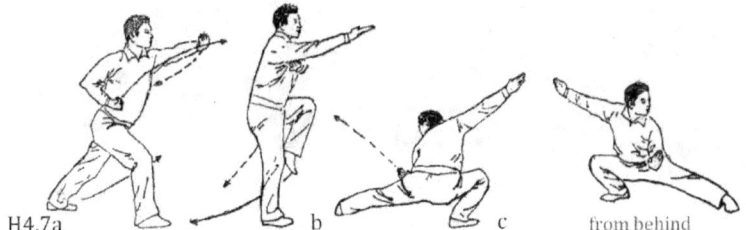

H4.7a　　b　　c　　from behind

8. Snap Kick And Push　　tántuǐ tuīzhǎng　　弹腿推掌

Shift to the left leg into a left bow stance, stabbing the left hand to the upper left. (image H4.8a) Bend the left elbow to make an upright palm. (image 8b)

207

Do a snap kick forward with the right leg, pushing forward with the left hand. Look at the left hand. (image 8c)

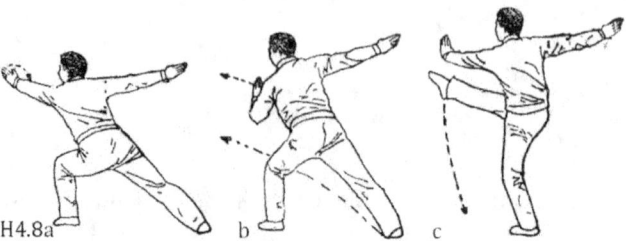

9. Step Around, Bow Stance Punch To The Sides
ráobù gōngbù cè chōngquán　　　　　　　　绕步弓步侧冲拳

Land the right foot forward and step the left foot forward. Step the right foot forward, passing by close to the left foot and turning the foot out, turning the torso slightly rightward. Swing the left hand down to the right and bring the right hand to the left, to cross the arms in front of the belly, left on the inside. Look to the lower front. (images H4.9a, 9b, 9c) Step the left foot around the right foot towards the right front, landing with the foot turned in. Step the right foot forward with the foot turned out. Gradually circle the hands in a clockwise circle with the stepping. Turn the right foot out more and turn the torso rightward. Bring the left hand up then chop down at the right. Bend the right elbow to tuck the hand into the left armpit. Look at the left hand. (images 9d, 9e, 9f) Step the left foot forward to the left and shift into a left bow stance, leaning the torso forward slightly. Clench the left hand and hook the arm down to the left, passing by in front of the left knee to raise out to level at the left side. (images 9g, 9h) Clench the right hand and bring the fist to the waist, then punch straight out to the right. Look at the right fist. (images 9i, 9j)

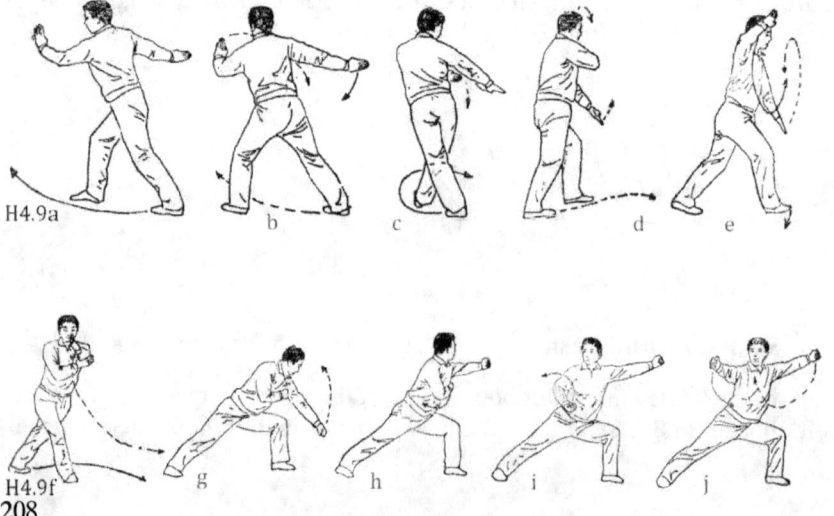

FOURTH FORM HONGQUAN

10. Horse Stance Punch Upwards mǎbù shàng chōngquán 马步上冲拳

Turn the torso rightward, bend the knees, and shift to sit into a horse stance. Bend the left elbow then punch straight up, knuckles at jaw height, fist eye in. Bring the right fist to the waist. Look at the left fist. (image H4.10)

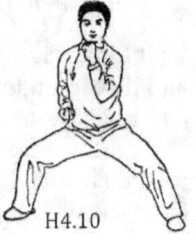

11. Horse Stance Three Punches mǎbù sān chōngquán 马步三冲拳

Punch the right fist down to the left in front of the belly. (image H4.11a) Bend the left elbow and cut across with the forearm down in front of the left side of the belly, fist eye down. Bring the right fist in to the waist. (image 11b) Punch the right fist out over the left forearm to the lower left, fist eye up. Bring the left fist in under the right elbow, fist heart down. (image 11c) Bring the right fist in to the waist with a hooking action. Bend the left elbow to cut across in front of the left side of the belly. (image 11d) Punch the right fist again to the lower left, bringing the left fist to inside the right upper arm. (image 11e)

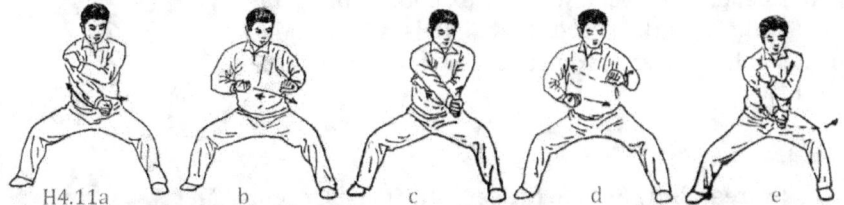

12. Brush Aside, Bow Stance Fan The Hand

lōushǒu gōngbù shǎnzhǎng   搂手弓步搧掌

Hook the left hand and slide along on top of the right arm, going down, then left and back, to brush aside by the left knee. Bring the right fist in to the waist. Look at the left hook hand. (image H4.12a) Shift to the right leg into a right bow stance and turn the torso right. Unclench the right hand and fan out to the right with a straight arm, the back of the hand facing the rear right, thumb up, palm at head height. Look at the right hand. (image 12b)

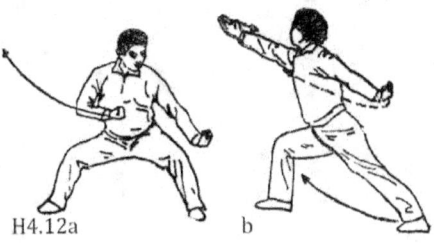

13. Driving Hop-Step, Arrow Kick Framing Block

zòngshēn jiàntán jiàzhǎng　　　　　纵身箭弹架掌

Shift to the right leg, bending and raising the left knee. Unhook the left hand and thread up to under the right elbow, cutting across with the elbow bent and the back of the hand facing up. Bend the right elbow to bring the hand in slightly. Hop forward on the right leg, then do a snap kick, landing on the left foot (or kick whilst airborne). Bring the right hand to the waist and do a framing block above the head with the left hand, palm facing forward. Look at the right foot. (images H4.13a, 13b)

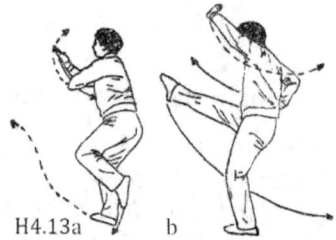

14. Bow Stance Brace To The Side　　gōngbù cè chēngzhǎng　弓步侧撑掌

Land the right foot behind into a left bow stance. Push forward with the right hand. Lower the left hand, bending the elbow, then extending the arm out to the rear to brace. Both hands are upright palms at head height. Look at the right hand. (image H4.14)

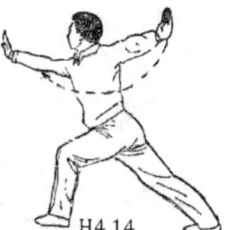

15. Retreat, Bow Stance Brace　　tuì gōngbù chēngzhǎng　退弓步撑掌

Thread the left hand in to the waist then forward to the right armpit, back of the hand up. Bend the right elbow and turn the palm up. (image H4.15a) Withdraw the left foot behind, touching the ball of the foot down. Do a framing block above the head with the left hand, bringing the right hand in to the waist, palm up. (image 15b) Withdraw the right foot back into a left bow stance. Push forward with the right hand and lower the left hand, bending the elbow, then extend the arm to brace out to the rear left. Both hands are vertical palms, at head height. Look at the right hand. (image 15c) Repeat. (images 15d, 15e, 15f)

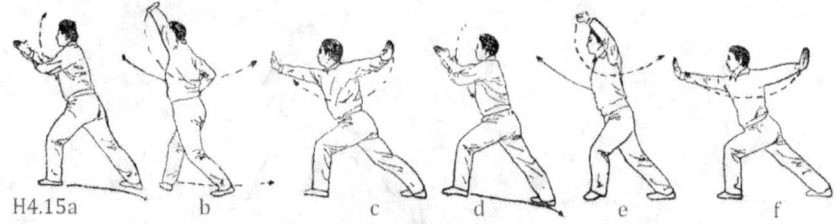

FOURTH FORM HONGQUAN

16. Drop Stance Thread The Hand, Arrow Kick

pūbù chuānzhǎng jiàntán   仆步穿掌箭弹

Thread the left hand forward over the right wrist. (image H4.16a) Bend the left leg fully and turn right into a right drop stance. Bring the right hand down, then thread along the inside of the right leg to the right foot. Look at the right hand. (image 16b) Shift forward to the right leg and push into both legs. Thread the right hand forward and up to the right side. (image 16c) Step the left foot forward and shift to the left leg, swinging the right leg up and pushing off the left leg, jumping up to do a left snap kick. Do a framing block with the right hand above the head at the right. Bend the left elbow to take a vertical palm by the right ear. Look past the left foot. (images 16d, 16e)

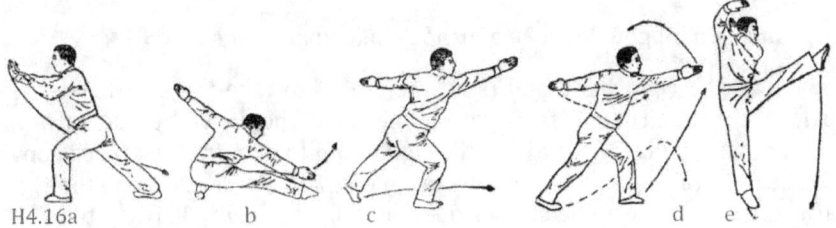

17. Closed Stance Framing Block And Punch

bīngbù jià chōngquán   并步架冲拳

Land the right foot and stand firmly, keeping the weight on the right leg, knee slightly bent. Land on the left foot, touching the toes down lightly, in a left high empty stance. Clench the left hand and bring the fist to the waist. (image H4.17a) Settle onto the left foot and bring the right foot in beside it, standing up. Punch the left fist directly to the left side, fist eye up. Maintain the framing block with the right hand above the head at the right. Look at the left fist. (image 17b)

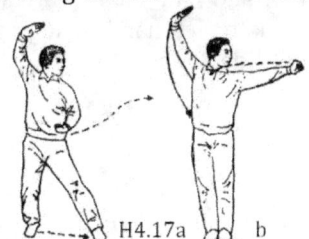

Section Two

18. Turn Around, Closed Stance Framing Block And Punch

zhuànshēn bīngbù jià chōngquán   转身并步架冲拳

Bend both knees to half-squat. Bend the left elbow and cut the forearm across to the right with the fist at jaw height and the forearm vertical, fist heart in. Clench the right hand and bring the fist to the waist. Look to the left side. (image H4.18a) Step the left foot across to the left and shift to the left leg, turning the torso leftward. Clench the left hand, bend the elbow, and cut up to the left with the forearm in front of the chest. (image 18b) Step the right foot forward, to the left, with the foot turned in, and turn the torso leftward. Bring the left foot in beside the right and stand up, turning the torso leftward. Do a straight punch with the right fist and do a framing block with the left hand above the head at the left. Look at the right fist. (image 18c, 18d)

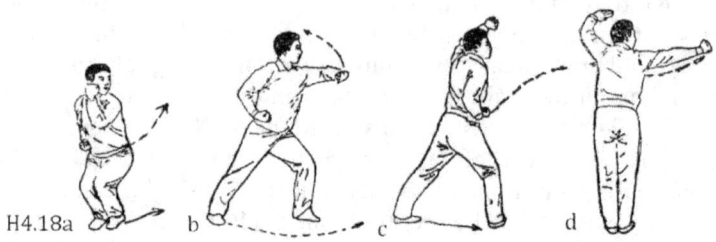

19. Turn Back, Closed Stance, Squat, Hook And Stab

huíshēn bīngbù dūnshēn gōushǒu chuānzhǎng 回身并步蹲身勾手穿掌

Unclench the right hand and bend the elbow to take the arm to the left, placing the forearm across in front of the chest, the hand at the left armpit, palm down. (image H4.19a) Lift the right hand to do a framing block above the head at the right, lowering the left hand past the chest inside the right arm to stop at the right side of the waist. (image 19b) Turn to the right around to face the rear, withdrawing the right foot to the left and shifting to the right leg with the turn. Chop downwards with the right hand on the right side in front of the head. Hold the left arm out to the lower rear. (image 19c) Step the left foot forward, then step the right foot forward, bringing the left hand over to chop down in front and bringing the right hand to the waist. (images 19d, 19e) Step the left foot up beside the right foot and half-squat. Thread the right hand up to do a framing block and hook the left hand, swinging it down and back to the lower rear. Look to the left side. (image 19f)

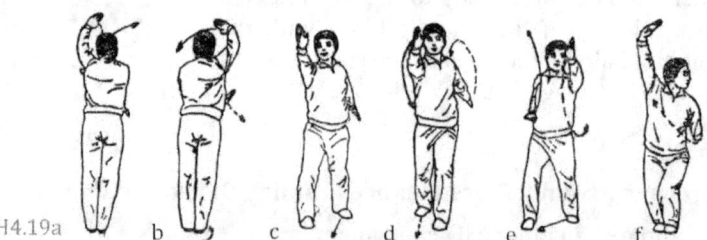

20. Turn Back, Closed Stance, Squat, Hook And Stab   huíshēn
bīngbù dūnshēn gōushǒu chuānzhǎng   回身并步蹲身勾手穿掌

Stand up. Unhook the left hand and bend the elbow, placing the forearm flat across in front of the chest, palm down. (image H4.20a) Withdraw the left foot and do a framing block up above the head with the left hand. Bend the right elbow to bring the hand to the waist, palm up. (image 20b) Turn to the

FOURTH FORM HONGQUAN

left, to face behind, shifting to the left leg. Chop down in front of the head with the left hand and extend the right arm out to the lower rear. (image 20c) Step the right foot forward, and then the left foot. Bring the right hand over to chop forward and bring the left hand in to the waist. (images 20d, 20e) Bring the right foot up to beside the left foot and half-squat. Thread the left hand up to do a framing block and hook the right hand, hooking it back and down. Look to the right. (image 20f)

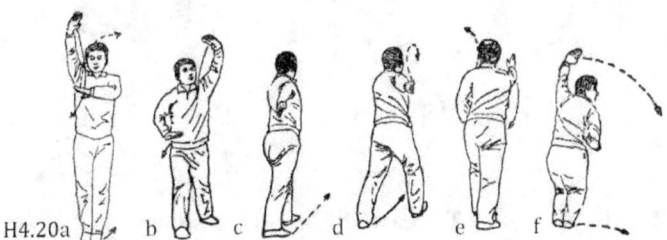

21. Right Bow Stance Press Down And Stab

yòu gōngbù àn chuānzhǎng   右弓步按穿掌

Stride the right foot across to the right and shift to the right leg, turning the torso rightward into a right bow stance. Press down in front of the chest with the left hand and bring the right hand to the waist. (image H4.21a) Thread the right hand out over the left hand, extending the arm to shoulder height. Tuck the left hand into the right armpit. Look at the right hand. (image 21b)

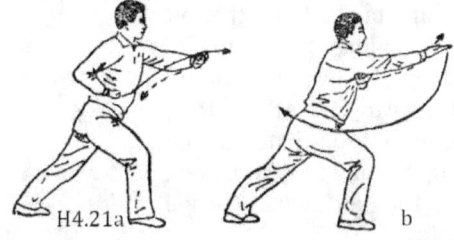

22. Angled Slap Kick   xié pāijiǎo   斜拍脚

Shift to the right leg, circling the right hand down and to the rear, and extending the left arm up in front. (image H4.22a) Do a straight swinging kick to chest height with the left foot, bringing the right hand over to the front to slap the foot. Bring the left hand to the waist, palm up. Look at the left foot. (image 22b)

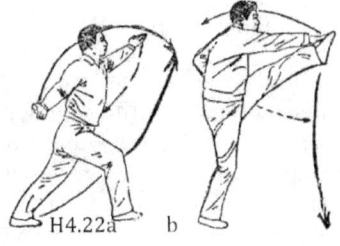

23. Left Bow Stance Punch   zuǒ gōngbù chōngquán   左弓步冲拳

Land the left foot in front and shift to the right foot, bending the knee to a half-squat and turning the torso rightward. Do a framing block with the right hand above the head and extend the left hand down to the left, palm up. (image H4.23a) Turn the torso slightly leftward and bend the left knee

CHAQUAN, VOLUME II

to take a left half horse stance. Clench the right hand and bring the fist to the waist. Bend the left arm and snap the wrist to set into a vertical palm, fingers at nose height. (image 23b) Shift to the left leg into a left bow stance and punch straight out with the right fist, fist eye up. Place the left hand at the right elbow. Look at the right punch. (image 23c)

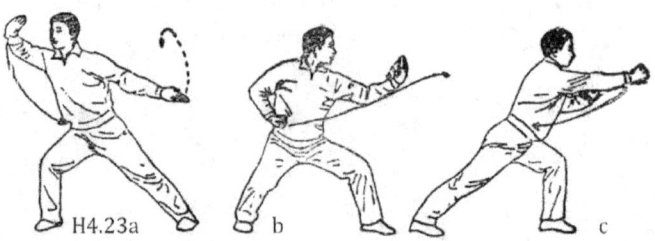

24. **Drop Stance Thread The Hand**   pūbù chuānzhǎng   仆步穿掌

Unclench the right hand and place it at the waist. Push the left hand to the front, palm down, edge forward. (image H4.24a) Shift to the right leg and raise the bent left knee. Thread the right hand forward over the left hand, palm up, and tuck the left hand into the right armpit, palm down. Look at the right hand. (image 24b) Land the left foot to the left and squat fully on the right leg to take a left drop stance. Slide the left hand along the inside of the left leg, to thread forward to the foot, thumb up. Extend the right arm up behind. Look at the left hand. (image 24c)

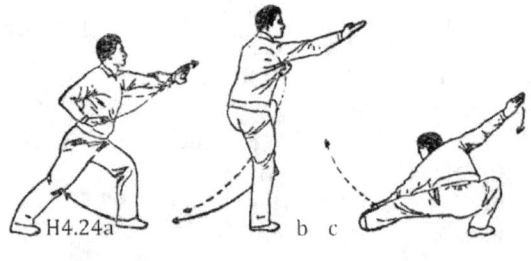

25. **Step Forward, Three Reaching Hands**

    shàngbù sān tànzhǎng   上步三探掌

Shift to the left leg and thread the left hand forward and up. (image H4.25a) Then shift back to the right leg and bring the left foot in, touching down the toes and bending the knee to take a left empty stance. Bend the left elbow to bring the hand in, palm down. (image 25b) Step the left foot forward and extend the left arm. (image 25c) Step the right foot forward and extend the right arm to reach forward, bringing the left hand to the waist. (image 25d) Step the left foot forward and extend the left arm to reach. Bring the right hand to the waist, palm up. Look at the left hand. (image 25e)

FOURTH FORM HONGQUAN

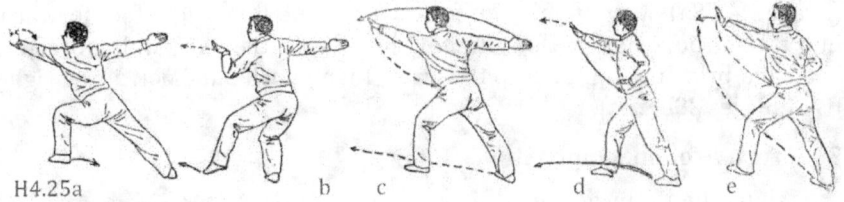

H4.25a b c d e

26. Slap Kick, Empty Stance Vertical Palm
pāijiǎo xūbù lìzhǎng   拍脚虚步立掌

Shift to the left leg and bring the left hand to the waist. Swing the right foot up with a swinging kick, reaching the right hand forward to slap the foot. Look at the right foot. (image H4.26a) Land the right foot forward, touching the toes down lightly, into a right empty stance. Bend the right elbow to set a vertical palm in front of the chest. Look at the right hand. (image 26b)

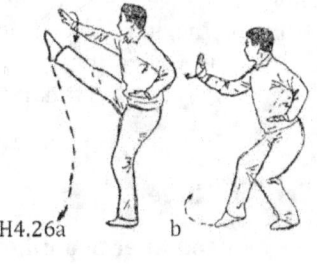

H4.26a b

27. Left Sweep Kick   zuǒ sǎotuǐ   左扫腿

Step the right foot a half-step forward with the foot turned out. Cut the right hand flat across in front of the chest. (image H4.27a) Squat on the right leg, then pivot on the right foot and extend the left leg to do a full-circle front sweep kick. (images 27b, 27c)

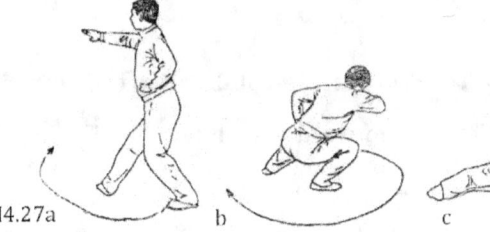

H4.27a b c

28. Bow Stance Framing Block And Punch
gōngbù jià chōngquán   弓步架冲拳

Push into the right leg to stand up into a half-squat. Bring the left foot in, touching the toes down lightly in a left empty stance. Clench the right hand and pound down in front of the belly. Lift the left hand to support under the back of the right hand.

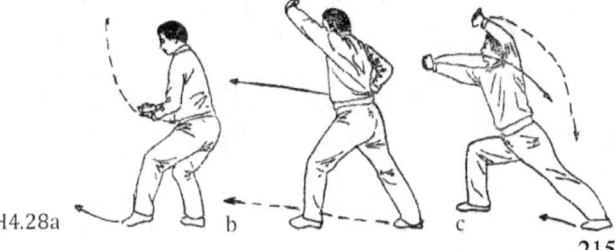

H4.28a b c

(image H4.28a) Step the left foot forward, then step the right foot forward into a right bow stance. Do a framing block with the left hand above the head and bring the right fist to the waist, then punch out. Look at the right fist. (images 28b, 28c)

29. Turn Around, Empty Stance Hook

zhuànshēn xūbù gōushǒu 转身虚步勾手

Turn around to the left to face behind, then bring the left foot in, touching the toes down to take a left empty stance. Change the left hand to a hook and lower it in front of the left knee. Unclench the right hand and bring it around with the turn, to stop in the left elbow crease. Look at the left hand. (image H4.29)

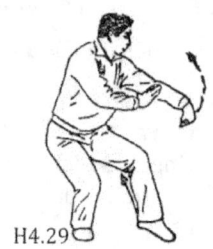
H4.29

Section Three

30. Raised Knee Scooping Snap   tíxī tiǎozhǎng   提膝挑掌

Push into the right leg and raise the bent left knee. Unhook the left hand and snap the wrist to do a scooping snap with a vertical palm, fingers at chest height, elbow slightly bent. Look past the left hand. (image H4.30)

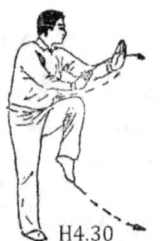
H4.30

31. Jump To Insertion Step Stab   tiào chābù chuānzhǎng   跳插步穿掌

Land the left foot forward and shift to the left leg. Thread the right hand forward, palm up, bringing the left hand to the waist. (image H4.27a) Step the right foot forward and push off, swinging the left foot up to jump up. Thread the left hand forward over the right hand, bringing the right hand to the chest. Land on the left foot first, then land the right foot behind the left leg to take a left insertion stance, weight on the left leg. Look at the left hand. (images 31b, 31c, 31d)

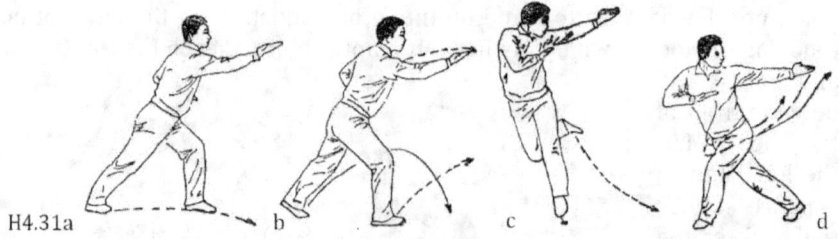
H4.31a   b   c   d

FOURTH FORM HONGQUAN

32. Turn Around, Bow Stance Double Lashes

zhuànshēn gōngbù shuāng bǎizhǎng 转身弓步双摆掌

Turn around one-eighty degrees to the right and shift to the right leg into a right bow stance. Bring the arms around with the turn, down, to the rear right, then up with a scooping lash. The right hand finishes in a vertical palm with the elbow slightly bent, fingers at nose height. The left hand finishes in the right elbow crease. Look past the right hand. (image H4.32)

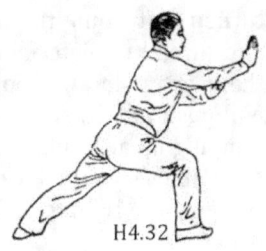

33. Retreat, Three Fanning Hands   tuìbù sān shānzhǎng   退步三搧掌

Circle the right hand to the right and down to hang. Circle the left hand left, up, then right, finishing with a vertical palm. (image H4.33a) Withdraw the right foot. Circle the right hand left, up, then right to fan with the back of the hand, fingers at nose height. Place the left hand in the right elbow crease. Look at the right hand. (image 33b) Withdraw the left foot, then withdraw the right foot, repeating the same fanning action with the hands. (images 33c, 33d) Circle the right hand right and down, to hang. Circle the left hand left, up, then right to a vertical palm. (image 33e) Withdraw the left foot to take a right bow stance. Circle the right hand left, up, then right to fan with the back of the hand, fingers at nose height. Bring the left hand to the right elbow crease. Look at the right hand. (image 33f)

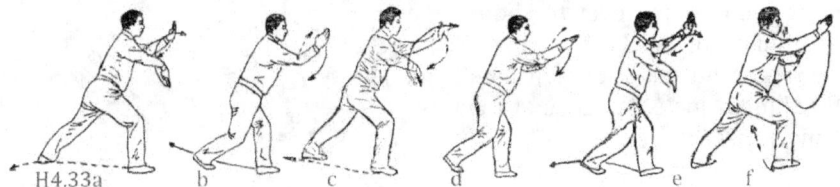

34. Raised Knee Scooping Snap   tíxī tiǎozhǎng   提膝挑掌

Push into the right leg and raise the bent knee, shifting to stand up firmly on the left leg. Bring the right hand to the right, down, then left past the right knee to scoop up in front of the chest with a bent elbow, fingers at nose height. Clench the left hand and bring the fist to the waist. Look at the right hand. (image H4.34 and from behind)

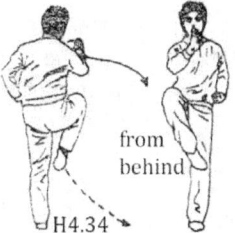

35. Walking Outside Crescent Kick   xíngbù bǎilián   行步摆莲

Land the right foot to the right, turned out, and turn the torso rightward. Bend the right elbow across to smear across levelly to the right. Step the left foot forward to the right and continue to smear the right hand across to the

217

CHAQUAN, VOLUME II

right. (images H4.35a, 35b) Take a front cross-over step with the right foot, moving forward. Laterally rotate the right hand and thread it first down to the waist then forward and up. Step the left foot forward with the foot turned in, turning the body rightward. (image 35c) Sit into a horse stance and thread the left hand out to the left, thumb up. Bring the right hand to the waist, palm up. Look at the left hand. (image 35d) Shift to the right leg and push into it, swinging the left foot up to the right with an inner swing, jumping up and spinning rightward. Extend the right leg to do an outwards swinging crescent kick. Swing the hands to the right, then to the left, slapping the right foot, first the left hand, then the right. (images 35e, 35f)

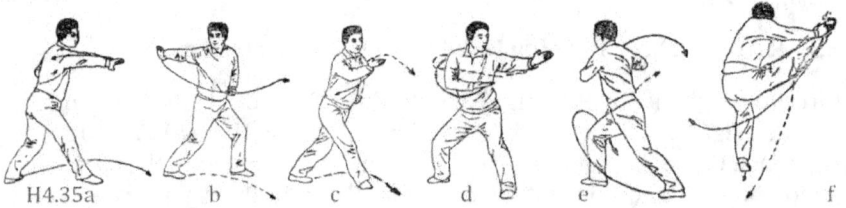

36. Closed Stance Chop   bīngbù pīzhǎng   并步劈掌

Land on the left foot then land the right foot to the right, shifting to the right leg and bending the knee. Hold the arms out levelly to either side. (image H4.36a) Bring the left foot in beside the right and half-squat in a closed stance. Bend the left elbow and bring the hand right and down to press down in front of the belly. Bring the right hand up and over to chop down in front of the belly. The right elbow contacts the back of the left hand, and the thumb side is up. Look at the right hand. (image 36b)

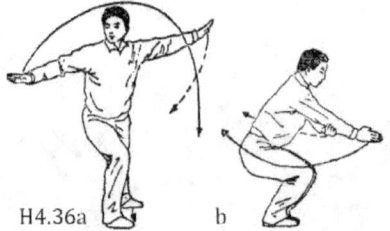

37. Double Flying Swallows   shuāng fēiyān   双飞燕

Swing the arms down and back, then swing them forward and up, pushing off with both legs. Do straight front swinging kicks at chest height whilst airborne, slapping the feet with the hands. (images H4.37a, 37b, 36c)

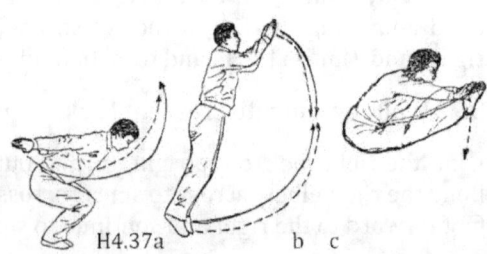

FOURTH FORM HONGQUAN

38. Horse Stance Double Chops   mǎbù shuāng pīzhǎng   马步双劈掌

Land on both feet, keeping them parallel, and bending the knees to sit into a horse stance. Separate the hands out to chop to either side with vertical palms. Look forward. (image H4.38)

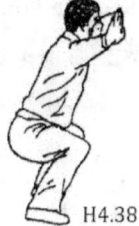

39. Bow Stance Scoop And Hook
gōngbù tiǎozhǎng gōushǒu   弓步挑掌勾手

Turn right and shift to the right leg into a right bow stance. Scoop up slightly with the right hand with a vertical palm, fingers at nose height. Hook the left hand and hold the arm out behind, low. Look at the right hand. (image H4.39)

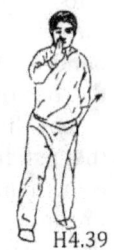

40. Snap Kick, Bow Stance Double Braces
tántuǐ gōngbù shuāng bǎizhǎng   弹腿弓步双撑掌

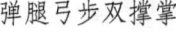

Shift to the right leg and do a snap kick forward with the left leg, landing the left foot behind, to take a right bow stance. Unhook the left hand and push out with both hands with vertical palms, left to the front and right to the rear. Look at the left hand. (images H4.40a, 40b)

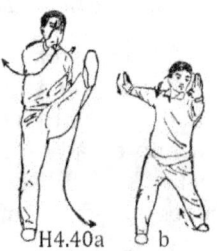

41. Empty Stance Double Framing Blocks
xūbù shuāng jiàzhǎng   虚步双架掌

Shift to the right leg, bending and raising the left knee. Swing the left hand to the right to in front of the right side of the chest. Bend the right elbow. (image H4.41a) Squat fully on the right leg and extend the left leg to a left drop stance. Thread both hands along inside the left leg, thumbs up. (image 41b) Push into the right leg, standing up with the leg slightly bent, turning the torso leftward and bringing the left foot in to sit into a left empty stance. Bend the arms to do framing blocks above the head at either side. Look

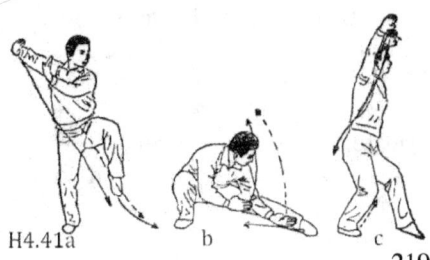

219

forward. (image 41c)

Section Four

42. Turn Around, Horse Stance Punch Upwards

zhuànshēn mǎbù shàng chōngquán   转身马步上冲拳

Shift to the left leg, bending and raising the right knee and turning the torso rightward. Lower the right hand and brush across to the right, pressing down by the right knee. (image H4.42a) Land the right foot to the right and shift to the right leg, turning the torso slightly rightward. Continue to turn to the right and step the left foot forward to the right, foot turned in, to sit into a horse stance. Clench the left hand as you turn, bending the elbow to bring the fist down, right, then up to punch at nose height with the fist heart in. Clench the right hand and bring the fist to the waist. Look at the left fist. (images 42b, 42c)

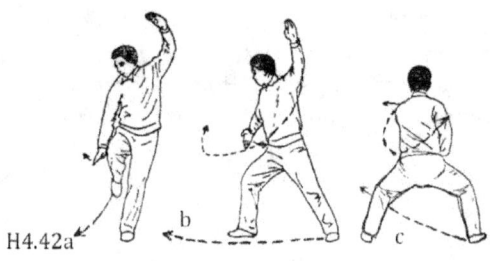

43. Turn Around, Horse Stance Elbow Butt

zhuànshēn mǎbù dǐngzhǒu   转身马步顶肘

Shift to the left leg and raise the bent right knee, turning leftward. Unclench both hands and separate them out levelly to either side. (image H4.43a) Land the right foot, foot turned in, and sit into a half horse stance. Clench the right fist and bend the elbow to cut it across in front of the chest, butting forward. Place the left hand at the right knuckles. Look to the right. (image 43b)

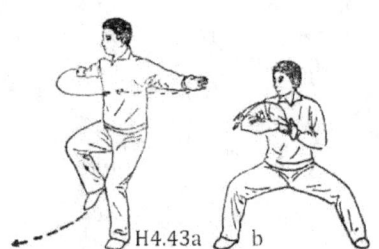

44. Bow Stance Cover And Stab   gōngbù gài chuānzhǎng   弓步盖穿掌

Shift to the right leg and turn the torso slightly rightward to take a right bow stance. Bend the left elbow and lift it, then press down across in front of the chest, palm down. (image H4.44a) Extend the right arm to stab forward over the left hand to jaw height, palm up. Look at the right hand. (image 44b)

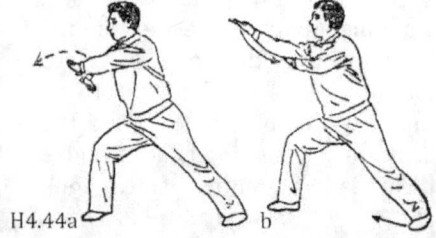

FOURTH FORM HONGQUAN

45. Snap Kick, Separate The Hands   tántuǐ fēnzhǎng   弹腿分掌

Turn the right foot out and bend the left knee, bringing the left foot a half-step forward towards the right foot, touching down the ball of the foot and turning the torso slightly rightward. Bring the right hand in, gathering the hands in front of the chest, palms facing, fingers up. (image H4.45a) Shift entirely to the right leg and do a snap kick forward with the left foot to chest height. Keep the back straight. Separate the hands and extend the arms to either side to chop level. Look at the left hand. (image 45b)

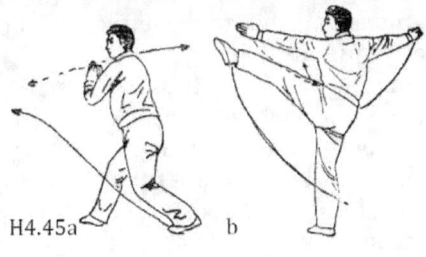

46. Jumping Turn Around, Close Stance Stab
tiào zhuànshēn bīngbù chuānzhǎng   跳转身并步穿掌

Land the left foot with the knee bent and turn the torso slightly leftwards. Whisk the back of the left hand on the left thigh. (image H4.46a) Push into the right leg to jump, turning to the rear left, opening both arms out. (image 46b) Land on the left foot, then the right, into a right bow stance. Bring the left hand over and down, bending the elbow to press down in front of the chest. Bend the right elbow to cut across in front of the chest. (image 46c) Bring the left foot in to beside the right. Stab the right hand out over the left hand, arm extended at shoulder height. Tuck the left hand into the right armpit, palm down. Look at the right hand. (image 46d)

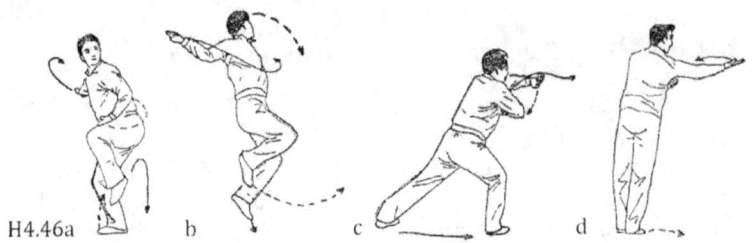

47. Snap Kick, Separate The Hands   tántuǐ fēnzhǎng   弹腿分掌

Step the right foot forward, turned out, and bend both knees to half-squat, turning the torso slightly rightward and shifting to the right leg. Gather the right hand in front of the chest together with the left hand, palms facing, fingers up. (image H4.47a) Do a snap kick with the left foot forward, to the left side. Separate the hands out to either side to chop with the arms level,

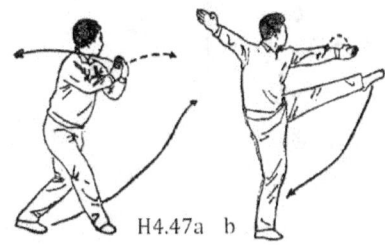

thumbs up. Look at the left hand. (image 47b)

48. Hitting Hop-Step Stab   jībù chuānzhǎng   击步穿掌

Bend the left knee to lower the foot. Bend the left elbow and hold it up in front of the left side of the chest. (image H4.48a) Place the left foot on the ground and shift to the left leg, turning the left palm up. (image 48b) Push off with the left leg to jump forward, hitting the right foot into the left foot and stabbing the left palm out to the left whilst airborne. Look at the left hand. (image 48c)

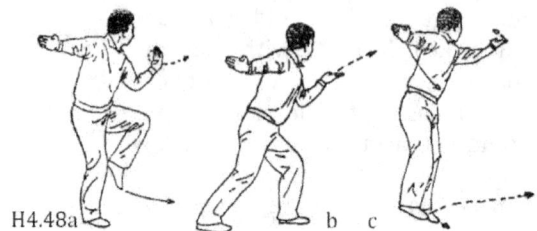

49. Raised Knee Right Punch   tíxī yòu chōngquán   提膝右冲拳

Land on the left foot, then land the right foot, stepping forward into a right bow stance. Place the left hand upright and clench the right fist, bringing the fist to the waist. (image H4.49a) Shift to the right leg and raise the bent left knee. Punch directly forward with the right fist and tuck the left hand into the right armpit. Look at the right fist. (image 49b)

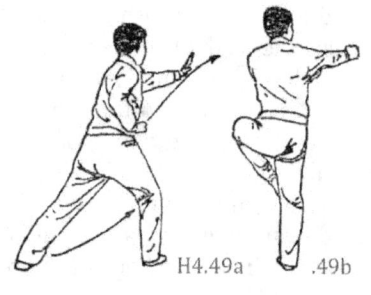

50. Hitting Hop-Step Stab   jībù chuānzhǎng   击步穿掌

Turn the head left. (image H4.50a) Land the left foot to the left, stepping forward and shifting to the left leg. Bend the left elbow and laterally rotate the hand in front of the chest, palm up. (image 50b) Push off with the left leg to jump up, tapping the right foot into the left whilst airborne. Land on the right foot, then the left, into a left bow stance. Stab the left hand straight forward. (images 50c, 50d) Step the right foot forward with the foot turned in and turn the torso leftward, sitting into a horse stance. Unclench the right hand and thread it over the left hand to the lower right. Bring the left hand

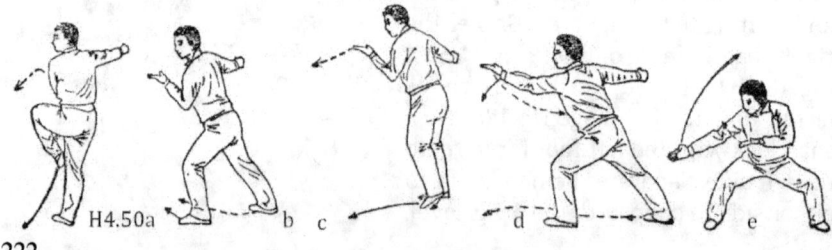

FOURTH FORM HONGQUAN

to the belly. Look at the right hand. (image 50e)

51. Tornado Kick, Horse Stance Chop

xuànfēngjiǎo mǎbù pīzhǎng   旋风脚马步劈掌

Shift to the right leg and push off with the right foot, swinging the left leg up to the rear and twisting the torso also to the rear, turning left. Swing the arms up to turn the body, jumping up. Do an inside crescent kick, slapping the right foot with the left hand whilst airborne. (images H4.51a, 51b) Land on the left foot, turn one-eighty degrees to the left, then land the right foot, turning it in, sitting into a horse stance. Chop down to the right side with the right hand, holding both arms out to the sides. Look at the right hand. (image 51c)

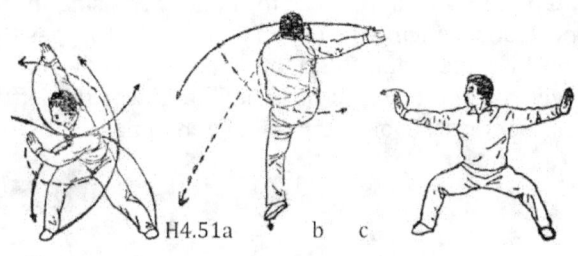

52. Jump To Insertion Stance Stab   tiào chābù chuānzhǎng   跳插步穿掌

Shift to the right leg and turn the torso slightly to the right. Thread the right hand out to the right, then push off with the right leg, swinging the left foot up, to jump up and spin rightward. Thread the left hand forward over the right hand. (images H4.52a, 52b) Land on the left foot then land the right foot behind the left leg, in an insertion step, touching down the ball of the foot. Turn the left foot out and hold the left arm out to the lower left, bringing the right hand to the chest, palm up. Look at the left hand. (image 52c)

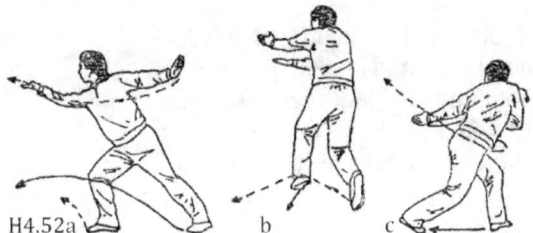

53. Turn Around, Closed Stance Lash

zhuànshēn bīngbù bǎizhǎng   转身并步摆掌

Turn one-eighty degrees around to the right, turning into the back, and withdraw the left foot to come in beside the right foot, standing up. As the body turns, swing the arms down, then to the upper right, the right arm slightly bent, out level at the right side, the left arm with the elbow bent, forearm across in front of the chest. Follow the action of the right hand while turning, then turn the head to look left. (images H4.53a, 53b)

CHAQUAN, VOLUME II

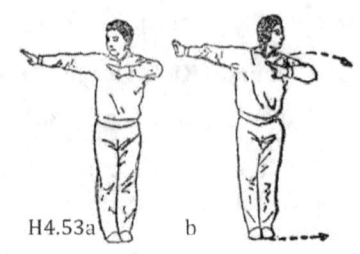

Section Five

54. Jump To Bow Stance Chop   tiào gōngbù pīzhǎng   跳弓步劈掌

Step the right foot across to the left, crossing in front of the left leg, then push off, swinging the leg up to jump up. (images H4.54a, 54b) Land on the left foot, then land the right, into a right bow stance. Bring the right hand over to chop down to nose height. Lower the left hand to set in the right elbow crease. Look at the right hand. (image 54c)

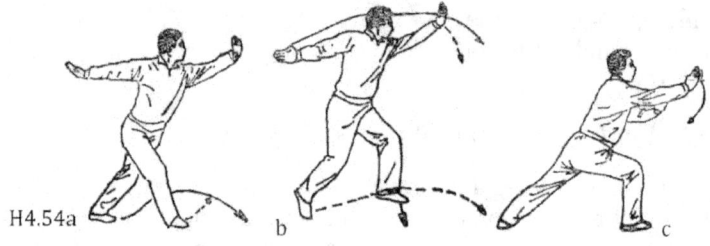

55. Hook, Turn Around, Stab
   gōushǒu zhuànshēn chuānzhǎng   勾手转身穿掌

Hook the right hand and lower it to brush and hook to the right, holding it angled down. (image H4.55) Turn left into a left bow stance. Thread the left hand in past the belly then extend up to the left side, to nose height, palm up. Look at the left hand. (image 55b)

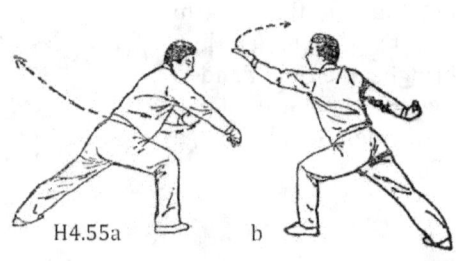

56. Closed Stance Stab   bīngbù chuānzhǎng   并步穿掌

Medially rotate the left arm to turn the palm up and block above the head. (image H4.56a) Turn the head to the right and shift to the right leg, turning the torso rightward. Unhook the right hand and bring it to the belly. Press down with the left hand to the right side. (image 56b) Step the left foot up to meet the right foot and stand up. Thread the right hand out over the left hand, extending the arm at shoulder height. Tuck the left hand into the right armpit, palm down. Look at the right hand. (image 56c)

FOURTH FORM HONGQUAN

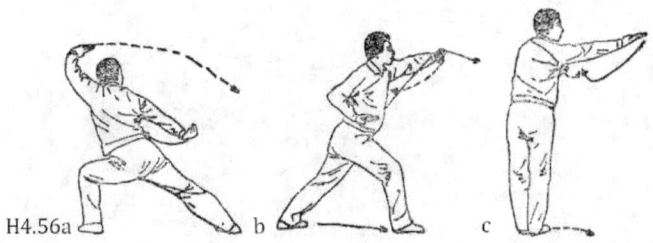

57. Snap Kick, Separate The Hands   tántuǐ fēnzhǎng   弹腿分掌

Step the right foot out to the right, turning the foot out, turning the body rightward, and bending both knees. Bring the right hand in to meet the left hand in front of the chest, palms facing, fingers pointing up. (image H4.57a) Shift to the right leg and do a snap kick with the left leg to the left side. Separate the hands out to either side, extending the arms to push out with vertical palms. Look past the left foot. (image 57b)

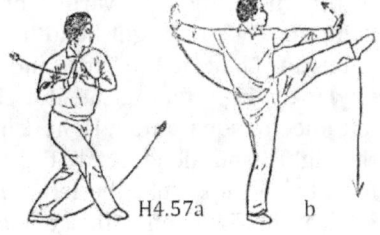

Section Six

58. Closed Stance Framing Block And Punch

bīngbù jià chōngquán   并步架冲拳

Land the left foot to the left and shift to the left leg, into a left bow stance. Bend the left elbow to do a framing block above the head, bringing the right hand to the waist. (image H4.58a) Bring the right foot up to meet the left foot. Clench the right hand and punch straight forward, fist eye up. Look at the right fist. (image 58b)

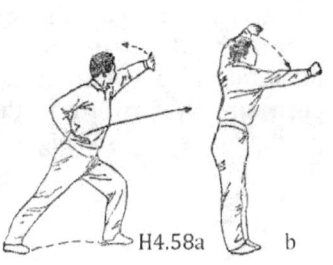

59. Open Bow Stance Hook And Flash The Hand

héngdāngbù gōushǒu liàngzhǎng   横裆步勾手亮掌

Lower the left hand to settle on top of the right wrist. (image H4.59a) Withdraw the right foot to the rear and shift to the right leg, half squatting, turning the torso rightward to a bow stance. Unclench the right hand, bend and relax the wrist, then circle back to the right to brush aside at the right knee. (image 59b) Turn the torso sharply to the left and raise the right hand, snapping the wrist to flash the palm above the head. Hold the left hook hand straight out to the side. Look to the left. (image 59c)

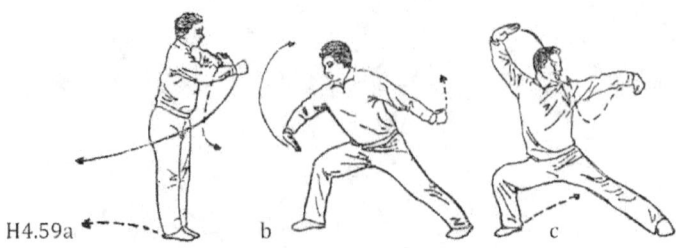

H4.59a   b   c

60. Drop Stance Thread The Hand   pūbù chuānzhǎng   仆步穿掌

Shift to the left leg, bending and raising the right knee. Press down with the right palm towards the forward left. Thread the left hand in to the left side of the chest, then forward over the right hand, palm up. Tuck the right hand into the left armpit, palm up. Look at the left hand. (image H4.60a) Lower the right foot to the rear right, bending the left knee to squat into a right drop stance. Thread the right hand along inside the right thigh to the foot, thumb up. Hold the left arm up at the left. Look at the right hand. (image 60b)

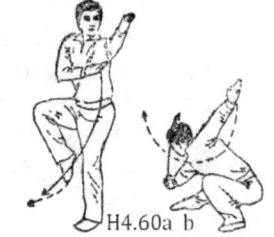

H4.60a b

61. Bow Stance Framing Block And Push

gōngbù jià tuīzhǎng   弓步架推掌

Shift to the right leg, bending the right knee and extending the left leg to take a right bow stance. Do a framing block over the head with the right hand, palm up and rightward. Bend the left elbow to bring the hand to the waist, then push directly forward, to the right side, with a vertical palm, fingers at nose height. Look at the left hand. (image H4.61)

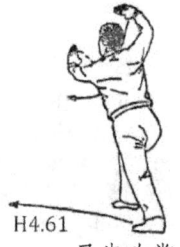

H4.61

62. Horse Stance Hack   mǎbù kǎnzhǎng   马步砍掌

Take a wide step across to the left with the left foot and bend both knees to sit into a horse stance. Hack down with the right hand to the lower left, in front of the left side of the chest, palm up. Place the left hand on top of the right forearm. Look at the right hand. (image H4.62)

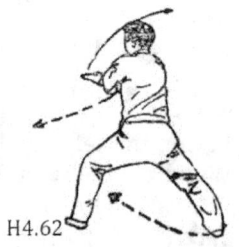

H4.62

63. Jumping Straddle Step, Horse Stance Hack

kuà tiàobù mǎbù kǎnzhǎng   跨跳步马步砍掌

Shift to the left leg and raise the bent right knee. Open the right arm out to the upper right and hold the left arm out to the lower left. (image H4.63a)

FOURTH FORM HONGQUAN

Step the right foot forward to the left, with a front cover step passing in front of the left leg. As soon as the right leg takes the weight, step the left foot across to the left into a horse stance. Hack down to the left with the right hand in front of the left side of the chest. Place the left hand on top of the right forearm. Look at the right hand. (image 63b)

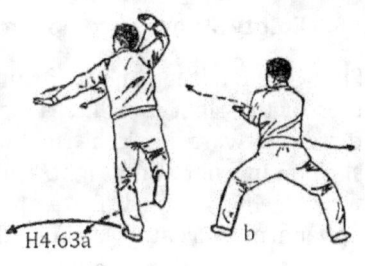

64. Jumping Turn Around, Bow Stance Hack

tiào zhuànshēn gōngbù kǎnzhǎng   跳转身弓步砍掌

Shift to the left leg. Brush the left hand forward, left, and up. Extend the right hand to the lower right so that the arm is held out to the lower rear. (image H4.64a) Push into the left foot and jump up, spinning one-eighty degrees whilst airborne. Swing the left arm up, right, then down, finishing low. Swing the right arm down and right, finishing high. (image 64b) Land on the right foot, then land the left, and continue to turn the torso leftward, sitting into a horse stance. Bring the right hand up to chop down in front of the chest, palm up. Bend the left elbow to place the hand on the right forearm, palm down. Look at the right hand. (image 64c)

65. Straddle Step Lash   kuàbù bǎizhǎng   跨步摆掌

Shift to the left leg and turn the torso slightly leftward. Lash the hands across to the left, hands at belly height, palms down. (image H4.65a) Step the right foot across to the left, past the left leg, with the foot turned out. Turn the torso slightly rightward. Swing the hands across to the right, hands at belly height, palms down. (image 65b) Step the left foot across to the left and turn the torso slightly leftward. Swing the hands again across to the left. Follow the actions of the hands with the eyes. (image 65c)

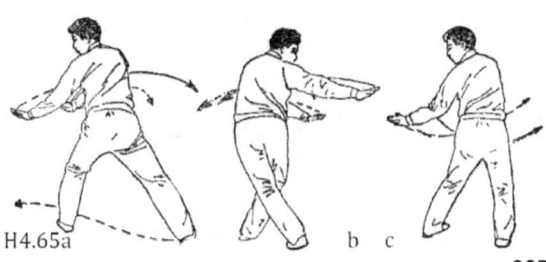

66. Empty Stance Slice Upwards Hook   xūbù liāogōushǒu   虚步撩勾手

Shift to the left leg and half-squat on it, touching down the toes of the right foot into a right empty stance. Turn the torso rightward, hook the right hand, and bring it down then slice up in front at the right. The hook is at belly height, the wrist facing forward. Place the left hand inside the right upper arm. Look at the right hook. (image H4.66)

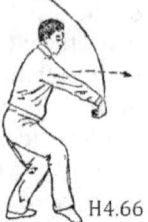

67. Empty Stance Scoop And Push   xūbù tiǎo tuīzhǎng   虚步挑推掌

Unhook the right hand and raise it. Push forward with the left hand in a vertical palm. Look at the left hand. (image H4.67)

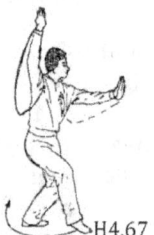

68. Closing Posture   shōu shì   收势

Withdraw the right foot to the rear, at the left, and shift to the left leg, taking a left bow stance, turning the torso rightward. Bend the elbows and bring the hands to the sides, then extend the arms levelly forward, palms up. (image H4.68a) Shift back to the right leg, then withdraw the left foot behind. Bring the hands to the sides. (image 68b) Bring the right foot in to meet the left and stand up. Clench the hands and bring the fists to the hips, fist eyes facing. Look to the left side. (image 68c) Unclench the hands and let the arms hang naturally, placing the palms on the thighs. Look forward. (image 68d)

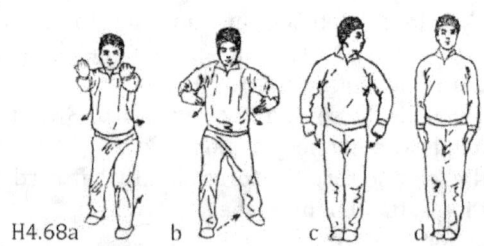

SEVENTH FORM HONGQUAN

七路洪拳

NAMES OF THE MOVEMENTS

Position Of Preparation
Section One
1. Closed Stance Flash Palm
2. Drop Stance Thread The Hand
3. Empty Stance Scooping Snap
4. Snap Kick
5. Leap To Snap Kick
6. Raised Knee Push
7. Drop Stance Thread The Hand
8. Curving Walk, Thread And Hook
9. Closed Stance Push

Section Two
10. Drop Stance Thread The Hand
11. Aerial Snap Kick
12. Separate The Hands, Side Thrust Kick
13. Closed Stance Push
14. Drop Stance Thread The Hand
15. Bow Stance Stab
16. Curving Walk, Thread And Hook
17. Closed Stance Push

Section Three
18. Drop Stance Thread The Hand
19. Two Rising Kicks
20. Empty Stance Stab
21. Bow Stance Stab
22. Wheel Over, Bow Stance Chop
23. Drop Stance Thread The Hand
24. Empty Stance Press Down

Section Four
25. Two Rising Kicks
26. Separate The Hands, Side Thrust Kick
27. Hitting Hop-Step Slice Upwards
28. Raised Knee Framing Block And Punch
29. Hitting Hop-Step Slice Upwards
30. Closed Stance Push

Section Five

31. Drop Stance Thread The Hand
32. Raised Knee Scooping Snap
33. Bow Stance Flash Palm
34. Curving Walk Slice Upwards And Hook
35. Closed Stance Stab
36. Closed Stance Hammerfist
37. Closed Stance Double Lashes
38. Snap Kick
39. Front Heel Kick
40. Leap To Snap Kick
41. Bow Stance Framing Block And Punch
42. Closed Stance Push

Section Six

43. Closed Stance Slice Upwards
44. Closed Stance Flash Palm
45. Raised Knee Press Down
46. Leap Forward To Bow Stance Stab
47. Leap Back To Bow Stance Punch
48. Leap Forward To Bow Stance Stab
49. Bow Stance Punch
50. Right Snap Kick
51. Left Snap Kick
52. Two Rising Kicks
53. Bow Stance Chop

Section Seven

54. Drop Stance Thread The Hand
55. Empty Stance Press Down
56. Empty Stance Double Lashes
57. Two Rising Kicks
58. Separate The Hands, Side Thrust Kick
59. Hitting Hop-Step Slice Upwards
60. Closed Stance Framing Block And Punch
61. Bow Stance Punch
62. Horse Stance Punches
63. Open Bow Stance Punch
64. Bow Stance Punches
65. Horse Stance Punch
66. Open Bow Stance Punch
67. Closed Stance Push

Section Eight

68. Drop Stance Thread The Hand

SEVENTH FORM HONGQUAN

69.   Raised Knee Scooping Snap
70.   Bow Stance Flash Palm
71.   Curving Walk, Slice Upwards And Hook
72.   Horse Stance Hammerfist
73.   Bow Stance Punch
74.   Horse Stance Framing Block And Punch
75.   Horse Stance Hammerfist
76.   Jump Switch-Step, Horse Stance Swinging Hammerfist
77.   Bow Stance Punch
78.   Horse Stance Framing Block And Punch

Section Nine

79.   Raised Knee Double Lashes
80.   Bow Stance Hack
81.   Advance, Reverse Snapped Palm
82.   Bow Stance Stab
83.   Empty Stance Scooping Snap
84.   Raised Knee Scooping Snap
85.   Hitting Hop-Step Slice Upwards
86.   Bow Stance Hack
87.   Empty Stance Flash Palm
88.   Closed Stance Facing Fists
89.   Closing Posture

0.   **Position Of Preparation**   yùbèi shì

Stand to attention with the feet together. (image H7.0)

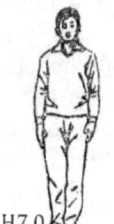

Section One

1.   **Closed Stance Flash Palm**   bīngbù liàngzhǎng   并步亮掌

Step the left foot forward, then step the right foot to the forward right. Lift up with the palms in front of the belly at either side. Continue on to lift up at either side. (images H7.1a, 1b) Step the left foot up to meet the right foot. Medially rotate the right hand above the head to flash the palm, and place the left hand in the right elbow crease. Look to the left. (image 1c)

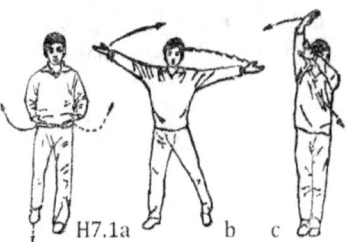

2. Drop Stance Thread The Hand   pūbù chuānzhǎng   仆步穿掌

Step the left foot out to the side and bend the right knee to take a right bow stance. Press the right hand down at the right side to shoulder height, palm down. Bring the left hand in to the waist, palm up. (image H7.2a) Step the right foot behind the left leg with an insertion step. Clench the right hand and bring the fist to the waist. Bring the left hand up to the forehead at the left then press down to shoulder height, palm down. (image 2b) Stand up and raise the bent left knee. Unclench the right hand and stab it forward to the right side, palm up. Tuck the left hand into the right armpit. Look at the right hand. (image 2c) Squat fully on the right leg and extend the left foot out to the side into a left drop stance. Thread the left hand along the left leg with the arm slightly bent, palm facing out, fingers forward. Keep the right hand back at the right side, thumb up. Look at the left hand. (image 2d)

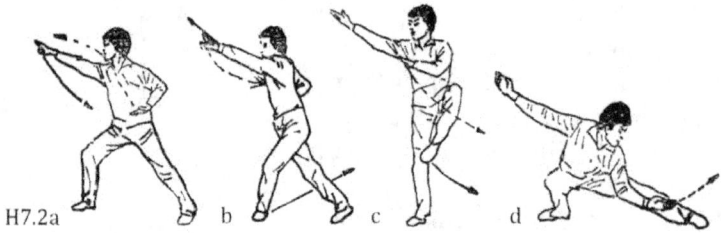

3. Empty Stance Scooping Snap   xūbù tiǎozhǎng   虚步挑掌

Straighten the right leg and bend the left knee to take a left bow stance. Scoop up with the left hand. (image H7.3a) Step the right foot forward, touching the toes down in a right empty stance. Clench the left hand and place the fist at the waist. Clench the right hand, bring the fist to the waist, then scoop forward with the elbow bent, knuckles forward. Look at the right fist. (image 3b)

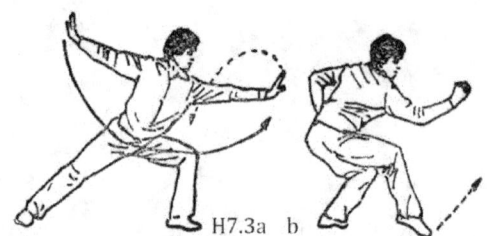

4. Snap Kick   tántītuǐ   弹踢腿

Stand up on the left leg. Do a right snap kick, ankle plantar-flexed. Look forward. (image H7.4)

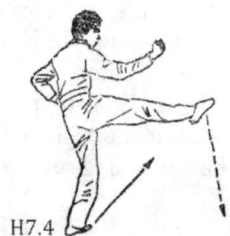

SEVENTH FORM HONGQUAN

5. Leap To Snap Kick   yuèbù tántī   跃步弹踢

Land the right foot forward and raise the left knee. (image H7.5a) Push off with the right leg to jump up and quickly do a snap kick whilst airborne. Look forward. (image 5b)

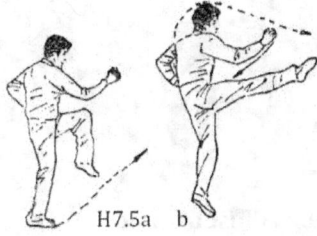

6. Raised Knee Push   tíxī tuīzhǎng   提膝推掌

Land on the left leg then land the right foot forward and bend the knee into a right bow stance. Bring the right fist in to the waist. Unclench the left hand and press down at the right side, palm down. (image H7.6a) Stand up on the right leg and lift the left knee. Unclench the right hand and push out to the right side with a vertical palm. Place the left hand in front of the right shoulder. Look at the right hand. (image 6b)

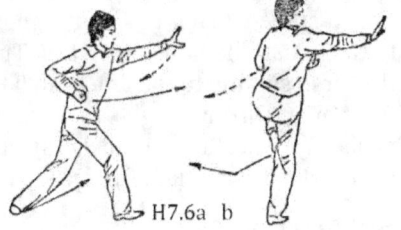

7. Drop Stance Thread The Hand   pūbù chuānzhǎng   仆步穿掌

Squat fully on the right leg and extend the left leg out to the left into a left drop stance. Thread the left hand forward along the left leg. (image H7.7a) Straighten the right leg and bend the left knee to take a left bow stance. Scoop upwards to shoulder height with the left hand, fingers up. Hold the right hand out behind, at the right side, about shoulder height. Look past the left hand. (image 7b)

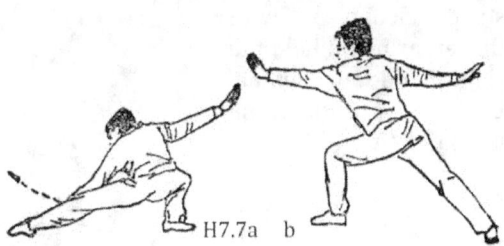

8. Curving Walk, Thread And Hook

húxíngbù chuān guàzhǎng   弧行步穿挂掌

Shift the left foot a bit, turning it out, and step the right foot forward. Laterally rotate the left arm to circle the palm down and in, then extend it forward again. (image H7.8a) Step the left foot forward, then the right, in all taking four to six curving steps. Swing the left hand up at the left side, over to behind. Bring the right hand past the waist to stab forward. (image 8b) When the right foot finishes in front, medially rotate the right arm to do a framing block, palm up. Look to the left. (image 8c)

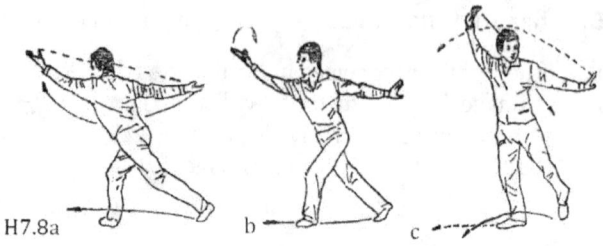

9. Closed Stance Push   bīngbù tuīzhǎng   并步推掌

As the curving walk finishes with the right foot forward, bring the left hand over the head to press down in front. Swing the right hand down at the right side to the rear. (image H7.9a) Bring the left foot up to meet the right in a closed stance. Bring the right hand in to the waist, then push forward. Turn the torso slightly to the left. Watch the movement of the right hand as it pushes forward, then quickly turn the head to look to the left. (image 9b)

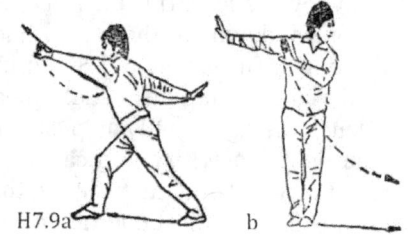

Section Two

10. Drop Stance Thread The Hand   pūbù chuānzhǎng   仆步穿掌

Squat fully on the right leg and extend the left foot out to the left side into a left drop stance. Thread the left hand forward along the left leg. (image H7.10a) Extend the right leg and bend the left knee to move to a left bow stance. Scoop up with the left arm and hold the right hand out behind. Look forward past the left hand. (image 10b)

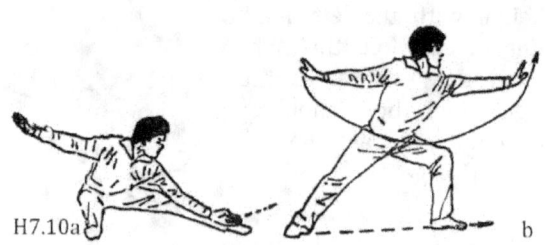

11. Aerial Snap Kick   téngkōng tántī   腾空弹踢

Step the right foot forward and bring the right hand through to scoop up in front. (image H7.11a) Swing the left leg up and push off with the right leg to jump up, quickly doing a right snap kick. Look forward. (image 11b)

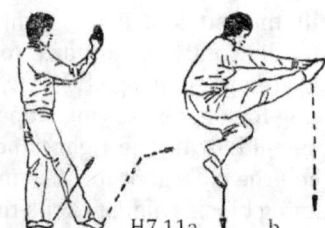

SEVENTH FORM HONGQUAN

12. Separate The Hands, Side Thrust Kick

fēnzhǎng cèchuāijiǎo   分掌侧踹脚

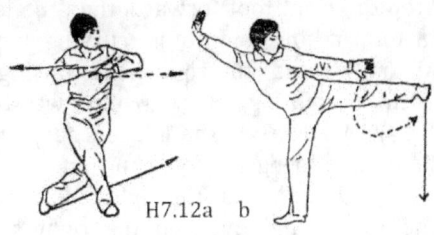

Land on the left leg then land the right foot, bending both knees to a half-squat. Cross both hands in front of the chest. (image H7.12a) Stand up on the right leg and do a left side kick. Simultaneously push the hands out to either side, palms out. (image 12b)

13. Closed Stance Push   bīngbù tuīzhǎng   并步推掌

Land the left foot and bend the knee, shifting the weight between the legs. Lower the left hand then slice up in front. (image H7.13a) Step the right foot forward then bring the left foot up to meet it in a closed stance. Medially

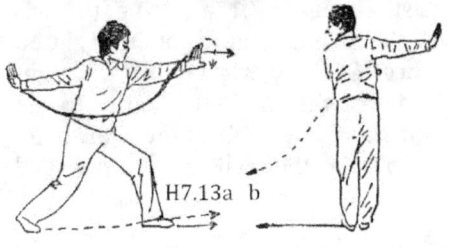

rotate the left arm to press down. Bring the right hand past the waist to push forward at shoulder height, palm edge out. Bring the left hand in to the right shoulder. Watch the right hand as it pushes, then quickly turn the head to look to the left. (image 13b)

14. Drop Stance Thread The Hand   pūbù chuānzhǎng   仆步穿掌

This is the same as move 10, but in the opposite direction. (images H7.14a, 14b)

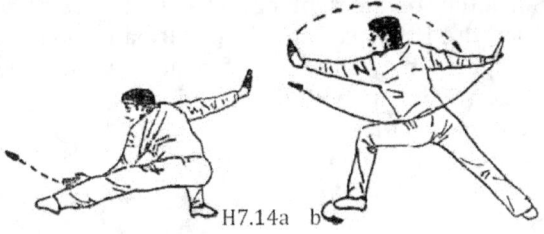

15. Bow Stance Stab   gōngbù chāzhǎng   弓步插掌

Turn the left foot out. Swing the left hand up and over on the left side to the rear at shoulder height, fingers up. Bring the right hand to the waist then stab forward, palm up. Look at the right hand. (image H7.15)

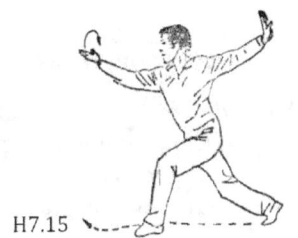

CHAQUAN, VOLUME II

16. Curving Walk, Thread And Hook

húxíngbù chuān guàzhǎng   弧行步穿挂掌

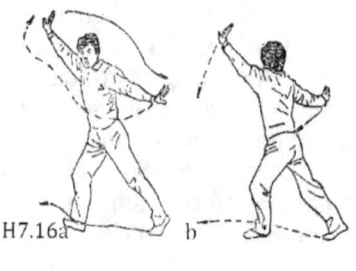

Step the right foot forward, then the left, in total taking four to six curving steps. Medially rotate the right hand, raising it with a framing block whilst walking. (image H7.16a) As the left foot takes the final step, bring the left hand up the left side to thread up at the right side. Swing the right hand over on the right side. Look forward. (image 16b)

17. Closed Stance Push   bīngbù tuīzhǎng   并步推掌

Step the right foot forward and bend the knee, shifting the weight forward. Medially rotate the left hand to press down. Bring the right hand in to the waist. (image H7.17a) Bring the left foot in to meet the right in a closed stance. Push forward with the right hand, bringing the left hand in to the right shoulder. Look at the right hand as it pushes, then quickly turn the head to look to the left. (image 17b)

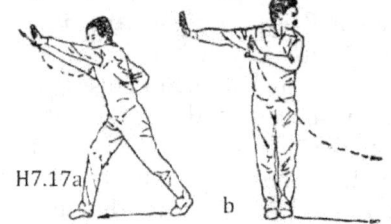

Section Three

18. Drop Stance Thread The Hand   pūbù chuānzhǎng   仆步穿掌

Squat fully on the right leg and extend the left foot out to the left side to take a left drop stance. Thread the left hand along the left leg. (image H7.18a) Straighten the right leg and bend the left knee to move into a left bow stance. Scoop up with the left hand to shoulder height with the fingers up. Hold the right hand out behind at shoulder height with a sideways palm. Look forward past the left hand. (image 18b)

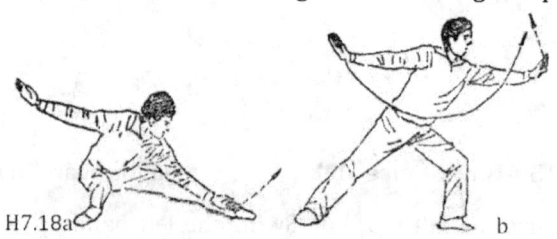

19. Two Rising Kicks   èrqǐjiǎo   二起脚

Shift forward, step the right foot forward, lifting the bent left knee. Lift the left hand and swing the right hand down on the right side, then forward and up to slap the back of the hand into the left palm with a sharp sound. Push off with the right leg to jump up, swinging the right foot up to kick. Slap the

SEVENTH FORM HONGQUAN

right foot with the right hand, swinging the left hand out to the left rear with a hook hand. Look forward. (images H7.19a, 19b, 19c)

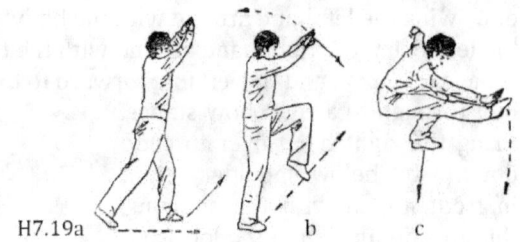

H7.19a   b   c

20. Empty Stance Stab   xūbù chāzhǎng   虚步插掌

Land on the left leg, then land the right foot, keeping the weight on the left leg. Swing the right hand up with a leading action at the right. Swing the left hand forward to press on the right elbow crease. (images H7.20a, 20b) Sit down into a right empty stance and hook the right hand, brushing to the right in front of the left knee. Keep the left hand at the right elbow crease. Look at the right hand. (image 20c) Shift to the right leg and step the left foot forward, touching the toes down in a left empty stance. Continue to hook the right hand rightward, back, and up to shoulder height, hook pointing down. Bring the left hand to the waist then stab directly forward, palm down, fingers up. Look past the left hand. (image 20d)

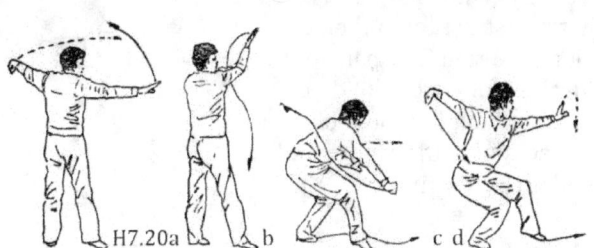

H7.20a   b   c   d

21. Bow Stance Stab   gōngbù chāzhǎng   弓步插掌

Extend the left foot forward and shift forward. Circle the left hand inward with a wrist-grabbing action. Unhook the right hand and bring it to the waist. (image H7.21a) Take a long step forward with the right foot to take a right bow stance. Stab the right hand forward and up, pressing the left hand down at the right armpit. Look at the right hand. (image 21b)

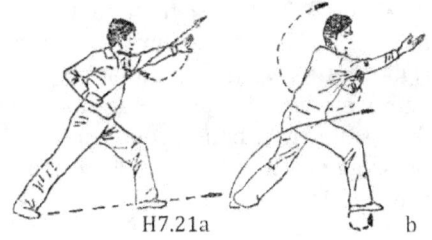

H7.21a   b

22. Wheel Over, Bow Stance Chop

fānshēn gōngbù pīzhǎng   翻身弓步劈掌

Turn a full three-sixty degrees around to the left, lifting the left knee, standing up on the right leg to pivot on the ball of the foot, turning the heel out. Swing the left hand around with the body, rising then chopping down at the left. Bring the right hand around with the turn, moving to the rear right. (image H7.22a) Land the left foot forward to the left side, then step the right foot through to a right bow stance. Bring the right hand over to chop down a bit below shoulder height in front, timed with the stepping, thumb side up. Swing the left hand back on the left side, finishing behind at shoulder height, thumb side up. Follow the action of the left hand, then turn the head to look at the right hand. (image 22b)

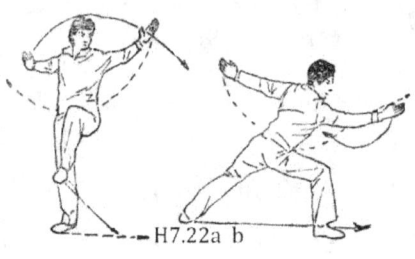

23. Drop Stance Thread The Hand pūbù chuānzhǎng 仆步穿掌

Step the left foot forward to take a left bow stance. Stab the left hand forward, passing by the waist. Press the right hand down at the left armpit. (image H7.23a) Squat fully on the left leg and sit down into a right drop stance. Thread the right hand past the torso then out along the right leg, palm out, fingers forward. Hold the left hand out behind. Follow the action of the right hand with the eyes. (image 23b)

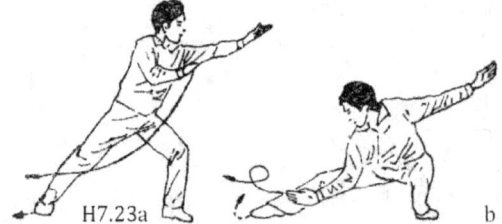

24. Empty Stance Press Down xūbù ànzhǎng 虚步按掌

Shift forward, moving the right foot a bit to take a right bow stance. Circle the right hand then stab forward, circling and laterally rotating the arm to turn the palm up. Look at the right hand. (image H7.24a) Step the left foot forward. Bring the left hand to the waist then stab forward, laterally rotating to turn the palm up. Look at the left hand. (image 24b) Step the right foot forward then squat on it, placing the left foot forward into a left empty stance. Medially rotate the left arm and lower it, hooking the hand. Swing the right hand around in a full circle at the right side, finishing by pressing down at the left elbow crease. Look forward past the hook hand. (image 24c)

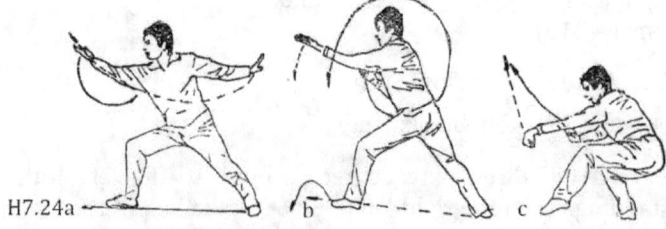

SEVENTH FORM HONGQUAN

Section Four

25. Two Rising Kicks   èrqǐjiǎo   二起脚

Shift forward, straightening the left leg. Unhook the left hand and swing it up. Swing up the right hand to slap the back of the hand into the left palm. (image H7.25a) Step the right foot forward and lift the bent left knee, pushing off with the right leg to jump up, quickly swinging the right leg up, keeping the left knee bent. Slap the right foot with the right hand, swinging the left hand up to the rear at shoulder height and hooking it, hook pointing down. Look at the slapping right hand. (images 25b, 25c)

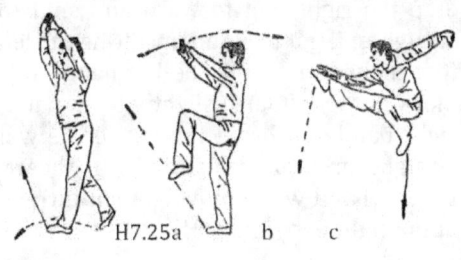

26. Separate The Hands, Side Thrust Kick

fēnzhǎng cèchuāijiǎo   分掌侧踹脚

Land on the left foot, then land the right. (image H7.26a) Step the right foot behind the left leg with an insertion step, then squat on both legs, taking a left resting stance. Laterally rotate the arms and circle them at the sides, continuing to circle until they cross in front of the chest with lifting palms, palms up. (image 26b) Stand up on the right leg, then do a side kick with the left leg to the left side. Medially rotate the arms and push out to either side. Look to the left. (image 26c)

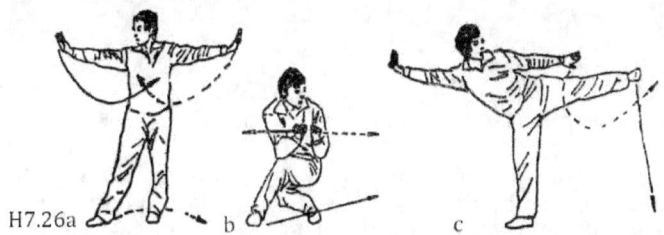

27. Hitting Hop-Step Slice Upwards   jībù liāozhǎng   击步撩掌

Land the left foot, swinging the left hand down, in order to slice up in front. (image H7.27a) Do a hitting hop-step, pushing off with the left leg and tapping the right foot into the left foot whilst airborne. Keep the

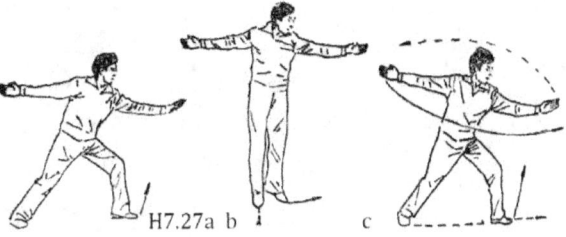

left hand in the slicing up position and hold the right arm out behind. (image 27b) Land the right foot, then the left, in front, without changing the arm positions. Look past the left hand. (image 27c)

28. Raised Knee Framing Block And Punch

tíxī jià chōngquán 提膝架冲拳

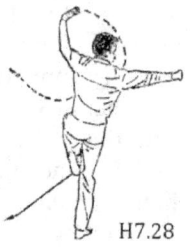

Step the right foot forward and shift to the right leg, straightening it to stand up, lifting the left knee with the foot tucked in. Swing the left hand up to do a framing block at the left, arm slightly bent, palm up. Clench the right hand and bring the fist to the waist then punch straight forward, arm straight, fist heart down. Look at the left hand while moving, then turn the head to look at the right fist. (image H7.28)

29. Hitting Hop-Step Slice Upwards jībù liāozhǎng 击步撩掌

Land the left foot to the left side, turning the body slightly to the left. Lower the left hand down in front of the right side of the chest, then slice up forward, to the left. (image H7.29a) Do a hitting hop-step, pushing off with the left foot and bumping the right foot behind the left foot whilst airborne. Bring the right fist to the waist. (image 29b) Land the right foot first, then the left, in front, shifting the weight between the legs. Look forward past the left hand. (image 29c)

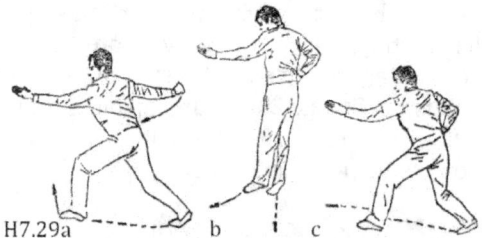

30. Closed Stance Push bīngbù tuīzhǎng 并步推掌

Step the right foot forward and shift forward. Do a wrist-grabbing action with the left hand. (image H7.30a) Bring the left foot up to meet the right, in a closed stance. Unclench the right hand and push out to the right with the palm edge, fingers up. Bring the left hand in to press down in front of the right shoulder. Look at the right hand as it pushes, then quickly turn the head to look left. (image 30b)

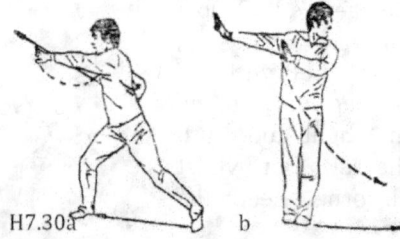

SEVENTH FORM HONGQUAN

Section Five

31. Drop Stance Thread The Hand   pūbù chuānzhǎng   仆步穿掌

Fully squat on the right leg and extend the left leg out to the left, into a left drop stance. Bring the left hand across the belly then along the left leg. Hold the right hand out at the right side at shoulder height. (image H7.31a) Push into the right leg and bend the left knee to take a left bow stance. Scoop up with the left hand to shoulder height, fingers up. Do not change the position of the right hand relative to the body. Look past the left hand. (image 31b)

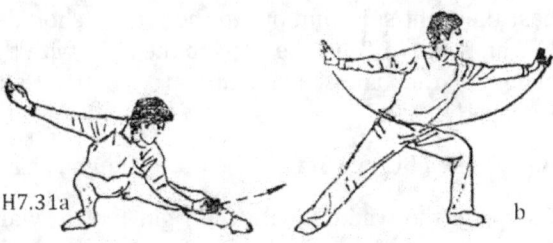

32. Raised Knee Scooping Snap   tíxī tiǎozhǎng   提膝挑掌

Swing the right hand along the right side to slice up in front, bringing the left hand in to tuck into the right elbow crease. (image H7.32a) Push into the left leg to lift the knee, shifting back to the right leg and standing up on it. With the weight shift, scoop up with the right arm, bringing the left arm along. Look forward. (image 32b)

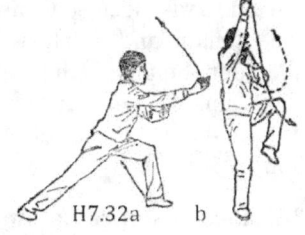

33. Bow Stance Flash Palm   gōngbù liàngzhǎng   弓步亮掌

Circle the left hand down and out to the upper left while circling the right hand out and down to inside the left knee. (image H7.33a) Circle the left hand down on the left side, hooking it as it passes to the rear. Scoop up with the right hand above the left knee. (image 33b) Land the left foot forward into a left bow stance. Raise the right hand, medially rotating the forearm, keeping the elbow slightly bent, palm up, to flash. Keep the left hand behind in a hook. Look forward. (image 33c)

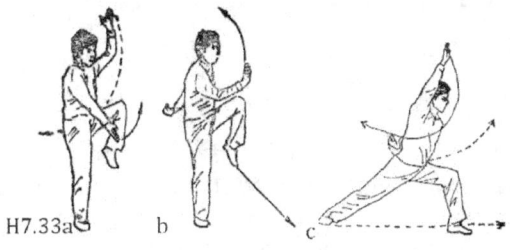

34. Curving Walk Slice Upwards And Hook

húxíngbù liāo guàzhǎng   弧行步撩挂掌

Step the right foot forward, then the left, walking forward with curving steps. Take four to six curving steps. Bring the left hand down at the left, then slice up to thread forward to the front, at head height, palm up. Swing the right hand down in front, past the right side, and out to the rear at shoulder height, palm up. Turn the body to the right with the action of the hands. Look forward, to the right. (image H7.34)

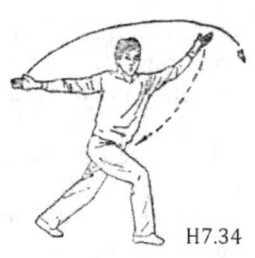

35. Closed Stance Stab   bīngbù chāzhǎng   并步插掌

Complete the walking with the right foot forward, then step the left foot forward into a bow stance. Bring the right hand over at the right side to press down in front at shoulder height, palm down. Clench the left hand and bring the fist to the waist. (image H7.35a) Bring the right foot up beside the left to take a closed stance. Unclench the left hand and stab forward and up to shoulder height, palm up. Press the right hand down, tucked into the left armpit. Look at the left hand. (image 35b)

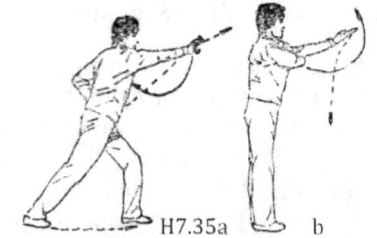

36. Closed Stance Hammerfist   bīngbù záquán   并步砸拳

Lift up the right hand, passing underneath the left arm, bringing in the left hand and lowering it. Both palms face up. (image H7.36a) Lift up with the left hand, passing outside the right hand, lowering the right hand. Both palms still face up. (image 36b) Clench the left hand and pound the fist down, lifting the right hand slightly to pound the back of the fist into the right palm. Watch the action of the hands. (image 36c)

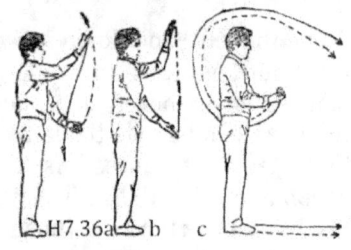

37. Closed Stance Double Lashes

bīngbù shuāng bǎizhǎng   并步双摆掌

Step the right foot forward, turning to the left. Unclench the left hand and lower both hands at the left side as you step forward. Then bring the left foot up beside the right into a closed stance. Continue to swing the arms up to the front at

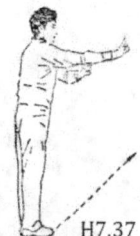

the right, right arm straight, left arm slightly bent so that the hand is tucked into the right elbow crease. Both hands are vertical palms, fingers up. Watch the hands as they circle, then look forward. (image H7.37)

38. Snap Kick   tántītuǐ   弹踢腿

Shift to the left leg and quickly do a snap kick with the right, ankle plantar-flexed. Look forward. (image H7.38)

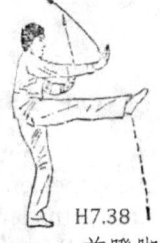

39. Front Heel Kick   qián dēngjiǎo   前蹬脚

Land the right foot, turning the hips and shoulders to the right and sitting down slightly. Lift the right hand to do a framing block. Press the left hand down in front of the right shoulder. (image H7.39a) Lift the left knee and do a heel kick to the front, pushing into the heel with the knee straight and the ankle dorsi-flexed. Push forward with the left hand along the leg. Look forward. (image 39b)

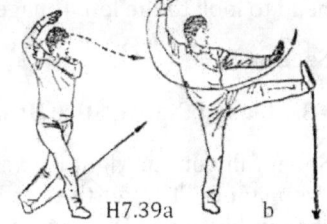

40. Leap To Snap Kick   yuèbù tántītuǐ   跃步弹踢腿

Land the left foot forward and shift forward. Lower the right hand at the back, then slice up and forward along the right side, finishing at shoulder height with the elbow bent and the fingers up. Bring the left hand in to press down at the right elbow crease. (image H7.40a) Step the right foot forward and lift the left knee, pushing into the right leg to jump up, quickly doing a snap kick with the right foot. Do not change the position of the hands. Look forward. (images 40b, 40c)

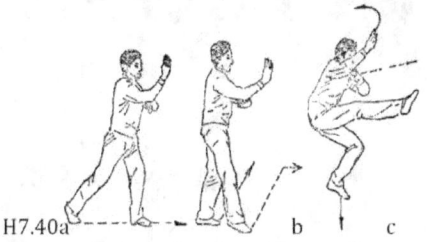

41. Bow Stance Framing Block And Punch

gōngbù jià chōngquán   弓步架冲拳

Land on the left leg, then step the right foot forward to take a right bow stance. Medially rotate the right arm to lead back on the right, then do a framing block upwards. Clench the left hand and bring the fist to the waist, then punch forward, extending the arm fully with the fist heart down. Look at the left fist. (image H7.41)

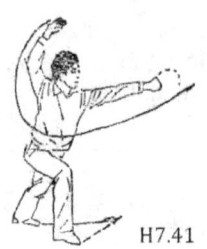

H7.41

42. Closed Stance Push   bīngbù tuīzhǎng   并步推掌

Step the right foot to the centre line of the form, then bring the left foot to meet it, standing up to a closed stance. Unclench the left hand and do a wrist-grabbing action. Push forward with the right hand, first passing the waist, palm edge forward, fingers up. Press down with the left hand in front of the right shoulder. Turn the head to look to the left. (image H7.42)

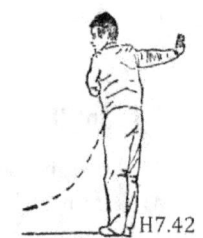

Section Six

43. Closed Stance Slice Upwards   bīngbù liāozhǎng   并步撩掌

Squat fully on the right leg and extend the left leg along the ground in a left drop stance. Thread the left hand along the left leg. (image H7.43.a) Bend the left leg and shift forward to a bow stance. Extend the left hand forward with a scoop. (image 43b) Bring the right foot up to the left, taking a closed stance with the knees bent in a half-squat. Swing the right hand on the right side to slice up in front, thumb side up. Bring the left hand in to the right elbow crease. Look forward past the right hand. (image 43c)

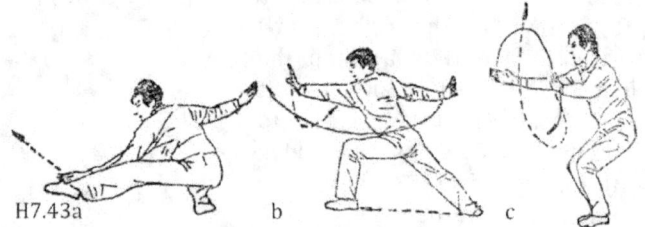

44. Closed Stance Flash Palm   bīngbù liàngzhǎng   并步亮掌

Circle the right hand up, out, then down to in front of the knees. Circle the left hand down, out, then up to above the head. (image H7.44a) Turn the torso slightly to the right and hook the left hand down past the left knee to the rear. Medially rotate the right hand to do a framing block / flash palm at the upper right. Look to the left. (image 44b)

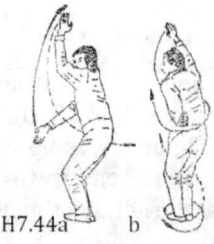

SEVENTH FORM HONGQUAN

45. Raised Knee Press Down   tíxī ànzhǎng   提膝按掌

Pivot on the ball of the left foot to turn two-seventy degrees around to the right. Then straighten the left leg and stand up, lifting the right knee with the foot tucked in. Bend the right elbow and lower it in front of the right chest, fingers up in a vertical palm. Keep the left hand hooking behind. Look forward. (image H7.45)

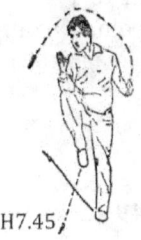

46. Leap Forward To Bow Stance Stab

qián yuè gōngbù chāzhǎng   前跃弓步插掌

Land the right foot forward and push off to jump up, swinging the left foot forward and across, to leap forward. Clench the right hand and bring the fist to the waist. Swing the left hand up past the head. (image H7.46a) Land on the left foot, then step the right foot forward to take a right bow stance. Bend the left elbow to press down with the palm. Unclench the right hand and thread it forward over the back of the left hand, finishing at shoulder height with the palm up. Look at the right hand. (image 46b)

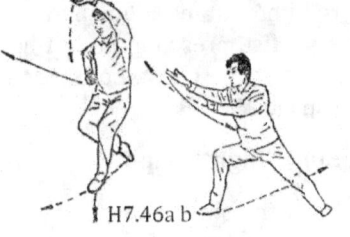

47. Leap Back To Bow Stance Punch

hòu yuè gōngbù chōngquán   后跃弓步冲拳

Push off with the right leg to swing backwards, shifting the body back, then pushing off with the left leg to jump up and back. Lift up with the left hand, palm down, with a framing block. Clench the right hand and bring the fist to the waist. (image H7.47a) Land on the right leg then step the left foot back, setting the right knee firmly into a right bow stance. Punch forward with the right fist. Press down with the left hand in front of the right side of the chest. Look at the right fist. (image 47b)

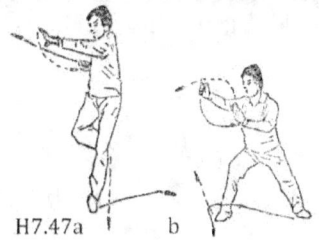

48. Leap Forward To Bow Stance Stab

qián yuè gōngbù chāzhǎng   前跃弓步插掌

Jump forward, pushing off and landing with the left leg. Push off with the right foot, lifting the knee. Bring the left hand over the right fist to press down in front. Bring the right fist to the waist. (image H7.48a) Land on the left leg, then land the right foot in front, setting the knee firmly to a right bow stance. Unclench the right hand and thread it out over the back of the left hand, palm up. Bring the left hand in to press down at the right armpit, palm down. Look at the right hand. (image 48b)

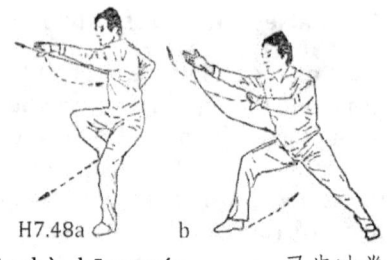

49. Bow Stance Punch   gōngbù chōngquán   弓步冲拳

Push with the right foot to lift the knee, shifting back to the left leg. Lift up with the left hand to do a framing block. Clench the right hand and bring it to the waist. (image H7.49a) Land the right foot firmly forward, bending the knee to a right bow stance. Punch forward with the right fist, pressing the left hand down in front of the chest. Look at the right fist. (image 49b)

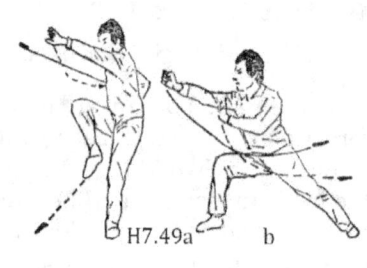

50. Right Snap Kick   yòu tántuǐ   右弹腿

Turn the shoulders and waist to the left and squat fully on the right leg, extending the left leg to a left drop stance. Brush aside with the left hand past the left foot. Unclench the right hand and swing it to press down in front of the left shoulder. (image H7.50a) Push into the right leg, lifting the heel, shifting forward and bending the left knee. Hook the left hand and swing the straight arm to the rear left side, hook pointing down at shoulder height. Do not change the position of the right hand. Turn the torso to the left. (image 50b) Lift the right knee then extend the leg with a snap kick, ankle plantar-flexed. Look forward. (image 50c)

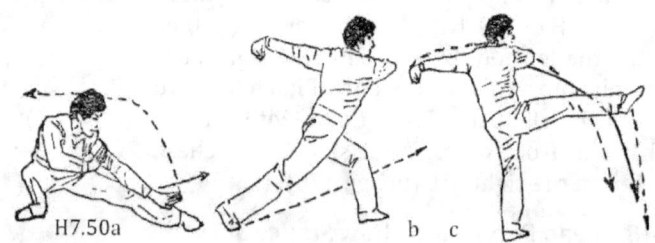

51. Left Snap Kick   zuǒ tántuǐ   左弹腿

Squat fully on the left leg and land the right foot forward, extending it to take a right drop stance. Swing the right hand to brush aside over the right foot. Unhook the left hand and press down in front of the right shoulder. (image H7.51a) Push into the left leg, lifting the heel and shifting forward,

SEVENTH FORM HONGQUAN

bending the right knee. Turn the torso to the right. Hook the right hand and swing it back on the right, hook pointing down at shoulder height. Keep the left hand pressing down in front of the right shoulder. (image 51b) Lift the left knee then extend it with a snap kick, ankle plantar-flexed. Look forward. (image 51c)

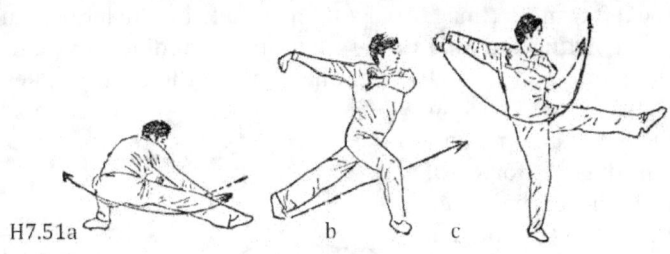

52. Two Rising Kicks   èrqǐjiǎo   二起脚

Land the left foot and shift forward. Swing the left hand down to swing forward and up. Unhook the right hand and swing it down on the right side to swing up to slap the back of the hand into the left palm. (image H7.52a) Step the right foot forward and lift the bent left knee, quickly pushing off with the right leg to jump up, swinging the right leg straight up in front. At the height of the jump, slap the right foot with the right hand. Hook the left hand and swing it out behind on the left side. Look forward. (images 52b, 52c)

53. Bow Stance Chop   gōngbù pīzhǎng   弓步劈掌

Land on the left foot and settle on it with the right knee still raised. Raise the right hand above the head. Unhook the left hand and hold it out behind at the left side. (image H7.53a) Land the right foot forward, bending the knee to take a right bow stance. Chop the right hand down in front to shoulder height, thumb side up. Keep the left hand extended out behind at shoulder height, fingers up. Look at the right hand. (53b)

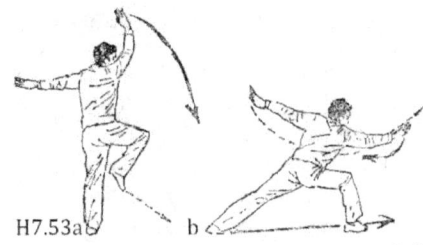

Section Seven

54. Drop Stance Thread The Hand   pūbù chuānzhǎng   仆步穿掌

Step the left foot forward into a left bow stance. Bring the left hand to the waist then thread forward. Press down with the right hand, bringing it to the left armpit. (image H7.54a) Squat fully on the left leg, turning the waist and twisting the hips to the right and extending the right leg into a right drop stance. Thread the right hand along the right leg, keeping the elbow slightly bent, palm facing out, fingers pointing forward. Hold the left hand out behind at shoulder height, fingers up. Look at the right hand. (image 54b)

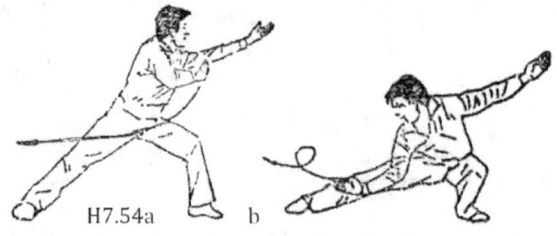

55. Empty Stance Press Down   xūbù ànzhǎng   虚步按掌

Shift forward, bending the right knee forward, shifting the foot a bit to take a right bow stance with the foot turned out. Circle the right hand out, then thread it forward, laterally rotating the arm to turn the palm up. (image H7.55a) Step the left foot forward. Bring the left hand to the waist then stab forward, laterally rotating to turn the palm up. Press down with the right hand. (image 55b) Step the right foot forward, bending the knee to a half-squat and moving the left foot forward to touch down in front in a left empty stance. Medially rotate the left hand, hooking the hand down. Swing the right hand down at the right, back, then up and over to press down in front at the left elbow crease. Follow the action of the right hand with the eyes, then look forward. (image 55c)

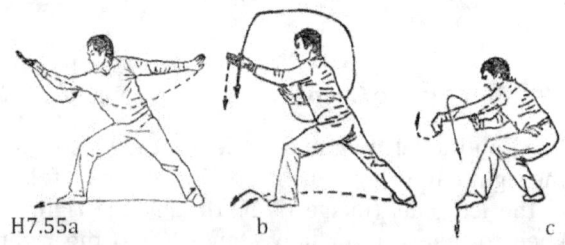

56. Empty Stance Double Lashes   xūbù shuāng bǎizhǎng   虚步双摆掌

Step the left foot across to the left side. Turn the torso to the left, turning the waist and hips. Swing the right hand over the left arm to hook down to the left side. Unhook the left hand and bend the elbow to tuck the hand in behind the right shoulder. (image H7.56a) Step the right foot across in front of the left foot. Laterally rotate the right arm and swing it to the left side, up, then right. Laterally rotate the left arm and swing it down, then up on the

SEVENTH FORM HONGQUAN

left side. Both palms face up at shoulder height. (image 56b) Step the left foot across to the left with a sideways step. Swing the left hand up over the head to the right, to stop at the right elbow crease. (image 56c) Shift to the left leg and half-squat on it, placing the right foot across to in front of the left foot, knee slightly bent, touching the toes down in a right empty stance. Lower both hands in front of the belly, swinging from the left, then up and over to the right side, turning the torso to the right. Keep the right arm extended and bend the left arm to keep the hand at the right elbow crease. Follow the action of the hands with the eyes, then look forward. (image 56d)

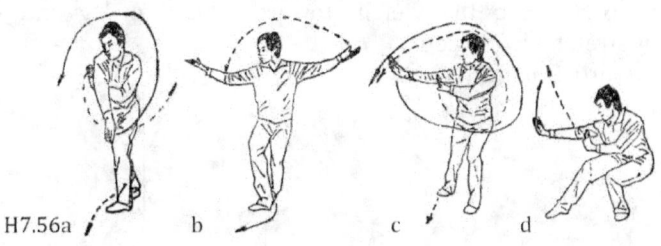

57. Two Rising Kicks   èrqǐjiǎo   二起脚

Push into the left leg, standing up and shifting forward. Swing both hands to lead upwards, the left moving a bit before the right, to slap the back of the right hand into the left palm. (image H7.57a) Swing the left leg up and push off with the right leg to quickly jump up and do a swinging kick, ankle plantar-flexed. Slap the right foot with the right hand. Hook the left hand and swing back on the left. (image 57b) Land on the left foot, then land the right foot forward. Keep the arms held out in the same positions, unhooking the left hand. Look forward. (image 57c)

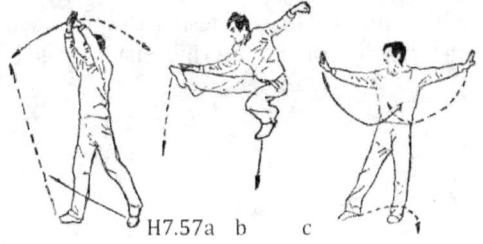

58. Separate The Hands, Side Thrust Kick
     fēnzhǎng cèchuāijiǎo   分掌侧踹脚

Do an insertion step with the right foot, tucking behind the left leg so that the legs are crossed, squatting down in a left resting stance. Lower the arms, then bring them to block with forearms crossed in front of the chest. (image H7.58a) Stand up on the right leg, straightening it. Bend and lift the left knee

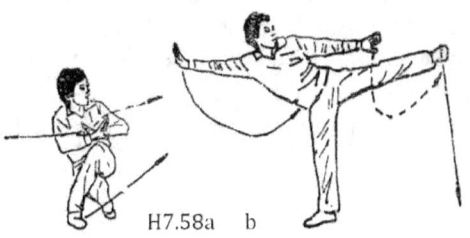

then do a side thrust kick to the left side. Push out to either side with the hands. Look to the left side. (image 58b)

59. Hitting Hop-Step Slice Upwards jībù liāozhǎng 击步撩掌

Land the left foot forward. Lower the left hand in order to slice up in front. Bring the right hand to the waist. (image H7.59a) Bring the right foot up to do a hitting hop-step, pushing off with the left foot and tapping the heel of the left foot with the right foot. Slice up with both hands to either side whilst airborne. (image 59b) Land on the right foot, then the left, keeping it in front. Keep the weight towards the rear leg and leave the arms outstretched. Look forward. (image 59c)

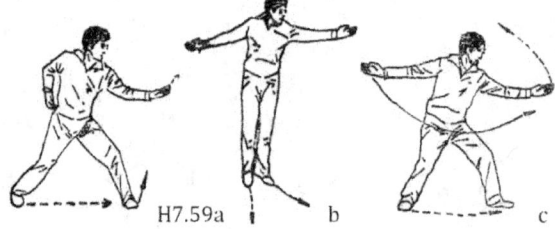

60. Closed Stance Framing Block And Punch bīngbù jià chōngquán 并步架冲拳

Bring the right foot up to meet the left foot, taking a closed stance in a half-squat. Do a framing block with the left hand, medially rotating the arm to turn the palm up. Clench the right hand and bring the fist to the waist, then punch out to the left side. Look at the right fist. (image H7.60)

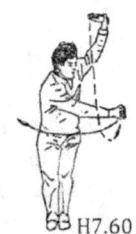

61. Bow Stance Punch gōngbù chōngquán 弓步冲拳

Do not change the stance. Hook with the left arm, passing in front, to the rear left of the body, medially rotating the arm and hooking the hand, fingers pointing up. Bring the right fist to the waist. (image H7.61a) Step the right foot out to the right side, turning the torso to the right, turning the waist and hips to take a right bow stance. Punch the right fist directly out to the front, to the right side. Clench the left hand and bring the fist to the waist. Look at the right fist. (image 61b)

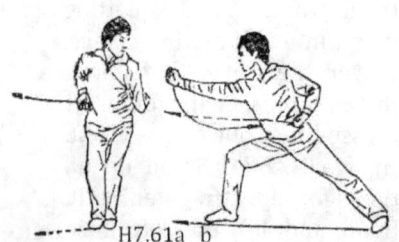

SEVENTH FORM HONGQUAN

62. Horse Stance Punches　　　mǎbù chōngquán　　马步冲拳

Step the left foot forward. Turn one-eighty degrees to the right and bend both knees to sit into a horse stance. Bring the right fist to the waist. Punch out to the left side with the left fist. Look at the left fist. (image H7.62a) Without changing the stance, bring the left fist to the waist and punch directly forward with the right fist. Look at the right fist. (image 62b)

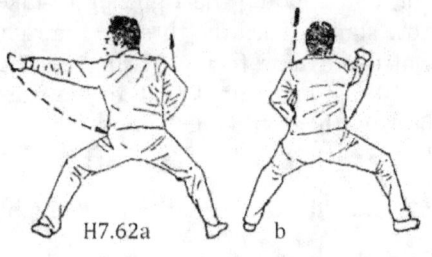

63. Open Bow Stance Punch　　　héngdāngbù chōngquán　　横裆步冲拳

Turn out the left heel and straighten the leg, pushing into the right knee. Turn the torso to the right, turning the waist and twisting the hips, to take a right open bow stance. Bring the right fist to the waist, fist heart up. Punch directly forward with the left fist, fist heart down. Look at the left fist. (image H7.63)

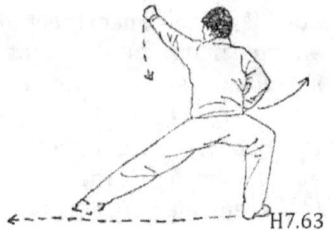

64. Bow Stance Punches　　　gōngbù chōngquán　　弓步冲拳

Retreat the right foot behind the left and turn the torso ninety degrees to the right, bending the left knee to take a left bow stance. Punch the right fist forward and bring the left fist to the waist. (image H7.64a) Punch forward with the left fist and bring the right fist to the waist. Look at the left fist. (image 64b)

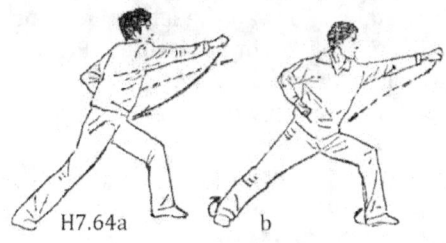

65. Horse Stance Punch　　　mǎbù chōngquán　　马步冲拳

Turn the left heel out and tuck in the left knee, bending the right knee and turning the waist to the right to sit into a horse stance. Bring the left fist to the waist and punch the right fist directly forward. Look at the right fist. (image H7.65)

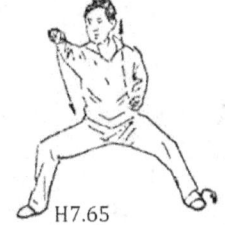

66. Open Bow Stance Punch   héngdāngbù chōngquán   横裆步冲拳

Straighten the left leg, pushing into left heel to turn it out, and bending the right leg to take a right open bow stance. Turn the torso to the right, twisting the waist and hips further. Bring the right fist to the waist, fist heart up. Punch to the front with the left fist, fist heart down. Look at the left fist. (image H7.66)

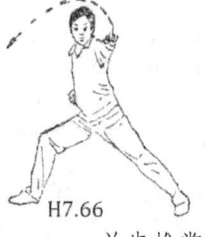

67. Closed Stance Push   bīngbù tuīzhǎng   并步推掌

Turn the torso ninety degrees to the right. Swing the left hand up and over to press down in front, to the right side, palm down, wrist cocked inward. (image H7.67a) Bring the left foot up to the right foot and stand up on both legs. Unclench the right hand and push out to the right side at shoulder height, palm edge out, fingers up. Bring the left hand in to in front of the right shoulder. Look at the right hand, then turn to look to the left side. (image 67b)

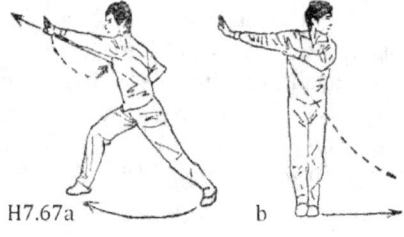

Section Eight

68. Drop Stance Thread The Hand   pūbù chuānzhǎng   仆步穿掌

Squat fully on the right leg and extend the left leg out to the left side in a left drop stance. Thread the left hand along the left leg. Hold the right arm out to the right side. (image H7.68a) Push into the right leg and bend the left leg to take a left bow stance. Scoop up with the left hand to shoulder height, fingers up. Keep holding the right arm out behind. Look past the left hand. (image 68b)

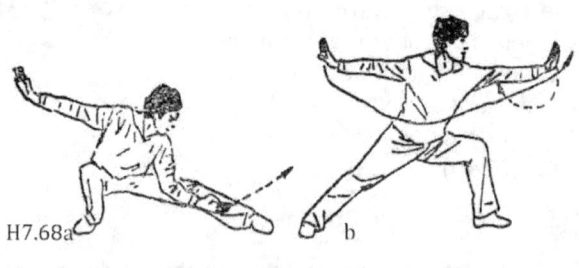

69. Raised Knee Scooping Snap   tíxī tiǎozhǎng   提膝挑掌

Swing the right hand down and along the right side to slice up in front. Tuck the left hand into the right elbow crease. (image H7.69a) Push into the left leg to raise the knee, shifting back

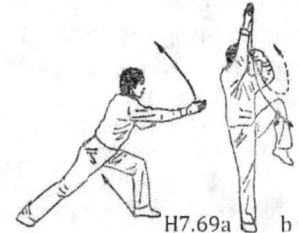

to the right leg and straightening it to stand upright. Raise the right arm, keeping it straight, bringing the left hand along with a scooping action. Look forward. (image 69b)

70. Bow Stance Flash Palm　　　gōngbù liàngzhǎng　　　弓步亮掌

Lower the left hand, circling it out to lift it on the left side. Circle the right hand out and down to inside the left knee. (image H7.70a) Swing the left hand down, then hook it as it passes by the left side towards the rear. Scoop up with the right hand. (image 70b) Land the left foot forward to a left bow stance. Extend the right arm forward, medially rotating to turn the palm up with a flash palm. Keep the left hand hooking back at the left side. Look forward. (image 70c)

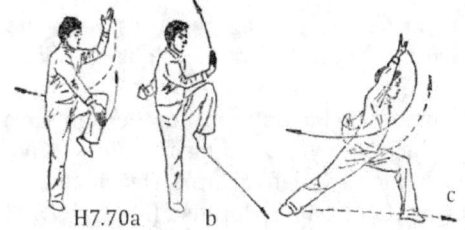

71. Curving Walk, Slice Upwards And Hook

húxíngbù liāo guàzhǎng　　　弧行步撩挂掌

Step the right foot forward with the foot turned out. Turn slightly to the right. Unhook the left hand and bring it down on the left side to slice up in front with a threading framing block. Lower the right hand in front, past the right side, and brush out behind on the right. Take four steps. (image H7.71a) After four steps, step the right foot forward again. Turn slightly leftward. Swing the right hand down on the right side, then slice up and thread forward to do a framing block. Swing the left hand at the left side to the rear. Look forward, following the turn of the body. (image 71b)

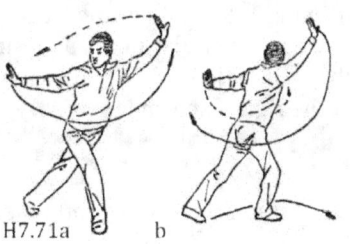

72. Horse Stance Hammerfist　　　mǎbù zāquán　　　马步砸拳

Step the left foot forward, shifting to a half-squat between the legs. Lower the left hand to press down in front of the right side of the chest. Circle the right hand down, out, and back to the right. (image H7.72a) Take a further half-step forward with the left foot. Extend the left hand out in front, palm forward, tiger's mouth angled down. Clench the right hand and bring the fist to the waist. (image 72b) Step the right foot forward and take a horse stance. Clench the left hand and bring the fist to the waist, fist heart up. Pound down with the right fist, first extending it up, then pounding down with the elbow bent, fist heart up. Look at the right fist. (image 72c)

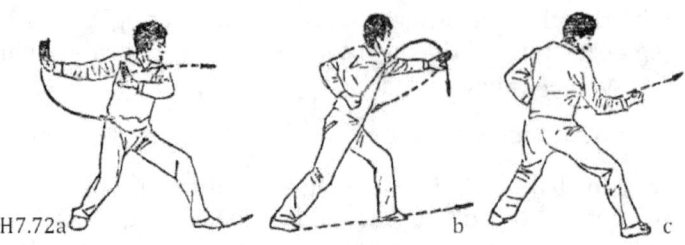

73. Bow Stance Punch   gōngbù chōngquán   弓步冲拳

Push into the left leg and press into the right knee, turning the waist to the right to take a right bow stance. Punch the left fist out over the right fist, fist heart down. Medially rotate the right arm to turn the fist heart down, bending the elbow and placing the fist under the left armpit. Reach the torso forward slightly. Look at the left fist. (image H7.73)

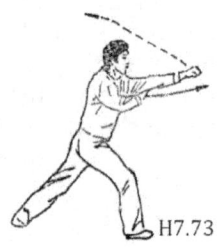

74. Horse Stance Framing Block And Punch
     mǎbù jià chōngquán   马步架冲拳

Push into the right heel to turn it out, tucking in the knee. Bend the left knee and turn to the left, turning the waist and half-squatting to a horse stance. Do a framing block above the head at the left with the left fist, arm bent, fist heart up. Punch the right fist out to the right side at shoulder height, fist heart down. Look at the right fist. (image H7.74)

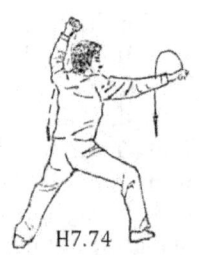

75. Horse Stance Hammerfist   mǎbù záquán   马步砸拳

Stay in the horse stance. Laterally rotate the right fist, raise it, then quickly pound down with the fist heart up. Laterally rotate the left fist and lower it to the waist, fist heart up. Look at the right fist. (image H7.75)

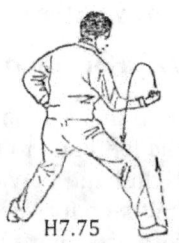

76. Jump Switch-Step, Horse Stance Swinging Hammerfist
     huàntiào mǎbù lūn záquán   换跳马步抡砸拳

Push into the right leg to lift the knee, shifting to the left leg and standing up on it. Swing the right fist in then out to pound outwards. (image H7.76a) Push off with the left leg to jump up, turn one-eighty degrees to the right,

SEVENTH FORM HONGQUAN

then land on the right foot and step the left out to the side into a horse stance. Swing the left arm up, then to the front to pound down, fist heart up. Bring the right fist to the waist. Look at the left fist. (image 76b)

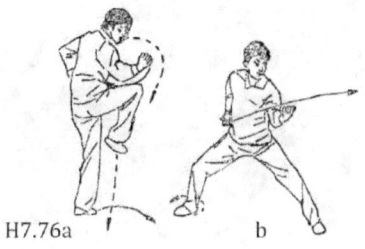

77. Bow Stance Punch   gōngbù chōngquán   弓步冲拳

Push into the right leg and press into the left knee, turning left into a left bow stance. Punch the right fist forward over the left fist, medially rotating the arm to turn the fist heart down. Medially rotate the left arm to turn the fist heart down, and bend the elbow to place the fist into the right armpit. Reach the torso forward slightly. Look at the right fist. (image H7.77)

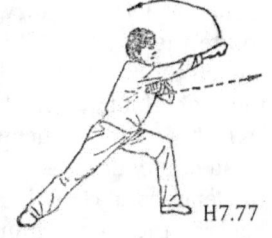

78. Horse Stance Framing Block And Punch

mǎbù jià chōngquán   马步架冲拳

Push into the left heel to turn it out, tucking in the knee. Bend the right knee and turn to the right, shifting between the legs and half-squatting to a horse stance. Do a framing block above the head with the right fist, elbow slightly bent and fist heart up. Punch out to the left side to shoulder height with the left fist, fist heart down. Look at the left fist. (image H7.78)

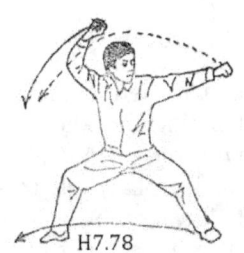

Section Nine

79. Raised Knee Double Lashes   tíxī shuāng bǎizhǎng   提膝双摆掌

Step the left foot across in front of the right foot towards the right side. Unclench the right hand and swing it down on the right side. Unclench the left hand and bring it over the head to the right side, tucking into the right elbow crease. Both hands are pointing up. (image H7.79a) Step the right foot across to the right side. Swing the hands together past the belly over to the upper left, tucking the right hand into the left elbow crease. Both hands point forward. (image 79b) Push into the left foot to lift the knee with the foot tucked in, shifting to the right leg and standing up on it. Swing the hands up and over to the right side, extending the right arm and bending the left arm to tuck the hand into the right elbow crease. Both hands point up. Follow the action of the right hand with the eyes. (image 79c)

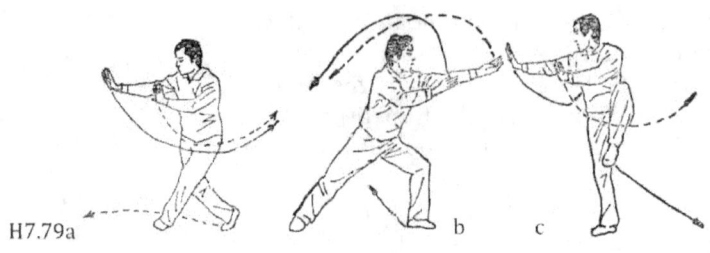

H7.79a   b   c

80. Bow Stance Hack gōngbù kǎnzhǎng 弓步砍掌

Land the left foot forward, to the left side, and turn leftward. Laterally rotate the left hand, bring it past the belly, then slice up to the left side. Clench the right hand and bring the fist to the waist. (image H7.80a) Step the right foot forward into a right bow stance, turning the torso ninety degrees to the left. Unclench the right hand and hack to the front, thumb side on top. Press down with the left hand at the right elbow crease. Look at the right hand. (image 80b)

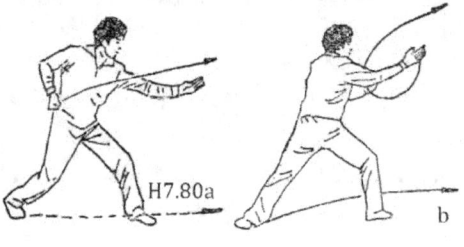

81. Advance, Reverse Snapped Palm jìnbù fǎn tánzhǎng 进步反弹掌

Step the left foot forward, turning the foot out and bending the knee, lifting the right heel slightly with the knee bent. Shift the weight to between the legs. Laterally rotate the right hand and bring it inwards, bring the hand down past the belly then up in front of the left arm, and forward to snap out upside down, palm angled in. Keep the left hand at the right elbow, fingers up. Look at the right hand. (image H7.81)

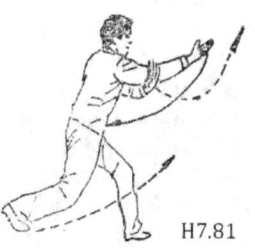

82. Bow Stance Stab gōngbù chāzhǎng 弓步插掌

Shift forward onto the left leg, bending the knee and lifting the right knee. Lift the left hand up and bring the right hand to the waist. (image H7.82a) Land the right foot forward with the knee bent, into a right bow stance. Stab the right hand out to shoulder height over the left arm, palm up. Bring the left hand in to press down at the right armpit, palm down. Look at the right hand. (image 82b)

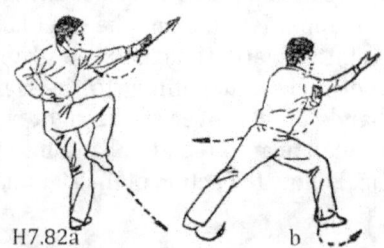

SEVENTH FORM HONGQUAN

83. Empty Stance Scooping Snap   xūbù tiǎozhǎng   虚步挑掌

Rotate the right foot out and turn ninety degrees to the left, shifting onto the right leg and half-squatting. Bring the left foot in a half-step to sit into a left empty stance. Bring the left hand in past the belly then scoop up to shoulder height on the left side, thumb side cocked, fingers up. Scoop up behind with the right hand at shoulder height. Look at the left hand. (image H7.83)

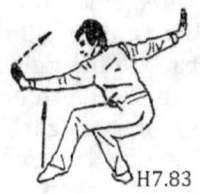

84. Raised Knee Scooping Snap   tíxī tiǎozhǎng   提膝挑掌

Straighten the right leg and lift the left knee. Scoop up with the left hand, bending the elbow, fingers up. Do not move the right hand. Look forward. (image H7.84)

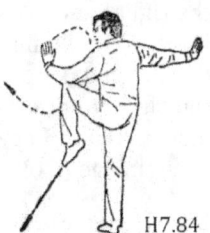

85. Hitting Hop-Step Slice Upwards   jībù liāozhǎng   击步撩掌

Land the left foot forward and shift forward. Lower the left hand then slice up in front. (image H7.85a) Jump up off the left foot, bringing the right foot up to tap the feet together whilst airborne, moving forward. Swing the arms naturally with the jump. (image 85b) Land on the right foot, then land the left foot ahead of it. Extend the left arm slightly to scoop up. Clench the right hand and bring the fist in to the waist. Look forward. (image 85c)

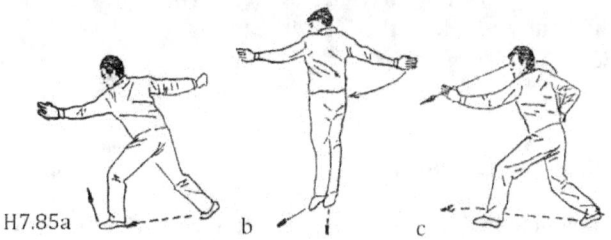

86. Bow Stance Hack   gōngbù kǎnzhǎng   弓步砍掌

Step the right foot forward into a right bow stance. Unclench the right hand and hack in front with an angled downward palm edge. Press down with the left hand at the right elbow crease. Look at the right hand. (image H7.86)

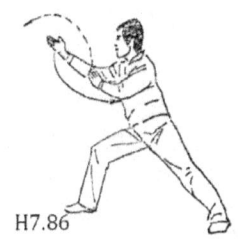

87. Empty Stance Flash Palm xūbù liàngzhǎng 虚步亮掌

Thread the left hand over top of the right arm, to circle out to the left, palm out. Draw in with the right hand to under the left armpit. (image H7.87a) Sit back to the right leg, half-squatting, and step the left foot across from the left side, touching the toes down to take a left empty stance. Turn the torso to face straight on. Swing the left hand flat out to the left side, medially rotating the arm to turn the palm down. Swing the right hand down and up to the right side, medially rotating the arm to turn the palm down. (image 87b) Lift the right hand at the right side, flashing the palm up. Swing the left hand up and over to the right, to press at the right elbow crease. Look to the left side. (image 87c)

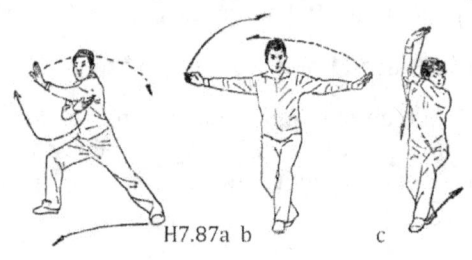

88. Closed Stance Facing Fists bīngbù duìquán 并步对拳

Withdraw the left foot. Laterally rotate the hands and lower them in front of the belly, palms up. (image H7.88a) Withdraw the right foot and bring the hands to either side at the hips. (image 88b) Bring the left foot to meet the right, to take a closed stance, and shift back, straightening both legs to stand up. Medially rotate the arms and circle the hands around, clenching the fists in front of the belly, fist hearts down. Look at the hands while they circle, then turn the head to look to the left side. (image 88c)

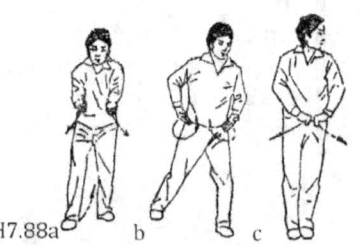

89. Closing Posture shōu shì 收势

Unclench the hands and place them on the thighs at their respective sides, standing to attention. Look straight forward. (image H7.89)

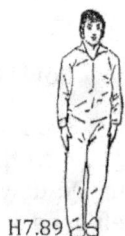

THIRD FORM HONGQUAN (IMAGES ONLY)
三路洪拳

0. **Position Of Preparation**
   yùbèi shì
   预备势

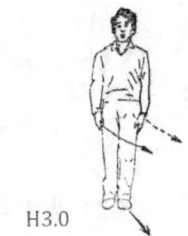

H3.0

Section One
1. **Step Forward Facing Fists**
   shàngbù duìquán
   上步对拳

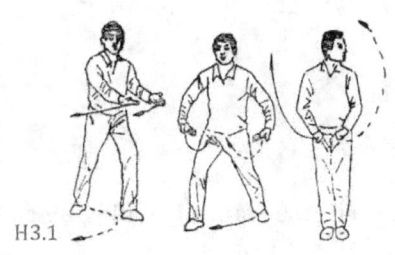

H3.1

2. **Closed Stance Flash Palm**
   bīngbù liàngzhǎng
   并步亮掌

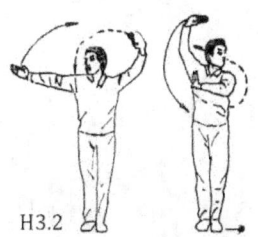

H3.2

3. **Right Empty Stance Scooping Snap**
   yòu xūbù tiǎozhǎng
   右虚步挑掌

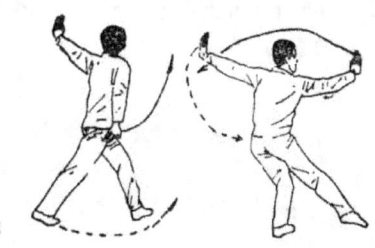

H3.3

4. **Left Empty Stance Scooping Snap**
   zuǒ xūbù tiǎozhǎng
   左虚步挑掌

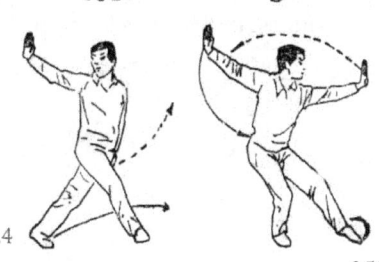

H3.4

5. **Right Empty Stance Scooping Snap**
   yòu xūbù tiǎozhǎng
   右虚步挑掌

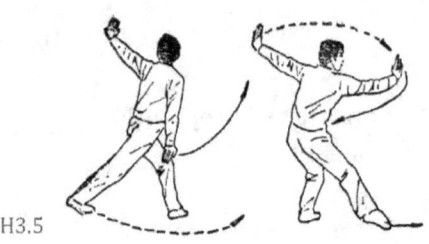

H3.5

6. **Right Bow Stance Press Down In Front**
   yòu gōngbù qián ànzhǎng
   右弓步前按掌

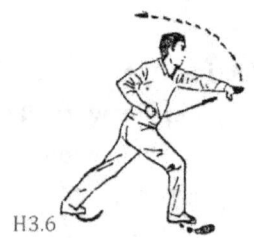

H3.6

7. **Horse Stance Framing Block And Hit**
   mǎbù jiàdǎ
   马步架打

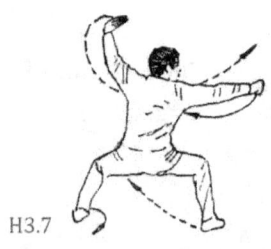

H3.7

8. **Raised Knee Stab**
   tíxī chuānzhǎng
   提膝穿掌

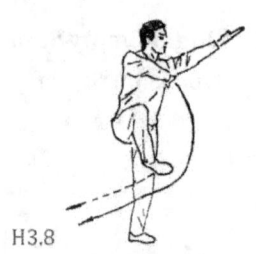

H3.8

9. **Right Drop Stance Thread The Hand**
   yòu pūbù chuānzhǎng
   右仆步穿掌

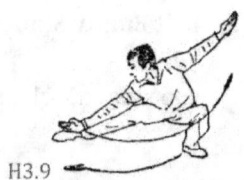

H3.9

THIRD FORM HONGQUAN (IMAGES ONLY)

10. Step Forward To Left Empty Stance Scooping Snap

shàngbù zuǒ xūbù tiǎozhǎng　　　　　　　　上步左虚步挑掌

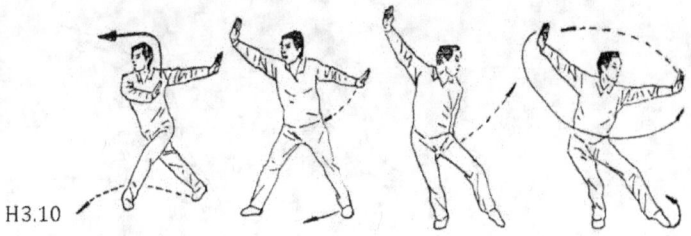

11. Resting Stance Vertical Palm

xiēbù lìzhǎng

歇步立掌

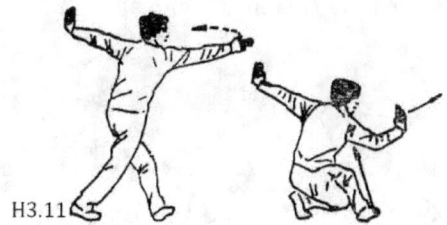

12. Raised Knee Push

tíxī tuīzhǎng

提膝推掌

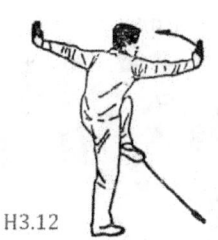

13. Right Bow Stance Character Ten Punches

yòu gōngbù shízìquán　　　　　　　　右弓步十字拳

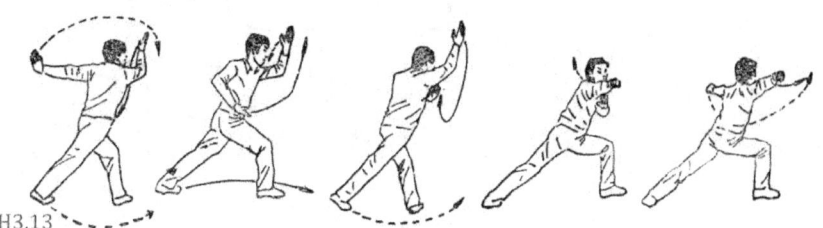

14. Wrist Wrap, Empty Stance Scooping Snap
chánwàn xūbù tiǎozhǎng   缠腕虚步挑掌

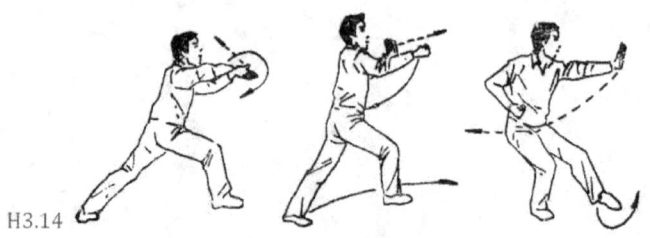

15. Jump Switch-Step, Horse Stance Low Planting Punch
huántiào mǎbù xià zāiquán   换跳马步下栽拳

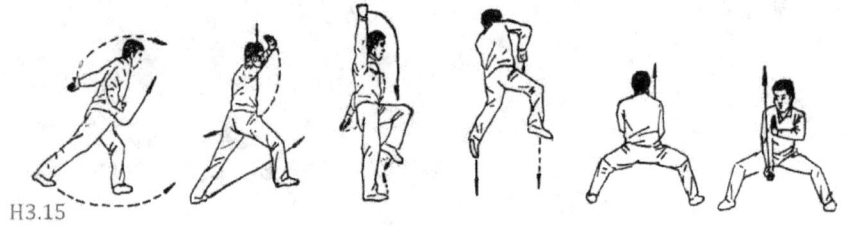

16. Horse Stance Upwards Punch
mǎbù shàng chōngquán
马步上冲拳

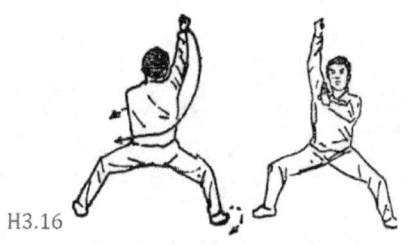

17. Separate The Hands, Snap Kick
fēnzhǎng tántuǐ
分掌弹腿

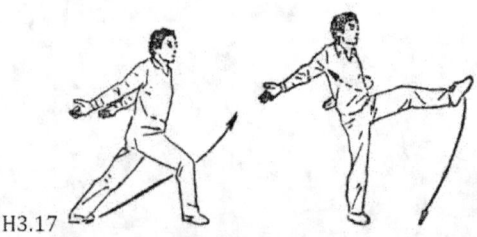

THIRD FORM HONGQUAN (IMAGES ONLY)

18. **Hitting Hop-Step, Horse Stance Hack**
    jībù mǎbù kǎnzhǎng 击步马步砍掌

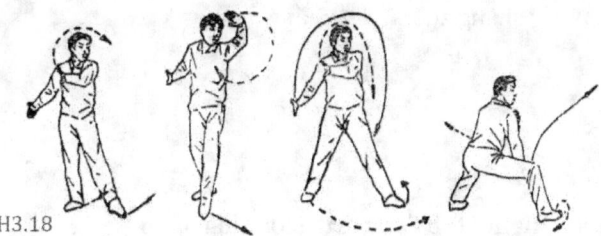

19. **Lean On The Mountain**
    kàoshānzhǎng
    靠山掌

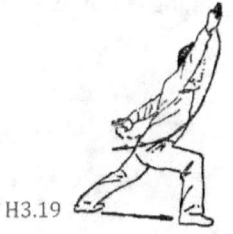

20. **Turn Around, Brush Aside, T Stance Flash Palm**
    zhuànshēn lōushǒu dīngbù liàngzhǎng 转身搂手丁步亮掌

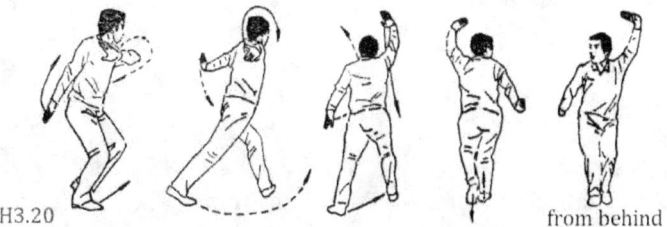

21. **Sounding Slap Kick**
    jīxiǎng pāijiǎo
    击响拍脚

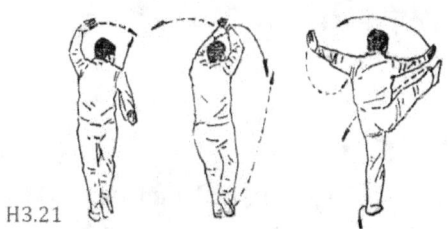

22. **Thread Hand, Raised Knee Flash Palm**
    chuānshǒu tíxī liàngzhǎng
    穿手提膝亮掌

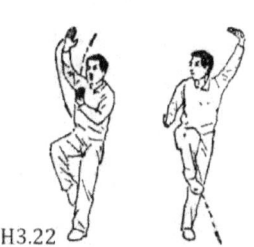

Section Two

23. Left Step Forward Scooping Snap
shàng zuǒbù tiǎozhǎng
上左步挑掌

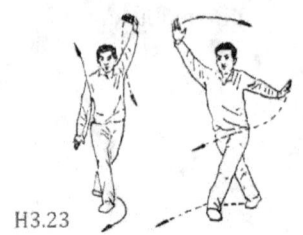
H3.23

24. Right Step Forward Scooping Snap
shàng yòubù tiǎozhǎng
上右步挑掌

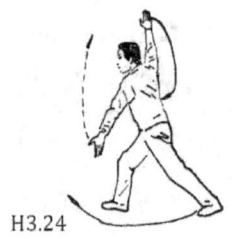
H3.24

25. Left Step Forward Scooping Snap
shàng zuǒbù tiǎozhǎng
上左步挑掌

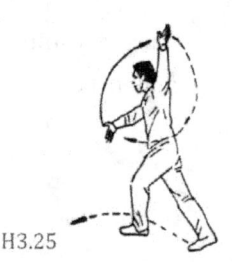
H3.25

26. Right Step Forward Scooping Snap
shàng yòubù tiǎozhǎng
上右步挑掌

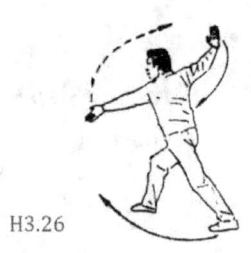
H3.26

27. Left Step Forward, Embracing Fist And Framing Block
shàng zuǒbù bāoquán jiàzhǎng
上左步抱拳架掌

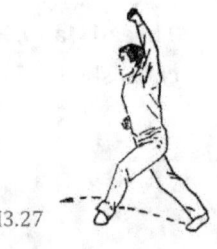
H3.27

THIRD FORM HONGQUAN (IMAGES ONLY)

28. **Left Raised Knee Push**
    zuǒ tíxī tuīzhǎng
    左提膝推掌

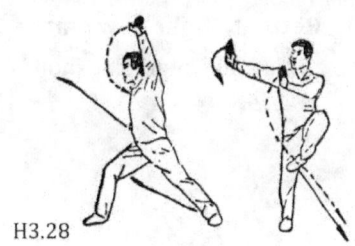

Section Three

29. **Left Drop Stance Thread The Hand**
    zuǒ pūbù chuānzhǎng
    左仆步穿掌

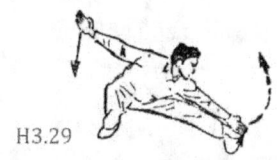

30. **Scooping Snap And Snap Kick**   tiǎozhǎng tántuǐ   挑掌弹腿

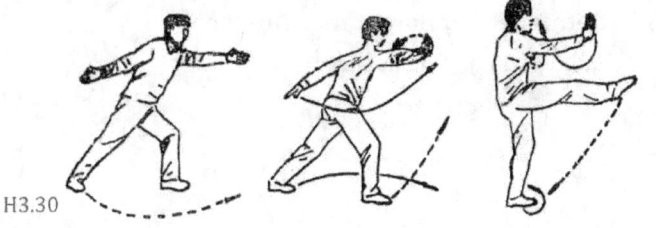

31. **T Stance Block**
    dīngbù gēzhǎng
    丁步格掌

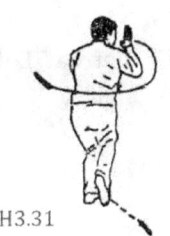

32. **Closed Stance Thread And Flash Palm**
    bīngbù chuānshǒu liàngzhǎng
    并步穿手亮掌

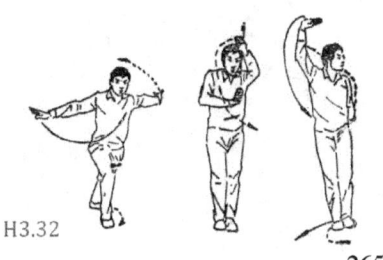

33. **Retreat, Right Bow Stance Dredge**
 tuìbù yòu gōngbù lāoshǒu
 退步右弓步捞手

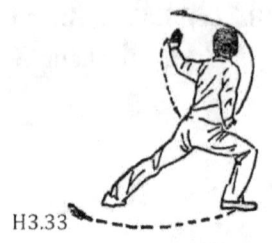

34. **Retreat, Left Bow Stance Dredge**
 tuìbù zǒu gōngbù lāoshǒu
 退步左弓步捞手

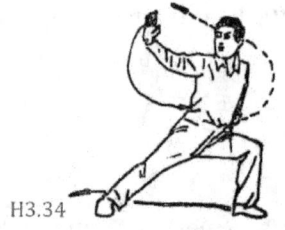

35. **Retreat, Right Bow Stance Dredge**
 tuìbù yòu gōngbù lāoshǒu
 退步右弓步捞手

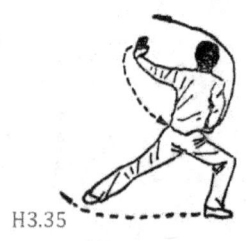

36. **Retreat, Left Bow Stance Dredge**
 tuìbù zǒu gōngbù lāoshǒu
 退左弓步捞手

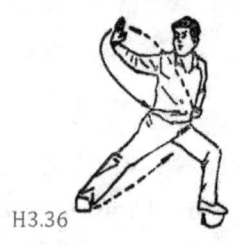

37. **Jump Switch-Step Press Down**
 huàntiàobù ànzhǎng
 换跳步按掌

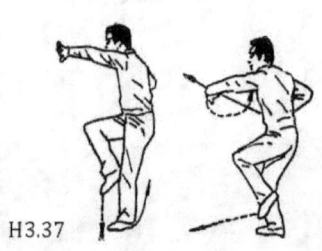

THIRD FORM HONGQUAN (IMAGES ONLY)

38. **Left Bow Stance Punch**
    zuǒ gōngbù chōngquán
    左弓步冲拳

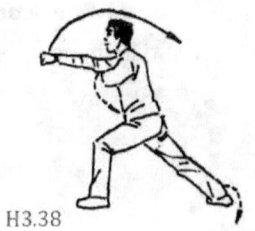
H3.38

39. **Turn Back, Bow Stance Back Hammerfist**
    huíshēn gōngbù fǎn záquán
    回身弓步反砸拳

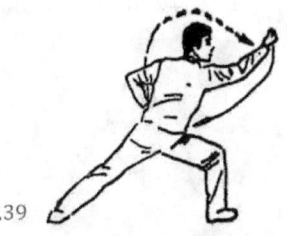
H3.39

40. **Right Bow Stance Forward Press Down**
    yòu gōngbù qián ànzhǎng
    右弓步前按掌

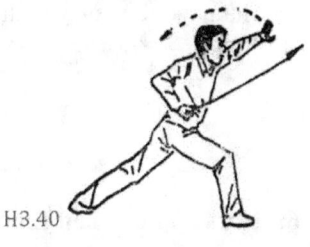
H3.40

41. **Horse Stance Framing Block And Punch**
    mǎbù jià chōngquán
    马步架冲拳

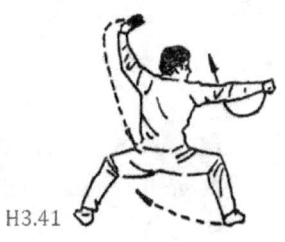
H3.41

Section Four

42. **Right Empty Stance Scooping Snap**
    yòu xūbù tiǎozhǎng
    右虚步挑掌

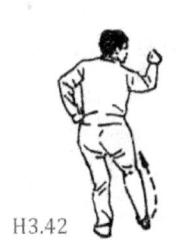
H3.42

CHAQUAN, VOLUME II

43. **Raised Knee Scooping Snap**
    tíxī tiǎozhǎng
    提膝挑掌

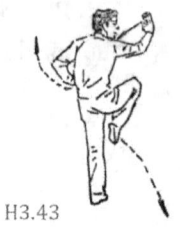
H3.43

44. **Left Step Forward, Left Elbow Tuck**
    shàng zuǒbù zuǒ yǎnzhǒu
    上左步左掩肘

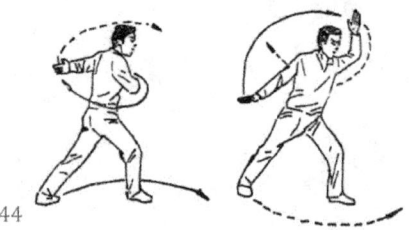
H3.44

45. **Right Step Forward, Right Elbow Tuck**
    shàng yòubù yòu yǎnzhǒu
    上右步右掩肘

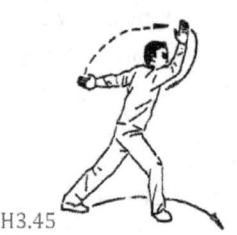
H3.45

46. **Horse Stance Left Elbow Tuck**
    mǎbù zuǒ yǎnzhǒu
    马步左掩肘

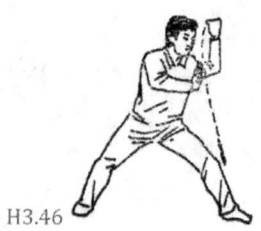
H3.46

47. **Left Bow Stance Lash Back**
    zuǒ gōngbù hòu bǎizhǎng
    左弓步后摆拳

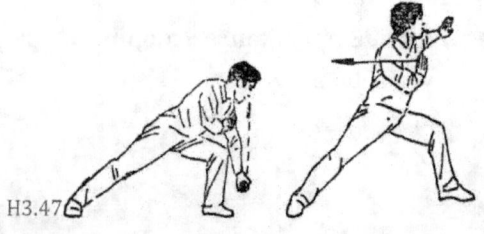
H3.47

THIRD FORM HONGQUAN (IMAGES ONLY)

48. **Left Bow Stance Character Ten Punches**
zuǒ gōngbù shízìquán
左弓步十字拳

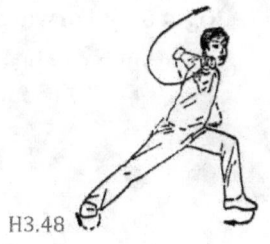

49. **Left Empty Stance Scooping Snap**
zuǒ xūbù tiǎozhǎng
左虚步挑掌

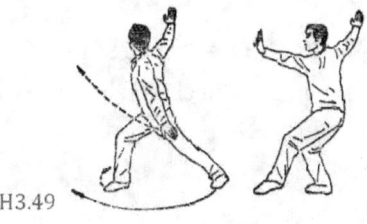

50. **Step Forward, Left Elbow Tuck**
shàngbù zuǒ yǎnzhǒu
上步左掩肘

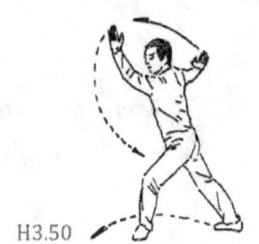

51. **Step Around Right Elbow Tuck**
ràoshàngbù yòu yǎnzhǒu
绕上步右掩肘

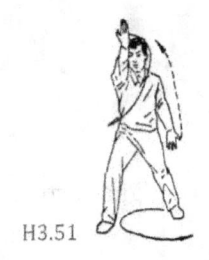

52. **Left Step Forward, Left Elbow Tuck**
shàng zuǒbù zuǒ yǎnzhǒu
上左步左掩肘

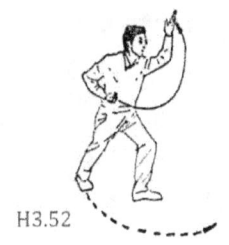

53. **Right Step Forward, Horse Stance Elbow Butt**
   shàng yòubù mǎbù dǐngzhǒu   上右步马步顶肘

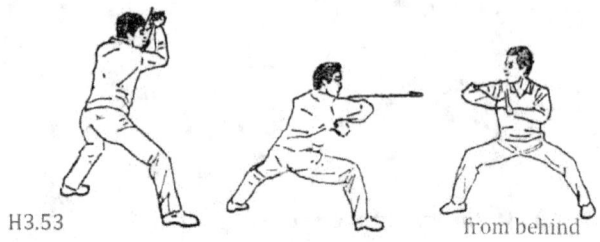

54. **Right Bow Stance Stab**
   yòu gōngbù chuānzhǎng
   右弓步穿掌

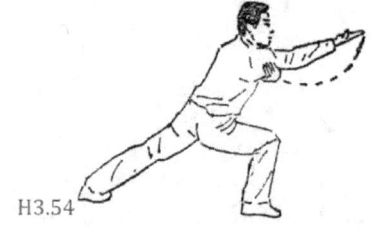

55. **Left Step Forward, Wrist Flowers To The Left**
   shàng zuǒbù shuāngshǒu zuǒ wànhuā   上左步双手左腕花

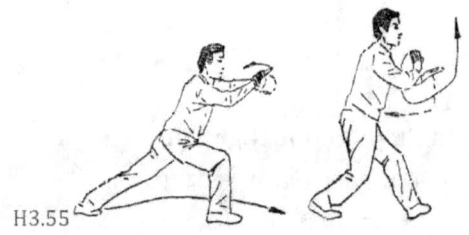

56. **Right Resting Stance Framing Block**
   yòu xiēbù jiàzhǎng
   右歇步架掌

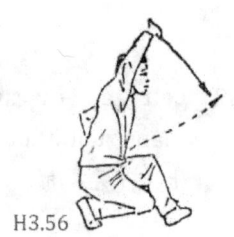

THIRD FORM HONGQUAN (IMAGES ONLY)

57. Right Step Forward, Wrist Flowers To The Right
shàng yòubù yòu shuāngshǒu yòu wànhuā   上右步双手右腕花

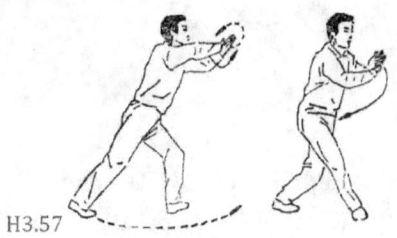

58. Left Resting Stance Framing Block
zuǒ xiēbù jiàzhǎng
左歇步架掌

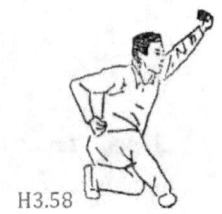

59. Right Bow Stance Crossed Fists
yòu gōngbù shízìquán
右弓步十字拳

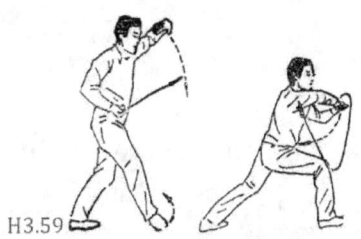

60. Right Bow Stance Scooping Snap
yòu gōngbù tiǎozhǎng
右弓步挑掌

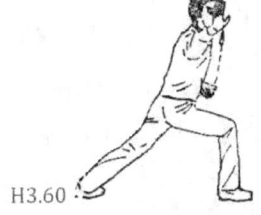

61. Right Bow Stance Character Ten Double Pushes
yòu gōngbù shízì shuāng tuīzhǎng
右弓步十字双推掌

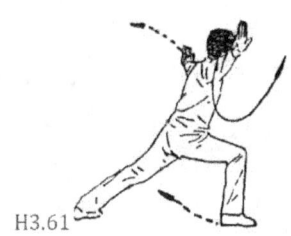

CHAQUAN, VOLUME II

62. **Right Empty Stance Scooping Snap**
    yòu xūbù tiǎozhǎng
    右虚步挑掌

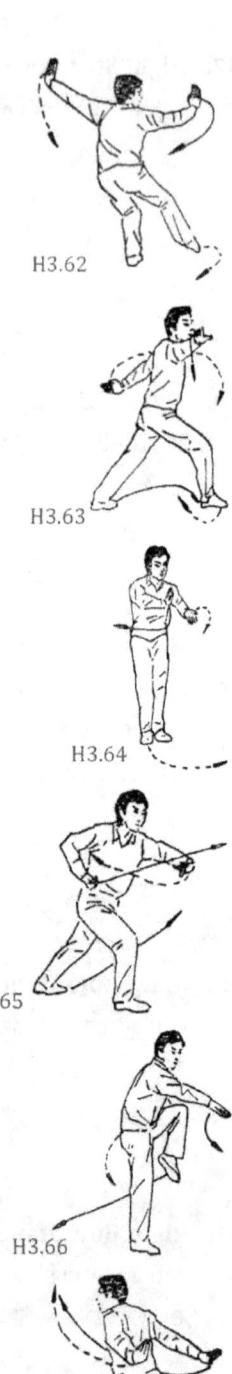

63. **Right Withdraw, Dredge**
    yòu chēbù lāoshǒu
    右撤步捞手

64. **Closed Stance Hack**
    bīngbù kǎnzhǎng
    并步砍掌

65. **Right Bow Stance Press Down**
    yòu gōngbù ànzhǎng
    右弓步按掌

66. **Left Raised Knee Stab**
    tíxī zuǒ chāzhǎng
    左提膝插掌

67. **Turn Back, Left Bow Stance Hook**
    huíshēn zuǒ gōngbù gōushǒu
    回身左弓步勾手

THIRD FORM HONGQUAN (IMAGES ONLY)

68. Right Step Forward, Roundhouse Punch

shàng yòubù guànquán

上右步贯拳

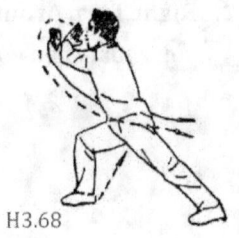

69. Jump Switch-Step, Planting Punch Down

huàntiàobù xià zāiquán

换跳步下栽拳

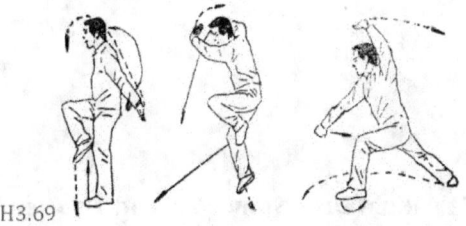

Section Five

70. Right Empty Stance Scooping Snap

yòu xūbù tiǎozhǎng

右虚步挑掌

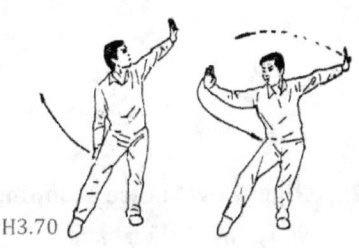

71. Step Forward, Character Ten Punches

shàngbù shízìquán

上步十字拳

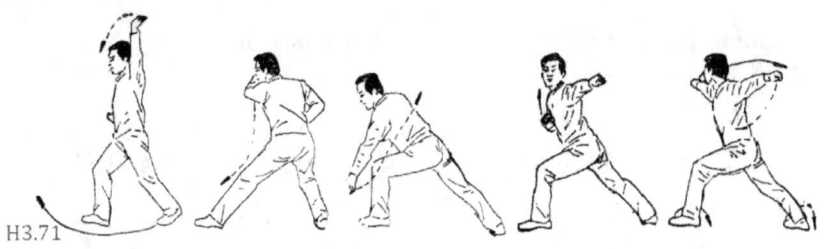

72. **Right Turn Around, Bow Stance Chop**
yòu zhuànshēn gōngbù pīzhǎng
右转身弓步劈掌

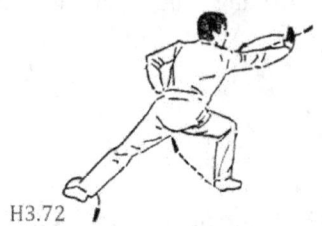

73. **Withdraw, Raised Knee Stab**
chèbù tíxī chuānzhǎng
撤步提膝穿掌

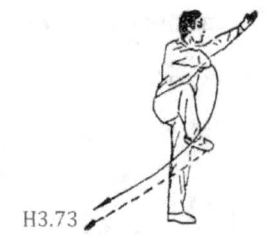

74. **Right Drop Stance Thread The Hand**
yòu pūbù chuānzhǎng
右仆步穿掌

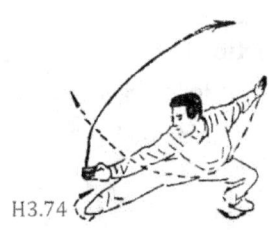

75. **Right Bow Stance Scooping Snap**
yòu gōngbù tiǎozhǎng
右弓步挑掌

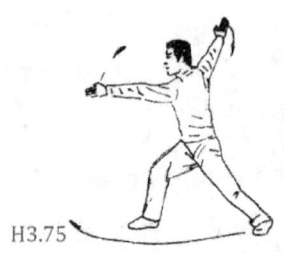

76. **Sounding Slap Kick** jīxiǎng pāijiǎo   击响拍脚

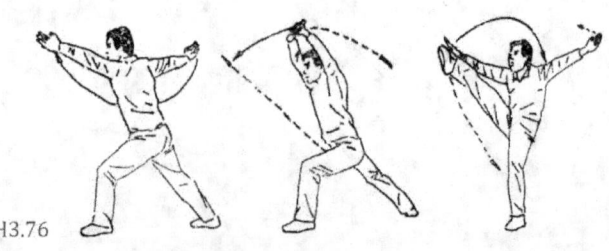

THIRD FORM HONGQUAN (IMAGES ONLY)

77. **Raise Knee Lash**
    tíxī bǎizhǎng
    提膝摆掌

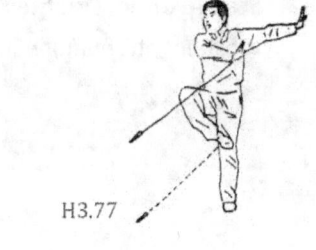

78. **Bow Stance Low Cut**
    gōngbù xià qiēzhǎng
    弓步下切掌

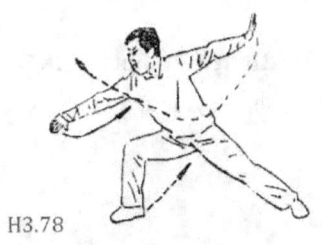

79. **Withdraw, Turn Back, Raised Knee Stab**
    chèbù huíshēn tíxī chuānzhǎng
    撤步回身提膝穿掌

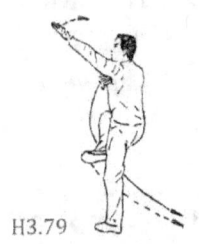

80. **Right Drop Stance Thread The Hand**
    yòu pūbù chuānzhǎng
    右仆步穿掌

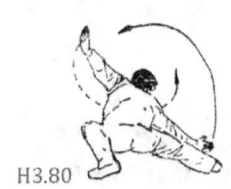

81. **Raised Knee Double Lashes**
    tíxī shuāng bǎizhǎng
    提膝双摆掌

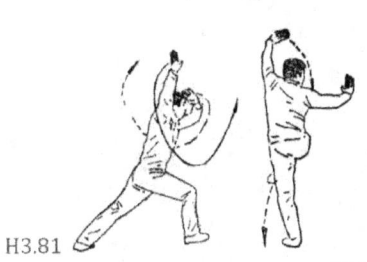

Section Six

82. **Step Around, Doubles Lashes**
    ràoshàngbù shuāng bǎizhǎng
    绕上步双摆掌

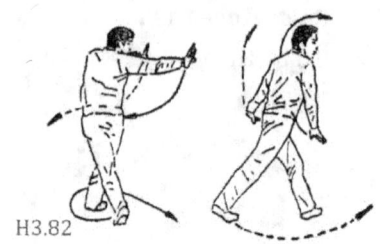

83. **Right Step Forward, Double Lashes**
    shàng yòubù shuāng bǎizhǎng
    上右步双摆掌

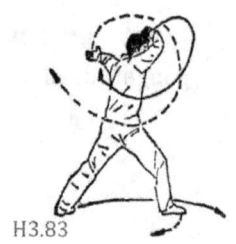

84. **Turn Around, Double Lashes**
    zhuànshēn shuāng bǎizhǎng
    转身双摆掌

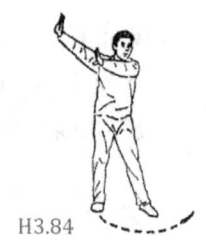

85. **Right Step Forward, Double Lashes**
    shàng yòubù shuāng bǎizhǎng
    上右步双摆掌

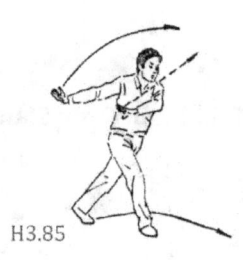

86. **Left Step Forward, Double Lashes**
    shàng zuǒbù shuāng bǎizhǎng
    上左步双摆掌

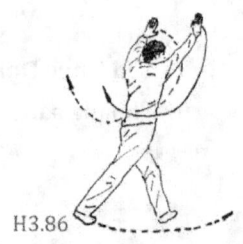

THIRD FORM HONGQUAN (IMAGES ONLY)

87. **Right Step Forward, Double Lashes**
shàng yòubù shuāng bǎizhǎng
上右步双摆掌

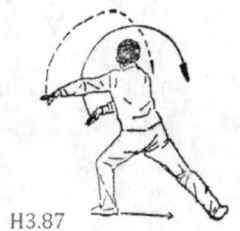
H3.87

88. **Closed Stance Double Lashes**
bīngbù shuāng bǎizhǎng
并步双摆掌

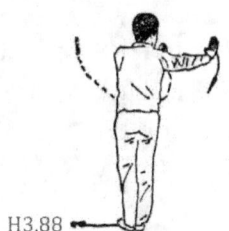
H3.88

89. **Left Bow Stance Scooping Snap**
zuǒ gōngbù tiǎozhǎng
左弓步挑掌

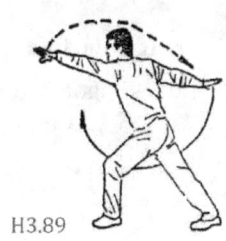
H3.89

90. **Resting Stance Vertical Palm**
xiēbù lìzhǎng
歇步立掌

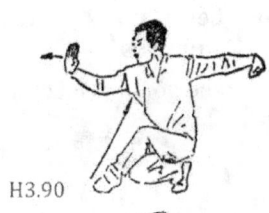
H3.90

Section Seven

91. **Raised Knee Push**
tíxī tuīzhǎng
提膝推掌

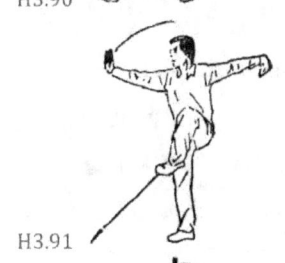
H3.91

92. **Step Forward, Left Bow Stance Elbow Tuck**
shàng zuǒbù gōngbù yǎnzhǒu
上左步弓步掩肘

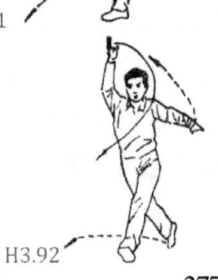
H3.92

93. Step Forward, Right Bow Stance Elbow Tuck

shàng yòubù gōngbù yǎnzhǒu

上右步弓步掩肘

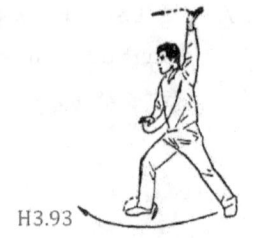
H3.93

94. Horse Stance Elbow Tuck

mǎbù yǎnzhǒu

马步掩肘

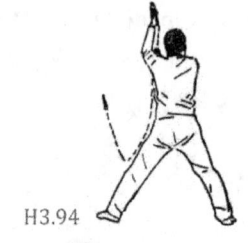
H3.94

95. Left Bow Stance Lash

zuǒ gōngbù bǎiquán

左弓步摆拳

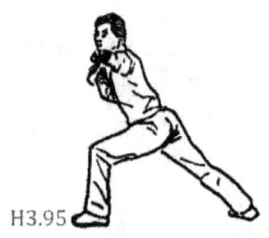
H3.95

96. Left Bow Stance Character Ten Punches

zuǒ gōngbù shízìquán

左弓步十字拳

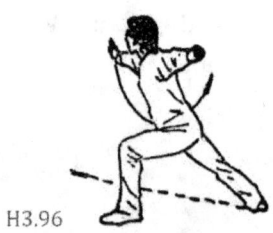
H3.96

97. Right Step Forward, Double Lashes

shàng yòubù shuāng bǎizhǎng

上右步双摆掌

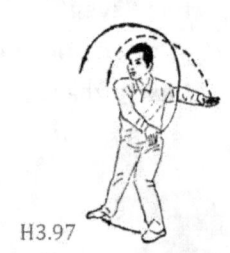
H3.97

98. Closed Stance Double Lashes

bīngbù shuāng bǎizhǎng

并步双摆掌

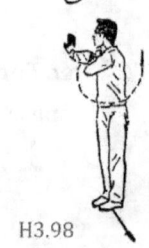
H3.98

THIRD FORM HONGQUAN (IMAGES ONLY)

99. Brush Aside, T Stance Hack
lōushǒu dīngbù kǎnzhǎng
搂手丁步砍掌

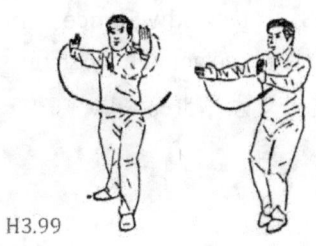

100. Jump Switch-Step Stab And Flash Palm
huàntiàobù chuānshǒu liàngzhǎng
换跳步穿手亮掌

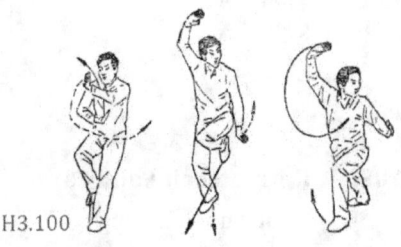

101. Front Cross-Over Stance Double Lashes
gàibù shuāng bǎizhǎng
盖步双摆掌

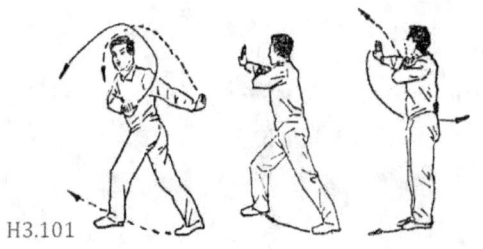

Section Eight

102. Thread The Hand, Front Sweep Kick
chuānshǒu qián sǎotuǐ
穿手前扫腿

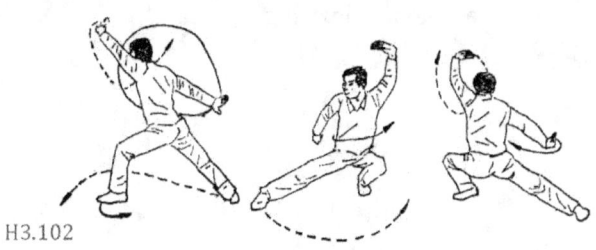

103. **Left Bow Stance Palm Carry**
zuǒ gōngbù tuōzhǎng
左弓步托掌

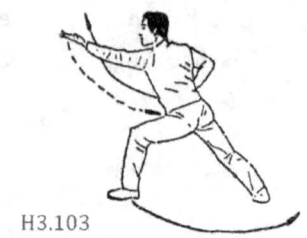

104. **Retreat, Right Palm Carry**
tuìbù yòu tuōzhǎng
退步右托掌

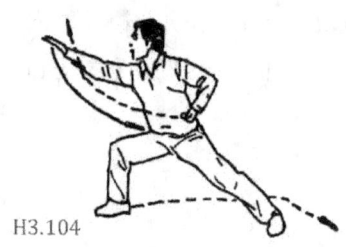

105. **Retreat, Left Palm Carry**
tuìbù zuǒ tuōzhǎng
退步左托掌

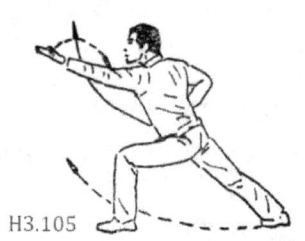

106. **Hooked Kick Scoop**
gōutī tiǎozhǎng
勾踢挑掌

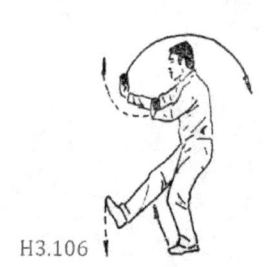

107. **Jump Switch-Step Scooping Snap**
huàntiàobù tiǎozhǎng
换跳步挑掌

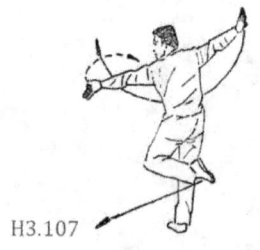

THIRD FORM HONGQUAN (IMAGES ONLY)

108. **Left Bow Stance Scooping Snap**
gōngbù zuǒ tiǎozhǎng
左弓步挑掌

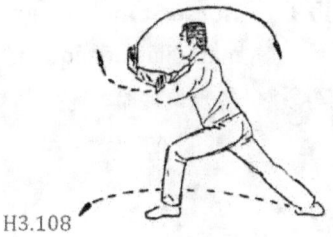

109. **Right Step Forward, Scooping Snap**
shàng yòubù tiǎozhǎng
上右步挑掌

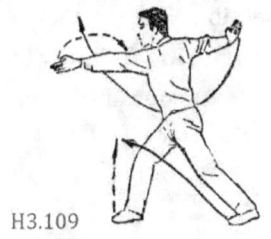

110. **Aerial Arrow Kick**
téngkōng jiàntán
腾空箭弹

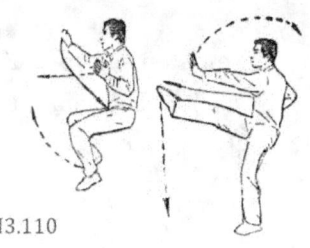

111. **Bow Stance Framing Block And Push**
gōngbù jià tuīzhǎng
弓步架推掌

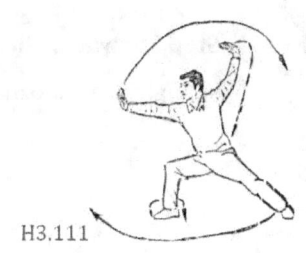

112. **Turn Back, Bow Stance Back Hammerfist**
huíshēn gōngbù fǎn záquán
回身弓步反砸拳

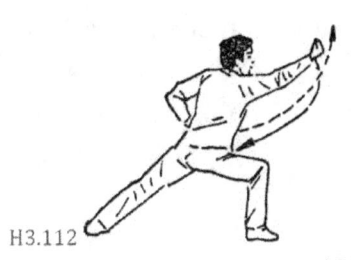

113. **Horse Stance Framing Block And Punch**
mǎbù jià chōngquán
马步架冲拳

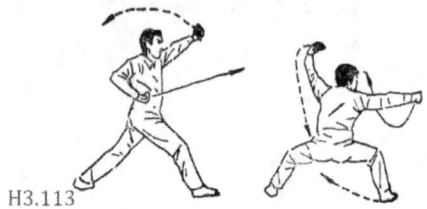

Section Nine

114. **Right Empty Stance Scoop Up**
yòu xūbù shàng tiǎozhǎng
右虚步上挑掌

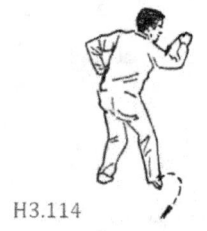

115. **Left Step Forward, Elbow Tuck**
shàng zuǒbù yǎnzhǒu
上左步掩肘

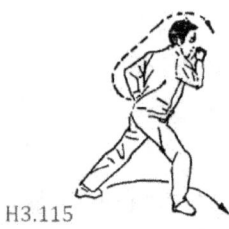 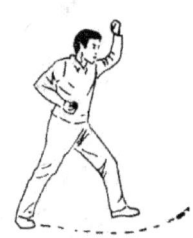

116. **Step Forward, Slice Upwards Behind**
shàngbù hòu liāozhǎng
上步后撩掌

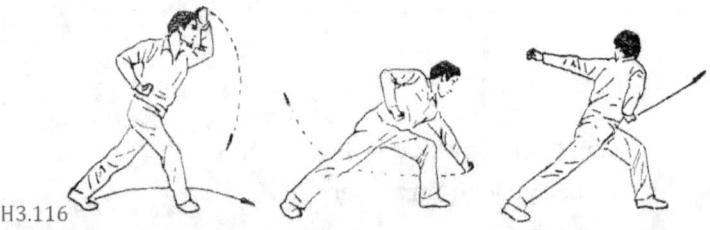

117. **Left Bow Stance Punch**
zuǒ gōngbù chōngquán
左弓步冲拳

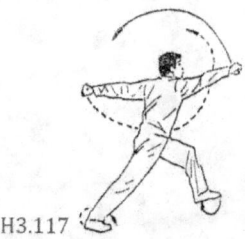

THIRD FORM HONGQUAN (IMAGES ONLY)

118. **Closed Stance Embrace Fists**
bīngbù bāoquán
并步抱拳

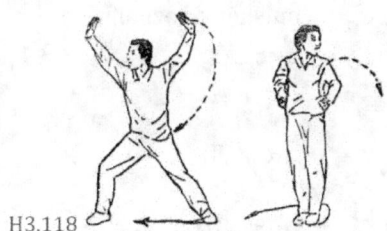

119. **Bow Stance Press Down**
gōngbù ànzhǎng
弓步按掌

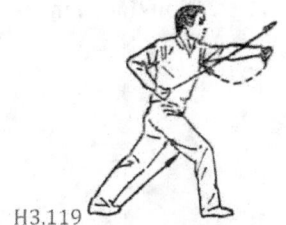

120. **Raised Knee Stab**
tíxī chuānzhǎng
提膝穿掌

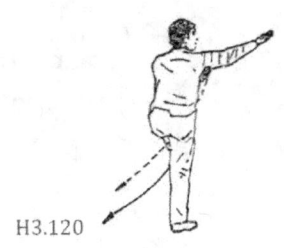

121. **Left Drop Stance Thread The Hand**
zuǒ pūbù chuānzhǎng
左仆步穿掌

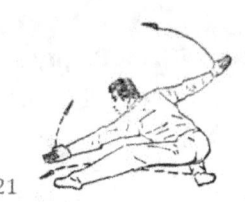

122. **Left Arm Flowers, Empty Stance Hack**
zuǒ bìhuā xūbù kǎnzhǎng   左臂花虚步砍掌

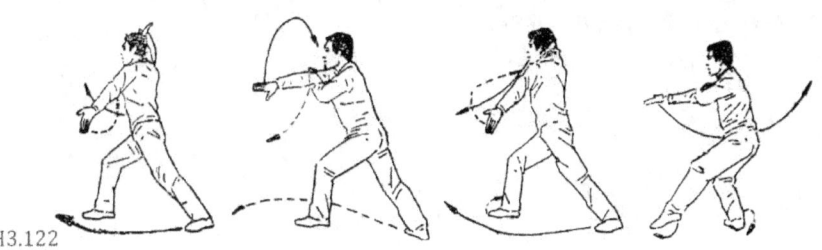

123. **Turn Back, Scooping Snap**
huíshēn tiǎozhǎng
回身挑掌

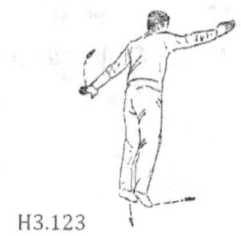

124. **Hitting Hop-Step Scooping Snap**
jībù tiǎozhǎng
击步挑掌

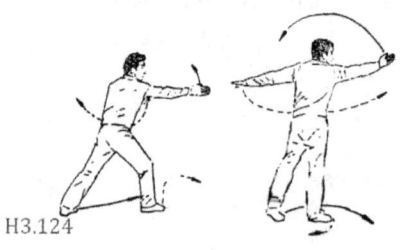

125. **Horse Stance Framing Block And Punch**
mǎbù jià chōngquán
马步架冲拳

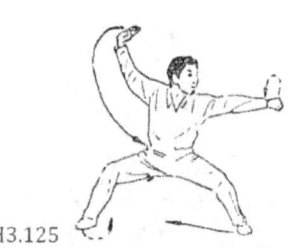

126. **Left Empty Stance Press Down**
zuǒ xūbù ànzhǎng
左虚步按掌

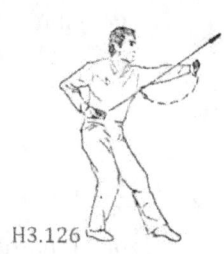

127. **Left Raised Knee Stab**
zuǒ tíxī chuānzhǎng
左提膝穿掌

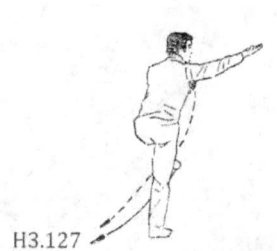

THIRD FORM HONGQUAN (IMAGES ONLY)

Section Ten

128. Left Drop Stance Thread The Hand
zuǒ pūbù chuānzhǎng
左仆步穿掌

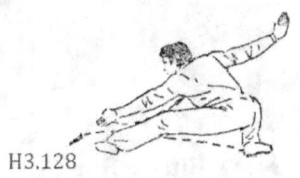

129. Front Cross-Over Stance Lash
gàibù gǎizhǎng
盖步摆掌

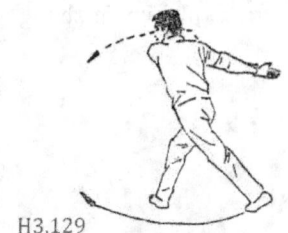

130. Left Step Forward, Chop
shàng zuǒbù pīzhǎng
上左步劈掌

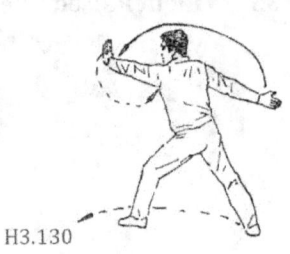

131. Right Step Forward, Chop
shàng yòubù pīzhǎng
上右步劈掌

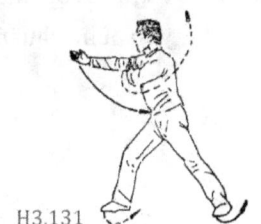

132. Turn Around, Hook And Flash Palm
zhuànshēn gōushǒu liàngzhǎng
转身勾手亮掌

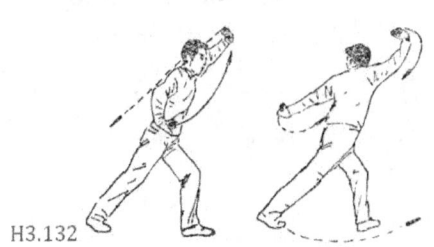

133. **Right Empty Stance Press With Palm**
yòu xūbù yāzhǎng
右虚步压掌

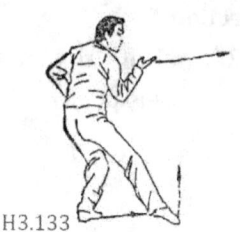

134. **Hitting Hop-Step Stab**
jībù chuānzhǎng
击步穿掌

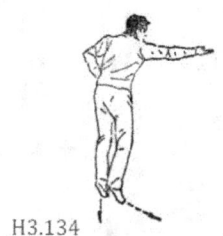

135. **Right Raised Knee Stab**
yòu tíxī chuānzhǎng
右提膝穿掌

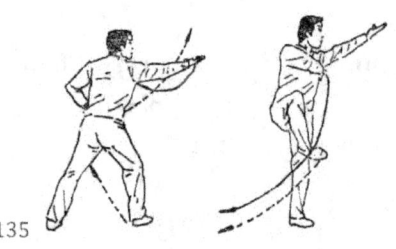

136. **Right Drop Stance Thread The Hand**
yòu pūbù chuānzhǎng
右仆步穿掌

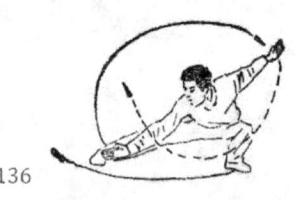

137. **Left Step Forward, Scooping Snap**
shàng zuǒbù tiǎozhǎng
上左步挑掌

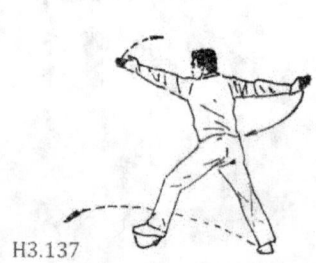

THIRD FORM HONGQUAN (IMAGES ONLY)

138. Horse Stance Palm Edge Strike
mǎbù jīzhǎng
马步击掌

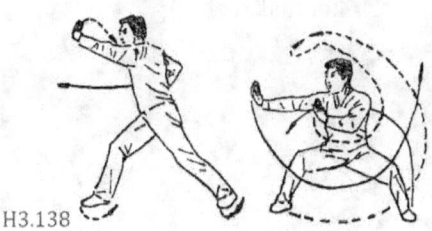

139. Tornado Kick On The Spot
yuándì xuànfēngjiǎo
原地旋风脚

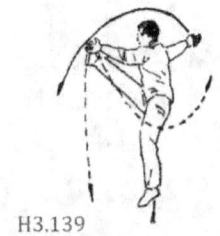

140. Horse Stance Double Vertical Palms
mǎbù shuāng lìzhǎng
马步双立掌

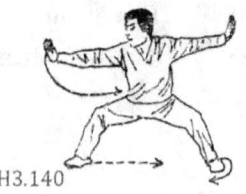

141. Step Forward, Push   shàngbù tuīzhǎng   上步推掌

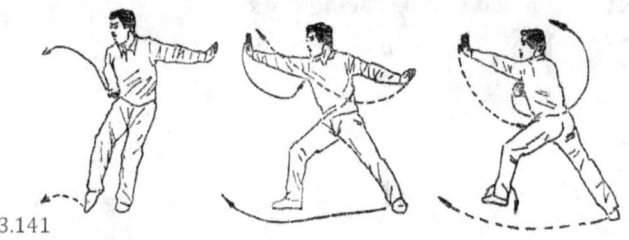

142. Turn Around, Tucked Leg Chop
zhuànshēn kòutuǐ pīzhǎng
转身扣腿劈掌

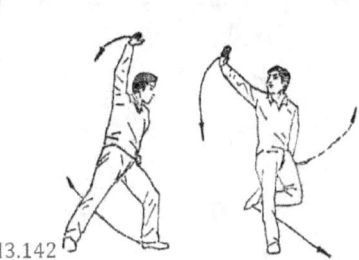

143. **Tucked Leg Slice Upwards**
kòutuǐ liāozhǎng
扣腿撩掌

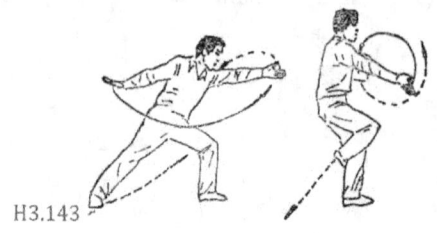

144. **Horse Stance Upward Scoop**
mǎbù shàng tiǎozhǎng
马步上挑拳

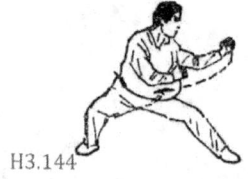

145. **Turn Around, Double Whisk**
zhuànshēn shuāng dǎnshǒu
转身双撣手

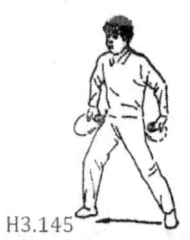

146. **Closed Stance Facing Fists**
bīngbù duìquán
并步对拳

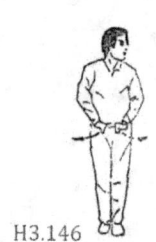

147. **Closing Posture**
shōu shì
收势

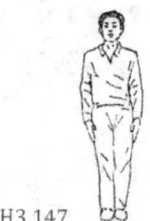

FIRST FORM TUIQUAN

头路腿拳

NAMES OF THE MOVEMENTS

Position Of Preparation
Section One
1. Stationary Closed Stance Facing Fists
2. Step Forward, Closed Stance Facing Fists
3. Closed Stance Roundhouse Punch
4. Drop Stance Thread The Hand
5. Left Bow Stance Punch
6. Hammerfist, Snap Kick
7. Aerial Snap Kick
8. Right Bow Stance Punch
9. Empty Stance Framing Block And Planting Punch
10. Bow Stance Swinging Chop
11. Hammerfist, Snap Kick
12. Snap Kick, Punch
13. Brace, Side Thrust Kick
14. Bow Stance Swinging Chop
15. Hammerfist, Snap Kick
16. Closed Stance Punch

Section Two
17. Turn Back, Snap Kick
18. Covering Jump, Double Stab
19. Aerial Side Thrust Kick
20. Insertion Step Side Thrust Kick
21. Bow Stance Framing Block And Punch
22. Turn Back, Step Forward To Snap Kick
23. Closed Stance Punch
24. Closed Stance Roundhouse Punch
25. Turn Around, Snap Kick
26. Closed Stance Stab
27. Curving Walk, Palm Carry
28. Drop Stance Thread The Hand
29. Stab, Snap Kick
30. Brace, Side Thrust Kick
31. Stab, Snap Kick
32. Closed Stance Roundhouse Punch

CHAQUAN, VOLUME II

Section Three
33. Step Forward, Raised Knee Stab
34. Step Forward, Punch
35. Hammerfist, Snap Kick
36. Turn Around, Snap Kick
37. Left And Right Snap Kicks
38. Front And Rear Bow Stance Punches
39. Raised Knee Stab
40. Push, Snap Kick
41. Step Forward, Aerial Snap Kick
42. Land To Bow Stance Punch
43. Turn Around, Elbow Tuck
44. Aerial Snap Kick
45. Closed Stance Punch Upwards
46. Guiding Hand, Bow Stance Roundhouse Punch
47. Press With Fist, Bow Stance Stab
48. Snap Kick Stab

Section Four
49. Front Cross-Over Stance Guiding Hand
50. Hop-Step, Wrist Wrap, Low Thrust Kick
51. Hop-Step, Wrist Wrap, Lean
52. Roundhouse Punch, Snap Kick
53. Bow Stance Push
55. Back Jump To Bow Stance Push
54. Back Jump To Bow Stance Push
56. Roundhouse Punch, Snap Kick
57. Hitting Hop-Step, Bow Stance Chop
58. Dodge, Bow Stance Low Punch
59. Turn Back, Block
60. Empty Stance Crossed Hands
61. Framing Block, Aerial Snap Kick
62. Step Around, Snap Kick
63. Bow Stance Swinging Chop
64. Raised Knee Punch To The Side
65. Land To Bow Stance Punch
66. Curving Walk, Hammerfist Snap Kick
67. Left And Right Bow Stance Punches
68. Withdraw, Roundhouse Punch
69. Withdraw, Facing Fists
70. Closing Posture

FIRST FORM TUIQUAN

0. **Position Of Preparation**   yùbèi shì

Stand to attention, looking forward. (image T1.0)

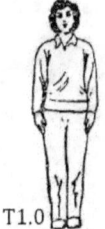

Section One

1. **Stationary Closed Stance Facing Fists**

   yuándì bīngbù duìquán   原地并步对拳

Laterally rotate the hands to turn the palms forward, then raise them to the front to navel height. (image T1.1a) Slap the thighs with the back of the hands at either side, then medially rotate the arms and clench the hands to place the fists in front of the belly, facing each other. Look to the left. (images 1b, 1c)

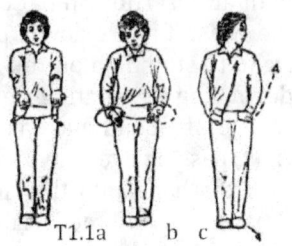

2. **Step Forward, Closed Stance Facing Fists**

   shàngbù bīngbù duìquán   上步并步对拳

Step the left foot forward on the left side, unclenching the hands and laterally rotating to circle forward and up to shoulder height, palms up. Look at the hands. (image T1.2a) Step the right foot out to the right side, circling by the left foot. Then step the left foot in together with the right foot. Lower the hands to either side, slapping the thighs with the back of the hands, then medially rotate the arms and clench the fists, facing each other in front of the belly. Look to the left. (images 2b, 2c)

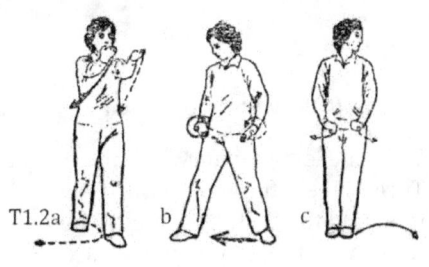

3. **Closed Stance Roundhouse Punch**   bīngbù guànquán   并步贯拳

Stride the left foot across to the left side. Laterally rotate the arms to turn the palms up. Look at the right hand. (image T1.3a) Bring the right foot in beside the left foot. Clench the right hand and circle it right and up to do a roundhouse punch inwards, stopping above the head at the right side. Circle the left hand to the left and up to place a vertical palm in front of the right shoulder, palm facing right, fingers up. Turn the head to look to the right. (image 3b)

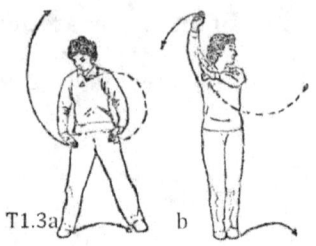

4. Drop Stance Thread The Hand   pūbù chuānzhǎng   仆步穿掌

Stride the left foot across to the left. Unclench the right hand and lower it at the right. Swing the left hand down and left. Look at the right hand. (image T1.4a) Step the right foot across to the left side, passing behind the left foot with an insertion step. Continue to circle the right hand, moving down to the waist, fingers down, palm forward. Circle the left hand up and to the right, to stop high on the right side, elbow bent, palm angled forward and down, fingers pointing right, palm edge up. Look forward, to the right side. (image 4b) Bend and raise the left knee. Thread the right hand up to the right, passing over the back of the left hand, palm up. Bend the left elbow to tuck the hand into the right armpit, palm down. Look at the right hand. (image 4c) Land the left foot to the left side and squat fully on the right leg to take a left drop stance. Laterally rotate the left hand to slide it along the inside of the left leg. Look to the lower left. (image 4d)

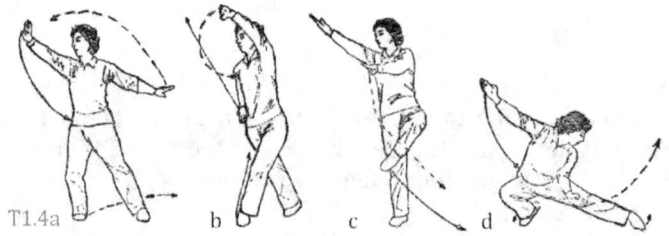

5. Left Bow Stance Punch   zuǒ gōngbù chōngquán   左弓步冲拳

Bend the left knee forward and extend the right leg to take a left bow stance. Thread the left hand forward, then circle up and over to the rear, clenching it behind the body at shoulder height. Clench the right hand, bring the fist in to the waist, then punch forward. Both fist hearts face down. Look forward. (images T1.5a, 5b)

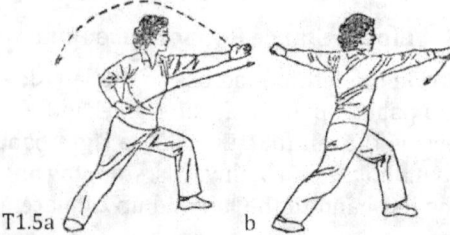

FIRST FORM TUIQUAN

6. **Hammerfist, Snap Kick**   záquán tántī   砸拳弹踢

Laterally rotate the right arm and bend the elbow to pound down, fist heart up, forearm level. Look at the right fist. (image T1.6a) Bend the right knee and do a snap kick forward, ankle plantar-flexed. Look forward. (image 6b)

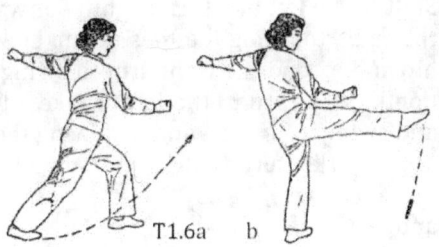

7. **Aerial Snap Kick**   téngkōng tántī   腾空弹踢

Land the right foot and raise the left knee, immediately pushing off the right foot to jump up. Whilst airborne, do a strong snap kick with the right foot, ankle plantar-flexed. Look forward. (images T1.7a, 7b, 7c)

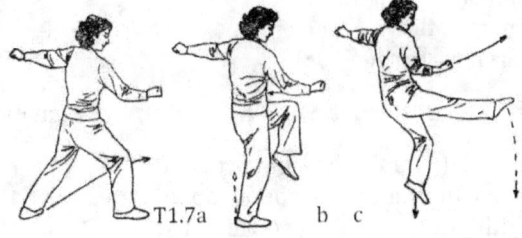

8. **Right Bow Stance Punch**   yòu gōngbù chōngquán   右弓步冲拳

Land on the left foot, still holding the right leg up. (image T1.8a) Land the right foot forward into a right bow stance. Medially rotate the right arm to punch forward at shoulder height, fist heart down. Look forward. (image 8b)

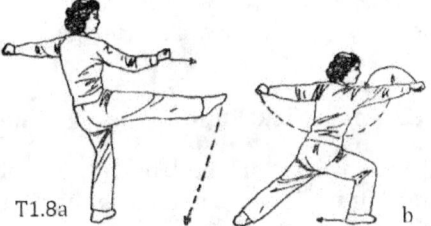

9. **Empty Stance Framing Block And Planting Punch**
    xūbù jià zāiquán   虚步架栽拳

Shift back, bringing the right foot back to take a right empty stance. Laterally rotate the right arm and bend the elbow to bring the fist to in front of the chest, fist heart in. Circle the left fist down and forward to outside the right fist, fist heart facing in. Look at the right fist. (image T1.9a) Do not change the stance. Medially rotate the right arm to punch down above the right knee, fist heart facing the rear right. Do a framing block above the head with the left fist. Look forward, to the right side. (image 9b)

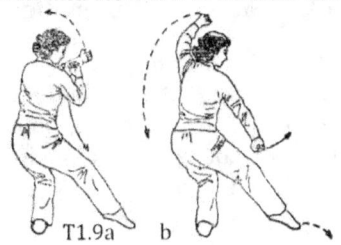

CHAQUAN, VOLUME II

10. Bow Stance Swinging Chop   gōngbù lūnpī   弓步抡劈

Shift to the left and turn slightly leftward, shifting the right foot slightly to the right, touching the toes down. Lower the left fist at the left side to the hip and extend the right arm to swing slightly to the right (image T1.10a) Continue to turn to the left to take a left bow stance. Lower the right fist, and swing it forward and up. Swing the left fist back. Look forward. (image 10b) Quickly turn to the right into a right bow stance. Swing the right arm up and over, back, and down to behind the body. Swing the left arm forward and over to in front of the body. Both fists are at shoulder height, fist hearts down. Look forward. (image 10c)

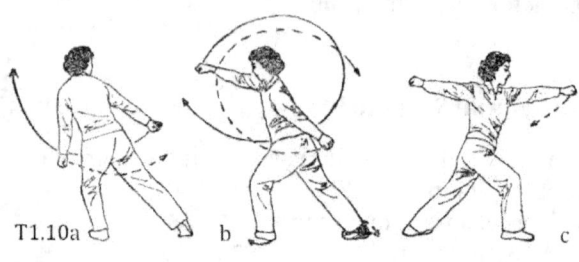

11. Hammerfist, Snap Kick   záquán tántī   砸拳弹踢

Laterally rotate the right arm and bend the elbow to pound down with the forearm level and fist heart up. Look forward. (image T1.11a) Do a snap kick with the left leg. Look forward. (image 11b)

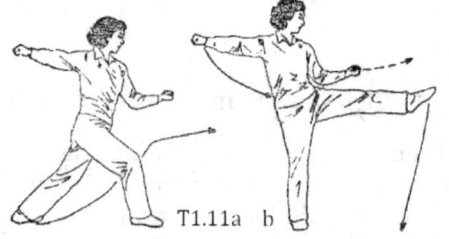

12. Snap Kick, Punch   tántuǐ chōngquán   弹腿冲拳

Land forward on the left foot. Extend the left fist forward and bring the right fist to the waist, fist heart up. Look forward. (image T1.12a) Do a snap kick with the right leg and punch with the right fist, fist eye up. Unclench the left hand and place a vertical palm in the right elbow crease. Look forward. (image 12b)

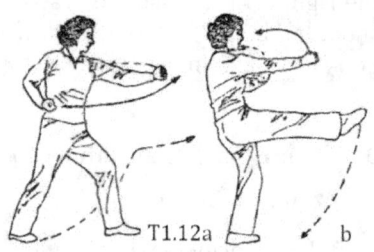

13. Brace, Side Thrust Kick   chēngzhǎng cèchuāi   撑掌侧踹

Land forward on the right foot, turning it out and turning the torso rightward. Clench the left hand and cross the bent arms in front of the chest, left hand on the inside, palms out. Look to the left side. (image T1.13a) Unclench both hands and circle them up and out to either side, continuing down and in, to once again cross in front of the chest. The left hand is again inside, the fingers point up. Look to the left side. (image 13b) Lift the left foot and do a side thrust kick to the left, foot flat, power going to the heel. Open the hands out to brace to either side, fingers forward, palms facing out to either side. Look to the left side. (image 13c)

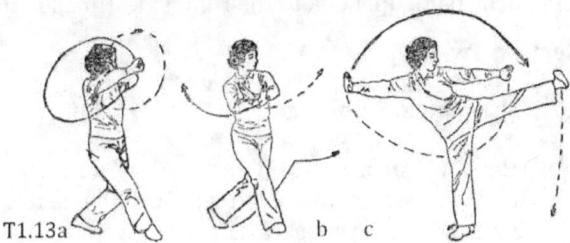

14. Bow Stance Swinging Chop gōngbù lūnpī 弓步抡劈

Turn to the left and land on the left foot into a left bow stance. Gradually clench the hands while circling them vertically, swinging the arms at either side until the right arm is in front and the left arm is behind. Both arms are fully extended at shoulder height, fist hearts down. Look forward. (image T1.14)

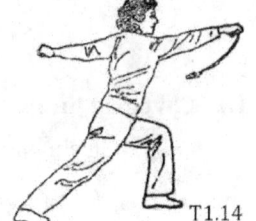

15. Hammerfist, Snap Kick záquán tántī 砸拳弹踢

This is the same as move 6. (images T1.15a, 15b)

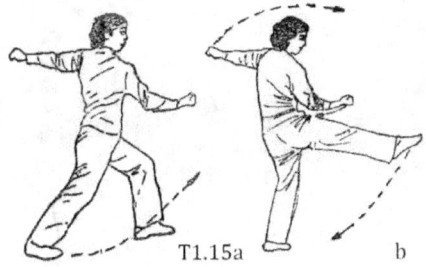

16. Closed Stance Punch bīngbù chōngquán 并步冲拳

Land the right foot in front with the foot turned in. Bring the right fist to the waist. Clench the left hand and bring it over, to come forward and then press down, palm down. Look at the left hand. (image T1.16a) Bring the left foot up to meet the right foot and stand up. Press the left hand down, and punch the right fist out to the right, passing over top of the back of the left hand, with a standing fist. Bring the left hand along

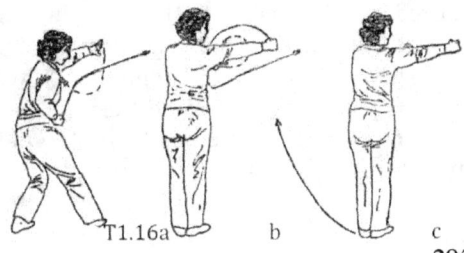

under the right arm, palm down. Look to the right side. (image 16b) Circle the right fist up to bring it in to the waist, then punch out to the right with a standing fist. Circle the left hand forward, then up, then bring it to inside the right arm, palm up. Look to the right side. (image 16c)

Section Two

17. Turn Back, Snap Kick   huíshēn tántī   回身弹踢

Hold the same arm position and quickly do a snap kick to the left side with the left leg. Turn the head to look to the left side. (image T1.17)

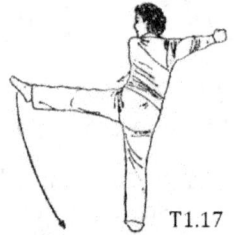

T1.17

18. Covering Jump, Double Stab

gài tiàobù shuāng chāzhǎng   盖跳步双插掌

Land the left foot forward and step the right foot across in front of the left leg, immediately pushing off to jump and swing the left foot to the left whilst airborne. (images T1.18a, 18b) Land on the left foot, then the right, taking a closed stance in half-squat. Bring the hands in to the waist then stab out to either side, palms forward. Look to the left side. (image 18c)

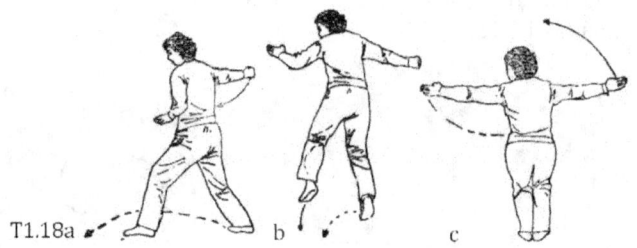

T1.18a   b   c

19. Aerial Side Thrust Kick   téngkōng cèchuāi   腾空侧踹

Swing the right hand up, then forward. Circle the left hand down to in front of the right side of the chest, palm in. (image T1.19a) Push off with both legs to jump up. Do a right side thrust kick to the right whilst airborne, the foot tucked in, power going to the heel. Hook the right hand down to the rear, arm straight, hook pointing up. Do a framing block with the left hand, passing inside the right arm, and finishing above the head with the palm angled up. Look to the right. (image 19b)

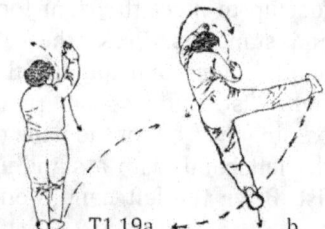

T1.19a   b

FIRST FORM TUIQUAN

20. Insertion Step Side Thrust Kick   chābù cèchuāi   插步侧踹

Land on the left foot, then land the right foot behind the left, crossing behind the left leg with an insertion step. Then do a left side thrust kick with the foot tucked in, power going to the heel. Hook the left hand down and back, passing in front of the belly, arm straight, hook pointing up. Unhook the right hand and slide it up the left arm to do a framing block above the head. Look to the left. (image T1.20)

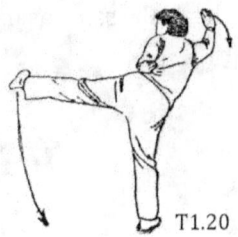

T1.20

21. Bow Stance Framing Block And Punch
    gōngbù jià chōngquán   弓步架冲拳

Land the left foot forward and bend the knee, extending the right leg to take a left bow stance. Unhook the left hand and do a block in front of the belly, palm in. (image T1.21a) Swing the left arm up to do a framing block above the head, palm up. Clench the right hand and do a straight punch forward, fist heart down. Look forward. (image 21b)

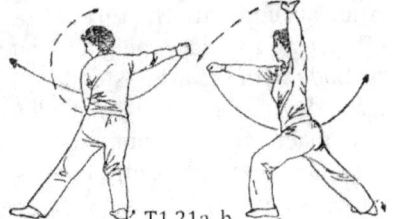

T1.21a b

22. Turn Back, Step Forward To Snap Kick
    huíshēn shàngbù tántī   回身上步弹踢

Pivot on the left heel to turn around one-eighty degrees to the right. Lift the right foot slightly to place it with the foot turned out. Lower the left arm to the side to shoulder height. Look to the right. (image T1.22a) Without moving the legs, laterally rotate the right arm and bend the elbow to pound down with the forearm level and fist heart up. Clench the left hand with the fist heart down. Look to the right. (image 22b) Step the left foot forward, then do a snap kick with the right foot. Look forward. (images 22c, 22d)

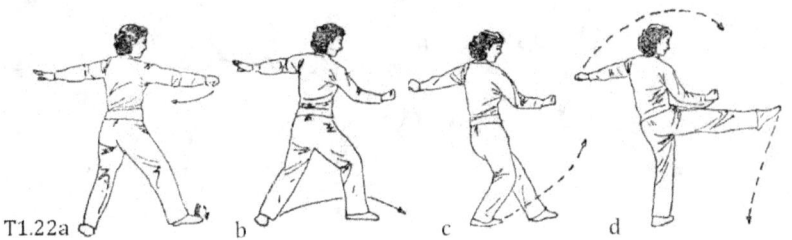

T1.22a   b   c   d

23. Closed Stance Punch bīngbù chōngquán 并步冲拳

This is the same as move 16. (images T1.23a, 23b, 23c, 23d)

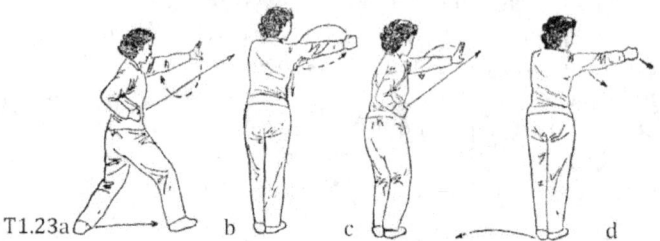

24. Closed Stance Roundhouse Punch bīngbù guànquán 并步贯拳

Stride the left foot across to the left and bend the right knee. Unclench the right hand and lower it, palm down. Look at the right hand. (image T1.24a) Pivot on the ball of the left foot to turn one-eighty degrees around to the left, then bring the right foot in beside the left foot and stand up. Swing the hands around with the turn to the left, then clench both of them. Place the left fist at shoulder height behind the body with the arm extended, fist heart down. Bend the right elbow and place it in front, doing a roundhouse punch with the right fist across in front of the chest, fist heart down. Look forward. (image 24b)

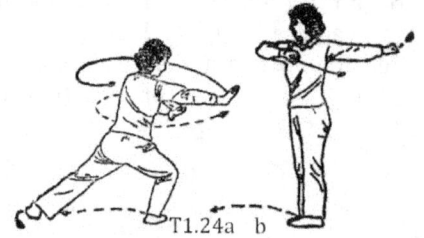

25. Turn Around, Snap Kick zhuànshēn tántī 转身弹踢

Pivot on the ball of the left foot to turn to the left, bending the left knee, and striding the right foot across to the right. Unclench both hands and press down, palms down. (image T1.25a) Turn to the right into an insertion stance. Swing the hands around with the turn, then bend the right elbow and clench the hand to bring the fist in front of the chest, fist heart down. Strike the left palm into the right fist, fingers up. Look to the left side. (image 25b) Shift forward and do a left snap kick with the ankle plantar-flexed. Continue to look to the left. (image 25c)

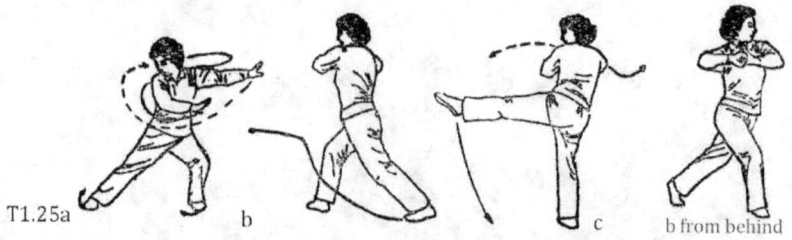

26. Closed Stance Stab   bīngbù chāzhǎng   并步插掌

Land the left foot forward. Unclench the right hand and extend the hands out to the sides, left palm down and right palm forward. (image T1.26a) Laterally rotate the left hand and bring it to the waist, palm up. Circle the right hand up and left, to stop high at the left side, fingers pointing left, palm edge leading. Look at the right hand. (image 26b) Bring the right foot in to meet the left foot. Stab the left hand out to the upper left, passing over the back of the right hand, palm up. Slide the right hand along under the left arm, then clench the fist and place it at the waist. Look at the left hand. (image 26c)

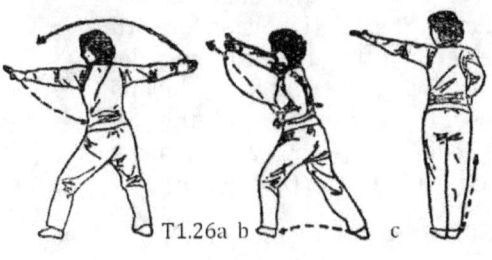

27. Curving Walk, Palm Carry   húxíngbù tuōzhǎng   弧形步托掌

Bend and raise the right knee. (image T1.27a) Land the right foot forward, turned out. (image 27b) Step in an arcing line with the left, then the right foot. Grind the right foot outwards slightly and step again with the left foot, tucking it in, to bring it up beside the right foot to take a closed stance. (The body has turned one-eighty degrees to the right during the walk.) Look at the left hand throughout the walk. (images 27c, 27d, 27e)

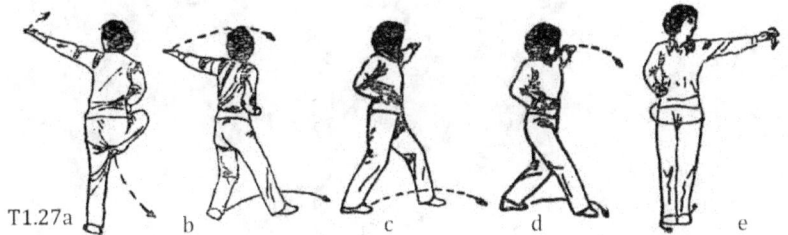

28. Drop Stance Thread The Hand   pūbù chuānzhǎng   仆步穿掌

Turn ninety degrees to the left. Medially rotate the left arm to turn the palm down. Look at the left hand. (image T1.28a) Bend and raise the left knee. Unclench the right hand and thread it out above the back of the left hand, extending the arm with the palm up. Press the left hand down under the right armpit, palm down. Look at the right hand. (image 28b) Land the left foot out to the left and fully squat on the right leg into a left drop stance. Laterally rotate the left hand and thread it forward

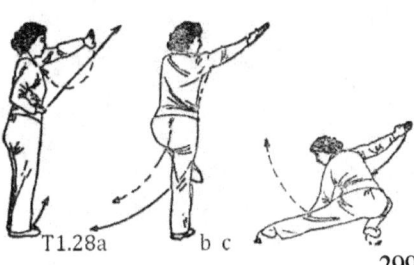

along the thigh, fingers forward. Look at the left hand. (image 28c)

29. Stab, Snap Kick   chāzhǎng tántī   插掌弹踢

Shift forward, pushing into the right leg to take a left bow stance. Scoop up with the left hand and bring the right hand to the waist, palm up. (image T1.29a) Do a snap kick forward with the right foot, ankle plantar-flexed. Stab the right hand forward, extending the arm with the palm up. Swing the left hand up and over to the rear, extending the arm to shoulder height, palm up. Look at the right hand. (image 29b)

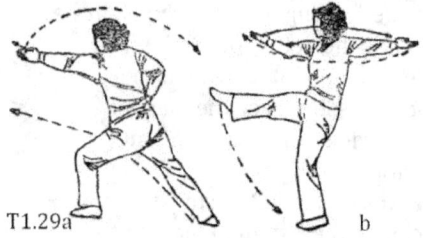

30. Brace, Side Thrust Kick   chēngzhǎng cèchuāi   撑掌侧踹

Land the right foot forward with the foot turned out and turn rightward into a cross stance. Medially rotate the arms, and, as the body turns, swing them flat out to either side. (image T1.30a) Stay in stance and bring the hands in and down, circling to lift with arms crossed in front of the chest with vertical palms, left hand inside. (image 30b) Do a side thrust kick to the left with the left foot, foot hooked in, power going to the heel. Brace out to the either side with the hands, palms out, fingers forward. Look to the left. (image 30c)

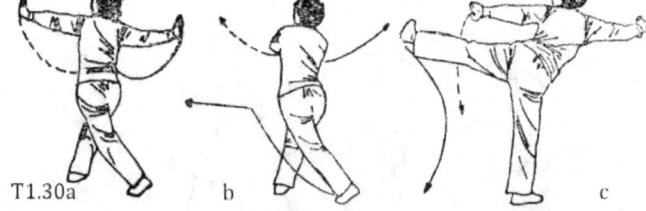

31. Stab, Snap Kick   chāzhǎng tántī   插掌弹踢

Land the left foot forward, turning it out. Lower the left hand to the thigh with the tiger's mouth forward. (image T1.31a) Shift forward and do a right snap kick forward. Scoop up with the left hand then continue circling up and back to behind the body, arm extended and palm up. Stab the right hand forward, palm up, first passing by the waist. Both hands are at shoulder height. Look at the right hand. (images 31b, 31c)

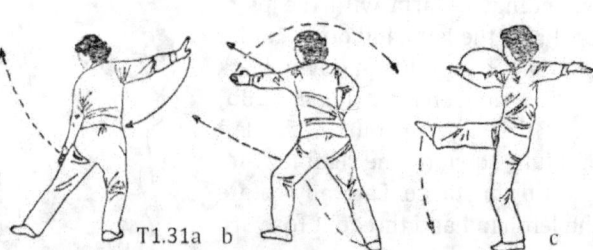

FIRST FORM TUIQUAN

32. Closed Stance Roundhouse Punch   bīngbù guànquán   并步贯拳

Land the right foot forward, tucked in, and squat on the left leg to take a right drop stance. Bring the right hand up and over to press down in front of the chest. (image T1.32a) Lean forward and brush the right hand across over the right foot, then form a hook as it moves towards the rear, hook pointing up. Look at the right foot. (image 32b) Shift forward, turning right, and step the left foot forward past the right foot, foot hooked in. (images 32c, 32d) Step the right foot up to meet the left foot and stand up. Clench the right hand and do roundhouse strikes with both hands, bringing them across to in front, slightly higher than the shoulders. The right fist heart faces in and the left palm covers the right knuckles. Look at the right fist. (image 32e, and from behind)

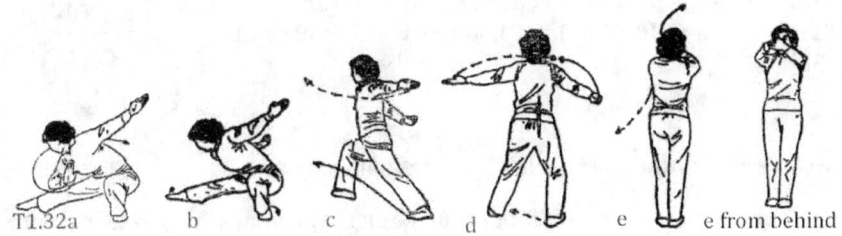

Section Three

33. Step Forward, Raised Knee Stab
shàngbù tíxī chuānzhǎng   上步提膝穿掌

Lift the right foot slightly. Unclench the right hand and circle it up, right, then down to the waist, palm up. Circle the left hand down, left, and up to above the head, palm down, fingers pointing right. Look at the left hand (images T1.33a, 33b) Land the right foot a half-step forward, hooked in, and lift the left knee. Thread the right hand forward over the back of the left hand, up to the right, palm up. Lower the left hand to tuck into the right armpit, palm down. Look at the right hand. (image 33c)

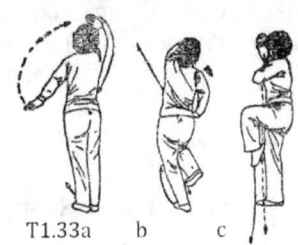

34. Step Forward, Punch   shàngbù chōngquán   上步冲拳

Extend the left leg along the ground with the foot turned in, and fully squat on the right leg to take a left drop stance. Thread the left hand along inside the left leg, tiger's mouth up. Look at the left hand. (image T1.34a) Shift forward and bring the right foot up to meet the left foot, standing up. Scoop up with the left hand, swinging the arm up then to the rear, clenching the fist and extending the arm. Bring the right hand to the waist, then clench the fist and punch forward, fist heart down. Both arms are at shoulder height. Look forward. (images 34b, 34c)

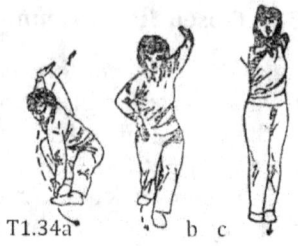

35. Hammerfist, Snap Kick   záquán tántī   砸拳弹踢

Step the left foot a half-step forward, foot turned out, legs slightly bent and crossed. Laterally rotate the right arm and bend the elbow to pound down with the fist heart up. Look at the right fist. (image T1.35a) Do a right snap kick. Look forward. (image 35b)

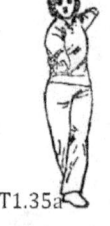 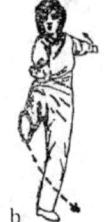

36. Turn Around, Snap Kick   zhuànshēn tántī   转身弹踢

Pivot on the ball of the left foot to turn quickly around a full circle leftward. Bend the right knee and do a hooking-in cover step to land in front of the left foot, foot turned out and touching down lightly. Swing the fists around without changing their relative positions. Look forward. (images T1.36a, 36b) Shift forward and settle on the right foot. Laterally rotate the left arm and bend the elbow to pound down. Extend the right arm out to the rear, fist heart down. Look forward. (image 36c) Do a left front snap kick. Look forward. (image 36d)

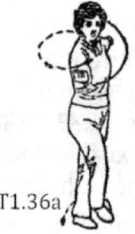 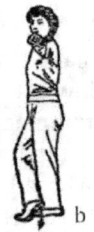 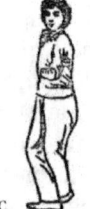 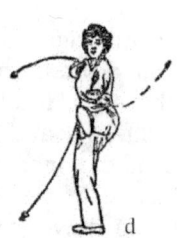

37. Left And Right Snap Kicks   zuǒ yòu tántī   左右弹踢

Land the left foot forward with a cover step past the right foot, foot turned out, and turn slightly rightward. Medially rotate the left arm to extend the fist out behind the body at shoulder height, fist heart down. Do a complete circle with the right fist, down, left, up, then down again, bending the elbow to pound, fist heart up. Look forward. (images T1.37a, 37b) Shift forward and do a right front snap kick. Look forward. (image 37c) Pivot on the ball of the left foot to turn one-eighty degrees around to the left. After the turn, step the right foot across in front of the left foot, turning the foot out. Medially rotate the right fist and extend the arm out to the rear at shoulder height, fist heart down. Laterally rotate the left arm and bend the elbow to pound down, fist heart up. (image 37d) Shift to the right leg and do a left front snap kick. Look forward. (image 37e)

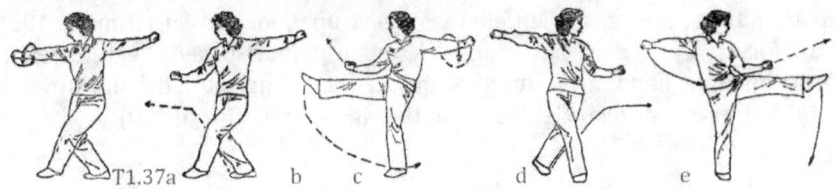

38. Front And Rear Bow Stance Punches

    qián hòu gōngbù chōngquán   前后弓步冲拳

Land on the left foot, extending the right leg into a left bow stance. Punch forward with the left fist, extending the arm at shoulder height, fist heart down. Bring the right fist to the waist, fist heart up. Look forward. (image T1.38a) Turn the torso one-eighty degrees rightward, extending the left leg to take a right bow stance. Punch forward with the right fist, extending the arm at shoulder height, fist heart down. Look forward. (image 38b)

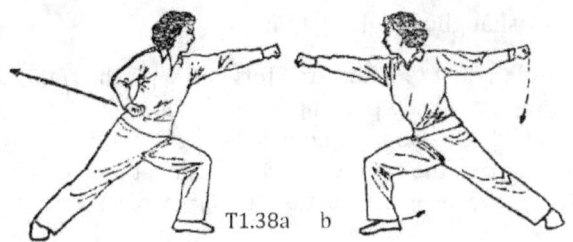

39. Raised Knee Stab   tíxī chuānzhǎng   提膝穿掌

Shift back and pivot on the ball of the left foot to turn slightly to the right. Unclench the fists. (image T1.39a) Bend and raise the right knee at the right side. Bring the left hand to the waist then thread it forward over top of the right hand, palm up. Bring the right hand along under the left arm to tuck into the left armpit, palm down. Look at the left fist. (image 39b)

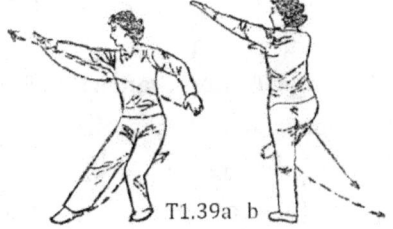

40. Push, Snap Kick   tuīzhǎng tántī   推掌弹踢

Squat fully on the left leg and extend the right leg out into a right drop stance, foot hooked in. Thread the right hand along inside the right leg, fingers forward. Medially rotate the left arm to turn the tiger's mouth up.

(image T1.40a) Shift forward into a right bow stance, extending the right arm. (image 40b) Lower the left hand, then slice up with a straight arm to in front, fingers forward, palm facing right. Circle the right hand forward and up, then bring it in to the left elbow, fingers up. Look forward. (image 40c) Shift forward and do a left snap kick, ankle plantar-flexed. Push forward with the right hand, arm straight, fingers up. Swing the left hand up and over to the rear, arm straight. Look at the right hand. (image 40d)

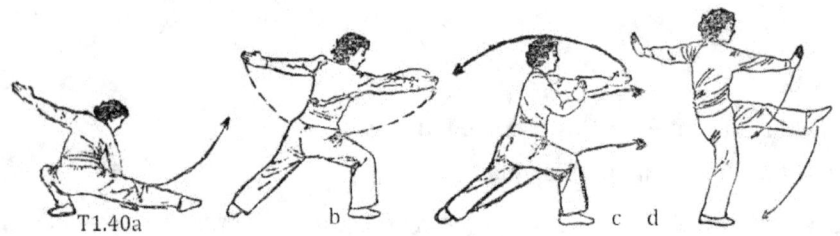

41. Step Forward, Aerial Snap Kick

shàngbù téngkōng tántī　　　　　　　　上步腾空弹踢

Land the left foot and step forward with the right, bending the left knee and lifting it, quickly pushing off with the right leg to jump up. Do a right snap kick whilst airborne. Lower the right hand slightly, then swing it forward, up, then to the rear in a vertical palm at shoulder height. Bring the left hand in to the waist then push it forward, extending the arm straight. Look forward.　　(images T1.41a, 41b, 41c)

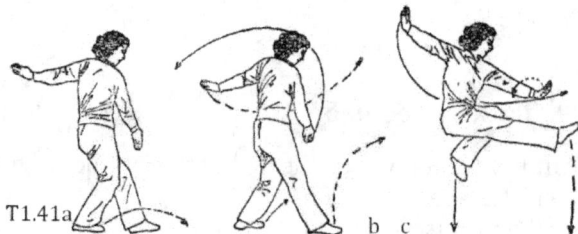

42. Land To Bow Stance Punch

luòdì gōngbù chōngquán　　　　　　　　落地弓步冲拳

Land on the left foot, then land the right foot forward into a right bow stance. Clench the right hand and bring it to the waist, then punch forward, extending the arm at shoulder height, fist eye up. Bring the left hand to the right elbow crease. Look forward. (image T1.42)

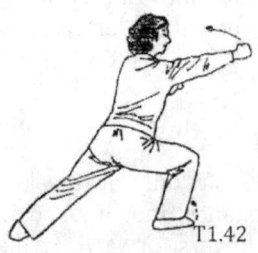

FIRST FORM TUIQUAN

43. Turn Around, Elbow Tuck   zhuànshēn yǎnzhǒu   转身掩肘

Shift to the left and bend the left leg, turning the right foot in. Laterally rotate the right arm and bend the elbow, turning the fist heart in. (image T1.43.a) Pivot on the ball of the right foot to turn ninety degrees to the left, raising the bent left knee. Cover inwards with the right elbow, then quickly do a framing block up above the head, fist heart up. Look forward. (image 43b)

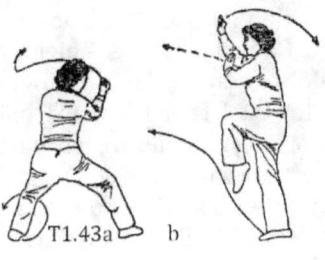

44. Aerial Snap Kick   téngkōng tántī   腾空弹踢

Push off with the right leg to jump up, and complete a right snap kick whilst airborne. During the kick, the right ankle is plantar-flexed and the left knee is bent. Push straight forward with the left hand, fingers up. Unclench the right hand and swing the arm out to shoulder height behind the body, fingers up. Look forward. (image T1.44)

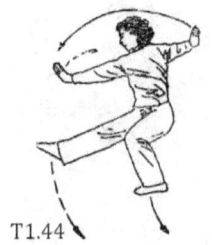

45. Closed Stance Punch Upwards
    bīngbù shàng chōngquán   并步上冲拳

Land on the left foot, and then the right, bending the left knee and tucking in the right foot. Swing the right hand flat across to the front and stab the left hand to under the right elbow, palm down. Look at the right hand. (image T1.45a) Shift to the right leg and circle the right hand left, up, and right past the face to stop at the waist on the right, elbow bent and fist heart up. Circle the left hand forward, left, and up to above the head at the right with a sideways palm, palm angled down. Look past the left hand. (image 45b) Bring the left foot across to beside the right foot. Punch the right fist directly up the side, passing inside the back of the left hand, extending the arm and turning the fist heart to face left. Tuck the left hand into the right armpit, palm facing right. Look to the left side. (image 45c)

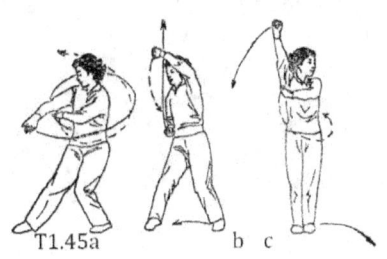

46. Guiding Hand, Bow Stance Roundhouse Punch
    yǐnzhǎng gōngbù guànquán   引掌弓步贯拳

Step the left foot forward to the left, foot pointing forward. Swing the left hand across the belly to the waist, fingers pointing forward. Lower the right fist behind to shoulder height, arm extended, fist eye up. (image T1.46a) Push off with the left leg to jump forward and up. Bump the right foot into the left heel whilst airborne. Stab the left hand forward, extending the arm just above shoulder height, fingers forward. Look at the left hand. (image 46b) Land on the right foot, keeping the left foot suspended. (image 46c) Step the left foot forward, pointing forward. Bring the left hand to the waist, fingers still pointing forward. (image 46d) Shift forward and step the right foot forward to take a right bow stance. Swing the right fist around to the front with a roundhouse punch, fist heart in. Circle the left hand back, left, then forward to swing into the right fist. Both arms are slightly bent. Look forward. (image 46e)

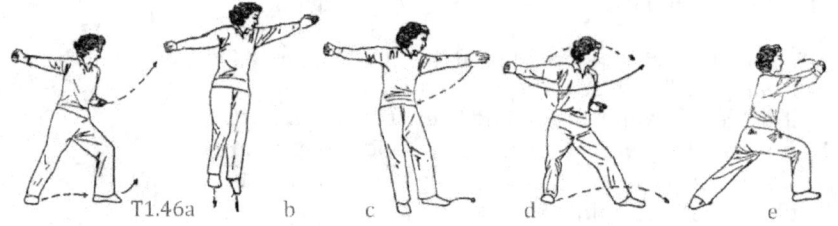

47. Press With Fist, Bow Stance Stab

yāquán gōngbù chuānzhǎng   压拳弓步穿掌

Shift to the left leg and sit into a half horse stance. Medially rotate the arms and press down at chest height. The right fist heart faces down. (image T1.47a) Shift forward and extend the left leg to take a right bow stance. Unclench the right hand and circle it up, forward, then down to the waist, palm up. Circle the left hand down and to the rear, then up and over to press down in front of the face, palm forward at eye height. (images 47b, 47c) Thread the right hand forward over the back of the left hand, extending the arm a bit above shoulder height, palm up. Tuck the left hand into the right armpit. Look at the right hand. (image 47d)

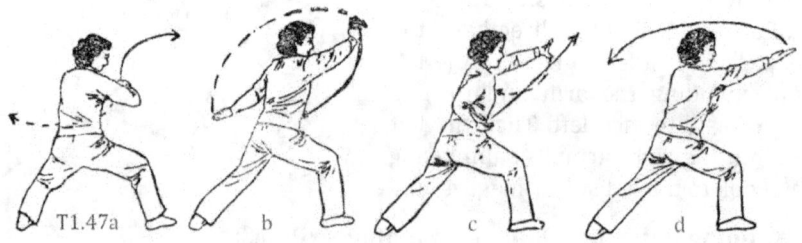

FIRST FORM TUIQUAN

48. Snap Kick Stab tántī chuānzhǎng 弹踢穿掌

Turn slightly rightward and do a left snap kick forward. Medially rotate the right hand and swing it up and to the rear to shoulder height. Bring the left hand down to the waist, then stab forward with the kick, palm up. Look forward. (images T1.48a, 48b) Land the left foot forward into a left bow stance. Bring the right hand in to the waist, palm up. Medially rotate the left hand and press down. (image 48c) Stab the right hand forward over the back of the left hand, palm up, a bit higher than the shoulders. Tuck the left hand into the right armpit, palm down. Look at the right hand. (image 48d)

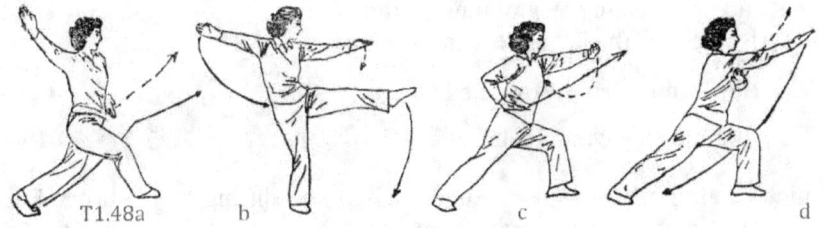

T1.48a b c d

Section Four

49. Front Cross-Over Stance Guiding Hand gàibù yǐnzhǎng 盖步引掌

Bend the left knee to squat, turning in the foot, and extend the right leg to take a right drop stance. Bring the right hand in, then thread it along inside the right leg. Extend the left hand out to the rear, palm angled forward. Look to the lower right (image T1.49a) Shift forward to a right bow stance. Scoop up with the right arm until both hands are at shoulder height. (image 49b) Shift forward to the right leg and lift the bent left knee forward. Guide back with the right hand, moving it up and back to the waist, fingers still pointing forward. Look forward. (image 49c) Land the left foot, foot turned out, to cross with the right leg. Stab the right hand forward, extending the arm, palm facing left, fingers forward. Look forward. (image 49d)

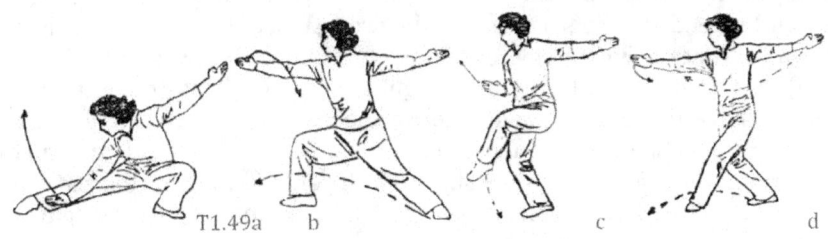

T1.49a b c d

50. Hop-Step, Wrist Wrap, Low Thrust Kick

diànbù chánwàn xiàchuāi   垫步缠腕下踹

Step the right foot forward. Bring the arms together in front of the body, placing the left hand under the right elbow, palm down. Look at the right hand. (image T1.50a) Push off with the right foot in a hop-step, lifting the left foot to kick forward with the foot turned out and the leg straight. Circle the left hand up, left, and down, finishing with the palm turned up. Circle the right hand down, right, and up, finishing by grabbing on top of the left wrist. Look at the left hand. (image 50b)

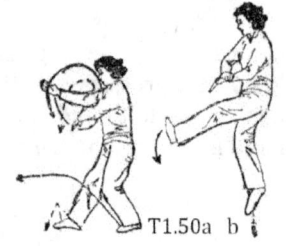

51. Hop-Step, Wrist Wrap, Lean

diànbù chánwàn kàoshēnzhǎng   垫步缠腕靠身掌

Land the left foot then immediately do a hop-step, lifting the bent right knee. Circle the right hand up, right, then down to stop inside the right thigh. Circle the left hand down, left, and up to the right elbow. Look at the right hand. (images T1.51a, 51b) Land the right foot, taking a right bow stance. Separate the hands up and down, swinging with the arms on a straight line with each other – the right arm angled up with the palm up and the left arm angled down with the palm down. Look at the right hand. (image 51c)

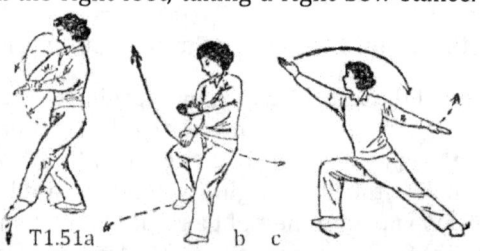

52. Roundhouse Punch, Snap Kick

guànquán tántī   贯拳弹踢

Shift back and turn left, pushing into the right leg to take a left bow stance. Hook the left hand and extend the arm out a bit above the shoulder, hook pointing down. Circle the right hand up and left, to come over to press down inside the left forearm. Look forward. (image T1.52a) Squat fully on the left leg and extend the right leg in a right drop stance. Press the right hand down in front of the left side of the belly. Look to the lower front. (image 52b) Push into the left leg to take a right bow stance. Brush the right hand across above the right foot and over to the rear right, then swing it back with a roundhouse punch. Unhook the left hand and swing it forward and to the right to in front of the right shoulder, fingers up, then hit the right fist into it. Look forward, to the left. (image 52c) Shift forward to the right leg and do a left front snap kick, without changing the hand position. Look forward. (image 52d, and from behind)

FIRST FORM TUIQUAN

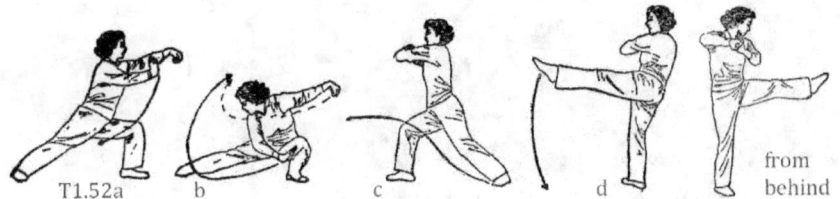

T1.52a   b   c   d   from behind

53. Bow Stance Push   gōngbù tuīzhǎng   弓步推掌

Land the left foot forward, squatting fully on the right leg into a left drop stance. Bring the right fist to the waist, fist heart up. Press the left hand down in front of the belly. (image T1.53a) Shift forward, pushing into the right leg to take a left bow stance. Brush the left hand forward over the left foot then hook and continue on to behind the body, hook pointing up. Unclench the right hand and push forward from the waist, arm straight and fingers up. Look forward. (image 53b)

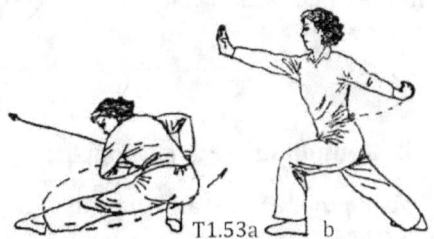

T1.53a   b

54. Back Jump To Bow Stance Push
hòu tiàobù gōngbù tuīzhǎng   后跳步弓步推掌

Unhook the left hand and bring it to the waist. (image T1.54a) Shift forward and do a right snap kick forward. Push forward with the left hand, extending the arm with the fingers up. Circle the right hand up and back, swinging to shoulder height with an extended arm, fingers up. Look forward. (image 54b) Withdraw the right foot into a bow stance. Push the right hand forward, passing by the waist, extending the arm with the fingers up. Swing the left hand up and back, hooking the hand with the arm extended, hook pointing up. Look forward. (image 54c) Shift forward, bending and lifting the left knee and pushing off with the right leg to jump up and back. Land on the left foot, then the right foot behind it, into a left bow stance. Circle the right hand up, back, down, and in to the waist, then push forward with a vertical palm, fingers pointing up. Unhook the left hand and circle it down, forward, up, and back, swinging in a full circle, then hook at the back, hook pointing up. Look forward. (images 54d, 54e)

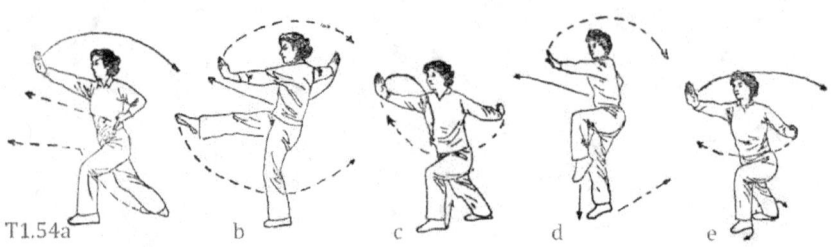

55. Back Jump To Bow Stance Push

hòu tiàobù gōngbù tuīzhǎng   后跳步弓步推掌

This is the same as move 54, but starting out from the bow stance, without the kick. (images T1.55a, 55b, 55c)

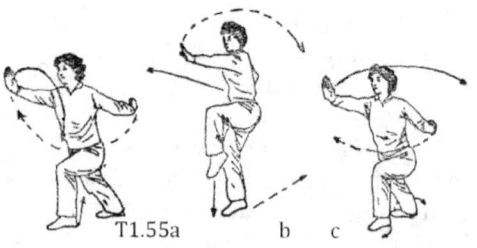

56. Roundhouse Punch, Snap Kick   guànquán tántī   贯拳弹踢

Pivot on the left heel and the ball of the right foot to turn around one-eighty degrees to the right. As the body turns, pull slightly upward with the right hand, keeping the arm naturally extended. Extend the left arm and unhook the hand, circling it forward and right to behind the body. Look at the right hand. (image T1.56a) Continue to turn the torso another ninety degrees rightward, twisting into a cross stance. Clench the right hand and punch right and down to in front of the chest, fist heart down. Bring the left hand to meet the right fist, fingers up. Look forward, to the left. (image 56b) Do a left snap kick to the front. Look forward, to the left. (image 56c)

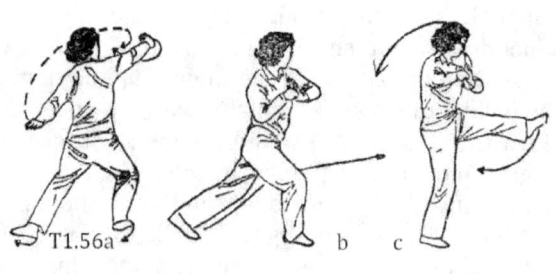

57. Hitting Hop-Step, Bow Stance Chop

jībù gōngbù pīquán   击步弓步劈拳

Keep standing on the right leg and bend the left knee to bring the foot in, ankle plantar-flexed. Lift the right fist to chop down on the right at shoulder height with the arm straight and fist eye up. Circle the left hand to in front of the right shoulder, fingers up, palm facing right. Look at the right fist. (image T1.57a) Turn the head left without moving anything else. Look forward, to the left side. (image 57b) Land the left foot and quickly push off to jump forward and up. Bump the right foot behind the left heel whilst airborne. Lower the left hand to the waist then stab forward until the arm is straight, fingers forward. Look forward. (images 57c, 57d) Land on the right foot, then the left, then step the right foot through to take a right bow stance. Bring the right hand over and forward to chop with the arm straight just above shoulder height, fist eye up. Circle the left hand down, out, then up, to lift under the right forearm. Look at the right fist. (images 57e, 57f)

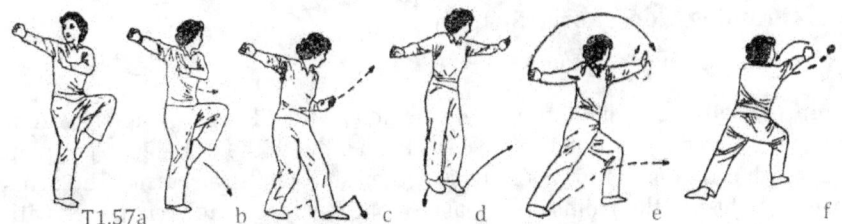

58. Dodge, Bow Stance Low Punch

shǎnshēn gōngbù xià chōngquán 闪身弓步下冲拳

Shift back and lean slightly back. Laterally rotate the right arm and bend the elbow to take the fist up and back, gathering in front of the face, fist heart in. Extend the left hand forward, palm up. (image T1.58a) Shift forward into a right bow stance. Medially rotate the right hand and bring it in, then punch forward and down, arm straight, fist heart down. Circle the left hand left and in to place the palm inside the right arm, fingers up. Look at the right fist. (image 58b)

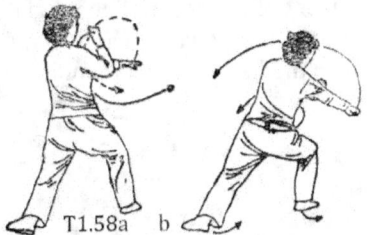

59. Turn Back, Block

huíshēn gédǎng 回身格挡

Pivot on the ball of the right foot to turn around leftward one-thirty-five degrees to face back. Straighten up, withdraw the left foot, and stand up, touching the toes of the left foot down in a high empty stance. Laterally rotate the right fist and bend the elbow to block inward, fist heart in, fist at nose height. Move the left hand to the right elbow crease. Look at the right fist. (image T1.59)

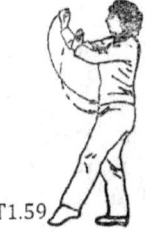

60. Empty Stance Crossed Hands

xūbù shízìshǒu 虚步十字手

Lift the left foot slightly, then immediately move it forward a half-step, touching the toes down. Sit on the right leg into a full empty stance. Unclench the right hand and circle the both hands down to either side of the hips, palms up, fingers angled downwards. Look at the right hand. (image

T1.60a) Separate the hands out to either side and up, circling until they come back down to cross in front of the chest with the fingers up. The right hand is on the inside. Look at the right hand. (image 60b)

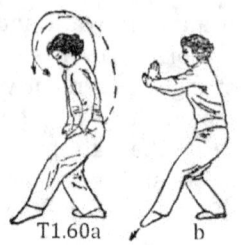

61. Framing Block, Aerial Snap Kick

jiàzhǎng téngkōng tántī   架掌腾空弹踢

Step the left foot a half-step forward. (image T1.61a) Step the right foot forward past the left foot. (image 61b) Push off with the right leg to jump up, separating the hands to block up to either side whilst airborne. The arms are straight and the palms up. (image 61c) Quickly to a right snap kick with the ankle plantar-flexed, then land on the left foot. (image 61d) Pivot on the ball of the left foot, lift the right knee and roll it inward, to turn one-thirty-five degrees around to the left. Swing the right hand high and extend the left hand low. (image 61e) Land the right foot to the right side and sit into a horse stance. Swing the straight right arm forward, down, then hook the hand to the rear, hook facing up. Bring the left hand to the belly then lift up in front of the chest, then medially rotate to do a framing block up above the head. Look down to the right. (image 61f) Without moving anything else, snap the head quickly to look straight forward. (image 61g)

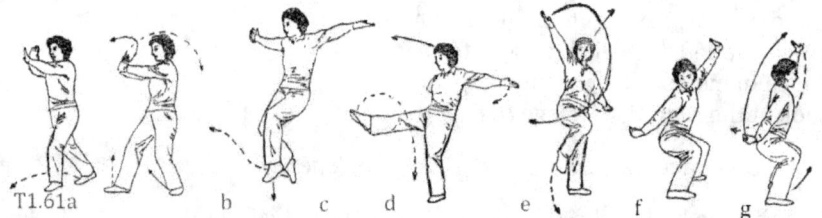

62. Step Around, Snap Kick   rào shàngbù tántī   绕上步弹踢

Shift to the right leg and lift the left foot, standing up straight. Take the left hand past in front of the body to hook down behind with the arm straight. Unhook the right hand and circle it up above the head at the right. (image T1.62a) Land on the left foot and lift the right foot. Sweep the right hand forward then down, hooking back behind the body with the arm straight (hand not hooked). Circle the left hand up above the head at the left. (image 62b)

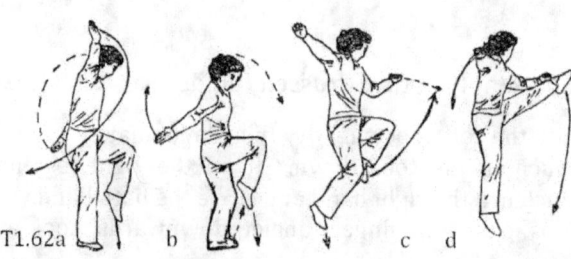

FIRST FORM TUIQUAN

Push into the left leg to jump up, quickly doing a front snap kick. Clench the left hand and bend the elbow to pound down, fist heart up. Clench the right hand and raise it up behind the head, arm straight, fist heart down. Look forward, to the left. (images 62c, 62d)

63. Bow Stance Swinging Chop   gōngbù lūnpīzhǎng   弓步抡劈拳

Land the right foot, keeping the weight on it, then bend it slightly and land the left foot to the forward left. Lower the left fist and medially rotate. Let the right fist naturally lower near the hip. (image T1.63a) Move the left foot across to the left and extend the right leg to take a left bow stance. Turn the body rightward then continue on to turn to the left. Swing the fists with the body turn, making vertical circles at either side of the body. The left arm stops behind, the right arm stops in front. Both arms are fully extended with the fist hearts down, at about shoulder height. Look forward. (image 63b)

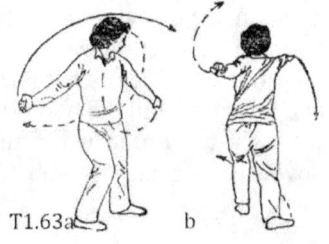

64. Raised Knee Punch To The Side   tíxī cè chōngquán   提膝侧冲拳

Step the right foot forward past the left foot, turning the foot in and bending the knee. Unclench both hands. Swing the left hand forward in front of the head at the left, palm forward. Swing the right hand back, angling it down. (image T1.64a) Clench the right hand and bring the fist to the waist. (image 64b) Stand up on the right leg and raise the bent left knee. Bring the left hand in to in front of the right shoulder, fingers up. Punch the right fist forward, arm straight, fist eye up. Look at the right fist. (image 64c)

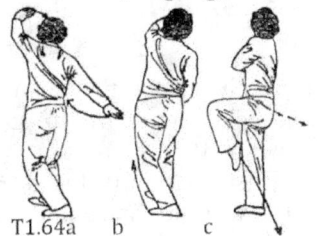

65. Land To Bow Stance Punch   luòdì gōngbù chōngquán   落地弓步冲拳

Land the left foot to the left into a bow stance. Clench the left hand and lower it to the waist, then punch out to the left with the arm extended a bit higher than the shoulder, fist eye up. Look at the left fist. (image T1.65a) Tuck in the hip and settle, turning the body slightly rightward, and turn the head straight. (image 65b and from the side)

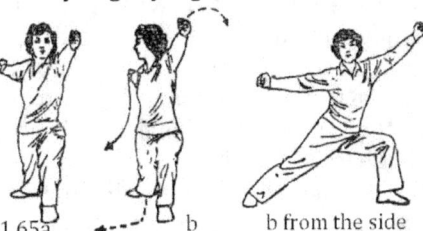

313

66. Curving Walk, Hammerfist Snap Kick

húxíngbù záquán tántī   弧形步砸拳 弹踢

Bring the right foot in past the left foot to take a curving step to the forward left. Bring the right fist down to the right hip then swing it to about waist height. (image T1.66a) Take a curving step with the left foot, going in the direction that the right foot points. Continue to swing the right fist up to shoulder height. (image 66b) Take a curving step with the right foot to the forward right. Continue to swing the right fist up and over to the rear. Bring the left fist in to the hip. (image 66c) Take a curving step with the left foot, going in the direction that the right foot points. Swing the fists, continuing in the direction that they are moving. (image 66d) Shift to a left bow stance. Continue to circle the left fist down, past in front of the belly, to the right, up, and left to behind the body, arm extended and fist eye up. Continue to swing the right fist up, forward, then chop down with a straight arm, fist heart down. Both arms are shoulder height. (image 66e) (Note: you may take three steps or five.)

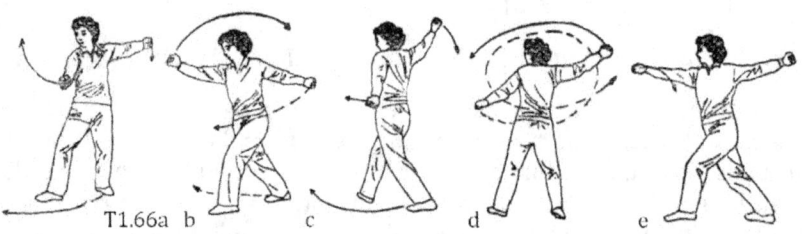

Laterally rotate the right fist and bend the elbow to pound down with the forearm level and fist heart up. (image 66f) Lift the right knee and do a snap kick, ankle plantar-flexed. Look forward. (image 66g)

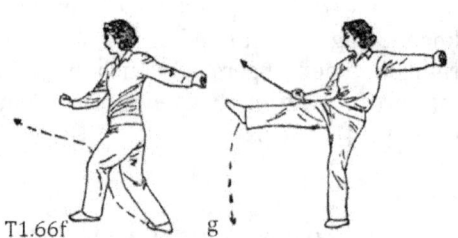

67. Left And Right Bow Stance Punches

zuǒ yòu gōngbù chōngquán   左右弓步冲拳

Land the right foot forward into a right bow stance. Medially rotate the right fist to punch forward, arm straight at shoulder height, fist heart down. Look at the right fist. (image T1.67a) Step the left foot forward into a left bow stance. Bring the left fist to the waist then punch forward, arm extended at shoulder height, fist heart down. Bring the right fist to the waist, fist heart up. Look forward. (image 67b) Shift back and turn one-eighty degrees rightward into a right bow stance. Punch the right fist forward, arm extended at shoulder height, fist heart down. Look forward. (image 67c)

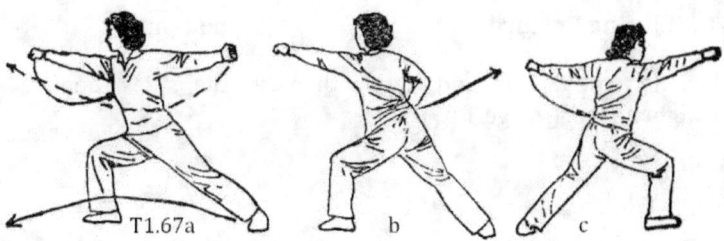

68. Withdraw, Roundhouse Punch   chèbù guànquán   撤步贯拳

Unclench both hands, turning the palms to face up. Bring the left hand to the waist. (image T1.68a) Withdraw the right foot behind the left, turned out. Thread the left hand forward over the right palm, palm up. Bring the right hand in to the waist, palm up. Look at the left hand. (image 68b) Bring the left foot in to beside the right foot and stand up. Clench the right hand and circle right, up, then left to do a roundhouse punch at the right side over the head. Circle the left hand up and in to in front of the right shoulder, fingers up. Look to the left. (image 68c)

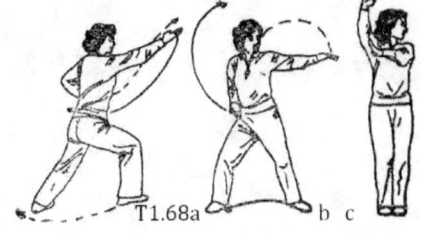

69. Withdraw, Facing Fists   chèbù duìquán   撤步对拳

Shift to the left leg and lift the right knee. (image T1.69a) Stamp with the right foot with the knee slightly bent, lifting the left foot as the right foot stamps. Place the left foot behind the right knee. (image 69b) Withdraw the left foot to the rear left. Unclench the right hand and lower both hands to either side, palms up. Look at the right hand. (image 69c) Withdraw the right foot to the rear right. Open out the hands to either side. (image 69d) Bring the left foot in beside the right foot and stand up. Continue to circle the hands up, in past the face, then down, gradually clenching fists to face each other in front of the belly, fist hearts down. The fists are about ten centimeters apart, and about ten centimeters in front of the belly. Look to the left. (image 69e)

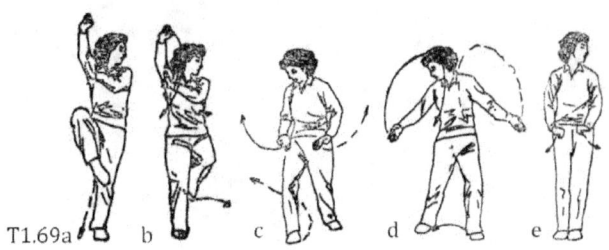

70. Closing Posture shōu shì 收势

Unclench the hands and lower them at the sides. Look straight ahead. (image T1.70)

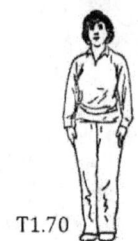
T1.70

SECOND FORM TUIQUAN

二路腿拳

Names Of The Movements

Position Of Preparation
Section One
1. Front Touch Stance Facing Fists
2. Step Forward, Facing Fists
3. Horse Stance Single Palm Carry
4. Resting Stance Hook
5. Horse Stance Double Palm Carries
6. Resting Stance Flash Palm
7. Raised Knee Stab
8. Drop Stance Thread The Hand
9. Aerial Arrow Kick
10. Bow Stance Low Punch

Section Two
11. Resting Stance Stab
12. Resting Stance Stab
13. Raised Knee Stab
14. Drop Stance Thread The Hand
15. Aerial Arrow Kick
16. Bow Stance Planting Punch Down

Section Three
17. Bow Stance Chop
18. Empty Stance Low Chop
19. Snap Kick Stab
20. Empty Stance Low Chop
21. Snap Kick Stab
22. Closed Stance Punch
23. Closed Stance Punch

Section Four
24. Raised Knee Stab
25. Drop Stance Thread The Hand
26. Aerial Arrow Kick
27. Closed Stance Stab

Section Five
28. Bow Stance Chop
29. Jump And Lash

30. Empty Stance Low Chop
31. Aerial Snap Kick
32. Aerial Stab
33. Empty Stance Low Chop
34. Aerial Snap Kick
35. Closed Stance Stab

Section Six
36. Raised Knee Stab
37. Drop Stance Thread The Hand
38. Aerial Snap Kick
39. Bow Stance Punch
40. Drop Stance Thread The Hand
41. Aerial Snap Kick
42. Bow Stance Double Pushes
43. Bow Stance Double Stabs
44. Raised Knee Scooping Snap
45. Aerial Raised Knee Stab
46. Drop Stance Chop
47. Inside Crescent Kick Push

Section Seven
48. Empty Stance Planting Punch Down
49. Bow Stance Chop
50. Snap Kick Hold The Fists
51. Inside Crescent Kick
52. Snap Kick Punch
53. Snap Kick Stab
54. Closed Stance Strike
55. Closed Stance Fist Strike

Section Eight
56. Raised Knee Stab
57. Drop Stance Thread The Hand
58. Bow Stance Scoop
59. Curving Walk
60. Snap Kick Embrace With The Fists
61. Bow Stance Punch
62. Closed Stance Punch Up
63. One-Legged Basin Squat Stance
64. Closing Posture

SECOND FORM TUIQUAN

0. Position Of Preparation yùbèi shì 预备势

Stand to attention. (image T2.0)

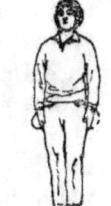

Section One

1. Front Touch Stance Facing Fists qiándiǎnbù duìquán 前点步对拳

Move the left foot to the forward right, touching the toes down to take a front touch stance. Clench both hands and place them facing in front of the belly, about ten centimeters apart. Look to the left. (image T2.1)

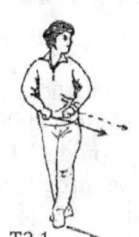

2. Step Forward, Facing Fists shàngbù duìquán 上步对拳

Stride the left foot out to the forward left, bending the knee. Unclench the hands and swing them forward at waist height, palms up. Look at the hands. (image T2.2a) Stride the right foot out to the forward right, then bring the left foot in to meet it. Clench the hands and medially rotate the arms, placing the fists to face each other about ten centimeters apart. Look to the left. (image 2b)

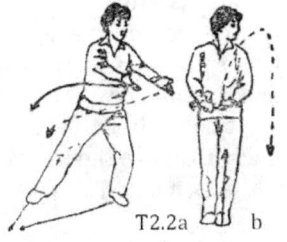

3. Horse Stance Single Palm Carry mǎbù dàn tuōzhǎng 马步单托掌

Lift the left knee with the ankle plantar-flexed to point the foot straight down. Swing the left hand up in front and out to the rear at the left side, then lower it to the outer edge of the left ankle, palm forward. Bend the right elbow to bring the fist to the waist, fist heart up. Look at the left hand. (image T2.3a) Land the left foot across the left to take a horse stance. Lift up with the left hand at shoulder height, palm up. Look forward. (image 3b)

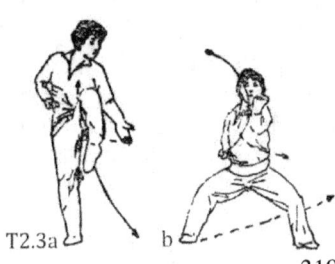

CHAQUAN, VOLUME II

4. **Resting Stance Hook**   xiēbù gōushǒu   歇步勾手

Take an insertion step with the right foot behind the left leg, crossing the legs with the knees bent in a left resting stance. Unclench the right hand and cross it with the left in front of the belly, elbows bent. Then hook the left hand and roll it under, extending it to the rear with the hook pointing up, and swing the right hand up the side of the body to flash above the head, palm up. Look to the left. (image T2.4)

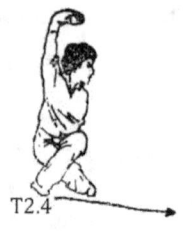

5. **Horse Stance Double Palm Carries**

   mǎbù shuāng tuōzhǎng   马步双托掌

Step the left foot across to the left into a half horse stance. Unhook the left hand and lift up in front to shoulder height, palm up. Lower the right hand, bending the elbow to place the palm, palm up, under the left elbow. Look forward. (image T2.5)

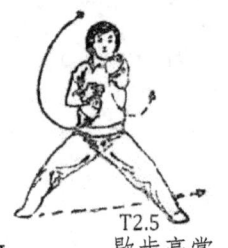

6. **Resting Stance Flash Palm**   xiēbù liàngzhǎng   歇步亮掌

Do an insertion step to the left with the right foot, passing behind the left leg, crossing the legs with the knees bent in a left resting stance. Hook the left hand and extend the arm to the rear, hook up. Bring the right hand down in front of the belly then flash the palm up above the head on the right, palm up. Look to the left. (image T2.6)

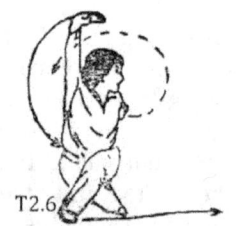

7. **Raised Knee Stab**   tíxī chuānzhǎng   提膝穿掌

Step the left foot across to the left side and turn ninety degree to the right, bending the right knee into a right bow stance. Bend the right elbow and bring the hand down along the right side to the waist, clenching it with the fist heart up. Unhook the left hand and circle it up, right, and to the front to the shoulder, arm bent, palm down. Look forward. (image T2.7a) Stand up on the right leg and raise the bent left knee, ankle plantar-flexed. Thread the right hand forward over the left hand, stopping at head height with the palm up. Slide the left hand in under the right arm, pressing down and bending the elbow to tuck the hand into the right armpit, palm down. Look at the right hand. (image 7b)

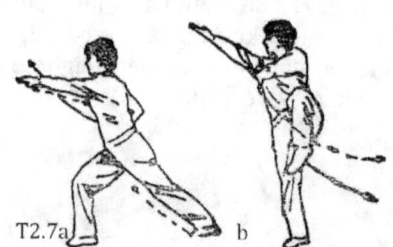

SECOND FORM TUIQUAN

8. Drop Stance Thread The Hand   pūbù chuānzhǎng   仆步穿掌

Extend the left leg along the ground to the left and squat fully on the right leg into a drop stance. Fully extend the left hand along the leg to above the foot, tiger's mouth up, fingers forward. Medially rotate the right arm to turn the tiger's mouth up. Reach the torso towards the left foot. Look at the left hand. (image T2.8)

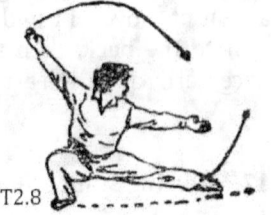

T2.8

9. Aerial Arrow Kick   téngkōng jiàntán   腾空箭弹

Push into the right leg to stand up and step forward, bending the knee. (image T2.9a) Shift forward on the ball of the right foot. Clench the left hand and bend the elbow to bring the fist to the waist. Extend the right arm forward, keeping it straight, to swing the hand up to shoulder height, palm up. Swing the left leg up. (image 9b) Push off with the right leg to jump up, then do a front snap kick whilst airborne, ankle plantar-flexed. Clench the right hand and bend the elbow to bring the fist to the waist, fist heart up. Unclench the left hand and extend the arm forward, fingers up. Look at the left hand. (image 9c)

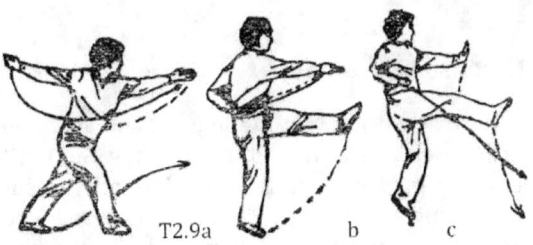

T2.9a   b   c

10. Bow Stance Low Punch   gōngbù xià chōngquán   弓步下冲拳

Land on the left foot and land the right foot forward into a right bow stance. Punch straight forward with the right fist, fist heart angled down to the left. Bend the left elbow to place the hand in the right elbow crease. Look at the right fist. (image T2.10)

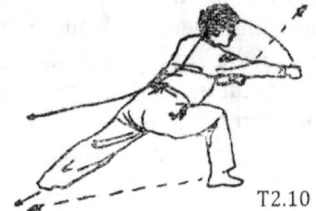

T2.10

Section Two

11. Resting Stance Stab   xiēbù chāzhǎng   歇步插掌

Withdraw the right foot behind, then do an insertion step with the left foot behind the right leg, so that the legs are crossed in a full squat. Turn one-eighty degrees to the right, sitting into a right resting stance. Unclench the right hand and bend the elbow to cross the arms in front of the chest, the right hand on top of the left. Then circle the right hand, straightening the arm and rolling it under, to stab downwards, palm facing the rear. Stab the left arm straight to the upper left, palm facing the front. Look to the left side.

(image T2.11) [Translator's note: Although the text says to face left, the image is facing right. The repeating action of moves 11 and 12 is often done with a look first to the back, then to the front. Since this is not necessarily a written error, I have left it as is.]

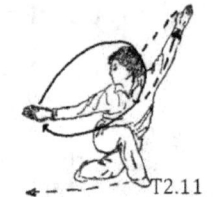

12. Resting Stance Stab   xiēbù chāzhǎng   歇步插掌

Straddle step the right foot across to the right, then do an insertion step with the left foot behind the right, squatting on the legs to take a right resting stance. Bring the left hand down in front of the body then stab up to the upper left, palm facing forward. Bring the right hand up and to the left past the body, then stab with a reverse stab to the lower right, palm facing the rear. Look at the right hand. (image T2.12)

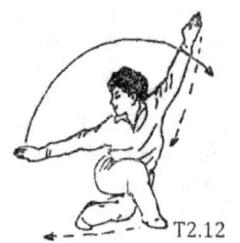

13. Raised Knee Stab   tíxī chuānzhǎng   提膝穿掌

Withdraw the right foot to the right and set to a left bow stance. Clench the left hand and bend the elbow to bring the fist to the waist, fist heart up. Circle the right hand in front of the body, to shoulder height, arm slightly bent, thumb side down, palm facing forward. Look forward. (image T2.13a) Stand up on the left leg and raise the bent right knee in front of the body, ankle plantar-flexed. Thread the left hand up to the front to above head height, passing over the right hand, palm up. Bend the right elbow to bring the hand along under the left arm to tuck into the left armpit, palm down, fingers pointing right. Look at the left hand. (image 13b)

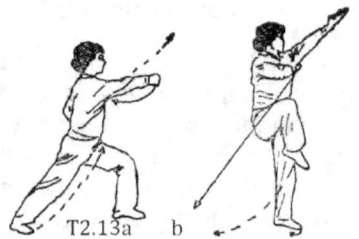

14. Drop Stance Thread The Hand   pūbù chuānzhǎng   仆步穿掌

Squat on the left leg and extend the right foot along the ground into a drop stance. Extend the right hand along the leg to the right foot, thumb side up, fingers pointing forward. Medially rotate the left arm to turn the thumb side up. Lean the torso towards the right foot. Look at the right hand. (image T2.14)

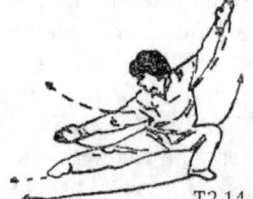

SECOND FORM TUIQUAN

15. Aerial Arrow Kick   téngkōng jiàntán   腾空箭弹

Push into the left leg and bend the right knee, standing up. Swing the arms, the left moving down and forward, the right moving down and back, to extend the arms at shoulder height, tiger's mouths up. (image T2.15a) Shift to the ball of the right foot. Clench the left hand and bend the elbow to bring the fist to the waist. Circle the right hand down and forward to shoulder height, palm up. Swing the left leg up to the front. (image 15b) Push into the right leg to jump up, doing a snap kick with the right foot, ankle plantar-flexed. Clench the right hand and bend the elbow to bring the fist to the waist, fist heart up. Unclench the left hand and push forward, fingers up. Look at the left hand. (image 15c)

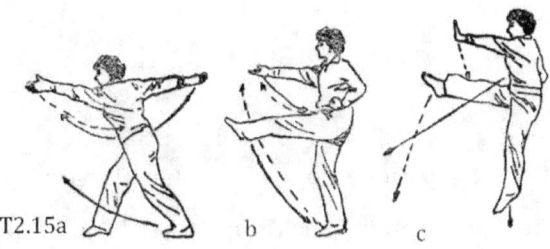

T2.15a   b   c

16. Bow Stance Planting Punch Down   gōngbù xià zāiquán   弓步下栽拳

Land on the left leg then land the right foot forward and push into a bent knee, to take a right bow stance. Punch forward and down with the right fist, fist heart down. Bend the left elbow to bring the hand to the right elbow crease. Look at the right fist. (image T2.16)

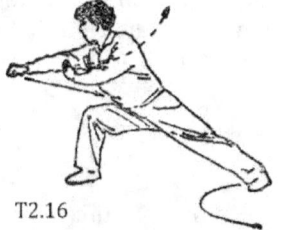

T2.16

Section Three

17. Bow Stance Chop   gōngbù pīzhǎng   弓步劈掌

Lift the left foot and do an arcing step, passing close by the inside of the right foot to step out to the forward left, foot turned out. Circle the left hand with a pulling motion to the forward left. Bend the right elbow to bring the fist to the waist, fist heart up. Look at the left hand. (image T2.17a) With an arcing step, step the right foot to in front of the left foot into a right bow stance. Unclench the right hand and swing it up the right side, over the head, then forward to chop a bit above shoulder height, palm edge down. Bend the left elbow to place the hand in the right elbow crease. Look at the right hand. (image 17b)

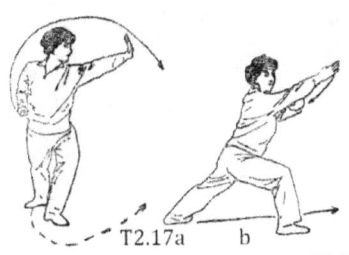

T2.17a   b

18. Empty Stance Low Chop   xūbù xià pīzhǎng   虚步下劈掌

Step the left foot to the forward left, foot turned out. Press the right hand down in front of the belly and place the back of the left hand under the right elbow, palm in. Look at the right hand. (image T2.18a) Step the right foot a half-step forward, touching down the toes and bending the left knee to take a right empty stance. Circle the right hand up and over to chop down in front with a straight arm. Circle the left hand along in front of the body, finishing tucked into the right elbow crease. The palms are facing each other. Look at the right hand. (image 18b)

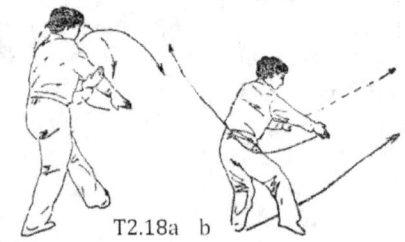

19. Snap Kick Stab   tántuǐ chāzhǎng   弹腿插掌

Step the right foot a half-step forward and lift the left foot to do a snap kick, ankle plantar-flexed. Bend both elbows to move the hands to in front of the belly, then separate them to stab forward and back. The left hand is in front, the right behind, palms angled up. Look at the left hand. (image T2.19)

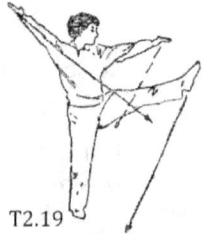

20. Empty Stance Low Chop   xūbù xià pīzhǎng   虚步下劈掌

Land the left foot in front of the right with the foot turned out, bending both knees. Lower both hands to cross in front of the belly, left hand on top of the right, palms angled inwards. Look at the left hand. (image T2.20a) Step the right foot across a half-step to the right then step the left foot a half-step to the forward left, touching down the toes in a left empty stance. Circle the left hand to the right and up, then over to chop forward. Circle the right hand down, to the right, then over, bending the elbow to tuck the hand into the left elbow crease. The palms are facing. Look at the left hand. (image 20b)

SECOND FORM TUIQUAN

21. Snap Kick Stab   tántuǐ chāzhǎng   弹腿叉掌

Settle the left foot a half-step forward and lift the right foot to do a snap kick, ankle plantar-flexed. Bend the elbows in front of the belly, then stab, the right hand stabbing forward, the left hand stabbing behind. The palms face up. Look at the right hand. (image T2.21)

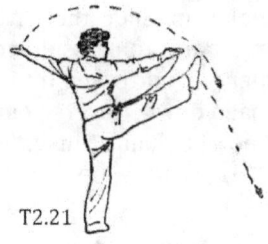

22. Closed Stance Punch   bīngbù chōngquán   并步冲拳

Land the right foot forward with the knee slightly bent. Clench the right hand and bend the elbow to bring the fist to the waist, fist heart up. Circle the left hand up and over to press down in front, arm at shoulder height, palm facing forward. Look at the left hand. (image T2.22a) Bring the left foot in to meet the right and stand up, reaching the torso slightly forward. Punch directly forward with the right fist, fist eye up, just above shoulder height. Bend the left elbow to tuck the hand into the right elbow crease. Look at the right fist. (image 22b)

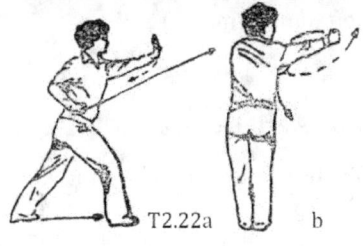

23. Closed Stance Punch   bīngbù chōngquán   并步冲拳

Do not move the feet. Circle the left hand upwards with a scooping palm, elbow bent. Bend the right elbow to tuck the hand into the left elbow crease, fist eye in. Look at the left hand. (image T2.23a) Punch the right fist forward, fist eye up. Tuck the left hand into the right elbow crease. Look at the right fist. (image 23b)

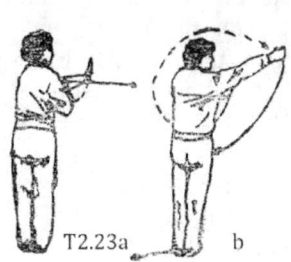

Section Four

24. Raised Knee Stab   tíxī chuānzhǎng   提膝穿掌

Withdraw the left foot to the left, bending the right knee into a right bow stance. Bend the left elbow to bring the hand to the waist, clenching it with the fist heart up. Bring the left hand past the front towards the right, circling it up to shoulder height with the elbow slightly bent, thumb side on the bottom, palm forward. Look forward. (image T2.24a) Stand up on the right leg and lift the bent left knee in front of the body, ankle plantar-flexed.

Unclench the right hand and thread over the left hand to stab forward and up, palm up. Slide the left hand below the right arm to press down with the elbow bent, hand tucked into the right armpit, palm down, fingers pointing left. Look at the right hand. (image 24b)

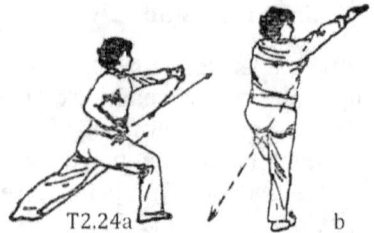

25. Drop Stance Thread The Hand　　pūbù chuānzhǎng　　仆步穿掌

Squat on the right leg and extend the left leg along the ground into a drop stance. Extend the left hand along the left leg to above the foot, thumb side on top, fingers pointing forward. Medially rotate the right hand to turn the thumb side up. Reach the torso towards the left foot. Look at the left hand. (image T2.25)

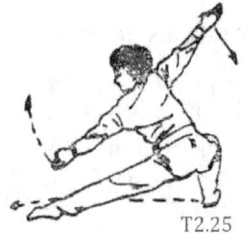

26. Aerial Arrow Kick　　téngkōng jiàntán　　腾空箭弹

Push into the right leg and step forward, turning the foot out and bending the knee, standing up. (image T2.26a) Shift to the ball of the right foot and swing the left leg forward and up. Clench the left hand and bend the elbow to bring the fist to the waist. Swing the right hand down then forward with a straight arm to shoulder height, palm up. (image 26b) Push off with the right leg to jump up and do a front snap kick with the ankle plantar-flexed. Clench the right hand and bend the elbow to bring the fist to the waist, fist heart up. Unclench the left hand and swing the straight arm forward, fingers up, palm forward. Look at the left hand. (image 26c)

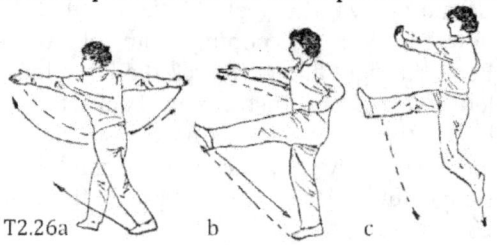

27. Closed Stance Stab　　bīngbù chāzhǎng　　并步插掌

Land on the left leg then land the right foot forward, bending the knee. Medially rotate the left hand to press down with the thumb side down and the palm forward. Look at the left hand. (image T2.27a) Hook the right foot in and bring the left foot up to meet it, turning the body ninety degrees to the left and

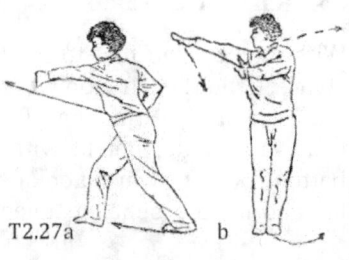

standing up. Reach the torso forward slightly. Bend the left elbow to tuck the hand into the right armpit, palm down. Unclench the right hand and stab it out over the back of the left hand to eye height, palm down. Look at the right hand. (image 27b)

Section Five

28. Bow Stance Chop   gōngbù pīzhǎng   弓步劈掌

Take an arcing step to the left with the left foot, turning the foot out. Circle the straight left arm to the forward left with a reaching hand. Lower the right hand to angle the arm downwards. Look forward. (image T2.28a) Step the right foot forward into a right bow stance. Clench the right hand and bring it up and over to chop in front at eye height, fist eye up. Bend the left elbow to tuck the hand into the right elbow crease. Look at the right fist. (image 28b)

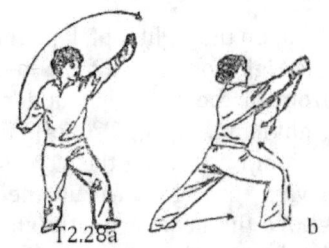

29. Jump And Lash   tiàoqǐ bǎizhǎng   跳起摆掌

Step the left foot forward and lift the bent right knee. Unclench the right hand and bend the elbow to cross the hands in front of the belly, the right hand under the left. Look at the left hand. (image T2.29a) Push off with the left leg to jump up, lifting the left foot whilst airborne. Lash with the left hand, swinging it up by the side to above the head with the arm straight, fingers forward. Lower the right hand down by the side, arm straight, fingers down. Look forward. (image 29b)

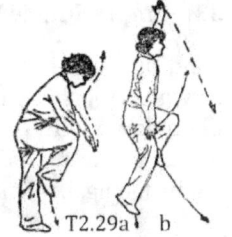

30. Empty Stance Low Chop   xūbù xià pīzhǎng   虚步下劈掌

Land on the right foot and land the left foot forward, touching down the toes to take an empty stance. Chop the left hand forward and down. Bend the right elbow to tuck the hand into the left elbow crease, palms facing. Look at the left hand. (image T2.30)

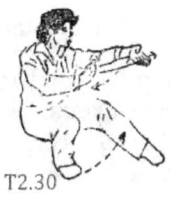

31. Aerial Snap Kick   téngkōng tántuǐ   腾空弹腿

Stand up on the left leg and lift the bent right knee. Straighten the right arm and extend it forward, thumb side on top. Bend the left elbow to place the hand at the waist. Push off with the left leg to jump up, doing a left snap kick whilst airborne. Bring the left hand forward and bring the right hand past the waist to simultaneously stab out to either side, left in front and right behind, palms angled up. Look at the left hand. (image T2.31)

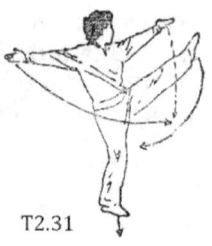

T2.31

32. Aerial Stab   téngkōng chāzhǎng   腾空叉掌

Land on the right foot, land the left foot in front, then take another step with the right foot and lift the bent left knee. Bring the arms down to cross in front of the belly, left under the right. Look at the right hand. (image T2.32a) Push off with the right leg to jump up, lifting the right foot up whilst airborne. Swing the right arm up the side in a circling lash above the head, arm straight, fingers up. Lower the left hand at the side, arm straight, fingers down. Look forward. (image 32b)

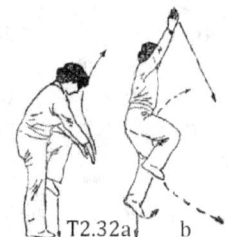

T2.32a   b

33. Empty Stance Low Chop   xūbù xià pīzhǎng   虚步下劈掌

Land on the left foot and step the right foot a half-step forward, touching down the toes in an empty stance. Chop down with the right arm to chest height. Bend the left elbow to tuck the hand into the right elbow crease, palms facing. Look at the right hand. (image T2.33)

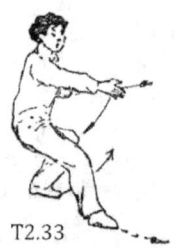

T2.33

34. Aerial Snap Kick   téngkōng tántuǐ   腾空弹腿

Step the right foot a half-step forward and stand up, lifting the bent left knee. Extend the left arm forward with the thumb side up. Bend the right elbow to bring the hand to the waist, palm up. Look at the left hand. (image T2.34a) Push off with the right leg to jump up, doing a right snap kick whilst airborne, with the ankle plantar-flexed. Bring the left hand in to the waist from the front then extend the arms out to either side, right in front and left behind, arms straight and palms up. Look at the right hand. (image 34b)

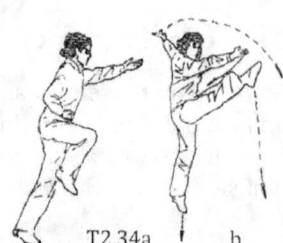

T2.34a   b

SECOND FORM TUIQUAN

35. Closed Stance Stab   bīngbù chāzhǎng   并步插掌

Land on the left foot then land the right foot forward with the knee bent. Clench the right hand and bend the elbow to bring the fist to the waist, fist heart up. Press down with the left hand to the front, arm at shoulder height, thumb side down, palm forward. Look at the left hand. (image T2.35a) Hook the right foot in then step the left foot in to meet it, turning the body ninety degrees to the left and standing up. Reach the torso slightly forward. Bend the left elbow to tuck the hand into the right armpit, palm down. Unclench the right hand and stab forward just above shoulder height, passing over the left hand, palm down. Look at the right hand. (image 35b)

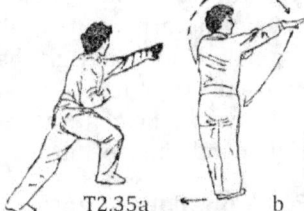

Section Six

36. Raised Knee Stab   tíxī chuānzhǎng   提膝穿掌

Withdraw the left foot to the left, bending the right knee to take a right bow stance. Bend the right elbow and clench the fist at the waist, fist heart up. Circle the left hand right and forward to lash, with the arm at shoulder height, the elbow slightly bent, the thumb edge down, and the palm forward. Look forward. (image T2.36a) Stand up on the right leg, bend and lift the left knee with the ankle plantar-flexed. Unclench the right hand and thread it forward over the left hand, palm up. Slide the left hand along the under the right arm to press down at the right armpit, palm down, fingers pointing right. Look at the right hand. (image 36b)

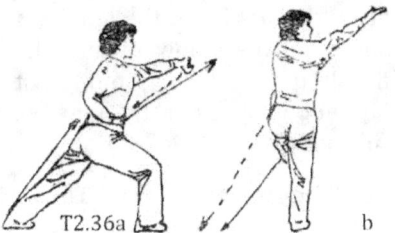

37. Drop Stance Thread The Hand   pūbù chuānzhǎng   仆步穿掌

Squat fully on the right leg and extend the left leg along the ground into a drop stance. Extend the left hand along the left leg to the foot, thumb side on top, fingers forward. Medially rotate the right arm to turn the thumb side up. Reach the torso towards the left foot. Look at the left hand. (image T2.37)

38. Aerial Snap Kick   téngkōng tántuǐ   腾空弹腿

Push into the right leg and bend the left knee to move forward, turning the left foot out. Step the right foot forward past the left foot. Scoop forward and up with the left hand. Lower the straight right arm, thumb side still up. Look past the left hand. (image T2.38a) Bend the left knee and swing it up, pushing off with the right leg to jump up, doing a snap kick with the right leg whilst airborne, ankle plantar-flexed. Bend the elbows to bring the hands to the waist at either side, then simultaneously extend the arms out to either side with the palms up. The right hand extends to above the right foot, the left hand extends to above the head at the rear. Look at the right hand. (image 38b)

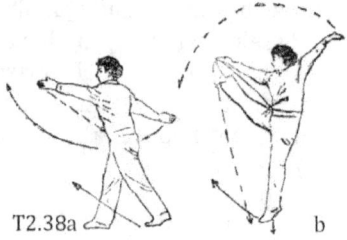

39. Bow Stance Punch   gōngbù chōngquán   弓步冲拳

Land on the left foot, then stomp with the right foot and lift the bent left knee in front. Clench the right hand and bend the elbow to bring the fist to the waist, fist heart up. Press forward and down with the left hand in front of the left knee, palm down. Look at the left hand. (image T2.39a) Land the left foot forward, bending the knee to take a left bow stance. Punch forward with the right fist to above shoulder height, fist heart down. Clench the left hand and bend the elbow to tuck the fist into the right armpit, fist heart down. Look at the right fist. (image 39b)

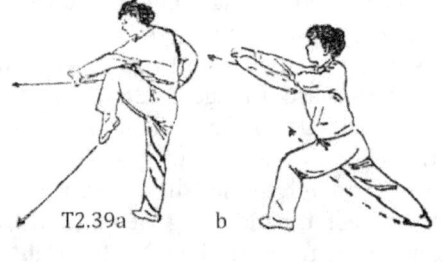

40. Drop Stance Thread The Hand   pūbù chuānzhǎng   仆步穿掌

Shift to the left leg and stand up, bending and lifting the right knee in front of the body. Unclench the right hand and bend the elbow to tuck the hand into the left armpit, palm down. Unclench the left hand and stab forward to above head height, passing over the back of the right hand, palm up. Look at the left hand. (image T2.40a) Squat fully on the left leg and extend the right leg along the ground with the foot turned in, taking a drop stance. Reach the right hand along the leg, extending the arm fully so that the hand is above the foot, thumb side up. Look at the right hand. (image 40b)

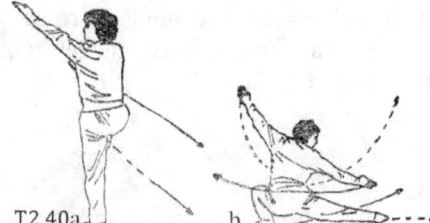

SECOND FORM TUIQUAN

41. Aerial Snap Kick   téngkōng tántuǐ   腾空弹腿

Turn right and push into the left leg, first extending it, then stepping forward past the right foot. Then step the right foot forward, bending the knee. Circle the straight left arm down, forward, and up. Swing the straight right arm back. The left hand swings to above the head in front and the right hand swings to a low position behind the body, both palms face right. Look forward. (image T2.41a) Shift to the right leg and swing the left foot forward and up, pushing off with the right leg to jump up. Whist airborne, do a right front snap kick, ankle plantar-flexed. Bring the left hand down and the right hand up, bending the elbows and clenching the hands to place the fists at the waist on either side, fist hearts up. Look forward. (image 41b)

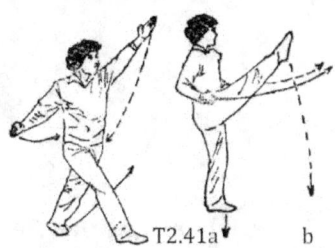

42. Bow Stance Double Pushes   gōngbù shuāng tuīzhǎng   弓步双推掌

Land on the left leg then land the right foot forward to take a right bow stance. Unclench both hands and push forward with both to shoulder height, palms forward, fingers up. Look forward. (image T2.42)

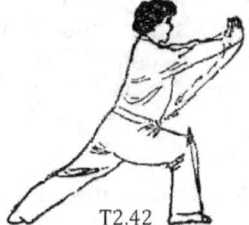

43. Bow Stance Double Stabs   gōngbù shuāng chāzhǎng   弓步双插掌

Stand up on the left leg, bending and lifting the right knee. Bend the elbows to bring the hands to either side of the waist, palms up. Look to the lower right side. (image T2.43.a) Land the right foot forward into a right bow stance. Stab forward with both hands to eye height, palms up. Look forward. (image 43.b)

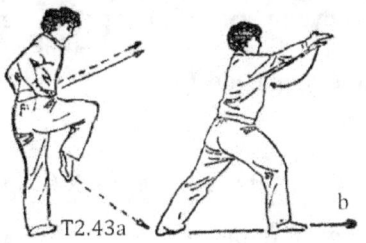

44. Raised Knee Scooping Snap   tíxī tiǎozhǎng   提膝挑掌

Step the left foot forward past the right foot, bending the knee. Turn ninety degrees rightward, keeping the left arm in the same position. Bend the right elbow to bring the right hand to the left armpit with the turn, palm up. Look at the left hand. (image T2.44a) Pivot on the right heel to turn a further ninety degrees to the right, then swing the left leg up in front to hip height, keeping it straight. Press the left hand down at shoulder height, palm down. Medially rotate the right arm to press down in front of the right knee, palm down. Look forward. (image 44b) Bend the left knee and hold it up tucked close to the body, ankle plantar-flexed. Hook the left hand with the hook pointing down. Scoop up with the right hand, passing the back of the hand along the outside of the left thigh, finishing at shoulder height with the palm forward. Look forward. (image 44c)

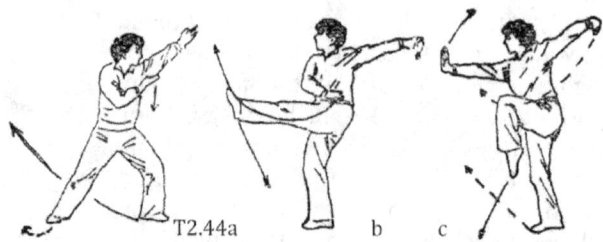

45. Aerial Raised Knee Stab téngkōng tíxī chāzhǎng 腾空提膝插掌

Land the left foot forward, bending and and raising the right knee in front, ankle plantar-flexed. Push off with the left leg to jump up. Swing the straight right arm up above the head, fingers up. Unhook the left hand and swing the arm down past the body then tuck the palm into the right armpit, tiger's mouth down, palm facing right. Look forward. (image T2.45)

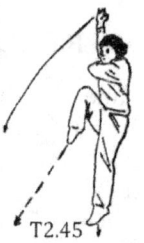

46. Drop Stance Chop pūbù pīzhǎng 仆步劈掌

Land on the left foot then squat fully on it and extend the right leg along the ground into a drop stance. Chop down with a straight right arm to above the right foot. Tuck the left hand into the right elbow crease. The palms are facing. Look at the right hand. (image T2.46)

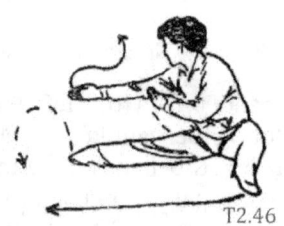

47. Inside Crescent Kick Push lǐhétuǐ tuīzhǎng 里合腿推掌

Push into the left leg to shift forward, turning out the right foot, then step the left foot forward and kick the right leg up to the side, then swing it inwards with a fanning action in front of the face. Push the hands out to either side, palms out, fingers up. Look forward. (image T2.47a) Bend the right knee and hold it up in front of the body. Clench the left hand, bend the elbow to bring the fist to the waist, then punch

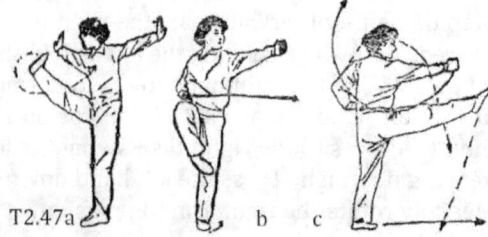

forward, fist eye up, arm at shoulder height. Clench the right hand and bring the fist to the waist, fist heart up. Look at the left fist. (image 47b) Pivot on the left foot to turn ninety degrees to the left, keeping the right knee up, then, after the turn, do a snap kick forward with the ankle plantar-flexed. Bring the left fist in to the waist, fist heart up. Punch the right fist forward to shoulder height, fist eye up. Look at the right fist. (image 47c)

Section Seven

48. Empty Stance Planting Punch Down

    xūbù xià zāiquán   虚步下栽拳

Land the right foot with the knee bent, then step the left foot forward a half-step, touching down the toes to take an empty stance. Circle the left fist up, forward, then down to just above the left knee, fist eye in. Circle the right fist back and up, medially rotating above the head to turn the fist heart up. Look forward. (image T2.48)

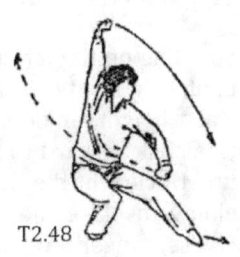

T2.48

49. Bow Stance Chop   gōngbù pīzhǎng   弓步劈掌

Step the left foot forward a half-step, bending the knee to take a left bow stance. Swing the left straight arm down and back behind the body to above the head, fist eye up. Bring the right straight arm over to chop just below shoulder height in front, fist eye up. Look at the right fist. (image T2.49)

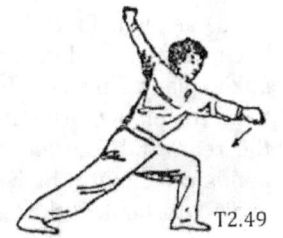

T2.49

50. Snap Kick Hold The Fists   tántuǐ bàoquán   弹腿抱拳

Hold the left arm steady and laterally rotate the right fist, bending the elbow to pound with the forearm level, fist heart up. Look at the right fist. (image T2.50a) Stand up on the left leg and lift the right leg to do a front snap kick, ankle plantar-flexed. Still not moving the left arm, bring the right fist to the waist, fist heart up. Look forward. (image 50b)

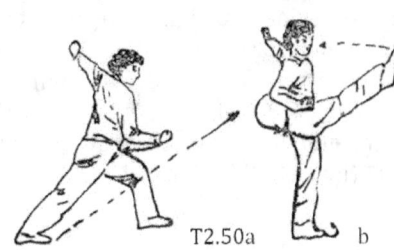

T2.50a   b

51. Inside Crescent Kick lǐhétuǐ 里合腿

Pivot three-sixty degrees on the left foot. As the body turns, do an inside fanning kick with the right leg, then tuck the foot in, keeping the knee up. Bring the left fist in to the waist while turning, then punch forward just above shoulder height after the turn, fist eye up. (image T2.51)

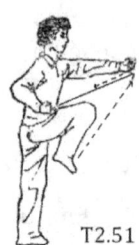

52. Snap Kick Punch tántuǐ chōngquán 弹腿冲拳

Standing on the left leg with the knee slightly bent, do a front snap kick with the right leg to waist height, ankle plantar-flexed. Punch the right fist forward to shoulder height, fist eye up. Unclench the left hand and bend the elbow to place the hand in the right elbow crease, fingers up. Look at the right fist. (image T2.52)

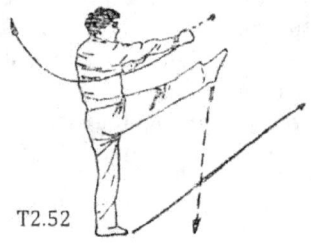

53. Snap Kick Stab tántuǐ chāzhǎng 弹腿插掌

Land the right foot directly down and bend the left knee, lifting it to do a front snap kick to waist height, ankle plantar-flexed. Unclench the right hand and bend the elbow, bring it past the side of the waist to the rear. Stab the left hand directly forward. Both hands are slightly higher than the shoulders, palms angled up. Look at the left hand. (image T2.53)

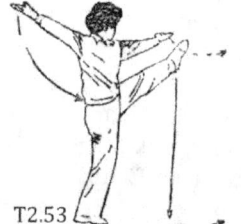

54. Closed Stance Strike bīngbù jīzhǎng 并步击掌

Land the left foot then step the right foot forward to take a right bow stance. Clench the right hand and bend the elbow to place the fist at the waist, fist heart up. Circle the left hand up and over to press down in front at shoulder height, fingers up. Look at the left hand. (image T2.54a) Bring the left foot up to beside the right foot and stand up. Punch forward to shoulder height with the right fist, fist eye up. Bend the left elbow to place the hand at the right elbow crease. Look at the right fist. (image 54b)

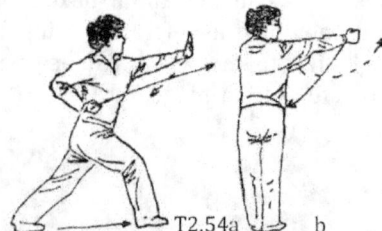

SECOND FORM TUIQUAN

55. Closed Stance Fist Strike   bīngbù jīquán   并步击拳

Standing without moving the legs, turn the torso slightly to the right while holding the left hand in place, bending the right elbow to tuck the fist into the left armpit, fist eye in. Look at the left hand. (image T2.55a) Punch forward to shoulder height with the right fist, fist eye up. Look at the right fist. (image 55b)

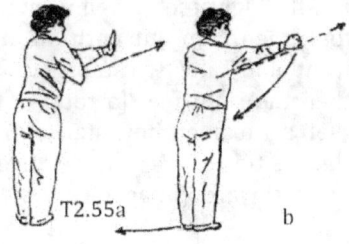

Section Eight

56. Raised Knee Stab   tíxī chuānzhǎng   提膝穿掌

Withdraw the left foot to the left side and bend the right knee to take a right bow stance. Bend the right elbow to bring the fist to the waist, fist heart up. Swing the left hand down, to the left, then up and over to shoulder height at the front, bending the elbow with the palm facing forward, tiger's mouth down. Look at the left hand. (image T2.56a) Stand up on the right leg and turn ninety degrees to the right, lifting the bent left knee in front of the body, ankle plantar-flexed. Thread the right hand out over top of the left hand to stab to the upper right, a bit higher than the head, palm up. Slide the left hand along the right arm to press down, bending the elbow to tuck the hand into the right armpit, palm down. Look at the right hand. (image 56b)

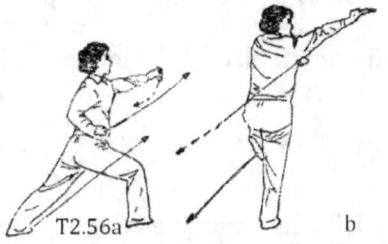

57. Drop Stance Thread The Hand   pūbù chuānzhǎng   仆步穿掌

Squat fully on the right leg and extend the left leg along the ground to take a drop stance. Extend the left hand along the left leg to above the foot, tiger's mouth up, fingers forward. Medially rotate the right arm to turn the tiger's mouth up. Reach the torso towards the left foot. Look at the left hand. (image T2.57)

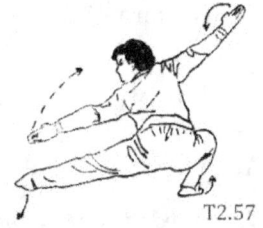

58. Bow Stance Scoop   gōngbù tiǎozhǎng   弓步挑掌

Shift forward into the left leg and step the right foot forward, angled to the right side, to a left bow stance. Clench both hands and scoop up with straight arms, the left fist above the head, the right fist at shoulder height., fist eyes angled upwards. Look to the right side. (image T2.58)

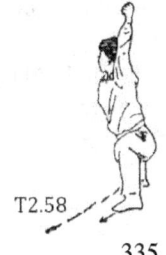

59. Curving Walk   húxíngbù   弧行步

Lift the right foot, bring it in beside the left foot, then step out with an arcing step in front of it. Take two steps each with the left, then the right feet (a total of fours steps), then set to a left bow stance. Do not change the position of the arms relative to the body. Look forward. (images T2.59a, 59b)

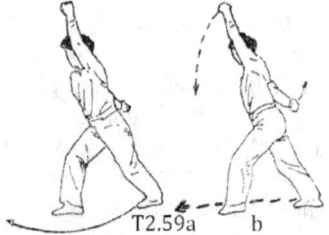

60. Snap Kick Embrace With The Fists   tántuǐ bàoquán   弹腿抱拳

Step the right foot forward, turning it out. Lift the right fist to shoulder height, fist eye up. Lower the left fist and bend the elbow to hit at waist height, fist heart up. Look past the left fist. (image T2.60a) Stand up on the right leg and lift the left leg to do a snap kick at waist height, ankle plantar-flexed. Lift the right fist slightly to just below head height, fist eye still up. Bring the left fist to the waist, fist heart still up. Look forward. (image 60b)

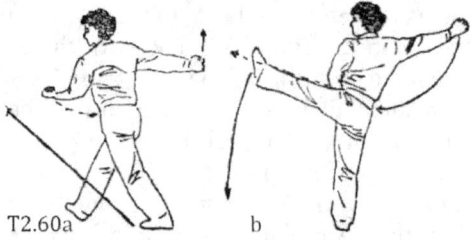

61. Bow Stance Punch   gōngbù chōngquán   弓步冲拳

Land the left foot forward and bend the knee to take a left bow stance. Bend the right elbow to bring the fist to the waist, fist heart up. Medially rotate the left arm and punch forward, fist eye up. Look at the left fist. (image T2.61)

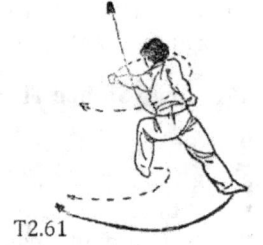

62. Closed Stance Punch Up   bīngbù shàng chōngquán   并步上冲拳

Turn the left foot in and turn one-eighty degrees to the right, then step the right foot across to the right. Finally, step the left foot in beside the right foot and stand up. Unclench the left hand and bend the elbow to place a vertical palm at the right armpit. Punch straight upward with the right fist, knuckles up. Look to the left side. (image T2.62)

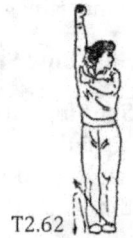

SECOND FORM TUIQUAN

63. One-Legged Basin Squat Stance   pántuǐ dúlì shì   盘腿独立势

Without changing the position of the arms, lift the right foot then place it down and bend the knee. Lift the left foot above the right knee, then medially rotate the left foot and open the hip to place the foot on top of the right knee. Look forward, to the left side. (image T2.63)

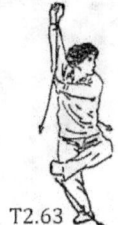

T2.63

64. Closing Posture   shōu shì   收势

Land the left foot beside the right and stand up. Unclench both hands and lower the arms at the sides to stand to attention. Look forward. (image T2.64)

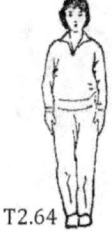

T2.64

PRONUNCIATION OF PINYIN, THE CHINESE NATIONAL PHONETIC ALPHABET (WITH INTERNATIONAL PHONETIC ALPHABET EQUIVALENTS)

INITIALS (words can start with these consonants, or have a zero initial)

PINYIN	IPA	ROUGH PRONUNCIATION GUIDE
p	p^h	Like English p̲et with a considerable puff of air.
b	p	Similar to the *pinyin* "p" but without the puff of air (unvoiced, neither English p̲et nor b̲et).
t	t^h	Like English t̲ag with a considerable puff of air.
d	t	Similar to the *pinyin* "t" but with no puff of air (unvoiced, not d̲og).
k	k^h	Like English k̲ill with a considerable puff of air.
g	k	Similar to the *pinyin* "k" but with no puff of air (unvoiced, not English g̲et).
c	ts^h	Like exaggerating English cat̲s̲.
z	ts	Like the *pinyin* "c" but without the puff of air (unvoiced).
ch	$tʂ^h$	Somewhat similar to English c̲h̲at with a puff of air, but with the tip of the tongue rolled back.
zh	tʂ	Like the *pinyin* "ch" but with no puff of air (unvoiced).
q	$tɕ^h$	Somewhat similar to English c̲h̲at with a puff of air, but with the front of the tongue raised and the tip on the lower teeth.
j	tɕ	Like the *pinyin* "q" but without the puff of air (unvoiced).
m	m	Like English m̲et.
n	n	Like English n̲et.
f	f	Similar to English f̲at, but with the teeth just touching lightly behind the lower lip.
s	s	Similar to English s̲et.
sh	ʂ	Somewhat similar to English s̲h̲ow, but with the same tongue placement as the *pinyin* "ch" and "zh."
x	ɕ	Somewhat similar to English s̲h̲ine but with the same tongue placement as the *pinyin* "q" and "j."
h	χ	Raise the back of the tongue and let the breath come through the obstructed passage without vibrating the vocal cords.
l	l	Like English l̲et.
r	ɻ	Like the *pinyin* "sh" but with voicing.

FINALS

n	n	Like English pin̲.
ng	ŋ	Like English sin̲g̲.

VOWELS

a	A a ɛ		Usually close to English f<u>a</u>ther (not p<u>a</u>t). Like y<u>e</u>t when written "-ian" or "yan."
e	ʏ e ɛ ə		Usually similar to English p<u>e</u>t, can tend towards a mid vowel.
i	i ɪ		Usually similar to English b<u>ee</u>. Similar to w<u>e</u>t when written "ui." After c, z, s, ch, zh, sh, and r it is similar to si<u>r</u>.
o	o u		Usually close to English r<u>o</u>ll. Similar to c<u>ow</u> when written "ao," and <u>owe</u> when in "ou."
u	u y		Usually similar t English o b<u>oo</u>t. After the *pinyin* "x", "q", and "j" and in the vowel groups starting with these consonants, it is pronounced "ü".
ü	y		Similar to French <u>ü</u>. It is written after "n" or "l," because these are the only positions where both "u" and "ü" are possible
y	i		Partially like an English 'y', tending towards i.
w	u		Partially like an English 'w', tending towards u.

INITIAL CONSONANTS

place of articulation	manner of articulation						
	Unaspirated Stops	Aspirated Stops	Unaspirated Affricates	Aspirated Affricates	Nasals	Fricatives	Voiced Continuants
bilabials	b	p			m		
labio-dentals						f	
dental-alveolars	d	t	z	c	n	s	l
retroflexes			zh	ch		sh	r
palatals			j	q		x	
velars	g	k				h	

TONES IN PINYIN			
NUMBER	PINYIN	NAME	RANGE
1	ˉ	high level	55
2	ˊ	high rising	35
3	ˇ	dipping	214
4	ˋ	high falling	51
none	˚ or blank	neutral	in context

With tone sandhi, tones may change according to the preceding or following tone.

The tone marking is put over the main vowel when there are two vowels written together (usually involving the pronunciation of y or w).

About the Translator

Andrea Falk has practised external and internal Chinese martial arts since 1972. She has studied Chinese art, geography, history, language, linguistics, literature, philosophy, politics, religion, and sociology since then, as well. She received a Bachelor of Arts majoring in Chinese (1978), a Bachelor of Physical Education (1980) and a Master of Physical Education with an emphasis on coaching science (1990) from the University of British Columbia. She trained in wushu full time on scholarship from 1980 to 1983 at the Beijing Physical Culture Institute, earning an Advanced Studies Diploma in Wushu under the tutelage of Professor Xia Bohua and instruction from Men Huifeng and others. There she learned the basics of Yang and Chen style Taijiquan, Baguazhang, Xingyiquan, Chaquan, Tongbeiquan, and modern Longfist (barehand and four standard weapons). Andrea spent two further extended summers at the Institute in 1984 and 1986.

Starting in 1984, Andrea gradually changed over to learning traditionally, visiting China on extended trips as often as possible to learn in parks, parking lots, and courtyards. She has trained and/or is training Chen style Taijiquan, Baguazhang, and Taiji Changquan as an inside apprentice of the late Huan Dahai (1924-2015) and elder martial brothers in Shanghai; Xingyiquan and Baguazhang as a close student and friend of Di Guoyong in Beijing; and Baguazhang from friends Li Baohua and Lu Yan. When not in China or traveling to teach, she is usually in Québec City or at a cabin in the Laurentian hills, Canada.

Andrea has taught and translated books about Chinese martial arts since 1983. She founded *the wushu centre* in Montreal in 1984, in Victoria in 1992, and in Quebec city in 2007. Andrea has taught Chen Taijiquan, Baguazhang, and Xingyiquan around the world, but mostly in Canada and England.

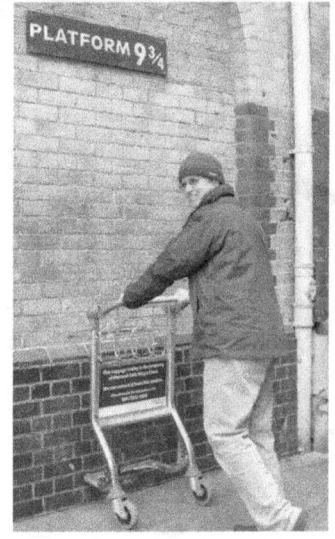

For years, Andrea translated books for her own students. In 2000, *tgl books* and the website www.thewushucentre.ca were established to bring these translations to a wider audience.

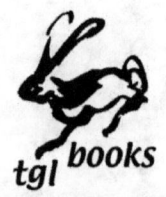

trois gros lapins traversent le chemin